CONFORMITY AND CONFLICT

Readings in cultural anthropology

CONFORMITY AND CONFLICT

Readings in cultural anthropology

Edited by
JAMES P. SPRADLEY
DAVID W. McCURDY
Macalester College

LITTLE, BROWN AND COMPANY BOSTON

LIBRARY OF CONGRESS CATALOG CARD NO. 79-147160

EIGHTH PRINTING

Published simultaneously in Canada
by Little, Brown & Company (Canada) Limited

PRINTED IN THE UNITED STATES OF AMERICA

To Barbara Spradley and Carolyn McCurdy

Contents

CONFORMITY AND CONFLICT

Readings in cultural anthropology

I

Culture and the contemporary world

Many students associate cultural anthropology with the study of primitive peoples. They picture the anthropologist as that slightly peculiar person who, dressed in khaki shorts and pith helmet, lives among some exotic tribe in order to record the group's bizarre and not altogether pleasant customs. Like most stereotypes, this one is not completely true but it does reflect our traditional interest in describing the culture of less complex societies. In the last century when anthropology became a recognized discipline, its members collected and analyzed the growing number of reports on non-Western peoples by missionaries, travelers, and colonial administrators. This tradition continued into the twentieth century, although the collection of data was refined by actual fieldwork. Impressed by the variety of human behavior, anthropologists sought to record these cultures which were vanishing before the onslaught of Western civilization. Such studies continue among remote groups, and reports of this research are regularly found in professional journals.

During recent decades anthropologists have broadened their research base. As primitive groups have been obliterated or assimilated, anthropologists have increasingly studied subcultures within more complex societies. Certainly World War II and the Cold War stimulated this trend. The American government employed anthropologists to describe societies in whose territories we fought. The Cold War years, marked by competition with the Russians for influence in developing agrarian nations, led to studies of peasant life styles and culture change.

However, the nature of the Cold War has changed. Americans have become less welcome in developing nations. Concurrently, problems in our country have multiplied and taken the center stage of national concern. Human rights, poverty, urban blight, violence, and environmental pollution are beginning to stimulate part of our research interest. The selections in this volume reflect this interest and include studies of poverty, Black ghettos, Mexican-Americans, modern warfare, urban courts, and other contemporary issues.

But what can anthropology contribute to an understanding of our own society? After all, other social scientists have been doing such studies for decades. Is there anything special about anthropology? In many ways the answer to this question is no. The various social-science disciplines share the same assumptions, methods, and interests. At the same time, as a result of their intensive cross-cultural experience, anthropologists have developed a unique perspective on the nature and significance of *culture*. This view has emerged from fieldwork among populations whose behavior dramatically differed from the anthropologists' own. For example, why did Iroquois women participate with apparent relish in the gruesome torture of prisoners? Why did Bhil tribesmen put chilli powder in the eyes of witches, blindfold them, and swing them over a smoky fire by their feet? What possessed Kwakiutl chiefs to publicly destroy their wealth at potlatch ceremonies? Why did Rajput widows cast themselves upon their husbands' funeral pyres? Why did Nagas engage in raids to acquire human heads? In every case, anthropologists were impressed by the fact that this "bizarre" behavior was intentional and meaningful to the participants. Bhils wanted to swing witches; to them it was appropriate. Kwakiutl chiefs made careful investments to increase the wealth they destroyed. These acts were planned; people had a notion of what they were going to do before they did it, and others shared their expectations.

This cognitive map — the categories, plans, and rules people employ to interpret their world and act purposefully within it — is called *culture*. Culture is not behavior itself, but the underlying rules, the grammar used to construct and interpret behavior. It is learned as children grow up in society and discover how their parents, and others around them, interpret the world. In our society we learn to distinguish objects such as cars, windows, houses, children, and food; to recognize attributes like sharp, hot, beautiful, and humid; to classify and perform different kinds of acts; to evaluate what is good and bad and to judge when a novel act is appropriate or inappropriate. How often have you heard a parent explain something about life to his child? Why do you think children forever ask why? During socialization the child learns his culture, and because he learns it from others, he *shares* it with others, a fact that makes human social existence possible.

Culture thus becomes the meaning system by which people design their own actions and interpret the behavior of others. It tells an American that eating with one's mouth closed is proper, while an Indian knows that to be polite he must eat with his mouth open. There is nothing preordained about cultural categories; they are arbitrary. The same act in separate cultures can have different meanings. For example, when adolescent Hindu boys walk holding hands, it signifies friendship, while to Americans the same act suggests homosexuality. This arbitrariness is particularly important to remember if we are to understand our own complex society. We tend to think that the norms we follow are part of "the American way of life" and that they represent the "natural" way human beings do things. Those who behave otherwise are judged morally wrong, a viewpoint anthropologists consider *ethnocentric,* which means that people think their own culture is the best, or at least the most appropriate, way for human beings to live.

However, in our complex society, while we share some cultural norms, each of us belongs to a number of groups possessing exclusive cultural rules. We share some categories and plans with family members alone. There is a distinctive culture of our occupational group, our ethnic group, our volunteer society, and our age group. Because of this, our multicultural society presents difficulties, which are discussed more fully in the final chapter. Instead of assuming that another's behavior is reasonable to him, that it is motivated by a different set of cultural norms, we frequently assume that he has intentionally violated accepted conventions. Americans who value the college experience as a way to learn and get ahead in life are highly critical of college students who protest and riot. Young people who are concerned about war, human rights, and pollution condemn their elders for being so preoccupied with physical appearance, deportment, and personal success. For many years anthropologists have identified the universality of ethnocentrism in their attempt to build bridges of understanding across cultural barriers. The study of subcultures in our society is making the same kind of contribution, as some of the selections in this volume indicate.

How do anthropologists discover and map another culture? Are their methods applicable in the United States? Typically anthropologists live among the people of the society that interests them. They learn the culture by observing, asking questions, and participating in daily activities — a process resembling childhood socialization or enculturation. Obviously, the anthropologist cannot become a child, and must try to learn the norms in a strange group despite his foreign appearance and his age. Those who study in the United States have followed a similar procedure. For example, Lincoln Keiser's research (part of the resulting data appears in Chapter 7) required that he "hang out" with the Vice Lords whose culture he sought to learn.

More than anything else, the study of culture separates anthropologists from other social scientists. Other scholars do not ignore culture; they assume their subjects have it, but their main interest is to account for human behavior by plotting correlations among variables. Some social scientists have explained the rise in the American divorce rate as a function of industrialization; this hypothesis can be tested by seeing if higher divorce rates are associated with industrialization and mobility. Anthropologists also share a concern for this kind of explanation; for example, many have employed the Human Relations Area Files, a collection of ethnographies describing several hundred societies, as data for testing more general hypotheses. However, almost every anthropologist starts with *ethnography*, the description of a particular culture, and such studies are required to understand the complexity and conflict within American society.

As anthropologists have encountered, studied, and compared the world's societies, they have learned more about the concept of culture itself. As already seen, culture is a plan for behavior, not behavior itself; it is arbitrary, learned, and shared. In addition, culture is adaptive. Human beings cope with their natural and social environment by means of their traditional categories and plans. Unlike other animals, if we are cold we can invent a coat and pass along the technique to our descendants. Culture allows for rapid adaptation because it is flexible and permits the invention of new strategies — although change often appears to be painfully slow to those who are in a hurry for it. By the same token, the adaptive nature of culture accounts for the enormous variety of the world's distinct societies.

Culture is a system of interrelated parts. If Americans were to give up automobiles, then other modes of travel, places for courtship, markers of status, and sources of income would have to be found. Culture meets personal needs; through it, man seeks security and a sense of control over his experience. Indeed, every tradition includes ways to cure the sick, prepare for the unexpected, and support the individual. In a complex society with many ways of life in contact, change is persistent. It may be an illusion that man can control the course of change, or modify the resulting culture conflict. Whatever the final verdict, if we can understand human cultures including our own, the illusion may become reality.

II

Conforming to culture

The customs we acquire as members of a society have a curious effect on us. While we find them difficult to learn at first, with practice we conform and feel that they are natural and right. In time, the rules for customary behavior fade from awareness, and men lose sight of the culture guiding their behavior. Ours is an effortless conformity which feels comfortable and secure. Each of us is a fluent speaker of his native language, yet we are often unable to state the rules of its grammar. Similarly, men abide by the rest of their culture with confidence but lack a knowledge of its structure. It is no accident that anthropologists, interested in understanding culture, have sought out groups with very different life styles. They have purposely chosen to study in these natural laboratories because of the realization that conformity to their own culture acts as a blinder. Even the nonconformist rejects little of his heritage — perhaps a few words in his speech, the style of his clothing, the length of his hair, the way he spends his time and money — but when compared with members of non-Western cultures, it is obvious that he has changed little. Even those who withdraw from the cultural mainstream create a new kind of conformity within their special groups.

How are we to learn about the power of culture in human experience? In the following selections we see the confusion that comes when individuals with one social map live in a society that operates in terms of another. This misunderstanding is an inevitable consequence of cultural differences, and leads to bewilderment, anxiety, and sometimes despair — a condition called "culture shock." But this shock of recognition can also produce insight into a universal phenomenon — conformity to culture. As anthropologists increase their study of complex societies, it is important to be reminded of the lessons learned through the study of cultures very different from our own.

1

Eating Christmas in the Kalahari

RICHARD BORSHAY LEE

What happens when an anthropologist living among the bushmen of Africa decides to be generous and to share a large animal with everyone at Christmastime? This compelling account of the misunderstanding and confusion that resulted takes the reader deeper into the nature of culture. Richard Lee carefully traces how the natives perceived his generosity and taught the anthropologist something about his own culture.

The !Kung Bushmen's knowledge of Christmas is thirdhand. The London Missionary Society brought the holiday to the southern Tswana tribes in the early nineteenth century. Later, native catechists spread the idea far and wide among the Bantu-speaking pastoralists, even in the remotest corners of the Kalahari Desert. The Bushmen's idea of the Christmas story, stripped to its essentials, is "praise the birth of white man's god-chief"; what keeps their interest in the holiday high is the Tswana-Herero custom of slaughtering an ox for his Bushmen neighbors as an annual goodwill gesture. Since the 1930's, part of the Bushmen's annual round of activities has included a December congregation at the cattle posts for trading, marriage brokering, and several days of trance-dance feasting at which the local Tswana headman is host.

As a social anthropologist working with !Kung Bushmen, I found that the Christmas ox custom suited my purposes. I had come to the Kalahari to study the hunting and gathering subsistence economy of the !Kung, and to accomplish this it was essential not to provide them with food, share my own food, or interfere in any way with their food-gather-

From "Eating Christmas in the Kalahari," *Natural History* 78 (December 1969): 14, 16, 18, 21–22, 60–63.

ing activities. While liberal handouts of tobacco and medical supplies were appreciated, they were scarcely adequate to erase the glaring disparity in wealth between the anthropologist, who maintained a two-month inventory of canned goods, and the Bushmen, who rarely had a day's supply of food on hand. My approach, while paying off in terms of data, left me open to frequent accusations of stinginess and hardheartedness. By their lights, I was a miser.

The Christmas ox was to be my way of saying thank you for the cooperation of the past year; and since it was to be our last Christmas in the field, I determined to slaughter the largest, meatiest ox that money could buy, insuring that the feast and trance dance would be a success.

Through December I kept my eyes open at the wells as the cattle were brought down for watering. Several animals were offered, but none had quite the grossness that I had in mind. Then, ten days before the holiday, a Herero friend led an ox of astonishing size and mass up to our camp. It was solid black, stood five feet high at the shoulder, had a five-foot span of horns, and must have weighed 1,200 pounds on the hoof. Food consumption calculations are my specialty, and I quickly figured that bones and viscera aside, there was enough meat — at least four pounds — for every man, woman, and child of the 150 Bushmen in the vicinity of /ai/ai who were expected at the feast.

Having found the right animal at last, I paid the Herero £20 ($56) and asked him to keep the beast with his herd until Christmas day. The next morning word spread among the people that the big solid black one was the ox chosen by/ontah (my Bushman name; it means, roughly, "whitey") for the Christmas feast. That afternoon I received the first delegation. Ben!a, an outspoken sixty-year-old mother of five, came to the point slowly.

"Where were you planning to eat Christmas?"

"Right here at /ai/ai," I replied.

"Alone or with others?"

"I expect to invite all the people to eat Christmas with me."

"Eat what?"

"I have purchased Yehave's black ox, and I am going to slaughter and cook it."

"That's what we were told at the well but refused to believe it until we heard it from yourself."

"Well, it's the black one," I replied expansively, although wondering what she was driving at.

"Oh, no!" Ben!a groaned, turning to her group. "They were right." Turning back to me she asked, "Do you expect us to eat that bag of bones?"

"Bag of bones! It's the biggest ox at /ai/ai."

"Big, yes, but old. And thin. Everybody knows there's no meat on that old ox. What did you expect us to eat off it, the horns?"

Everybody chuckled at Ben!a's one-liner as they walked away, but all I could manage was a weak grin.

That evening it was the turn of the young men. They came to sit at our evening fire. /gaugo, about my age, spoke to me man-to-man.

"/ontah, you have always been square with us," he lied. "What has happened to change your heart? That sack of guts and bones of Yehave's will hardly feed one camp, let alone all the Bushmen around /ai/ai." And he proceeded to enumerate the seven camps in the /ai/ai vicinity, family by family. "Perhaps you have forgotten that we are not few, but many. Or are you too blind to tell the difference between a proper cow and an old wreck? That ox is thin to the point of death."

"Look, you guys," I retorted, "that is a beautiful animal, and I'm sure you will eat it with pleasure at Christmas."

"Of course we will eat it; it's food. But it won't fill us up to the point where we will have enough strength to dance. We will eat and go home to bed with stomachs rumbling."

That night as we turned in, I asked my wife, Nancy: "What did you think of the black ox?"

"It looked enormous to me. Why?"

"Well, about eight different people have told me I got gypped; that the ox is nothing but bones."

"What's the angle?" Nancy asked. "Did they have a better one to sell?"

"No, they just said that it was going to be a grim Christmas because there won't be enough meat to go around. Maybe I'll get an independent judge to look at the beast in the morning."

Bright and early, Halingisi, a Tswana cattle owner, appeared at our camp. But before I could ask him to give me his opinion on Yehave's black ox, he gave me the eye signal that indicated a confidential chat. We left the camp and sat down.

"/ontah, I'm surprised at you: you've lived here for three years and still haven't learned anything about cattle."

"But what else can a person do but choose the biggest, strongest animal one can find?" I retorted.

"Look, just because an animal is big doesn't mean that it has plenty of meat on it. The black one was a beauty when it was younger, but now it is thin to the point of death."

"Well I've already bought it. What can I do at this stage?"

"Bought it already? I thought you were just considering it. Well, you'll have to kill it and serve it, I suppose. But don't expect much of a dance to follow."

My spirits dropped rapidly. I could believe that Ben!a and /gaugo just might be putting me on about the black ox, but Halingisi seemed to be an impartial critic. I went around that day feeling as though I had bought a lemon of a used car.

In the afternoon it was Tomazo's turn. Tomazo is a fine hunter, a top trance performer . . ., and one of my most reliable informants. He approached the subject of the Christmas cow as part of my continuing Bushman education.

"My friend, the way it is with us Bushmen," he began, "is that we love meat. And even more than that, we love fat. When we hunt we always search for the fat ones, the ones dripping with layers of white fat: fat that turns into a clear, thick oil in the cooking pot, fat that slides down your gullet, fills your stomach and gives you a roaring diarrhea," he rhapsodized.

"So, feeling as we do," he continued, "it gives us pain to be served such a scrawny thing as Yehave's black ox. It is big, yes, and no doubt its giant bones are good for soup, but fat is what we really crave and so we will eat Christmas this year with a heavy heart."

The prospect of a gloomy Christmas now had me worried, so I asked Tomazo what I could do about it.

"Look for a fat one, a young one . . . smaller, but fat. Fat enough to make us *//gom* ('evacuate the bowels'), then we will be happy."

My suspicions were aroused when Tomazo said that he happened to know of a young, fat, barren cow that the owner was willing to part with. Was Toma working on commission, I wondered? But I dispelled this unworthy thought when we approached the Herero owner of the cow in question and found that he had decided not to sell.

The scrawny wreck of a Christmas ox now became the talk of the /ai/ai water hole and was the first news told to the outlying groups as they began to come in from the bush for the feast. What finally convinced me that real trouble might be brewing was the visit from u!au, an old conservative with a reputation for fierceness. His nickname meant spear and referred to an incident thirty years ago in which he had speared a man to death. He had an intense manner; fixing me with his eyes, he said in clipped tones:

"I have only just heard about the black ox today, or else I would have come here earlier. /ontah, do you honestly think you can serve meat like that to people and avoid a fight?" He paused, letting the implications sink in. "I don't mean fight you, /ontah; you are a white man. I mean a fight between Bushmen. There are many fierce ones here, and with such a small quantity of meat to distribute, how can you give everybody a fair share? Someone is sure to accuse another of taking too much or hogging all the choice pieces. Then you will see what happens when some go hungry while others eat."

The possibility of at least a serious argument struck me as all too real. I had witnessed the tension that surrounds the distribution of meat from a kudu or gemsbok kill, and had documented many arguments that sprang up from a real or imagined slight in meat distribution. The owners of a kill may spend up to two hours arranging and rearranging the piles of meat under the gaze of a circle of recipients before handing them out. And I also knew that the Christmas feast at /ai/ai would be bringing together groups that had feuded in the past.

Convinced now of the gravity of the situation, I went in earnest to search for a second cow; but all my inquiries failed to turn one up.

The Christmas feast was evidently going to be a disaster, and the incessant complaints about the meagerness of the ox had already taken the fun out of it for me. Moreover, I was getting bored with the wisecracks, and after losing my temper a few times, I resolved to serve the beast anyway. If the meat fell short, the hell with it. In the Bushmen idiom, I announced to all who would listen:

"I am a poor man and blind. If I have chosen one that is too old and too thin, we will eat it anyway and see if there is enough meat there to quiet the rumbling of our stomachs."

On hearing this speech, Ben!a offered me a rare word of comfort. "It's thin," she said philosophically, "but the bones will make a good soup."

At dawn Christmas morning, instinct told me to turn over the butchering and cooking to a friend and take off with Nancy to spend Christmas alone in the bush. But curiosity kept me from retreating. I wanted to see what such a scrawny ox looked like on butchering, and if there *was* going to be a fight, I wanted to catch every word of it. Anthropologists are incurable that way.

The great beast was driven up to our dancing ground, and a shot in the forehead dropped it in its tracks. Then, freshly cut branches were heaped around the fallen carcass to receive the meat. Ten men volunteered to help with the cutting. I asked /gaugo to make the breast bone cut. This cut, which begins the butchering process for most large game, offers easy access for removal of the viscera. But it also allows the hunter to spot-check the amount of fat on the animal. A fat game animal carries a white layer up to an inch thick on the chest, while in a thin one, the knife will quickly cut to bone. All eyes fixed on his hand as /gaugo, dwarfed by the great carcass, knelt to the breast. The first cut opened a pool of solid white in the black skin. The second and third cut widened and deepened the creamy white. Still no bone. It was pure fat; it must have been two inches thick.

"Hey /gau," I burst out, "that ox is loaded with fat. What's this about the ox being too thin to bother eating? Are you out of your mind?"

"Fat?" /gau shot back, "You call that fat? This wreck is thin, sick, dead!" And he broke out laughing. So did everyone else. They rolled on the ground, paralyzed with laughter. Everybody laughed except me; I was thinking.

I ran back to the tent and burst in just as Nancy was getting up. "Hey, the black ox. It's fat as hell! They were kidding about it being too thin to eat. It was a joke or something. A put-on. Everyone is really delighted with it!"

"Some joke," my wife replied. "It was so funny that you were ready to pack up and leave /ai/ai."

If it had indeed been a joke, it had been an extraordinarily convincing one, and tinged, I thought, with more than a touch of malice as many jokes are. Nevertheless, that it was a joke lifted my spirits considerably, and I returned to the butchering site where the shape of the ox was rapidly disappearing under the axes and knives of the butchers. The atmosphere had become festive. Grinning broadly, their arms covered with blood well past the elbow, men packed chunks of meat into the big cast-iron cooking pots, fifty pounds to the load, and muttered and chuckled all the while about the thinness and worthlessness of the animal and /ontah's poor judgment.

We danced and ate that ox two days and two nights; we cooked and distributed fourteen potfuls of meat and no one went home hungry and no fights broke out.

But the "joke" stayed in my mind. I had a growing feeling that something important had happened in my relationship with the Bushmen and that the clue lay in the meaning of the joke. Several days later, when most of the people had dispersed back to the bush camps, I raised the question with Hakekgose, a Tswana man who had grown up among the !Kung, married a !Kung girl, and who probably knew their culture better than any other non-Bushman.

"With us whites," I began, "Christmas is supposed to be the day of friendship and brotherly love. What I can't figure out is why the Bushmen went to such lengths to criticize and belittle the ox I had bought for the feast. The animal was perfectly good and their jokes and wisecracks practically ruined the holiday for me."

"So it really did bother you," said Hakekgose. "Well, that's the way they always talk. When I take my rifle and go hunting with them, if I miss, they laugh at me for the rest of the day. But even if I hit and bring one down, it's no better. To them, the kill is always too small or too old or too thin; and as we sit down on the kill site to cook and eat the liver, they keep grumbling, even with their mouths full of meat. They say things like, 'Oh this is awful! What a worthless animal! Whatever made me think that this Tswana rascal could hunt!' "

"Is this the way outsiders are treated?" I asked.

"No, it is their custom; they talk that way to each other too. Go and ask them."

/gaugo had been one of the most enthusiastic in making me feel bad about the merit of the Christmas ox. I sought him out first.

"Why did you tell me the black ox was worthless, when you could see that it was loaded with fat and meat?"

"It is our way," he said smiling. "We always like to fool people about that. Say there is a Bushman who has been hunting. He must not come home and announce like a braggard, 'I have killed a big one in the bush!' He must first sit down in silence until I or someone else comes up to his fire and asks, 'What did you see today?' He replies quietly, 'Ah, I'm no good for hunting. I saw nothing at all [pause] just a little tiny one.' Then I smile to myself," /gaugo continued, "because I know he has killed something big.

"In the morning we make up a party of four or five people to cut up and carry the meat back to the camp. When we arrive at the kill we examine it and cry out, 'You mean to say you have dragged us all the way out here in order to make us cart home your pile of bones? Oh, if I had known it was this thin I wouldn't have come.' Another one pipes up, 'People, to think I gave up a nice day in the shade for this. At home we may be hungry but at least we have nice cool water to drink.' If the horns are big, someone says, 'Did you think that somehow you were going to boil down the horns for soup?'

"To all this you must respond in kind. 'I agree,' you say, 'this one is not worth the effort; let's just cook the liver for strength and leave the rest for the hyenas. It is not too late to hunt today and even a duiker or a steenbok would be better than this mess.'

"Then you set to work nevertheless; butcher the animal, carry the meat back to the camp and everyone eats," /gaugo concluded.

Things were beginning to make sense. Next, I went to Tomazo. He corroborated /gaugo's story of the obligatory insults over a kill and added a few details of his own.

"But," I asked, "why insult a man after he has gone to all that trouble to track and kill an animal and when he is going to share the meat with you so that your children will have something to eat?"

"Arrogance," was his cryptic answer.

"Arrogance?"

"Yes, when a young man kills much meat he comes to think of himself as a chief or a big man, and he thinks of the rest of us as his servants or inferiors. We can't accept this. We refuse one who boasts, for someday his pride will make him kill somebody. So we always speak of his meat as worthless. This way we cool his heart and make him gentle."

"But why didn't you tell me this before?" I asked Tomazo with some heat.

"Because you never asked me," said Tomazo, echoing the refrain that has come to haunt every field ethnographer.

The pieces now fell into place. I had known for a long time that in situations of social conflict with Bushmen I held all the cards. I was the only source of tobacco in a thousand square miles, and I was not incapable of cutting an individual off for noncooperation. Though my boycott never lasted longer than a few days, it was an indication of my strength. People resented my presence at the water hole, yet simultaneously dreaded my leaving. In short I was a perfect target for the charge of arrogance and for the Bushmen tactic of enforcing humility.

I had been taught an object lesson by the Bushmen; it had come from an unexpected corner and had hurt me in a vulnerable area. For the big black ox was to be the one totally generous, unstinting act of my year at /ai/ai, and I was quite unprepared for the reaction I received.

As I read it, their message was this: There are no totally generous acts. All "acts" have an element of calculation. One black ox slaughtered at Christmas does not wipe out a year of careful manipulation of gifts given to serve your own ends. After all, to kill an animal and share the meat with people is really no more than Bushmen do for each other every day and with far less fanfare.

In the end, I had to admire how the Bushmen had played out the farce — collectively straight-faced to the end. Curiously, the episode reminded me of the *Good Soldier Schweik* and his marvelous encounters with authority. Like Schweik, the Bushmen had retained a thoroughgoing skepticism of good intentions. Was it this independence of spirit, I wondered, that had kept them culturally viable in the face of generations of contact with more powerful societies, both black and white? The thought that the Bushmen were alive and well in the Kalahari was strangely comforting. Perhaps, armed with that independence and with their superb knowledge of their environment, they might yet survive the future.

2

Shakespeare in the bush

LAURA BOHANNAN

Cultural anthropologists are all concerned with meaning, *with the difficult task of translation from one language to another. In this classic of anthropology, Laura Bohannan shows the difficulty of translating the meaning of* Hamlet *to the Tiv in West Africa. The article forcefully demonstrates the way in which different cultures provide distinct and separate worlds of meaning for those who have learned to live by them.*

Just before I left Oxford for the Tiv in West Africa, conversation turned to the season at Stratford. "You Americans," said a friend, "often have difficulty with Shakespeare. He was, after all, a very English poet, and one can easily misinterpret the universal by misunderstanding the particular."

I protested that human nature is pretty much the same the whole world over; at least the general plot and motivation of the greater tragedies would always be clear — everywhere — although some details of custom might have to be explained and difficulties of translation might produce other slight changes. To end an argument we could not conclude, my friend gave me a copy of *Hamlet* to study in the African bush: it would, he hoped, lift my mind above its primitive surroundings, and possibly I might, by prolonged meditation, achieve the grace of correct interpretation.

It was my second field trip to that African tribe, and I thought myself ready to live in one of its remote sections — an area difficult to cross even on foot. I eventually settled on the hillock of a very knowledgeable old man, the head of a homestead of some hundred and forty people, all

From "Shakespeare in the Bush," *Natural History* 75 (August–September 1966): 28–33.

of whom were either his close relatives or their wives and children. Like the other elders of the vicinity, the old man spent most of his time performing ceremonies seldom seen these days in the more accessible parts of the tribe. I was delighted. Soon there would be three months of enforced isolation and leisure, between the harvest that takes place just before the rising of the swamps and the clearing of new farms when the water goes down. Then, I thought, they would have even more time to perform ceremonies and explain them to me.

I was quite mistaken. Most of the ceremonies demanded the presence of elders from several homesteads. As the swamps rose, the old men found it too difficult to walk from one homestead to the next, and the ceremonies gradually ceased. As the swamps rose even higher, all activities but one came to an end. The women brewed beer from maize and millet. Men, women, and children sat on their hillocks and drank it.

People began to drink at dawn. By midmorning the whole homestead was singing, dancing, and drumming. When it rained, people had to sit inside their huts: there they drank and sang or they drank and told stories. In any case, by noon or before, I either had to join the party or retire to my own hut and my books. "One does not discuss serious matters when there is beer. Come, drink with us." Since I lacked their capacity for the thick native beer, I spent more and more time with *Hamlet*. Before the end of the second month, grace descended on me. I was quite sure that *Hamlet* had only one possible interpretation, and that one universally obvious.

Early every morning, in the hope of having some serious talk before the beer party, I used to call on the old man at his reception hut — a circle of posts supporting a thatched roof above a low mud wall to keep out wind and rain. One day I crawled through the low doorway and found most of the men of the homestead sitting huddled in their ragged cloths on stools, low plank beds, and reclining chairs, warming themselves against the chill of the rain around a smoky fire. In the center were three pots of beer. The party had started.

The old man greeted me cordially. "Sit down and drink." I accepted a large calabash full of beer, poured some into a small drinking gourd, and tossed it down. Then I poured some more into the same gourd for the man second in seniority to my host before I handed my calabash over to a young man for further distribution. Important people shouldn't ladle beer themselves.

"It is better like this," the old man said, looking at me approvingly and plucking at the thatch that had caught in my hair. "You should sit and drink with us more often. Your servants tell me that when you are not with us, you sit inside your hut looking at a paper."

The old man was acquainted with four kinds of "papers": tax receipts, bride price receipts, court free receipts, and letters. The messenger who brought him letters from the chief used them mainly as a badge of office, for he always knew what was in them and told the old man. Personal letters for the few who had relatives in the government or mission stations were kept until someone went to a large market where there was a letter writer and reader. Since my arrival, letters were brought to me to be read. A few men also brought me bride price receipts, privately, with requests to change the figures to a higher sum. I found moral arguments were of no avail, since in-laws are fair game, and the technical hazards of forgery difficult to explain to an illiterate people. I did not wish them to think me silly enough to look at any such papers for days on end, and I hastily explained that my "paper" was one of the "things of long ago" of my country.

"Ah," said the old man. "Tell us."

I protested that I was not a storyteller. Storytelling is a skilled art among them; their standards are high, and the audiences critical — and vocal in their criticism. I protested in vain. This morning they wanted to hear a story while they drank. They threatened to tell me no more stories until I told them one of mine. Finally, the old man promised that no one would criticize my style "for we know you are struggling with our language." "But," put in one of the elders, "you must explain what we do not understand, as we do when we tell you our stories." Realizing that here was my chance to prove *Hamlet* universally intelligible, I agreed.

The old man handed me some more beer to help me on with my storytelling. Men filled their long wooden pipes and knocked coals from the fire to place in the pipe bowls; then, puffing contentedly, they sat back to listen. I began in the proper style, "Not yesterday, not yesterday, but long ago, a thing occurred. One night three men were keeping watch outside the homestead of the great chief, when suddenly they saw the former chief approach them."

"Why was he no longer their chief?"

"He was dead," I explained. "That is why they were troubled and afraid when they saw him."

"Impossible," began one of the elders, handing his pipe on to his neighbor, who interrupted, "Of course it wasn't the dead chief. It was an omen sent by a witch. Go on."

Slightly shaken, I continued. "One of these three was a man who knew things" — the closest translation for scholar, but unfortunately it also meant witch. The second elder looked triumphantly at the first. "So he spoke to the dead chief saying, 'Tell us what we must do so you may rest in your grave,' but the dead chief did not answer. He vanished, and they could see him no more. Then the man who knew things — his name was Horatio — said this event was the affair of the dead chief's son, Hamlet."

There was a general shaking of heads round the circle. "Had the dead chief no living brothers? Or was this son the chief?"

"No," I replied. "That is, he had one living brother who became the chief when the elder brother died."

The old men muttered: such omens were matters for chiefs and elders, not for youngsters; no good could come of going behind a chief's back; clearly Horatio was not a man who knew things.

"Yes, he was," I insisted, shooing a chicken away from my beer. "In our country the son is next to the father. The dead chief's younger brother had become the great chief. He had also married his elder brother's widow only about a month after the funeral."

"He did well," the old man beamed and announced to the others, "I told you that if we knew more about Europeans, we would find they really were very like us. In our country also," he added to me, "the younger brother marries the elder brother's widow and becomes the father of his children. Now, if your uncle, who married your widowed mother, is your father's full brother, then he will be a real father to you. Did Hamlet's father and uncle have one mother?"

His question barely penetrated my mind; I was too upset and thrown too far off balance by having one of the most important elements of *Hamlet* knocked straight out of the picture. Rather uncertainly I said that I thought they had the same mother, but I wasn't sure — the story didn't say. The old man told me severely that these genealogical details made all the difference and that when I got home I must ask the elders about it. He shouted out the door to one of his younger wives to bring his goatskin bag.

Determined to save what I could of the mother motif, I took a deep breath and began again. "The son Hamlet was very sad because his mother had married again so quickly. There was no need for her to do so, and it is our custom for a widow not to go to her next husband until she has mourned for two years."

"Two years is too long," objected the wife, who had appeared with the old man's battered goatskin bag. "Who will hoe your farms for you while you have no husband?"

"Hamlet," I retorted without thinking, "was old enough to hoe his mother's farms himself. There was no need for her to remarry." No one looked convinced. I gave up. "His mother and the great chief told Hamlet not to be sad, for the great chief himself would be a father to Hamlet. Furthermore, Hamlet would be the next chief: therefore he must stay to learn the things of a chief. Hamlet agreed to remain, and all the rest went off to drink beer."

While I paused, perplexed at how to render Hamlet's disgusted soliloquy to an audience convinced that Claudius and Gertrude had behaved in the best possible manner, one of the younger men asked me who had married the other wives of the dead chief.

"He had no other wives," I told him.

"But a chief must have many wives! How else can be brew beer and prepare food for all his guests?"

I said firmly that in our country even chiefs had only one wife, that they had servants to do their work, and that they paid them from tax money.

It was better, they returned, for a chief to have many wives and sons who would help him hoe his farms and feed his people; then everyone loved the chief who gave much and took nothing — taxes were a bad thing.

I agreed with the last comment, but for the rest fell back on their favorite way of fobbing off my questions: "That is the way it is done, so that is how we do it."

I decided to skip the soliloquy. Even if Claudius was here thought quite right to marry his brother's widow, there remained the poison motif, and I knew they would disapprove of fratricide. More hopefully I resumed, "That night Hamlet kept watch with the three who had seen his dead father. The dead chief again appeared, and although the others were afraid, Hamlet followed his dead father off to one side. When they were alone, Hamlet's dead father spoke."

"Omens can't talk!" The old man was emphatic.

"Hamlet's dead father wasn't an omen. Seeing him might have been an omen, but he was not." My audience looked as confused as I sounded. "It *was* Hamlet's dead father. It was a thing we call a "ghost."" I had to use the English word, for unlike many of the neighboring tribes, these people didn't believe in the survival after death of any individuating part of the personality.

"What is a 'ghost?' An omen?"

"No, a 'ghost' is someone who is dead but who walks around and can talk, and people can hear him and see him but not touch him."

They objected. "One can touch zombis."

"No, no! It was not a dead body the witches had animated to sacrifice and eat. No one else made Hamlet's dead father walk. He did it himself."

"Dead men can't walk," protested my audience as one man.

I was quite willing to compromise. "A 'ghost' is the dead man's shadow."

But again they objected. "Dead men cast no shadows."

"They do in my country," I snapped.

The old man quelled the babble of disbelief that arose immediately and told me with that insincere, but courteous, agreement one extends to the fancies of the young, ignorant, and superstitious, "No doubt in your country the dead can also walk without being zombis." From the depths of his bag he produced a withered fragment of kola nut, bit off one end to show it wasn't poisoned, and handed me the rest as a peace offering.

"Anyhow," I resumed, "Hamlet's dead father said that his own brother, the one who became chief, had poisoned him. He wanted Hamlet to avenge him. Hamlet believed this in his heart, for he did not like his father's brother." I took another swallow of beer. "In the country of the great chief, living in the same homestead, for it was a very large one, was an important elder who was often with the chief to advise and help him. His name was Polonius. Hamlet was courting his daughter, but her father and her brother . . . [I cast hastily about for some tribal analogy] warned her not to let Hamlet visit her when she was alone on her farm, for he would be a great chief and so could not marry her."

"Why not?" asked the wife, who had settled down on the edge of the old man's chair. He frowned at her for asking stupid questions and growled, "They lived in the same homestead."

"That was not the reason," I informed them. "Polonius was a stranger who lived in the homestead because he helped the chief, not because he was a relative."

"Then why couldn't Hamlet marry her?"

"He could have," I explained, "but Polonius didn't think he would. After all, Hamlet was a man of great importance who ought to marry a chief's daughter, for in his country a man could have only one wife. Polonius was afraid that if Hamlet made love to his daughter, then no one else would give a high price for her."

"That might be true," remarked one of the shrewder elders, "but a chief's son would give his mistress's father enough presents and patronage to more than make up the difference. Polonius sounds like a fool to me."

"Many people think he was," I agreed. "Meanwhile Polonius sent his son Laertes off to Paris to learn the things of that country, for it was the homestead of a very great chief indeed. Because he was afraid that Laertes might waste a lot of money on beer and women and gambling, or get into trouble by fighting, he sent one of his servants to Paris secretly, to spy out what Laertes was doing. One day Hamlet came upon Polonius's daughter Ophelia. He behaved so oddly he frightened her. Indeed" — I was fumbling for words to express the dubious quality of Hamlet's madness — "the chief and many others had also noticed that when Hamlet talked one could understand the words but not what they meant. Many people thought that he had become mad." My audience suddenly became much more attentive. "The great chief wanted to know what was wrong with Hamlet, so he sent for two of Hamlet's age mates [school friends would have taken long explanation] to talk to Hamlet and find out what troubled his heart. Hamlet, seeing that they had been bribed by the chief to betray him, told them nothing. Polonius, however, insisted that Hamlet was mad because he had been forbidden to see Ophelia, whom he loved."

"Why," inquired a bewildered voice, "should anyone bewitch Hamlet on that account?"

"Bewitch him?"

"Yes, only witchcraft can make anyone mad, unless, of course, one sees the beings that lurk in the forest."

I stopped being a storyteller, took out my notebook and demanded to be told more about these two causes of madness. Even while they spoke and I jotted notes, I tried to calculate the effect of this new factor on the plot. Hamlet had not been exposed to the beings that lurk in the forest. Only his relatives in the male line could bewitch him. Barring relatives not mentioned by Shakespeare, it had to be Claudius who was attempting to harm him. And, of course, it was.

For the moment I staved off questions by saying that the great chief also refused to believe that Hamlet was mad for the love of Ophelia and nothing else. "He was sure that something much more important was troubling Hamlet's heart."

"Now Hamlet's age mates," I continued, "had brought with them a famous storyteller. Hamlet decided to have this man tell the chief and all his homestead a story about a man who had poisoned his brother because he desired his brother's wife and wished to be chief himself. Hamlet was sure the great chief could not hear the story without making a sign if he was indeed guilty, and then he would discover whether his dead father had told him the truth."

The old man interrupted, with deep cunning, "Why should a father lie to his son?" he asked.

I hedged: "Hamlet wasn't sure that it really was his dead father." It was impossible to say anything, in that language, about devil-inspired visions.

"You mean," he said, "it actually was an omen, and he knew witches sometimes send false ones. Hamlet was a fool not to go to one skilled in reading omens and divining the truth in the first place. A man-who-sees-the-truth could have told him how his father died, if he really had been poisoned, and if there was witchcraft in it; then Hamlet could have called the elders to settle the matter."

The shrewd elder ventured to disagree. "Because his father's brother was a great chief, one-who-sees-the-truth might therefore have been afraid to tell it. I think it was for that reason that a friend of Hamlet's father — a witch and an elder — sent an omen so his friend's son would know. Was the omen true?"

"Yes," I said, abandoning ghosts and the devil; a witch-sent omen it would have to be. "It was true, for when the storyteller was telling his tale before all the homestead, the great chief rose in fear. Afraid that Hamlet knew his secret he planned to have him killed."

The stage set of the next bit presented some difficulties of translation. I began cautiously. "The great chief told Hamlet's mother to find out from her son what he knew. But because a woman's children are always first in her heart, he had the important elder Polonius hide behind a cloth that hung against the wall of Hamlet's mother's sleeping hut. Hamlet started to scold his mother for what she had done."

There was a shocked murmur from everyone. A man should never scold his mother.

"She called out in fear, and Polonius moved behind the cloth. Shouting, 'A rat!' Hamlet took his machete and slashed through the cloth." I paused for dramatic effect. "He had killed Polonius!"

The old men looked at each other in supreme disgust. "That Polonius truly was a fool and a man who knew nothing! What child would not know enough to shout, 'It's me!' " With a pang, I remembered that these people are ardent hunters, always armed with bow, arrow, and machete; at the first rustle in the grass an arrow is aimed and ready, and the hunter shouts "Game!" If no human voice answers immediately, the arrow speeds on its way. Like a good hunter Hamlet had shouted, "A rat!"

I rushed in to save Polonius's reputation. "Polonius did speak. Hamlet heard him. But he thought it was the chief and wished to kill him to avenge his father. He had meant to kill him earlier that evening. . . ." I broke down, unable to describe to these pagans, who had no belief in individual afterlife, the difference between dying at one's prayers and dying "unhousell'd, disappointed, unaneled."

This time I had shocked my audience seriously. "For a man to raise his hand against his father's brother and the one who has become his father — that is a terrible thing. The elders ought to let such a man be bewitched."

I nibbled at my kola nut in some perplexity, then pointed out that after all the man had killed Hamlet's father.

"No," pronounced the old man, speaking less to me than to the young men sitting behind the elders. "If your father's brother has killed your father, you must appeal to your father's age mates; *they* may avenge him. No man may use violence against his senior relatives." Another thought struck him. "But if his father's brother had indeed been wicked enough to bewitch Hamlet and make him mad that would be a good story indeed, for it would be his fault that Hamlet, being mad, no longer had any sense and thus was ready to kill his father's brother."

There was a murmur of applause. *Hamlet* was again a good story to them, but it no longer seemed quite the same story to me. As I thought over the coming complications of plot and motive, I lost courage and decided to skim over dangerous ground quickly.

"The great chief," I went on, "was not sorry that Hamlet had killed Polonius. It gave him a reason to send Hamlet away, with his two treacherous age mates, with letters to a chief of a far country, saying that Hamlet should be killed. But Hamlet changed the writing on their papers, so that the chief killed his age mates instead." I encountered a reproachful glare from one of the men whom I had told undetectable forgery was not merely immoral but beyond human skill. I looked the other way.

"Before Hamlet could return, Laertes came back for his father's funeral. The great chief told him Hamlet had killed Polonius. Laertes swore to kill Hamlet because of this, and because his sister Ophelia, hearing her father had been killed by the man she loved, went mad and drowned in the river."

"Have you already forgotten what we told you?" The old man was reproachful. "One cannot take vengeance on a madman; Hamlet killed Polonius in his madness. As for the girl, she not only went mad, she was drowned. Only witches can make people drown. Water itself can't hurt anything. It is merely something one drinks and bathes in."

I began to get cross. "If you don't like the story, I'll stop."

The old man made soothing noises and himself poured me some more beer. "You tell the story well, and we are listening. But it is clear that the elders of your country have never told you what the story really means. No, don't interrupt! We believe you when you say your marriage customs are different, or your clothes and weapons. But people are the same everywhere; therefore, there are always witches and it is we, the elders, who know how witches work. We told you it was the great chief who wished to kill Hamlet, and now your own words have proved us right. Who were Ophelia's male relatives?"

"There were only her father and her brother." Hamlet was clearly out of my hands.

"There must have been many more; this also you must ask of your elders when you get back to your country. From what you tell us, since

Polonius was dead, it must have been Laertes who killed Ophelia, although I do not see the reason for it."

We had emptied one pot of beer, and the old men argued the point with slightly tipsy interest. Finally one of them demanded of me, "What did the servant of Polonius say on his return?"

With difficulty I recollected Reynaldo and his mission. "I don't think he did return before Polonius was killed."

"Listen," said the elder, "and I will tell you how it was and how your story will go, then you may tell me if I am right. Polonius knew his son would get into trouble, and so he did. He had many fines to pay for fighting, and debts from gambling. But he had only two ways of getting money quickly. One was to marry off his sister at once, but it is difficult to find a man who will marry a woman desired by the son of a chief. For if the chief's heir commits adultery with your wife, what can you do? Only a fool calls a case against a man who will someday be his judge. Therefore Laertes had to take the second way: he killed his sister by witchcraft, drowning her so he could secretly sell her body to the witches."

I raised an objection. "They found her body and buried it. Indeed Laertes jumped into the grave to see his sister once more — so, you see, the body was truly there. Hamlet, who had just come back, jumped in after him."

"What did I tell you?" The elder appealed to the others. "Laertes was up to no good with his sister's body. Hamlet prevented him, because the chief's heir, like a chief, does not wish any other man to grow rich and powerful. Laertes would be angry, because he would have killed his sister without benefit to himself. In our country he would try to kill Hamlet for that reason. Is this not what happened?"

"More or less," I admitted. "When the great chief found Hamlet was still alive, he encouraged Laertes to try to kill Hamlet and arranged a fight with machetes between them. In the fight both the young men were wounded to death. Hamlet's mother drank the poisoned beer that the chief meant for Hamlet in case he won the fight. When he saw his mother die of poison, Hamlet, dying, managed to kill his father's brother with his machete."

"You see, I was right!" exclaimed the elder.

"That was a very good story," added the old man, "and you told it with very few mistakes. There was just one more error, at the very end. The poison Hamlet's mother drank was obviously meant for the survivor of the fight, whichever it was. If Laertes had won, the great chief would have poisoned him, for no one would know that he arranged Hamlet's death. Then, too, he need not fear Laertes' witchcraft; it takes a strong heart to kill one's only sister by witchcraft.

"Sometime," concluded the old man, gathering his ragged toga about him, "you must tell us some more stories of your country. We, who are elders, will instruct you in their true meaning, so that when you return to your own land your elders will see that you have not been sitting in the bush, but among those who know things and who have taught you wisdom."

3

Intercultural communication

EDWARD T. HALL, JR.
WILLIAM FOOTE WHYTE

In any culture the rules and plans that individuals learn provide a frame of reference for all behavior. When Americans attempt to work in other cultures, they are often misunderstood and misunderstand, because of their different definitions of space, time, body contact, and gestures. Edward Hall and William Whyte explore how people in every society conform to their culture, even when they are least aware of such conformity. Understanding this fact will facilitate cross-cultural communication.

How can anthropological knowledge help the man of action in dealing with people of another culture? We shall seek to answer that question by examining the process of intercultural communication.

Anthropologists have long claimed that a knowledge of culture is valuable to the administrator. More and more people in business and government are willing to take this claim seriously, but they ask that we put culture to them in terms they can understand and act upon.

When the layman thinks of culture, he is likely to think in terms of (1) the way people dress, (2) the beliefs they hold, and (3) the customs they practice — with an accent upon the esoteric. Without undertaking any comprehensive definition, we can concede that all three are aspects of culture, and yet point out that they do not get us very far, either theoretically or practically.

Dress is misleading, if we assume that differences in dress indicate differences in belief and behavior. If that were the case, then we should expect to find people dressed like ourselves to be thinking and acting like ourselves. While there are still peoples wearing "colorful" apparel quite

From "Intercultural Communication: A Guide to Men of Action," *Human Organization* 19, no. 1 (1960): 5–12. Reprinted by permission of the Society for Applied Anthropology and the authors. Footnotes are omitted.

different from ours, we find in many industrializing societies that the people with whom we deal dress much as we do — and yet think and act quite differently.

Knowledge of beliefs may leave us up in the air because the connections between beliefs and behavior are seldom obvious. In the case of religious beliefs, we may know, for example, that the Mohammedan must pray to Allah a certain number of times a day and that therefore the working day must provide for praying time. This is important, to be sure, but the point is so obvious that it is unlikely to be overlooked by anyone. The administrator must also grasp the less dramatic aspects of everyday behavior, and here a knowledge of beliefs is a very imperfect guide.

Customs provide more guidance, providing we do not limit ourselves to the esoteric and also search for the pattern of behavior into which a given custom fits. The anthropologist, in dealing with customary behavior, is not content with identifying individual items. To him, these items are not miscellaneous. They have meaning only as they are fitted together into a pattern.

But even assuming that the pattern can be communicated to the administrator, there is still something important lacking. The pattern shows how the people act — when among themselves. The administrator is not directly concerned with that situation. Whatever background information he has, he needs to interpret to himself how the people act *in relation to himself*. He is dealing with a cross-cultural situation. The link between the two cultures is provided by acts of communication between the administrator, representing one culture, and people representing another. If communication is effective, then understanding grows with collaborative action. If communication is faulty, then no book knowledge of culture can assure effective action.

This is not to devalue the knowledge of culture that can be provided by the anthropologist. It is only to suggest that the point of implementation of the knowledge must be in the communication process. Let us therefore examine the process of intercultural communication. By so doing we can accomplish two things: (A) Broaden knowledge of ourselves by revealing some of our own unconscious communicative acts. (B) Clear away heretofore almost insurmountable obstacles to understanding in the cross-cultural process. We also learn that communication, as it is used here, goes far beyond words and includes many other acts upon which judgments are based of what is transpiring and from which we draw conclusions as to what has occurred in the past.

Culture affects communication in various ways. It determines the time and timing of interpersonal events, the places where it is appropriate to discuss particular topics, the physical distance separating one speaker from another, the tone of voice that is appropriate to the subject matter.

Culture, in this sense, delineates the amount and type of physical contact, if any, which convention permits or demands, and the intensity of emotion which goes with it. Culture includes the relationship of *what is said to what is meant* — as when "no" means "maybe" and "tomorrow" means "never." Culture, too, determines whether a given matter — say, a business contract — should be initially discussed between two persons or hacked out in a day-long conference which includes four or five senior officials from each side, with perhaps an assist from the little man who brings in the coffee.

These are important matters which the businessman who hopes to trade abroad ignores at his peril. They are also elusive, for every man takes his own culture for granted. Even a well-informed national of another country is hard put to explain why, in his own land, the custom is thus-and-so rather than so-and-thus; as hard put, indeed, as you would probably be if asked what is the "rule" which governs the precise time in a relationship that you begin using another man's first name. One "just knows." In other words, you do not know and cannot explain satisfactorily because you learn this sort of thing unconsciously in your upbringing, in your culture, and you take such knowledge for granted. Yet the impact of culture on communication can be observed and the lessons taught.

Since the most obvious form of communication is by language, we will first consider words, meanings, voice tones, emotions, and physical contact; then take up, in turn, the cultural impact of time, place, and social class relations on business situations in various lands. Finally, we will suggest what the individual administrator may do to increase his effectiveness abroad, and what students of culture may do to advance this application of anthropology.

Beyond language

Americans are often accused of not being very good at language, or at least not very much interested in learning foreign languages. There is little evidence that any people are inherently "better" at languages than any other, given the opportunity and incentive to learn. The West and Central European who has since childhood been in daily contact with two or three languages learns to speak them all, and frequently to read and write them as well. Under similar conditions, American children do the same. Indeed, a not uncommon sight on the backroads of Western Europe is a mute, red-faced American military family lost on a Sunday drive while the youngest child, barely able to lisp his own English, leans from the window to interpret the directions of some gnarled farmer whose dialect is largely unintelligible to most of his own countrymen.

We should not underestimate the damage our lack of language facility as a nation has done to our relations all over the world. Obviously, if you cannot speak a man's language, you are terribly handicapped in communicating with him.

But languages can be learned and yet most, if not all, of the disabling errors described in this article could still be made. Vocabulary, grammar, even verbal facility are not enough. Unless a man understands the subtle cues that are implicit in language, tone, gestures and expression, he will not only consistently misinterpret what is said to him, but he may offend irretrievably without knowing how or why.

Do they mean what they say?

Can't you believe what a man says? We all recognize that the basic honesty of the speaker is involved. What we often fail to recognize, however, is that the question involves cultural influences that have nothing to do with the honesty or dependability of the individual.

In the United States we put a premium on direct expression. The "good" American is supposed to say what he means and to mean what he says. If, on important matters, we discover that someone spoke deviously or evasively, we would be inclined to regard him thereafter as unreliable if not out-and-out dishonest.

In some other cultures, the words and their meanings do not have such a direct connection. People may be more concerned with the emotional context of the situation than with the meaning of particular words. This leads them to give an agreeable and pleasant answer to a question when a literal, factual answer might be unpleasant or embarrassing.

This situation is not unknown in our culture, of course. How many times have you muttered your delighted appreciation for a boring evening? We term this simple politeness and understand each other perfectly.

On the other hand, analogous "polite" behavior on a matter of factory production would be incomprehensible. An American businessman would be most unlikely to question another businessman's word if he were technically qualified and said that his plant could produce 1000 gross of widgets a month. We are "taught" that it is none of our business to inquire too deeply into the details of his production system. This would be prying and might be considered an attempt to steal his operational plans.

Yet this cultural pattern has trapped many an American into believing that when a Japanese manufacturer answered a direct question with the reply that he could produce 1000 gross of widgets, he meant what he said. If the American had been escorted through the factory and saw quite clearly that its capacity was, at the most, perhaps 500 gross of widgets per month, he would be likely to say to himself:

> Well, this fellow probably has a brother-in-law who has a factory who can make up the difference. He isn't telling the whole story because he's

afraid I might try to make a better deal with the brother-in-law. Besides, what business is it of mine, so long as he meets the schedule?

The cables begin to burn after the American returns home and only 500 gross of widgets arrive each month.

What the American did not know was that in Japanese culture one avoids the direct question unless the questioner is absolutely certain that the answer will not embarrass the Japanese businessman in any way whatsoever. In Japan for one to admit being unable to perform a given operation or measure up to a given standard means a bitter loss of face. Given a foreigner who is so stupid, ignorant, or insensitive as to ask an embarrassing question, the Japanese is likely to choose what appears to him the lesser of two evils.

Americans caught in this cross-cultural communications trap are apt to feel doubly deceived because the Japanese manufacturer may well be an established and respected member of the business community.

Excitable people?

Man communicates not by words alone. His tone of voice, his facial expressions, his gestures all contribute to the infinitely varied calculus of meaning. But the confusion of tongues is more than matched by the confusion of gesture and other culture cues. One man's nod is another man's negative. Each culture has its own rich array of meaningful signs, symbols, gestures, emotional connotations, historical references, traditional responses and — equally significant — pointed silences. These have been built up over the millennia as (who can say?) snarls, growls, and love murmurs gathered meaning and dignity with long use, to end up perhaps as the worn coinage of trite expression.

Consider the Anglo-Saxon tradition of preserving one's calm. The American is taught by his culture to suppress his feelings. He is conditioned to regard emotion as generally bad (except in weak women who can't help themselves) and a stern self-control as good. The more important a matter, the more solemn and outwardly dispassionate he is likely to be. A cool head, granite visage, dispassionate logic — it is no accident that the Western story hero consistently displays these characteristics.

In the Middle East it is otherwise. From childhood, the Arab is permitted, even encouraged, to express his feelings without inhibition. Grown men can weep, shout, gesture expressively and violently, jump up and down — and be admired as sincere.

The modulated, controlled Anglo-Saxon is likely to be regarded with suspicion — he must be hiding something, practicing to deceive.

The exuberant and emotional Arab is likely to disturb the Anglo-Saxon, cause him to writhe inwardly with embarrassment — for isn't this childish behavior? And aren't things getting rather out of hand?

Then, again, there is the matter of how loudly one should talk.

In the Arab world, in discussions among equals, the men attain a decibel level that would be considered aggressive, objectionable, and obnoxious in the United States. Loudness connotes strength and sincerity among Arabs; a soft tone implies weakness, deviousness. This is so "right" in the Arab culture that several Arabs have told us they discounted anything heard over the "Voice of America" because the signal was so weak!

Personal status modulates voice tone, however, even in Arab society. The Saudi Arab shows respect to his superior — to a sheik, say — by lowering his voice and mumbling. The affluent American may also be addressed in this fashion, making almost impossible an already difficult situation. Since in the American culture one unconsciously "asks" another to raise his voice by raising one's own, the American speaks louder. This lowers the Arab's tone more and increases the mumble. This triggers a shouting response in the American — which cues the Arab into a frightened "I'm not being respectful enough" tone well below audibility.

They are not likely to part with much respect for each other.

To touch or not to touch?

How much physical contact should appropriately accompany social or business conversation?

In the United States we discourage physical contact, particularly between adult males. The most common physical contact is the handshake and, compared to Europeans, we use it sparingly.

The handshake is the most detached and impersonal form of greeting or farewell in Latin America. Somewhat more friendly is the left hand placed on another man's shoulder during a handshake. Definitely more intimate and warm is the *"doble abrazo"* in which two men embrace by placing their arms around each other's shoulders.

These are not difficult conventions to live with, particularly since the North American can easily permit the Latin American to take the initiative in any form of contact more intimate than the handshake. Far more difficult for the North American to learn to live with comfortably are the less stylized forms of physical contact such as the hand on one's arm during conversation. To the North American this is edging toward what in his culture is an uncomfortable something — possibly sexual — which inhibits his own communication.

Yet there are cultures which restrict physical contact far more than we do. An American at a cocktail party in Java tripped over the invisible cultural ropes which mark the boundaries of acceptable behavior. He was seeking to develop a business relationship with a prominent Javanese and seemed to be doing very well. Yet, when the cocktail party ended, so apparently did a promising beginning. For the North American spent nearly six months trying to arrange a second meeting. He finally learned, through pitying intermediaries, that at the cocktail party he had momentarily placed his arm on the shoulder of the Javanese — and in the presence of other people. Humiliating! Almost unpardonable in traditional Javanese etiquette.

In this particular case, the unwitting breach was mended by a graceful apology. It is worth noting, however, that a truly cordial business relationship never did develop.

The five dimensions of time

If we peel away a few layers of cultural clothing, we begin to reach almost totally unconscious reactions. Our ideas of time, for example, are deeply instilled in us when we are children. If they are contradicted by another's behavior, we react with anger, not knowing exactly why. For the businessman, five important temporal concepts are: appointment time, discussion time, acquaintance time, visiting time, and time schedules.

Anyone who has travelled abroad or dealt at all extensively with non-Americans learns that punctuality is variously interpreted. It is one thing to recognize this with the mind; to adjust to a different kind of *appointment time* is quite another.

In Latin America, you should expect to spend hours waiting in outer offices. If you bring your American interpretation of what constitutes punctuality to a Latin-American office, you will fray your temper and elevate your blood pressure. For a forty-five-minute wait is not unusual — no more unusual than a five-minute wait would be in the United States. No insult is intended, no arbitrary pecking order is being established. If, in the United States, you would not be outraged by a five-minute wait, you should not be outraged by the Latin-American's forty-five-minute delay in seeing you. The time pie is differently cut, that's all.

Further, the Latin American doesn't usually schedule individual appointments to the exclusion of other appointments. The informal clock of his upbringing ticks more slowly and he rather enjoys seeing several people on different matters at the same time. The three-ring circus atmosphere which results, if interpreted in the American's scale of time and propriety, seems to signal him to go away, to tell him that he is not being properly treated, to indicate that his dignity is under attack. Not so. The clock on the wall may look the same but it tells a different sort of time.

The cultural error may be compounded by a further miscalculation. In the United States, a consistently tardy man is likely to be considered undependable, and by our cultural clock this is a reasonable conclusion. For you to judge a Latin American by your scale of time values is to risk a major error.

Suppose you have waited forty-five minutes and there is a man in his office, by some miracle alone in the room with you. Do you now get down to business and stop "wasting time"?

If you are not forewarned by experience or a friendly advisor, you may try to do this. And it would usually be a mistake. For, in the American culture, *discussion* is a means to an end: the deal. You try to make your point quickly, efficiently, neatly. If your purpose is to arrange some major affairs, your instinct is probably to settle the major issues first, leave the details for later, possibly for the technical people to work out.

For the Latin American, the discussion is a part of the spice of life. Just as he tends not to be overly concerned about reserving you your specific segment of time, he tends not as rigidly to separate business from non-business. He runs it all together and wants to make something of a social event out of what you, in your culture, regard as strictly business.

The Latin American is not alone in this. The Greek businessman, partly for the same and partly for different reasons, does not lean toward the "hit-and-run" school of business behavior, either. The Greek businessman adds to the social element, however, a feeling about what length of discussion time constitutes good faith. In America, we show good faith by ignoring the details. "Let's agree on the main points. The details will take care of themselves."

Not so the Greek. He signifies good will and good faith by what may seem to you an interminable discussion which includes every conceivable detail. Otherwise, you see, he cannot help but feel that the other man might be trying to pull the wool over his eyes. Our habit, in what we feel to be our relaxed and friendly way, of postponing details until later smacks the Greek between the eyes as a maneuver to flank him. Even if you can somehow convince him that this is not the case, the meeting must still go on a certain indefinite — but, by our standards, long — time or he will feel disquieted.

The American desire to get down to business and on with other things works to our disadvantage in other parts of the world, too; and not only in business. The head of a large, successful Japanese firm commented: "You Americans have a terrible weakness. We Japanese know about it and exploit it every chance we get. You are impatient. We have learned that if we just make you wait long enough, you'll agree to anything."

Whether this is literally true or not, the Japanese executive singled out a trait of American culture which most of us share and which, one may assume from the newspapers, the Russians have not overlooked, either.

By *acquaintance time* we mean how long you must know a man before you are willing to do business with him.

In the United States, if we know that a salesman represents a well-known, reputable company, and if we need his product, he may walk away from the first meeting with an order in his pocket. A few minutes conversation to decide matters of price, delivery, payment, model of product — nothing more is involved. In Central America, local custom does not permit a salesman to land in town, call on the customer and walk away with an order, no matter how badly your prospect wants and needs your product. It is traditional there that you must see your man at least three times before you can discuss the nature of your business.

Does this mean that the South American businessman does not recognize the merits of one product over another? Of course it doesn't. It is just that the weight of tradition presses him to do business within a circle of friends. If a product he needs is not available within his circle, he does not go outside it so much as he enlarges the circle itself to include a new friend who can supply the want. Apart from his cultural need to "feel right" about a new relationship, there is the logic of his business system. One of the realities of his life is that it is dangerous to enter into business with someone over whom you have no more than formal, legal "control." In the past decades, his legal system has not always been as firm as ours and he has learned through experience that he needs the sanctions implicit in the informal system of friendship.

Visiting time involves the question of who sets the time for a visit. George Coelho, a social psychologist from India, gives an illustrative case. A U.S. businessman received this invitation from an Indian businessman: "Won't you and your family come and see us? Come anytime." Several weeks later, the Indian repeated the invitation in the same words. Each time the American replied that he would certainly like to drop in — but he never did. The reason is obvious in terms of our culture. Here "come any time" is just an expression of friendliness. You are not really expected to show up unless your host proposes a specific time. In India, on the contrary, the words are meant literally — that the host is putting himself at the disposal of his guest and really expects him to come. It is the essence of politeness to leave it to the guest to set a time at his convenience. If the guest never comes, the Indian naturally assumes that he does not want to come. Such a misunderstanding can lead to a serious rift between men who are trying to do business with each other.

Time schedules present Americans with another problem in many parts of the world. Without schedules, deadlines, priorities, and timetables, we tend to feel that our country could not run at all. Not only are they essential to getting work done, but they also play an important role in the informal communication process. Deadlines indicate priorities and priorities signal the relative importance of people and the processes they control. These are all so much a part of our lives that a day hardly passes without some reference to them. "I have to be there by 6:30." "If

I don't have these plans out by 5:00 they'll be useless." "I told J. B. I'd be finished by noon tomorrow and now he tells me to drop everything and get hot on the McDermott account. What do I do now?"

In our system, there are severe penalties for not completing work on time and important rewards for holding to schedules. One's integrity and reputation are at stake.

You can imagine the fundamental conflicts that arise when we attempt to do business with people who are just as strongly oriented away from time schedules as we are toward them.

The Middle Eastern peoples are a case in point. Not only is our idea of time schedules no part of Arab life but the mere mention of a deadline to an Arab is like waving a red flag in front of a bull. In his culture, your emphasis on a deadline has the emotional effect on him that his backing you into a corner and threatening you with a club would have on you.

One effect of this conflict of unconscious habit patterns is that hundreds of American-owned radio sets are lying on the shelves of Arab radio repair shops, untouched. The Americans made the serious cross-cultural error of asking to have the repair completed by a certain time.

How do you cope with this? How does the Arab get another Arab to do anything? Every culture has its own ways of bringing pressure to get results. The usual Arab way is one which Americans avoid as "bad manners." It is needling.

An Arab businessman whose car broke down explained it this way:

> First, I go to the garage and tell the mechanic what is wrong with my car. I wouldn't want to give him the idea that I didn't know. After that, I leave the car and walk around the block. When I come back to the garage, I ask him if he has started to work yet. On my way home from lunch I stop in and ask him how things are going. When I go back to the office I stop by again. In the evening I return and peer over his shoulder for a while. If I didn't keep this up, he'd be off working on someone else's car.

If you haven't been needled by an Arab, you just haven't been needled.

A place for everything

We say that there is a time and place for everything, but compared to other countries and cultures we give very little emphasis to place distinctions. Business is almost a universal value with us; it can be discussed almost anywhere, except perhaps in church. One can even talk business on the church steps going to and from the service. Politics is only slightly more restricted in the places appropriate for its discussion.

In other parts of the world, there are decided place restrictions on the discussion of business and politics. The American who is not conscious of the unwritten laws will offend if he abides by his own rather than by the local rules.

In India, you should not talk business when visiting a man's home. If you do, you prejudice your chances of ever working out a satisfactory business relationship.

In Latin America, although university students take an active interest in politics, tradition decrees that a politician should avoid political subjects when speaking on university grounds. A Latin American politician commented to anthropologist Allan Holmberg that neither he nor his fellow politicians would have dared attempt a political speech on the grounds of the University of San Marcos in Peru — as did Vice-President Nixon.

To complicate matters further, the student body of San Marcos, anticipating the visit, had voted that Mr. Nixon would not be welcome. The University Rector had issued no invitation, presumably because he expected what did, in fact, happen.

As a final touch, Mr. Nixon's interpreter was a man in full military uniform. In Latin American countries, some of which had recently overthrown military dictators, the symbolism of the military uniform could hardly contribute to a cordial atmosphere. Latin Americans need no reminder that the United States is a great military power.

Mr. Nixon's efforts were planned in the best traditions of our own culture: he hoped to improve relations through a direct, frank, and face-to-face discussion with students — the future leaders of their country. Unfortunately, this approach did not fit in at all with the culture of the host country. Of course, elements hostile to the United States did their best to capitalize upon this cross-cultural misunderstanding. However, even Latin Americans friendly to us, while admiring the Vice President's courage, found themselves acutely embarrassed by the behavior of their people and ours in the ensuing difficulties.

Being comfortable in space

Like time and place, differing ideas of space hide traps for the uninformed. Without realizing it, almost any person raised in the United States is likely to give an unintended snub to a Latin American simply in the way we handle space relationships, particularly during conversations.

In North America, the "proper" distance to stand when talking to another adult male you do not know well is about two feet, at least in a formal business conversation. (Naturally at a cocktail party, the distance shrinks, but anything under eight to ten inches is likely to provoke an apology or an attempt to back up.)

To a Latin American, with his cultural traditions and habits, a distance of two feet seems to him approximately what five feet would to us.

To him, we seem distant and cold. To us, he gives an impression of pushiness.

As soon as a Latin American moves close enough for him to feel comfortable, we feel uncomfortable and edge back. We once observed a conversation between a Latin and a North American which began at one end of a forty-foot hall. At intervals we noticed them again, finally at the other end of the hall. This rather amusing displacement had been accomplished by an almost continual series of small backward steps on the part of the American, trying unconsciously to reach a comfortable talking distance, and an equal closing of the gap by the Latin American as he attempted to reach his accustomed conversation space.

Americans in their offices in Latin America tend to keep their native acquaintances at our distance — not the Latin American's distance — by taking up a position behind a desk or typewriter. The barricade approach to communication is practiced even by old hands in Latin America who are completely unaware of its cultural significance. They know only that they are comfortable without realizing that the distance and equipment unconsciously make the Latin American uncomfortable.

How class channels communication

We would be mistaken to regard the communication patterns which we observe around the world as no more than a miscellaneous collection of customs. The communication pattern of a given society is part of its total culture pattern and can only be understood in that context.

We cannot undertake here to relate many examples of communication behavior to the underlying culture of the country. For the businessman, it might be useful to mention the difficulties in the relationship between social levels and the problem of information feedback from lower to higher levels in industrial organizations abroad.

There is in Latin America a pattern of human relations and union-management relations quite different from that with which we are familiar in the United States. Everett Hagen of MIT has noted the heavier emphasis upon line authority and the lesser development of staff organizations in Latin-American plants when compared with North American counterparts. To a much greater extent than in the United States, the government becomes involved in the handling of all kinds of labor problems.

These differences seem to be clearly related to the culture and social organization of Latin America. We find there that society has been much more rigidly stratified than it has with us. As a corollary, we find a greater emphasis upon authority in family and the community.

This emphasis upon status and class distinction makes it very difficult for people of different status levels to express themselves freely and frankly in discussion and argument. In the past, the pattern has been for the man of lower status to express deference to his superior in any face-to-face contact. This is so even when everyone knows that the subordinate dislikes the superior. The culture of Latin America places a great premium upon keeping personal relations harmonious on the surface.

In the United States, we feel that it is not only desirable but natural to speak up to your superior, to tell the boss exactly what you think, even when you disagree with him. Of course, we do not always do this, but we think that we should, and we feel guilty if we fail to speak our minds frankly. When workers in our factories first get elected to local union office, they may find themselves quite self-conscious about speaking up to the boss and arguing grievances. Many of them, however, quickly learn to do it and enjoy the experience. American culture emphasizes the thrashing-out of differences in face-to-face contacts. It de-emphasizes the importance of status. As a result, we have built institutions for handling industrial disputes on the basis of the local situation, and we rely on direct discussion by the parties immediately involved.

In Latin America, where it is exceedingly difficult for people to express their differences face-to-face and where status differences and authority are much more strongly emphasized than here, the workers tend to look to a third party — the government — to take care of their problems. Though the workers have great difficulty in thrashing out their problems with management, they find no difficulty in telling government representatives their problems. And it is to their government that they look for an authority to settle their grievances with management.

Status and class also decide whether business will be done on an individual or a group basis.

In the United States, we are growing more and more accustomed to working as members of large organizations. Despite this, we still assume that there is no need to send a delegation to do a job that one capable man might well handle.

In some other parts of the world, the individual cannot expect to gain the respect necessary to accomplish this purpose, no matter how capable he is, unless he brings along an appropriate number of associates.

In the United States, we would rarely think it necessary or proper to call on a customer in a group. He might well be antagonized by the hard sell. In Japan — as an example — the importance of the occasion and of the man is measured by whom he takes along.

This practice goes far down in the business and government hierarchies. Even a university professor is likely to bring one or two retainers along on academic business. Otherwise people might think that he was a nobody and that his affairs were of little moment.

Even when a group is involved in the U.S., the head man is the spokesman and sets the tone. This is not always the case in Japan. Two young Japanese once requested an older American widely respected in Tokyo to accompany them so that they could "stand on his face." He was not expected to enter into the negotiation; his function was simply to be present as an indication that their intentions were serious.

Adjustment goes both ways

One need not have devoted his life to a study of various cultures to see that none of them is static. All are constantly changing and one element of change is the very fact that U.S. enterprise enters a foreign field. This is inevitable and may be constructive if we know how to utilize our knowledge. The problem is for us to be aware of our impact and to learn how to induce changes skillfully.

Rather than try to answer the general question of how two cultures interact, we will consider the key problem of personnel selection and development in two particular intercultural situations, both in Latin cultures.

One U.S. company had totally different experiences with "Smith" and "Jones" in the handling of its labor relations. The local union leaders were bitterly hostile to Smith, whereas they could not praise Jones enough. These were puzzling reactions to higher management. Smith seemed a fair-minded and understanding man; it was difficult to fathom how anyone could be bitter against him. At the same time, Jones did not appear to be currying favor by his generosity in giving away the firm's assets. To management, he seemed to be just as firm a negotiator as Smith.

The explanation was found in the two men's communication characteristics. When the union leaders came in to negotiate with Smith, he would let them state their case fully and freely — without interruption, but also without comment. When they had finished, he would say, "I'm sorry. We can't do it." He would follow this blunt statement with a brief and entirely cogent explanation of his reasons for refusal. If the union leaders persisted in their arguments, Smith would paraphrase his first statement, calmly and succinctly. In either case, the discussion was over in a few minutes. The union leaders would storm out of Smith's office complaining bitterly about the cold and heartless man with whom they had to deal.

Jones handled the situation differently. His final conclusion was the same as Smith's — but he would state it only after two or three hours of discussion. Furthermore, Jones participated actively in these discussions, questioning the union leaders for more information, relating the case in question to previous cases, philosophizing about labor relations and human rights and exchanging stories about work experience. When the discussion came to an end, the union leaders would leave the office, commenting on how warmhearted and understanding he was, and how confident they were that he would help them when it was possible for him to do so. They actually seemed more satisfied with a negative decision from Jones than they did with a hard-won concession with Smith.

This was clearly a case where the personality of Jones happened to match certain discernible requirements of the Latin American culture. It was happenstance in this case that Jones worked out and Smith did not, for by American standards both were top-flight men. Since a talent for the kind of negotiation that the Latin American considers graceful and acceptable can hardly be developed in a grown man (or perhaps even in a young one), the basic problem is one of personnel selection in terms of the culture where the candidate is to work.

The second case is more complicated because it involves much deeper intercultural adjustments. The management of the parent U.S. company concerned had learned — as have the directors of most large firms with good-sized installations overseas — that one cannot afford to have all of the top and middle-management positions manned by North Americans. It is necessary to advance nationals up the overseas-management ladder as rapidly as their abilities permit. So the nationals have to learn not only the technical aspects of their jobs but also how to function at higher levels in the organization.

Latin culture emphasizes authority in the home, church, and community. Within the organization this produces a built-in hesitancy about speaking up to one's superiors. The initiative, the acceptance of responsibility which we value in our organizations had to be stimulated. How could it be done?

We observed one management man who had done a remarkable job of building up these very qualities in his general foremen and foremen. To begin with, he stimulated informal contacts between himself and these men through social events to which the men and their wives came. He saw to it that his senior North American assistants and their wives were also present. Knowing the language, he mixed freely with all. At the plant, he circulated about, dropped in not to inspect or check up, but to joke and to break down the great barrier that existed in the local traditions between authority and the subordinates.

Next, he developed a pattern of three-level meetings. At the top, he himself, the superintendents, and the general foremen. At the middle level, the superintendents, general foremen, and foremen. Then the general foremen, foremen, and workers.

At the top level meeting, the American management chief set the pattern of encouraging his subordinates to challenge his own ideas, to come up with original thoughts. When his superintendents (also North Americans) disagreed with him, he made it clear that they were to state their objections fully. At first, the general foreman looked surprised and uneasy. They noted, however, that the senior men who argued with the boss were encouraged and praised. Timorously, with great hesitation, they began to add their own suggestions. As time went on, they more and more accepted the new convention and pitched in without inhibition.

The idea of challenging the boss with constructive new ideas gradually filtered down to the second and third level meetings. It took a lot of time and gentle handling, but out of this approach grew an extraordinary morale. The native general foremen and foremen developed new pride in themselves, accepted new responsibilities, even reached out for more. They began to work to improve their capacities and to look forward to moving up in the hierarchy.

Conformity or adjustment?

To work with people, must we be just like them? Obviously not. If we try to conform completely, the Arab, the Latin American, the Italian, whoever he might be, finds our behavior confusing and insincere. He suspects our motive. We are expected to be different. But we are also expected to respect and accept the other people as they are. And we may, without doing violence to our own personalities, learn to communicate with them by observing the unwritten patterns they are accustomed to.

To be aware that there are pitfalls in cross-cultural dealings is the first big step forward. And to accept the fact that our convictions are in no respect more eternally "right" than someone else's is another constructive step. . . .

4

A friend who misunderstands

ROBERT B. EDGERTON

The interpersonal processes that occur during culture contact often involve misunderstanding — even among those who sincerely desire to be friends. Using data from Africa and North America, Robert Edgerton traces the development of friendship across cultures and through early encounters, testing, outrage, and final disillusionment of "pseudo-friendship." He relates the study of friendship to larger theoretical issues pertaining to the psychological processes of culture contact.

The vast literature concerning culture contact and culture change includes many competent studies of psychological factors. However, the interpersonal processes that underline culture contact are still too seldom analyzed. Where interpersonal process has been considered, for the most part the literature describes relatively impersonal, stereotyped, brief and superficial transactions between "donors" and "recipients" in acculturative contacts. True enough, acculturative relations are frequently of just this "recipient-donor" kind, but there are occasions when intimate and prolonged contact does occur and though relatively few in number these contacts can be of crucial importance to the course of subsequent acculturation.

In many acculturative situations, personal and prolonged contact does take place between "European" employer and "Native" employee, missionary and convert, teacher and student, colonial government officer and "Native" political leader, "old settler" and "Native" neighbor, trader and client, and, not least, between anthropologist and interpreter or informant. In some of these relationships, the "European" insists that he is

From "Some Dimensions of Disillusionment in Culture Contact," *Southwestern Journal of Anthropology* 21 (1965):231–243. Reprinted by permission of the author and of the editors of the *Southwestern Journal of Anthropology*. Most of the footnotes, the bibliographic citations, and the bibliography are omitted.

not like other "Europeans" who "dislike" or "mistreat" the "Natives" and he attempts to develop a close and friendly relationship with a particular "Native."

This kind of acculturative relationship is significant for what it tells us about disillusionment, both as it affects the course of culture change and as it implicates general features of interpersonal process. Although the process of disillusionment to be discussed here is directed to a particular culture contact situation, the general relevance of the process of disillusionment for a variety of interpersonal relations will also be pointed out.

Dimensions of disillusionment

Fieldwork with the Menomini Indians of Wisconsin in 1959 and with four East African tribes in 1961-62 led to the conviction that the process of disillusionment in culture contact in both areas was remarkably similar in most respects and identical in its essential characteristics. In both areas, a "Native" population was dominated politically, economically, and culturally by a "European" population. In both areas, members of the "Native" population were seeking and achieving political and social amelioration. Obviously, the details differ, but the ways in which the situations are alike are so impressive that, unless otherwise noted, the two areas will be considered one for the purposes of this discussion. Consequently, when the word "Native" is used it will refer both to the Menomini and the East Africans, and "European" will refer alike to the Americans of Wisconsin and the British of Uganda, Kenya, and Tanganyika. Although neither of these terms is wholly satisfactory, available synonyms were even less acceptable.

Antecedents of pseudo-friendship

The possibility of disillusionment in acculturation arises when a European member of the superordinate population presents himself to one or more Natives as a "friend," a "good guy," a "fair man," etc. That is, he describes himself as not typical of Europeans, as someone for whom the old rules of European-Native interaction do not apply, as someone who is fair, decent, trustworthy, unprejudiced and willing to treat Natives as he would "any other" men.

Given the status dominance of the European, only he can make this opening move. In most circumstances, the Native will not reject the offer; indeed, often he cannot do so. In any case, once the offer of friendship has been made, the rules have been changed, although neither Native nor European can at this point anticipate just how they have changed. Before examining this new relationship, it is necessary to see what these partners in pseudo-friendship bring with them to the encounter. Four major antecedents will be mentioned: (1) prestige and power differentials, (2) stereotyped misperceptions of the other, (3) ignorance of the culture of the other, and (4) mistrust.

Prestige and power differentials. The prestige gulf between European and Native is enormous. The European holds himself in every sense inviolably superior; he commands respect, deference, and distance from the Native while reciprocating none of these to him. For example, the European "first names" the Native who in turn must address the European in most respectful terms. And this pattern is followed regardless of the relative rank of the European in the European system or the Native in his system; with few exceptions, a low-ranking European is superior to a high-ranking Native.

Both in Wisconsin and East Africa, the Natives are exquisitely sensitive to status degradation *beyond* that accepted as being in the nature of things. This explosive touchiness has been reported by many observers for both areas. For the Indian, it may take the form of a bitter and elaborate defense against an assumed accusation. For example, Menomini are acutely sensitive to suggestions that their skin may be naturally dark rather than tanned by the sun. Similar responses have been noted by other writers; for example, for the Wisconsin Ojibwa by James: [1] "When 'kidded' about his 'sun-tanned neck' by a local White resorter he replied in cold anger, 'I may be black on the outside, but I'm White on the inside and that's more than you can say.' "

For the East African, the most innocent allusion to stealing is likely to provoke the Native to a furious defense which may well reflect innocence rather than self-incrimination. Experienced Europeans, who in the course of everyday life consistently inflict status insults upon Africans, nonetheless recognize that Africans are unusually sensitive about stealing, and attempt to avoid loose talk on the subject.

On his part, the European expects deference, and takes it for granted. He is often incredulous when it fails to appear, and is likely to turn to his sources of power for punishment. If the status breach is great enough, the European may turn to the courts or the police, both of which the Native believes him to control. If the insult is insufficient to warrant formal action, a wide range of economic penalties can be imposed; rarely will an individual Native have any economic power with which to retaliate. Finally, the European can employ a number of viciously wounding epithets. Natives may be devastated by words such as "boy," "nigger," "red nigger," "chief," "wog," etc., whereas the European is not vulnerable to any words the Natives can employ.

[1] B. James, "Social-psychological Dimensions of Ojibwa Acculturation," *American Anthropologist* 63 (1961):721–746.

Stereotyped misperceptions. The prevailing European stereotype of the Native describes him as lazy, drunken, immoral, stupid, primitive, magical, irresponsible, ungrateful, sexually promiscuous, and so forth. No European can be unaware that Natives are generally so regarded. The European may avoid becoming committed to all or part of this stereotyped view, but he always runs the risk of "slipping" and seeming to subscribe to the stereotype, or of reacting so strenuously against it that similar damage is done, for the Native is also aware that the stereotype exists and is alert to the slightest evidence that it is being brought into play against him.

On the other hand, the Native stereotype regards the European as aloof, greedy, wealthy but stingy, exploitative, excessively vain, and the like. Not all Europeans are aware that these perceptions exist. Those who are aware of the stereotype may be variously indifferent, indignant, or simply amused. But the European who initiates the pseudo-friend relationship cannot ignore the stereotype. He will probably admit that some of his fellow Europeans deserve to be characterized in such a manner, but he will be at pains to demonstrate that he is none of these things himself.

The friendly European is also aware that the stereotype has its own reality — that it perpetuates itself — but he almost certainly will not understand precisely what actions contribute to this perpetuation. He may feel that he knows when a fellow European is being coldly impolite, but without doubt some acts which he would consider completely proper will be read by the Native as overbearing or haughty. The converse, of course, is also true, and this brings up the third problem that underlies the process of acculturative disillusionment.

Ignorance of the other's culture. Accounts of acculturation throughout the world bear eloquent witness to the part that cultural misunderstanding can play in generating conflict, and of these gross misunderstandings no more need to be said here. In the course of disillusionment, however, slight and subtle ignorance of the other's culture is the greater danger. In most cases, parties to the pseudo-friend relationship know a great deal about each other's culture (greatly unacculturated persons are not likely to become involved in such relationships) and typically do not make obvious cultural blunders. But even should they do so, this kind of gaffe is so patent that it can easily be made to appear amusing and need not seriously disrupt the relationship.

However, where both parties are convinced that they have a good (if not perfect) understanding of the other's culture, minor misunderstandings may occur that may not be recognized by the offender, and are difficult for the offended to bring into the open. These misunderstandings may occur in any of hundreds of kinds of circumstances but some that seem repeatedly to cause trouble involve matters of privacy, sharing (especially of food), begging, gratitude (especially for small favors), presence or absence of reciprocal obligations to certain kin, cleanliness, honesty, and cruelty (especially to animals).

Rules and roles can be deceptively simple, and what may seem to one actor to be a full understanding may in fact be a considerably less than adequate one. For example, the Native may conclude that because the European appears to understand a certain role, he therefore understands it completely. In all probability, the European is not aware of the rich variations and flexibility in the role performance nor of the ambiguity in the many options attached to it; neither can he always display the appropriate affect. His consequently imperfect role performance can easily be interpreted by the Native as indicative of indifference, insincerity, or disrespect; worse, it can be read as evidence of bad faith or as verification of some aspect of the "stereotype."

Mistrust. Pervading all relations between Native and European is a profound sense of mistrust. The Native regards the history of European contact as one of unrelieved exploitation. He points to military aggression, land alienation, repression of traditional or "sacred" practices, and economic "enslavement" as evidence of his exploitation by the Europeans. And, of course, a literal reading of history will provide ample documentation of these and other charges. For his part, the European is likely to recognize these past abuses and feel some guilt regarding them, but he may offer extenuating reasons for the abuses and point out that there were also many benefits. The European views *pax* (either Britannica or Americana), medical care, education, and the introduction of a new technology as positive benefits and feels some lingering sense of puzzlement over the Natives' refusal always to view them with equal enthusiasm. As a result, the European is more likely than ever to feel that Natives generally cannot be trusted to behave reasonably or decently.

Each, then, reads the past differently, finds in it reason for dissatisfaction, and carries mistrust into the contacts of the present day. This legacy of mistrust is of fundamental importance in the process of disillusionment.

The pseudo-friend relationship

The actual contact between a Native and his European "friend" has the compellingness of the inevitable about it, for even should the Native not particularly care to have the European as a "friend" he is nonetheless obliged to test the European's offer of friendship if he is to remain in interaction with him. By being a "friend," by presenting himself as something different from other Europeans, the European has altered the currently accepted rules of conduct and the Native is unsure how he is expected to behave. Of course, a Native may welcome the offer of friendship as a possible route to status equality, for economic favors, or simply out of curiosity about the previously distant and sacrosanct European. In any case, the Native cannot behave correctly or comfortably until he has tested the limits of the friendship — until he knows where he stands. The superordinate European experiences little initial discomfort from the offer of friendship; it is the Native who is unsure and anxious and hopeful, and it is he who must take action to define the nature of the friendship offered to him. The Native must solve two puzzles: first, how to behave in this new role; second, why the European should propose such a role in the first place. To solve these puzzles he must test the European.

Testing for trust. The initial move in the test is likely to be a delicate lamentation consisting of a recitation of past grievances suffered at the hands of Europeans. Often, a specific European, rather than Europeans in general, is singled out for criticism. For example, here is a typical Menomini lament:

> Old Reverend ______, he done nothing but cause trouble. Always coming around and preaching against Indian ways. One day he called my wife a dirty squaw and when I come along he told me I was ignorant and full of stupid superstitions and unless I saw the truth I'd go straight to hell where I was headed. He always treated us like we was trash.

Or that of a Kamba of Kenya:

> Bwana ______ is a very kali [hot-tempered] man. When I worked for him he always called me, "Boy," and when I made a mistake he would call me bad names. One day I was late to work and he abused me in front of many people and when I protested that I was delayed by the sickness of my wife, he hit me in my face.

By a series of such laments the Native can elicit responses that suggest some preliminary guideliness for the new "friendship" relationship. Typically, the European will respond to these tales of abuse with sympathy; when he does, the Native responds with enthusiastic praise, assuring the European that he is, indeed, different and that theirs will be a sincere friendship. The result of this sort of preliminary exchange is to provide the Native with some information and to embolden the European in his offer of friendship.

As the relationship continues, the Native must acquire more information concerning the limitations of "friendship"; to do so he tests the European *indirectly*. Indirection is the technique of choice for two reasons. First, for the Native, indirection is *the* basis of everyday life. In a world peopled by powerful sorcerers and witches whose identity is never certain, indirection and concealment are more than simply proper — they are imperative. For the Menomini and throughout much of East Africa, social conduct proceeds upon a foundation of indirection where motives are concealed, wishes are obliquely expressed, and goals are hidden. But there is another equally compelling reason for being indirect; namely, that it has proven over the years to be the most successful way the Native can deal with the European. The European has great power both to hurt or punish openly and to degrade and discredit subtly. The Native must maneuver deviously, for privilege, knowledge, acceptance, and prestige are all contingent upon concealment of motives and goals. The Natives express their understanding of the necessity for such an approach quite clearly. Said one Menomini:

> An Indian has two faces — one for his own people and one for the white man. White man won't let you say what you feel, or do what you want, so you gotta lie to him — fool him so's he won't know what you're after or he won't let you get it. If he figures you out, you'll never get anywhere.

A Sebei of Uganda agrees:

> When I am with Europeans I must be so careful — I cannot say my mind to them, I must be sly and trick them. I must lie and make up stories in order to advance myself. I know what happens when an African talks straight out to a European. He is abused for not being polite and he does not get what he wants.

We find then, a Native who is vastly subordinate in power and prestige to the European, who misunderstands him and mistrusts him, attempting both to understand what is meant by an offer of friendship and what benefits this offer, if real, might entail. Of course, as the European interacts with the Native, he provides covert and pointed bits of information about himself, European in general, and what relations between men ought to be like. The chances are, however, that this information, no matter how sincerely and carefully communicated, will be insufficient for the needs of the Native. Words, after all, speak less convincingly than actions. The Native as yet has insufficient grounds for trust, for revealing himself to the yet potentially dangerous European. To establish grounds for trust he must test further.

The traditional test. The next move is likely to involve a test which in its formalized, repetitive character may be regarded as traditional. For the Menomini, as for many American Indian reservation groups, the test involves liquor. The European is asked to purchase liquor and transport it into the reservation. As such action is in violation of law, it serves dramatically to determine the willingness of the European to violate both the law and the general belief that Indians cannot "hold" their liquor and therefore should not drink alcoholic beverages. The Menomini refer to this test as "proof that you are a friend of the Indian." Lemert[2] describes an identical test among the Kwakiutl.

For the East African, the traditional test involves money rather than alcohol. The Native asks the European to lend him a sum of money (usually less than five dollars) promising only to repay the loan when he can. The common European belief insists that money so lent may just as well be considered a gift, for repayment will never occur. The Native is, of course, aware that the European feels this way.

In both cases, the request — for alcohol or money — is so contrary either to law or custom that the European cannot fail to understand that he is being tested. Presumably a few Europeans, by their refusal, fail this test but probably most are willing to comply with the request in an effort to demonstrate the sincerity of their friendship. The test is typically not repeated at this point; a single act of compliance seems to be sufficient evidence of good faith for the moment and the Native is still reluctant to antagonize the European unduly.

Hinting. What usually follows is a period of renewed indirection. The Native returns to his devious techniques of hinting, wishing, suggesting, alluding, dissembling, and so forth, both for his own short-term profit and in order to test the long-range possibilities of friendship.

Hinting, although but one of the devices of deviousness, is both basic to the Native and relatively foreign to the male European. For example, in the Native world of social reality, the hint often stands as a virtual obligation. Both for the Menomini and the East African, hints are generally to be understood as requests to be acted upon lest the hinter be gravely offended. Yet the hinter himself is protected against being committed to having made a request. As the psychiatrist Szasz[3] has put it: "The main advantage of hinting over more direct modes of communication is the protection it affords the speaker by enabling him to communicate without committing himself to what he says."

Obviously, the natural protection given by hinting when dealing with Europeans commends the practice to Natives. James[4] in a quotation from a "white informant married to an Ojibwa woman" could easily be writing about the Menomini:

> They never come right out with anything they want. You have to understand them if you want to get along with them. You got to always figure out what's on their mind. Sometimes they come around and you can't figure out what for, and if you can't tell what they're after they go

[2] E. Lemert, *Alcohol and the Northwest Coast Indians* (Berkeley: University of California Publications in Culture and Society, 1954).

[3] Thomas S. Szasz, *The Myth of Mental Illness* (New York: Hoerber-Harper, 1961).

[4] James, *op. cit.*, p. 738.

away without ever telling you what they want. But they'll be mad at you. You got to guess what they want from the hints they give.

Both the Menomini and East Africans are explicit about the necessity of approaching Europeans with hints to avoid being held accountable for the full implications of a forthright request. A Hehe man of Tanganyika put it this way:

> I never speak out to a European exactly what I have in my mind. There are reasons why this is so. Europeans do not understand how to say "no" politely — they simply say "no" straight out and this is a very bad thing. Also, they are not generous people and do not like to give things so I know that if I ask for something they will not agree so I only hint and if they should be good people and give me what I need then I am very happy but should they not give it, I have lost nothing.

What is true of the Ojibwa is true of their neighbors the Menomini as well as the distant East Africans — when a hint is not understood and acted upon, the hinter is disappointed and angry.

For his part, the European tends to resent the continued deviousness of the Native. While Europeans obviously understand that deviousness regularly occurs in European social relations, it is generally nothing to be proud of and is indeed usually disvalued. Certainly, men who are friends should not be devious with each other; they should "speak their minds," be direct and honest with each other. Although Europeans actually behave in a wondrous variety of ways, they tend to value honesty and direct communication; the Native regards both as impossibly ineffective and downright dangerous. After continued contact between the devious Native and his, ideally at least, direct European friend, tensions are apt to accumulate. Additionally, both parties display continued ignorance of each other's expectations for proper conduct, with the result that basic motives are once again called into question.

By this point, the European begins to question the wisdom of treating the Native as a friend, and the Native is increasingly frustrated in his efforts to test the meaning of "friendship" with his indirect methods. The stage is now set for the climactic scene.

The outrage. Occasionally in their writings and often in their conversations, anthropologists have discussed their disappointment when a "friend" among the people they were studying "suddenly" did something outrageous. As Stephen Boggs has put it: [5]

> Such slips seem to be caused by excessive anxiety. In my experience and in others that I have heard about from fieldworkers, they seem par-

[5] Quoted by James, *op. cit.*, p. 736.

ticularly likely to happen with whites who have established a good relation with the individual. Why? I suggest because there is more anxiety involved in relations with these whites because there is something to hope for from them.

It is true that the outrageous act is determined by hope — the problem for the Native is that he does not know *what* he can hope for. Boggs notes that "slips" occur as the "relationship progressed," an observation which accords with my own; the "outrage" occurs when all other tests have proven insufficient. The Native has been unable to learn the limits of the friendship offered him or whether in fact the European can be trusted to fullfill any of the assumed obligations of "friendship."

The Native must determine how far he can go. Is there a point at which the European will reveal his "true" motives by rejecting or "using" the Native? Will the European finally reveal that the entire relationship is but an elaborate exploitation of some sort? Sometimes as a frustrated "slip" but more often as an intentional test, the Native commits an "outrage."

One of the most common "outrages" is the blatant lie. This lie is obviously transparent and is not really offered as an acceptable explanation for the conduct in question; it is a challenge to the European to accept the explanation despite its clear falsehood. The bold-faced lie says to the European, "If you are the friend that you purport to be you will accept even this lie." A European teacher in Kenya recalled this pattern:

> Several times over the years I've grown quite attached to students and become just like a mother to them but after a point they simply destroy it all — they begin to misbehave, they lie terribly, and even steal. They become suspicious of me and refuse to believe that I only want to help them. It is just like they want to provoke me.

Outrageous demands also occur. The East African Native suddenly asks for a prized and valuable possession, or a Menomini appears in the middle of the night to insist that he be driven to a town thirty miles distant so that he may "visit a friend." These demands, like the lies, have the appearance of challenges: "If you are truly my friend you will do this thing even though I know that you do not want to do it." And, of course, no excuse, however reasonable, is sufficient; refusal is betrayal of the pledge of friendship.

When the outrage is met with refusal by the European the Native may respond with a ventilation of his accumulated anger and pour abuse upon the European, but usually he will simply withdraw convinced *not* that he has exceeded the limits of this friendship but that the friendship was a fraudulent, pseudo-friendship.

Disillusionment

A frequent consequence of the outrage is disillusionment. The Native retreats convinced at last that Europeans cannot be trusted and must truly be dealt with as always — suspiciously, deviously, and antagonistically.

Only rarely, however, will the antagonism erupt into overt aggression — the Europeans' sanctions against aggression are still to be feared. Typically, the sense of bitter disillusionment, the confirmation of exploitation, produces a passively hostile withdrawal into alienation or nativism.

The European is equally disillusioned. He has suffered a personal confirmation of the European stereotype's dictum that "if you give them an inch, they'll take a mile." He is certain that he gave his friendship, that he went more than half-way, and it was not appreciated. He too withdraws, and rather than risk another "outrage," he will probably be reluctant to offer friendship again.

Both Native and European receive enthusiastic support in their withdrawal. Other Natives shake their heads sadly and with commiserative zeal reaffirm their creed: "Never trust a European." Other Europeans readily reinforce the disillusionment by their insistence that an "outrage" is the inevitable result of any attempt to treat the Natives as equals or anything close to it. Thus, the conventional wisdom of both the Natives and the Europeans insisted that such an experiment in friendship, i.e., in trust, would fail. Despite hope and good will, it did fail. The consequence of disillusioning failure under such conditions can only increase the mistrust and antagonism between Europeans and Natives, and it will probably do so to a disproportionately great extent.

Summary and conclusion

The process of disillusionment as visualized here may be regarded as simply one variant of a more general form of interpersonal conflict. This conflict develops from unsuccessful attempts to establish trust between two persons or, more accurately, persons from two different categories. It has these essential features: (1) there is a differential in rights, privileges, prestige, and power, (2) the status superior has a typical biography involving the use of his prestige and power to punish, discomfit, or discredit a status inferior, (3) there are mutually derogatory stereotypes which ascribe improper, irresponsible, or hostile conduct to both the status superior and inferior, (4) as a consequence, both parties are mistrustful of the other, (5) the status superior offers to suspend the established relationships and behave as a friend, although not necessarily as a status equal, (6) the status inferior must probe to determine to what extent he can trust the superior, (7) because of basic mistrust and status inequality, this probing will be indirect and devious. With these features operative, the probability of failure, disillusionment, and heightened mistrust is great.

All or most of these features are commonly present in many relationships in the United States: for example, between soldiers and officers, employees and employers, patients and psychiatrists, Negroes and Whites, wives and husbands, and, of course, children and parents. But for the anthropologist perhaps the prototypically characteristic example of the friendship-mistrust-disillusionment process is the one elaborated here — the superordinate European and the subordinate Native.

It is contended that our accumulated knowledge of acculturation, while substantial in many respects, is deficient in some of the social-psychological dimensions of interpersonal process. It is further asserted that an important and neglected type of acculturative interpersonal process is the personal and prolonged interaction that occurs between a few Europeans and a few Natives.

This idealized reconstruction of the process that follows an offer of friendship has stressed misunderstanding, mistrust, indirection, and the "outrage" as crucial steps toward the final disillusionment of both partners in "pseudo-friendship." This process occurs often and with striking similarity in many areas of East Africa and among the Menomini of Wisconsin. It is presumed that it also occurs in many other parts of the world. Where it does occur, the outcome of disillusionment must serve to increase the misunderstanding and mistrust present in the acculturative context.

If this analysis is correct, then mistrust, indirection, and disillusionment are phenomena of considerable significance in an understanding of the interpersonal relationships which can be so critical in determining the course of culture contact.

III

Language and communication

Culture is a system of symbols that enables man to represent and communicate his experience. We are surrounded by symbols — the flag, a cap and gown, a beard, a hard hat — and all have special meaning in our society. In fact, since a symbol is anything that stands for something else, almost everything we experience holds symbolic meaning. Every symbol has a referrent which it calls to our attention. The words hard hat *refer to an object worn on the heads of construction workers; this object, in turn, is a symbol to many of hard work and patriotism. But, as with all symbols and referrents, these relationships are arbitrary.* Hard hat *could refer to a supernatural diety, and the laborers' headgear symbolic of the teachings of Chairman Mao. The fact that man assigns meaning to his experience in an arbitrary fashion gives rise to the cultural variation described in the last chapter.*

Symbols greatly simplify communication. Once we learn what barn *stands for, we can communicate about this object, even though it is beyond our sensory experience. Symbols make it possible to communicate the immense variety of human experience, whether past or present, tangible or intangible, good or bad. There are many channels available to man for symbolic com-*

munication — sound, sight, touch, and smell. Language, man's most highly developed communication system, uses the channel of sound. Linguists have developed techniques for discovering the rules for the formation of symbols (phonology), their combination (grammar), and their interpretation (semantics).

The selections that follow reflect the fact that anthropologists are going beyond descriptions of sound and grammar to study meaning and style. The way the body is adorned, the length of one's hair, the style of one's speech, all convey meaning. Whatever channel is used — gestures, body adornment, morse code, writing, braille, or language — all are based upon man's capacity to create and use symbols.

5

How to ask for a drink in Subanun

CHARLES O. FRAKE

Language fluency means more than a knowledge of sounds and grammar; styles of speech are also important. In this article Charles Frake discusses the different styles of speech the Subanun of the Philippines use to define and manipulate social relationships. The stages of discourse during a drinking encounter — "invitation," "jar talk," "discussion," and "display of verbal art" — constitute a set of instructions for asking for a drink in this culture. The result is a brief, elegant ethnography of speaking, which shows the function and meaning of speech styles in this culture and provides an excellent contrast with the next selection by Thomas Kochman.

Ward Goodenough [1] has proposed that a description of a culture — an ethnography — should properly specify what it is that a stranger to a society would have to know in order appropriately to perform any role in any scene staged by the society. If an ethnographer of Subanun culture were to take this notion seriously, one of the most crucial sets of instructions to provide would be that specifying how to ask for a drink. Anyone who cannot perform this operation successfully will be automatically excluded from the stage upon which some of the most dramatic scenes of Subanun life are performed.

To ask appropriately for a drink among the Subanun it is not enough to know how to construct a grammatical utterance in Subanun translatable in English as a request for a drink. Rendering such an utterance might elicit praise for one's fluency in Subanun, but it probably would not

Reproduced by permission of Charles O. Frake and the American Anthropological Association from the *American Anthropologist:* Vol. 66 (2), pp. 127–132, 1964. A note, the bibliographic citations, and the bibliography are omitted.

[1] Ward G. Goodenough, "Cultural Anthropology and Linguistics," in *Report of the Seventh Annual Round Table Meeting on Linguistics and Language Study*, Paul L. Garvin, ed., Georgetown University Monograph Series on Language and Linguistics 9 (1957):167–173.

get one a drink. To speak appropriately it is not enough to speak grammatically or even sensibly (in fact some speech settings may require the uttering of nonsense as is the case with the semantic-reversal type of speech play common in the Philippines.) Our stranger requires more than a grammar and a lexicon; he needs what Hymes [2] has called an ethnography of speaking: a specification of what kinds of things to say in what message forms to what kinds of people in what kinds of situations. Of course an ethnography of speaking cannot provide rules specifying exactly what message to select in a given situation. If messages were perfectly predictable from a knowledge of the culture, there would be little point in saying anything. But when a person selects a message, he does so from a set of appropriate alternatives. The task of an ethnographer of speaking is to specify what the appropriate alternatives are in a given situation and what the consequences are of selecting one alternative over another.

Drinking defined. Of the various substances which the Subanun consider "drinkable," we are here concerned only with a subset called *gasi,* a rice-yeast fermented beverage made of a rice, manioc, maize, and/or Job's tears mash. *Gasi,* glossed in this paper as "beer," contrasts in linguistic labelling, drinking technique, and social context with all other Subanun beverages (*tebaq* "toddy," *sebug* "wine," *binu,* "liquor," *sabaw* "juice-broth," *tubig* "water").

The context of drinking. Focused social gatherings among the Subanun fall into two sharply contrasted sets: festive gatherings or "festivities" and nonfestive or informal gatherings. The diagnostic feature of a festivity is the consumption of a festive meal as a necessary incident in the encounter. A "meal" among the Subanun necessarily comprises a serving of a cooked starchy-staple food, the "main dish," and ordinarily also includes a "side dish" of vegetables, fish, or meat. A festive meal, or "feast," is a meal with a meat side dish. A "festivity" comprises all socially relevant events occurring between the arrival and dispersal of participants in a feast. Apart from a feast, the necessary features of a festivity are (1) an occasioning event, (2) multi-family participation, and (3) beer. The drinking of beer, unlike the consumption of any other beverage, occurs only during a festivity and must occur as part of any festivity. It occupies a crucial position as a focus of formal social gatherings.

Drinking technique. "Beer," uniquely among Subanun drinks, is drunk with bamboo straws inserted to the bottom of a Chinese jar containing the fermented mash. Just prior to drinking, the jar is filled to the rim with water. Except in certain types of game drinking, one person

[2] Dell H. Hymes, "The Ethnography of Speaking," in *Anthropology and Human Behavior,* T. Gladwin and W. C. Sturtevant, eds. (Washington: Anthropological Society of Washington, 1962), pp. 15–53.

drinks at a time, after which another person replenishes the water from an agreed-upon "measure." As one sucks on the straw, the water disappears down through the mash where it picks up a surprising amount of alcohol and an indescribable taste. After initial rounds of tasting, drinking etiquette requires one to gauge his consumption so that when a full measure of water is added, the water level rises exactly even with the jar rim.

The drinking encounter. Each beer jar provided for a festivity becomes the focus of a gathering of persons who take turns drinking. A *turn* is a single period of continuous drinking by one person. Each change of drinkers marks a new turn. A circuit of turns through the gathering is a *round.* As drinking progresses, rounds change in character with regard to the number and length of constituent turns and to variations in drinking techniques. Differences in these features among successive sets of rounds mark three distinct stages of the drinking encounter: tasting, competitive drinking, and game drinking (Table I).

The first round is devoted to *tasting,* each person taking a brief turn with little regard to formal measurement of consumption. Successive turns become longer and the number of turns per round fewer, thus cutting out some of the participants in the encounter. These individuals go to other jars if available or withdraw from drinking during this stage of *competitive drinking.* Measurement is an important aspect of competitive rounds, participants keeping a mental record of each other's consumption. Within a round, successive drinkers must equal the consumption of the drinker who initiated the round. In later rounds, as the brew becomes weaker, the measure tends to be raised. Continued competitive drinking may assume an altered character signaled by accompanying music, dancing, and singing. The scope of the gathering may enlarge and turns become shorter. Special types of drinking games occur: "chugalug" *(saŋgayuq)* and dual-drinking by opposite-sexed partners under the cover of a blanket. These rounds form a stage of *game drinking.*

Drinking talk. The Subanun expression for drinking talk, *taluq bwat dig beksuk* "talk from the straw," suggests an image of the drinking straw as a channel not only of the drink but also of drinking talk. The two activities, drinking and talking, are closely interrelated in that how one talks bears on how much one drinks and the converse is, quite obviously, also true. Except for "religious offerings," which must precede drinking, whatever business is to be transacted during a festivity occurs during drinking encounters. Consequently drinking talk is a major medium of interfamily communication. Especially for an adult male, one's role in the society at large, insofar as it is subject to manipulation, depends to a considerable extent on one's verbal performance during drinking encounters.

Subanun society contains no absolute, society-wide status positions or offices which automatically entitle their holder to deference from and

TABLE I. *Subanun drinking talk*

Encounter stages	*Discourse stages*	*Focus of speech acts*	*Function*
1. Tasting	1. Invitation—permission	Role expression	Assignment of role distances and authority relations to participants
2. Competitive drinking	2. Jar talk	Role expression and context definition	Allocation of encounter resources (turns at drinking and talking)
	3. Discussion 3.1 Gossip 3.2 Deliberation	Topic	Exchange of information; disputation, arbitration; deciding issues on basis of cogent argument
3. Game drinking	4. Display of verbal art	Stylistic	Establishment of euphoria. Deciding issues on basis of skill in use of special styles of discourse (singing, verse)

Segments of a drinking encounter:
1. A turn (continuous drinking by one person)
2. A round (a set of related turns)
3. Encounter stage (a set of related rounds)

Segments of drinking talk:
1. An utterance (continuous speech by one person)
2. An exchange (a set of related utterances)
3. Discourse stage (a set of related exchanges)

authority over others. The closest approximation to such a formal office is the status of religious specialist or "medium" who is deferred to in religious matters but who has no special voice in affairs outside his domain. Assumption of decision-making roles in legal, economic, and ecological domains depends not on acquisition of an office but on continuing demonstration of one's ability to make decisions within the context of social encounters. This ability in turn depends on the amount of deference one can evoke from other participants in the encounter. Although relevant, no external status attributes of sex, age, or wealth are sufficient to guarantee such deference; it must be elicited through one's skill in the use of speech. Apart from age, sex, and reputation from performances in previous encounters, the most salient external attributes brought to an encounter by a participant are his relational roles based on kinship, neighborhood, and friendship with specific other participants. Because of consanguineal endogamy and residential mobility, the relationship ties between an ego and any given alter are likely to be multiple and complex, giving wide latitude for manipulation of roles within particular encounters. Moreover, most kinship roles permit a range of interpretation depending upon other features of the relationship such as friendship and residential proximity.

The strategy of drinking talk is to manipulate the assignment of role relations among participants so that, within the limits of one's external status attributes, one can maximize his share of encounter resources (drink and talk), thereby having an opportunity to assume an esteem-attracting and authority-wielding role. Variations in the kinds of messages sent during periods devoted to different aspects of this strategic plan mark four distinct *discourse stages* within the drinking talk of the encounter: invitation-permission, jar talk, discussion, and display of verbal art (Table I). The constituents of a discourse stage are *exchanges:* sets of utterances with a common topic focus. (Boundaries of exchanges in American speech are often marked by such expressions as "Not to change the subject, but . . ." or "By the way, that reminds me . . .".) The constituents of exchanges are *utterances:* stretches of continuous speech by one person.

1. Invitation-Permission. The Subanun designate the discourse of the initial tasting round as "asking permission." The provider of the jar initiates the tasting round by inviting someone to drink, thereby signaling that this person is the one to whom he and those closest to him in the encounter owe the greatest initial deference on the basis of external status attributes. The invited drinker squats before the jar and asks permission to drink of the other participants. He has two variables to manipulate: the order in which he addresses the other participants and the terms of address he employs. Apart from the latter variable, message form remains relatively constant: *naa, A, sep pa u* "Well, *A*, I will be drinking." (*A*

represents a term of address.) Role relations with persons who are not lineal consanguineal or lineal affinal kin (Mo, F, Ch, Sp, SpPr, ChSp, ChSpPr) permit a variety of forms of address each with different implications for social distance with respect to ego. The drinker's final opportunity to express role relations comes when he finishes tasting and invites another (ordinarily the person who invited him) to drink.

2. Jar talk. As competitive drinking begins, asking permission is reduced in scope and importance, and there is an increase in messages sent during drinking itself. The topic focus of these exchanges is the drink being consumed. The drinker responds to queries about the taste and strength of the beer, explanations are advanced for its virtues and defects, and the performance of drinkers is evaluated. During this stage the topic of messages is predictable. The informative aspect of the messages is the quantity and quality of verbal responses a drinker can elicit. This information signals the amount of drinking and talking time the gathering will allot him. Those who receive little encouragement drop out, and the encounter is reduced generally to less than half-a-dozen persons, who can thereby intensify their interaction with each other and with the beer straw.

3. Discussion. As the size and role-structure of the gathering becomes defined, discourse changes in topic to removed referents, usually beginning with relatively trivial gossip, proceeding to more important subjects of current interest, and, finally, in many cases arriving at litigation. Since there are no juro-political offices in Subanun society, a legal case is not only a contest between litigants, but also one between persons attempting to assume a role of legal authority by settling the case. Success in effecting legal decisions depends on achieving a commanding role in the encounter and on debating effectively from that position. Since there are no sanctions of force legally applicable to back up a decision, the payment of a fine in compliance with a decision is final testimony to the prowess in verbal combat of the person who made the decision.

4. Display of verbal art. If drinking continues long enough, the focus of messages shifts from their topics to play with message forms themselves, following stylized patterns of song and verse composition. Songs and verses are composed on the spot to carry on discussions in an operetta-like setting. Even unsettled litigation may be continued in this manner, the basis for decision being shifted from cogent argument to verbal artistry. The most prestigious kinds of drinking songs require the mastery of an esoteric vocabulary by means of which each line is repeated with a semantically equivalent but formally different line. Game drinking is a frequent accompaniment to these displays of verbal art. Together they help assure that the festivity will end with good feelings among all participants, a goal which is explicitly stated by the Subanun. Participants

who have displayed marked hostility toward each other during the course of drinking talk may be singled out for special ritual treatment designed to restore good feelings.

The Subanun drinking encounter thus provides a structured setting within which one's social relationships beyond his everyday associates can be extended, defined, and manipulated through the use of speech. The cultural patterning of drinking talk lays out an ordered scheme of role play through the use of terms of address, through discussion and argument, and through display of verbal art. The most skilled in "talking from the straw" are the de facto leaders of the society. In instructing our stranger to Subanun society how to ask for a drink, we have at the same time instructed him how to get ahead socially.

6

"Rapping" in the Black ghetto

THOMAS KOCHMAN

Although the urban subcultures of the United States often use the sounds of English grammar, their styles of speaking are different. Achievement in the ghetto involves the verbal abilities of "rapping," "shucking," "jiving," "running it down," "gripping," "copping a plea," "signifying," and "sounding." With vivid examples, each of these verbal styles is described. Thomas Kochman also shows how individuals establish their personalities, show their respect for power, and stir up excitement by careful manipulation af these verbal abilities.

"Rapping," "shucking," "jiving," "running it down," "gripping," "copping a plea," "signifying," and "sounding" are all part of the Black ghetto idiom and describe different kinds of talking. Each has its own distinguishing features of form, style, and function; each is influenced by, and influences, the speaker, setting, and audience; and each sheds light on the Black perspective and the Black condition — on those orienting values and attitudes that will cause a speaker to speak or perform in his own way within the social context of the Black community.

I was first introduced to Black idiom in New York City, and, as a professional linguist interested in dialects, I began to compile a lexicon of such expressions. My real involvement, however, came in Chicago, while preparing a course on Black idiom at the Center for Inner City studies, the southside branch of Northeastern Illinois State College.

Here I began to explore the full cultural significance of this kind of verbal behavior. My students and informants within Black Chicago, through their knowledge of these terms, and their ability to recognize and categorize the techniques, and to give examples, gave me much reliable

From "'Rapping' in the Black Ghetto," *Trans*-action 6 (February 1969): 26–34. Illustrations are omitted.

data. When I turned for other or better examples to the literature — such as the writings of Malcolm X, Robert Conot, and Iceberg Slim — my students and informants were able to recognize and confirm their authenticity.

While often used to mean ordinary conversation, rapping is distinctively a fluent and a lively way of talking, always characterized by a high degree of personal style. To one's own group, rapping may be descriptive of an interesting narration, a colorful rundown of some past event. An example of this kind of rap is the answer from a Chicago gang member to a youth worker who asked how his group became organized:

> Now I'm goin to tell you how the jive really started. I'm going to tell you how the club got this big. 'Bout 1956 there used to be a time when the Jackson Park show was open and the Stony show was open. Sixty-six street, Jeff, Gene, all of 'em, little bitty dudes, little bitty . . . Gene wasn't with 'em then. Gene was cribbin (living) over here. Jeff, all of 'em, real little bitty dudes, you dig? All of us were little.
>
> Sixty-six (the gang on sixty-sixth street), they wouldn't allow us in the Jackson Park show. That was when the parky (?) was headin it. Everybody say, If we want to go to the show, we go! One day, who was it? Carl Robinson. He went up to the show . . . and Jeff fired on him. He came back and all this was swelled up 'bout yay big, you know. He come back over to the hood (neighborhood). He told (name unclear) and them dudes went up there. That was when mostly all the main sixty-six boys was over here like Bett Riley. All of 'em was over here. People that quit gang-bangin (fighting, especially as a group), Marvell Gates, people like that.
>
> They went on up there, John, Roy and Skeeter went in there. And they start humbuggin (fighting) in there. That's how it all started. Sixty-six found out they couldn't beat us, at *that* time. They couldn't *whup* seven-o. Am I right Leroy? You was cribbin over here then. Am I right? We were dynamite! Used to be a time, you ain't have a passport, Man, you couldn't walk through here. And if didn't nobody know you it was worse than that. . . .

Rapping to a woman is a colorful way of "asking for some pussy." "One needs to throw a lively rap when he is 'putting the make' on a broad." (John Horton, "Time and Cool People," *Trans*-action, April, 1967.)

According to one informant the woman is usually someone he has just seen or met, looks good, and might be willing to have sexual intercourse with him. My informant says the term would not be descriptive of talk between a couple "who have had a relationship over any length of time." Rapping then, is used at the beginning of a relationship to create a favorable impression and be persuasive at the same time. The man who has the reputation for excelling at this is the pimp, or mack man. Both terms describe a person of considerable status in the street hierarchy, who, by his lively and persuasive rapping ("macking" is also used in this context) has acquired a stable of girls to hustle for him and give him money. For most street men and many teenagers he is the model whom they try to emulate. Thus, within the community you have a pimp walk, pimp style boots and clothes, and perhaps most of all "pimp talk," is a colorful literary example of a telephone rap. One of my informants regards it as extreme, but agrees that it illustrates the language, style and technique of rapping. "Blood" is rapping to an ex-whore named Christine in an effort to trap her into his stable:

> Now try to control yourself baby. I'm the tall stud with the dreamy bedroom eyes across the hall in four-twenty. I'm the guy with the pretty towel wrapped around his sexy hips. I got the same hips on now that you X-rayed. Remember that hump of sugar your peepers feasted on?
>
> She said, "Maybe, but you shouldn't call me. I don't want an incident. What do you want? A lady doesn't accept phone calls from strangers."
>
> I said, "A million dollars and a trip to the moon with a bored, trapped, beautiful bitch, you dig? I'm no stranger. I've been popping the elastic on your panties ever since you saw me in the hall. . . ."

Rapping between men and women often is competitive and leads to a lively repartee with the women becoming as adept as the men. An example follows:

> A man coming from the bathroom forgot to zip his pants. An unescorted party of women kept watching him and laughing among themselves. The man's friends "hip" (inform) him to what's going on. He approaches one woman — "Hey baby, did you see that big black Cadillac with the full tires? ready to roll in action just for you." She answers — "No mother-fucker, but I saw a little gray Volkswagen with two flat tires." Everybody laughs. His rap was "capped" (excelled, topped).

When "whupping the game" on a "trick" or "lame" (trying to get goods or services from someone who looks like he can be swindled), rapping if often descriptive of the highly stylized verbal part of the maneuver. In well established "con games" the rap is carefully prepared and used with great skill in directing the course of the transaction. An excellent illustration came from an adept hustler who was playing the "murphy" game on a White trick. The "murphy" game is designed to get the *trick* to give his money to the hustler, who in this instance poses as a "steerer" (one who directs or steers customers to a brothel), to keep the whore from stealing it. The hustler then skips with the money.

> Look Buddy, I know a fabulous house not more than two blocks away. Brother you ain't never seen more beautiful, freakier broads than

> are in that house. One of them, the prettiest one, can do more with a swipe than a monkey can with a banana. She's like a rubber doll; she can take a hundred positions."
>
> At this point the sucker is wild to get to this place of pure joy. He entreats the con player to take him there, not just direct him to it.
>
> The "murphy" player will prat him (pretend rejection) to enhance his desire. He will say, "Man, don't be offended, but Aunt Kate, that runs the house don't have nothing but highclass White men coming to her place. . . . You know, doctors, lawyers, big-shot politicians. You look like a clean-cut White man, but you ain't in that league are you? (Iceberg Slim, *Pimp: The Story of My Life.*)

After a few more exchanges of the "murphy" dialogue, "the mark is separated from his scratch."

An analysis of rapping indicates a number of things.

For instance, it is revealing that one raps *to* rather than *with* a person supporting the impression that rapping is to be regarded more as a performance than verbal exchange. As with other performances, rapping projects the personality, physical appearance and style of the performer. In each of the examples given, the intrusive "I" of the speaker was instrumental in contributing to the total impression of the rap.

The combination of personality and style is usually best when "asking for some pussy." It is less when "whupping the game" on someone or "running something down."

In "asking for some pussy" for example, where personality and style might be projected through nonverbal means: stance, clothing, walking, looking, one can speak of a "silent rap." The woman is won here without the use of words, or rather, with words being implied that would generally accompany the nonverbal components.

As a lively way of "running it down" the verbal element consists of personality and style plus information. To someone *reading* my example of the gang member's narration, the impression might be that the information would be more influential in directing the listener's response. The youth worker might be expected to say "So that's how the gang got so big," instead of "Man, that gang member is *bad* (strong, brave)" in which instance he would be responding to the personality and style of the rapper. However, if the reader would *listen* to the gang member on tape or could have been present when the gang member spoke he more likely would have reacted more to personality and style as my informants did.

Remember that in attendance with the youth worker were members of the gang who *already knew* how the gang got started (e.g., "Am

I right Leroy? You was cribbin' over here then") and for whom the information itself would have little interest. Their attention was held by the *way* the information was presented.

The verbal element in "whupping the game" on someone, in the preceding example, was an integral part of an overall deception in which information and personality-style were skillfully manipulated for the purpose of controlling the "trick's" response. But again, greater weight must be given to personality-style. In the "murphy game" for example, it was this element which got the trick to trust the hustler and leave his money with him for "safekeeping."

The function of rapping in each of these forms is *expressive*. By this I mean that the speaker raps to project his personality onto the scene or to evoke a generally favorable response. When rapping is used to "ask for some pussy" or to "whup the game" on someone its function is *directive*. By this I mean that rapping becomes an instrument to manipulate and control people to get them to give up or to do something. The difference between rapping to a "fox" (pretty girl) for the purpose of "getting inside her pants" and rapping to a "lame" to get something from him is operational rather than functional. The latter rap contains a concealed motivation where the former does not.

"Shucking," "shucking it," "shucking and jiving," "S-ing" and "J-ing" or just "jiving," are terms that refer to language behavior practiced by the Black when confronting "the Man" (the White man, the establishment, or *any* authority figure), and to another form of language behavior practiced by Blacks with each other on the peer group level.

In the South, and later in the North, the Black man learned that American society had assigned to him a restrictive role and status. Among Whites his behavior had to conform to this imposed station and he was constantly reminded to "keep his place." He learned that it was not acceptable in the presence of white people to show feelings of indignation, frustration, discontent, pride, ambition, or desire; that real feelings had to be concealed behind a mask of innocence, ignorance, childishness, obedience, humility and deference. The terms used by the black to describe the role he played before White folks in the South was "tomming" or "jeffing." Failure to accommodate the white Southerner in this respect was almost certain to invite psychological and often phsycial brutality. A description related by a Black psychiatrist, Alvin F. Poussaint, is typical and revealing:

> Once last year as I was leaving my office in Jackson, Miss., with my Negro secretary, a White policeman yelled, "Hey, boy! Come here!" Somewhat bothered, I retorted: "I'm no boy!" He then rushed at me,

> inflamed, and stood towering over me, snorting "What d'ja say, boy?" Quickly he frisked me and demanded, "What's your name boy?" Frightened, I replied, "Dr. Poussaint. I'm a physician." He angrily chuckled and hissed, "What's your first name, boy?" When I hesitated he assumed a threatening stance and clenched his fists. As my heart palpitated, I muttered in profound humiliation, "Alvin."
>
> He continued his psychological brutality, bellowing, "Alvin, the next time I call you, you come right away, you hear? You hear?" I hesitated. "You hear me, boy?" My voice trembling with helplessness, but *following my instincts of self-preservation,* I murmured, "Yes, sir." *Now fully satisfied that I had performed and acquiesced to my "boy" status,* he dismissed me with, "Now, boy, go on and get out of here or next time we'll take you for a little ride down to the station house! (Alvin F. Poussaint, "A Negro Psychiatrist Explains the Negro Psyche," *The New York Times Magazine,* August 20, 1967 [emphasis mine]).

In the northern cities the Black encountered authority figures equivalent to Southern "crackers": policemen, judges, probation officers, truant officers, teachers and "Mr. Charlies" (bosses), and soon learned that the way to get by and avoid difficulty was to shuck. Thus, he learned to accommodate "the Man," to use the total orchestration of speech, intonation, gesture and facial expression for the purpose of producing whatever appearance would be acceptable. It was a technique and ability that was developed from fear, a respect for power, and a will to survive. This type of accommodation is exemplified by the Uncle Tom with his "Yes sir, Mr. Charlie," or "Anything you say, Mr. Charlie."

Through accommodation, many Blacks became adept at concealing and controlling their emotions and at assuming a variety of postures. They became competent actors. Many developed a keen perception of what affected, motivated, appeased or satisfied the authority figures with whom they came into contact. Shucking became an effective way for many Blacks to stay out of trouble, and for others a useful artifice for avoiding arrest or getting out of trouble when apprehended. Shucking it with a judge, for example, would be to feign repentance in the hope of receiving a lighter or suspended sentence. Robert Conot reports an example of shucking in his book, *Rivers of Blood, Years of Darkness:* Joe was found guilty of possession of narcotics. But he did an excellent job of shucking it with the probation officer.

The probation officer interceded for Joe with the judge: "His own attitude toward the present offense appears to be serious and responsible and it is believed that the defendant is an excellent subject for probation."

Some field illustrations of shucking to get out of trouble came from some seventh-grade children from an inner-city school in Chicago. The children were asked to talk their way out of a troublesome situation.

You are cursing at this old man and your mother comes walking down the stairs. She hears you.

To "talk your way out of this":

"I'd tell her that I was studying a scene in school for a play."

What if you were in a store stealing something and the manager caught you?

"I would start stuttering. Then I would say, 'Oh, Oh, I forgot. Here the money is.' "

A literary example of shucking comes from Iceberg Slim's autobiography. Iceberg, a pimp, shucks before "two red-faced Swede rollers (detectives)" who catch him in a motel room with his whore. My italics identify which elements of the passage constitute the shuck.

> I put my shaking hands into the pajama pockets . . . *I hoped I was keeping the fear out of my face. I gave them a wide toothy smile.* They came in and stood in the middle of the room. Their eyes were racing about the room. Stacy was open mouthed in the bed.
>
> I said, *"Yes gentlemen, what can I do for you?"*
>
> Lanky said, "We wanta see your I.D."
>
> I went to the closet and got the phony John Cato Fredrickson I.D. I put it in his palm. I felt cold sweat running down my back. They looked at it, then looked at each other.
>
> Lanky said, "You are in violation of the law. You signed the motel register improperly. Why didn't you sign your full name? What are you trying to hide? What are you doing here in town? It says here you're a dancer. We don't have a club in town that books entertainers."
>
> I said, *"Officers, my professional name is Johnny Cato. I've got nothing to hide. My full name had always been too long for the marquees. I've fallen into the habit of using the shorter version.*
>
> *"My legs went out last year. I don't dance anymore: My wife and I decided to go into business. We are making a tour of this part of the country. We think that in your town we've found the ideal site for a Southern fried chicken shack. My wife has a secret recipe that should make us rich up here."* (Iceberg Slim, *Pimp: The Story of My Life.*)

Another example of shucking was related to me by a colleague. A Black gang member was coming down the stairway from the club room with seven guns on him and encountered some policemen and detectives coming up the same stairs. If they stopped and frisked him he and others would have been arrested. A paraphrase of his shuck follows: "Man, I gotta get away from up there. There's gonna be some trouble and I don't want no part of it." This shuck worked on the minds of the policemen. It anticipated their questions as to why he was leaving the club room, and why he would be in a hurry. He also gave *them* a reason for wanting to get up to the room fast.

It ought to be mentioned at this point that there was not uniform agreement among my informants in characterizing the above examples as shucking. One informant used shucking only in the sense in which it is used among peers, e.g., bull-shitting, and characterized the above examples as jiving or whupping game. Others however, identified the above examples as shucking, and reserved jiving and whupping game for more offensive maneuvers. In fact, one of the apparent features of shucking is that the posture of the Black when acting with members of the establishment be a *defensive* one.

Frederick Douglass, in telling of how he taught himself to read, would challenge a White boy with whom he was playing, by saying that he could write as well as he. Whereupon he would write down all the letters he knew. The White boy would then write down more letters than Douglass did. In this way, Douglass eventually learned all the letters of the alphabet. Some of my informants regarded the example as whupping game. Others regarded it as shucking. The former were perhaps focusing on the manuever rather than the language used. The latter may have felt that any maneuvers designed to learn to read were justifiably defensive. One of my informants said Douglass was "shucking *in order to* whup the game." This latter response seems to be the most revealing. Just as one can rap to whup the game on someone, so one can shuck or jive for the same purpose; that is, assume a guise or posture or perform some action in a certain way that is designed to work on someone's mind to get him to give up something.

"Whupping game" to con whitey

The following examples from Malcolm X illustrate the shucking and jiving in this context though jive is the term used. Today, whupping game might also be the term used to describe the operation. Whites who came at night got a better reception; the several Harlem nightclubs they patronized were geared to entertain and jive (flatter, cajole) the night white crowd to get their money. (Malcolm X, *The Autobiography of Malcolm X.)*

The maneuvers involved here are clearly designed to obtain some benefit or advantage.

> Freddie got on the stand and went to work on his own shoes. Brush, liquid polish, brush, paste wax, shine rag, lacquer sole dressing . . . step by step, Freddie showed me what to do.
>
> "But you got to get a whole lot faster. You can't waste time!" Freddie showed me how fast on my own shoes. Then because business was tapering off, he had time to give me a demonstration of how to make

> the shine rag pop like a firecracker. "Dig the action?" he asked. He did it in slow motion. I got down and tried it on his shoes. I had the principle of it. "Just got to do it, faster," Freddie said. *"It's a jive noise, that's all. Cats tip better, they figure you're knocking yourself out!"* (Malcolm X, *The Autobiography of Malcolm X.*)

An eight-year-old boy whupped the game on me one day this way:

> My colleague and I were sitting in a room listening to a tape. The door to the room was open and outside was a soda machine. Two boys came up in the elevator, stopped at the soda machine, and then came into the room.
>
> "Do you have a dime for two nickels?" Presumably the soda machine would not accept nickels. I took out the change in my pocket, found a dime and gave it to the boy for two nickels.
>
> After accepting the dime, he looked at the change in my hand and asked, "Can I have two cents? I need carfare to get home." I gave him the two cents.

At first I assumed the verbal component of the maneuver was the rather weak, transparently false reason for wanting the two cents. Actually, as was pointed out to me later, the maneuver began with the first question which was designed to get me to show my money. He could then ask me for something that he knew I had, making my refusal more difficult. He apparently felt that the reason need not be more than plausible because the amount he wanted was small. Were the amount larger, he would no doubt have elaborated on the verbal element of the game. The form of the verbal element could be in the direction of rapping or shucking and jiving. If he were to rap the eight-year-old might say, "Man, you know a cat needs to have a little bread to keep the girls in line." Were he to shuck and jive he might make the reason for needing the money more compelling, look hungry, etc.

The function of shucking and jiving as it refers to Blacks and "the Man" is designed to work on the mind and emotions of the authority figure for the purpose of getting him to feel a certain way or give up something that will be to the other's advantage. Iceberg showed a "toothy smile" which said to the detective, "I'm glad to see you" and "Would I be glad to see you if I had something to hide?" When the maneuvers seem to be *defensive* most of my informants regarded the language behavior as shucking. When the maneuvers were *offensive* my informants tended to regard the behavior as "whupping the game."

Also significant is that the first form of shucking described, which developed out of accommodation, is becoming less frequently used today by many blacks, because of a new-found self-assertiveness and pride, challenging the system. The willingness on the part of many Blacks to accept the psychological and physical brutality and general social consequences of not "keeping one's place" is indicative of the changing self-concept of the Black man. Ironically, the shocked reaction of some Whites to the present militancy of the black is partly due to the fact that the Black was so successful at "putting Whitey on" via shucking in the past. This new attitude can be seen from a conversation I recently had with a shoe-shine attendant at O'Hare Airport in Chicago.

I was having my shoes shined and the Black attendant was using a polishing machine instead of the rag that was generally used in the past. I asked whether the machine made his work any easier. He did not answer me until about ten seconds had passed and then responded in a loud voice that he "never had a job that was easy," that he would give me "one hundred dollars for any *easy* job" I could offer him, that the machine made his job "faster" but not "easier." I was startled at the response because it was so unexpected and I realized that here was a new "breed of cat" who was not going to shuck for a big tip or ingratiate himself with "Whitey" anymore. A few years ago his response probably would have been different.

The contrast between this "shoe-shine" scene and the one illustrated earlier from Malcolm X's autobiography, when "shucking Whitey" was the common practice, is striking.

Shucking, jiving, shucking and jiving, or S-ing and J-ing, when referring to language behavior practiced by Blacks, is descriptive of the talk and gestures that are appropriate to "putting someone on" by creating a false impression. The terms seem to cover a range from simply telling a lie, to bullshitting, to subtly playing with someone's mind. An important difference between this form of shucking and that described earlier is that the same talk and gestures that are deceptive to "the Man" are often transparent to those members of one's own group who are able practitioners at shucking themselves. As Robert Conot has pointed out, "The Negro who often fools the White officer by 'shucking it' is much less likely to be successful with another Negro. . . ." Also, S-ing and J-ing within the group often has play overtones in which the person being "put on" is aware of the attempts being made and goes along with it for enjoyment or in appreciation of the style.

"Running it down" is the term used by speakers in the ghetto when it is their intention to give information, either by explanation, narrative, or giving advice. In the following literary example, Sweet Mac is "running this Edith broad down" to his friends:

> Edith is the "saved" broad who can't marry out of her religion . . . or do anything else out of her religion for that matter, especially what I wanted her to do. A bogue religion, man! So dig, for the last couple weeks I been quoting the Good Book and all that stuff to her; telling

her I am now saved myself, you dig. (Woodie King, Jr., "The Game," *Liberator,* August, 1965.)

The following citation from Claude Brown uses the term with the additional sense of giving advice:

> If I saw him (Claude's brother) hanging out with cats I knew were weak, who might be using drugs sooner or later, I'd run it down to him.

It seems clear that running it down has simply an informative function, that of telling somebody something that he doesn't already know.

"Gripping" is of fairly recent vintage, used by Black high school students in Chicago to refer to the talk and facial expression that accompanies a *partial* loss of face or self-possession, or showing of fear. Its appearance alongside "copping a plea," which refers to a total loss of face, in which one begs one's adversary for mercy, is a significant new perception. In linking it with the street code which acclaims the ability to "look tough and inviolate, fearless, secure, 'cool,' " it suggests that even the slightest weakening of this posture will be held up to ridicule and contempt. There are always contemptuous overtones attached to the use of the term when applied to the others' behavior. One is tempted to link it with the violence and toughness required to survive on the street. The intensity of both seems to be increasing. As one of my informants noted, "Today, you're *lucky* if you end up in the hospital" — that is, are not killed.

REACTION TO FEAR AND SUPERIOR POWER

Both gripping and copping a plea refer to behavior produced from fear and a respect for superior power. An example of gripping comes from the record *"Street and Gangland Rhythms"* (Band 4 Dumb Boy). Lennie meets Calvin and asks him what happened to his lip. Calvin says that a boy named Pierre hit him for copying off him in school. Lennie, pretending to be Calvin's brother, goes to confront Pierre. Their dialogue follows:

> Lennie: "Hey you! What you hit my little brother for?"
> Pierre: "Did he tell you what happen man?"
> Lennie: "Yeah, he told me what happened."
> Pierre: "But you . . . but you . . . but you should tell your people to teach him to go to the school, man." (Pause) I, I know, I know I didn't have a right to hit him."

Pierre, anticipating a fight with Lennie if he continued to justify his hitting of Calvin, tried to avoid it by "gripping" with the last line.

Copping a plea, originally meant "to plead guilty to a lesser charge to save the state the cost of a trial" (with the hope of receiving a lesser or suspended sentence), but is now generally used to mean "to beg," "plead for mercy," as in the example "Please cop, don't hit me. I give." (*Street and Gangland Rhythms*, Band 1 "Gang Fight.") This change of meaning can be seen from its use by Piri Thomas in *Down These Mean Streets.*

> The night before my hearing, I decided to make a prayer. It had to be on my knees, 'cause if I was gonna cop a plea to God, I couldn't play it cheap.

The function of gripping and copping a plea is obviously to induce pity or to acknowledge the presence of superior strength. In so doing, one evinces noticeable feelings of fear and insecurity which also result in a loss of status among one's peers.

Signifying is the term used to describe the language behavior that, as Abrahams has defined it, attempts to "imply, goad, beg, boast by indirect verbal or gestural means." (Roger D. Abrahams, *Deep Down in the Jungle.*) In Chicago it is also used as a synonym to describe language behavior more generally known as "sounding" elsewhere.

Some excellent examples of signifying as well as of other forms of language behavior come from the well known "toast" (narrative form) "The Signifying Monkey and the Lion" which was collected by Abrahams from Negro street corner bards in Philadelphia. In the above toast the monkey is trying to get the lion involved in a fight with the elephant:

> Now the lion came through the jungle one peaceful day,
> When the signifying monkey stopped him, and that is what he started
> to say:
> He said, "Mr. Lion," he said, "A bad-assed mother-fucker down your
> way,"
> He said, "Yeah! The way he talks about your folks is a certain shame.
> I even heard him curse when he mentioned your grandmother's
> name."
> The lion's tail shot back like a forty-four
> When he went down that jungle in all uproar.

Thus the monkey has goaded the lion into a fight with the elephant by "signifying," that is, indicating that the elephant has been "sounding on" (insulting) the lion. When the lion comes back, thoroughly beaten up, the monkey again "signifies" by making fun of the lion:

> . . . lion came back through the jungle more dead than alive,
> When the monkey started some more of that signifying jive.
> He said, "Damn, Mr. Lion, you went through here yesterday, the jungle
> rung.
> Now you come back today, damn near hung."

The monkey, of course, is delivering this taunt from a safe distance away on the limb of a tree when his foot slips and he falls to the ground, at which point,

> Like a bolt of lightning, a stripe of white heat,
> The lion was on the monkey with all four feet.

In desperation the monkey quickly resorts to "copping a plea":

> The monkey looked up with a tear in his eyes,
> He said, "Please, Mr. Lion, I apologize."

His "plea" however, fails to move the lion to show any mercy so the monkey tries another verbal ruse, "shucking":

> He said, "You lemme get my head out of the sand,
> Ass out the grass, I'll fight you like a natural man."

In this he is more successful as,

> The lion jumped back and squared for a fight.
> The mother-fucking monkey jumped clear out of sight.

A safe distance away again, the monkey returns to "signifying":

> He said, "Yeah, you had me down, you had me at last,
> But you left me free, now you can still kiss my ass."

This example illustrates the methods of provocation, goading and taunting artfully practiced by a signifier.

Interestingly, when the *function* of signifying is *directive* the *tactic* employed is *indirection*, i.e., the signifier reports or repeats what someone else has said about the listener; the "report" is couched in plausible language designed to compel belief and arouse feelings of anger and hostility. There is also the implication that if the listener fails to do anything about it — what has to be "done" is usually quite clear — his status will be seriously compromised. Thus the lion is compelled to vindicate the honor of his family by fighting or else leave the impression that he is afraid, and that he is not "king" of the jungle. When used for the purpose of directing action, "signifying" is like "shucking" in also being deceptive and subtle in approach and depending for success on the naiveté or gullibility of the person being "put on."

When the function of signifying is to arouse feelings of embarrassment, shame, frustration or futility, to diminish someone's status, the tactic employed is direct in the form of a taunt, as in the example where the monkey is making fun of the lion.

"Sounding" to relieve tensions

Sounding is the term which is today most widely known for the game of verbal insult known in the past as "Playing the Dozens," "The Dirty Dozens" or just "The Dozens." Other current names for the game have regional distribution: Signifying or "Sigging" (Chicago), Joning (Washington, D.C.), Screaming (Harrisburg), etc. In Chicago, the term "sounding" would be descriptive of the initial remarks which are designed to sound out the other person to see whether he will play the game. The verbal insult is also subdivided, the term "signifying" applying to insults which are hurled directly at the person and "the dozens" applying to results hurled at your opponent's family, especially, the mother.

Sounding is often catalyzed by signifying remarks referred to earlier such as "Are you going to let him say that about your mama" to spur an exchange between members of the group. It is begun on a relatively low key and built up by verbal exchanges. The game goes like this:

> One insults a member of another's family; others in the group make disapproving sounds to spur on the coming exchange. The one who has been insulted feels at this point that he must reply with a slur on the protagonist's family which is clever enough to defend his honor (and therefore that of his family). This, of course, leads the other (once again, more due to pressure from the crowd than actual insult) to make further jabs. This can proceed until everyone is bored with the whole affair, until one hits the other (fairly rare), or until some other subject comes up that interrupts the proceedings (the usual state of affairs). (Roger D. Abrahams, "Playing the Dozens," *Journal of American Folklore*, July–September, 1962.)

Mack McCormick describes the dozens as a verbal contest:

> . . . in which the players strive to bury one another with vituperation. In the play, the opponent's mother is especially slandered. . . . Then, in turn fathers are identified as queer and syphilitic. Sisters are whores, brothers are defective, cousins are "funny" and the opponent is himself diseased. (Mack McCormick, "The Dirty Dozens," book jacket in the record album *The Unexpurgated Folksongs of Men*, Arhoolie Records.)

An example of the "game" collected by one of my students goes:

> Frank looked up and saw Leroy enter the Outpost.
>
> Leroy walked past the room where Quinton, "Nap," "Pretty Black," "Cunny," Richard, Haywood, "Bull" and Reese sat playing cards. As Leroy neared the T.V. room, Frank shouted to him.
>
> Frank: "Hey Leroy, your mama — calling you man."
>
> Leroy turned and walked toward the room where the sound came from. He stood in the door and looked at Frank.
>
> Leroy: "Look mother-fuckers, I don't play that shit."
>
> Frank (signifying): "Man, I told you cats 'bout that mama jive" (as if he were concerned about how Leroy felt).
>
> Leroy: "That's all right Frank; you don't have to tell these funky mother-fuckers nothing; I'll fuck me up somebody yet."
>
> Frank's face lit up as if he were ready to burst his side laughing. "Cunny" became pissed at Leroy.

"Cunny": "Leroy, you stupid bastard, you let Frank make a fool of you. He said that 'bout your mama."

"Pretty Black": "Aw, fat ass head 'Cunny' shut up."

"Cunny": Ain't that some shit. This Black slick head motor flicker got nerve 'nough to call somebody 'fat-head.' Boy, you so black, you sweat Permalube Oil."

This eased the tension of the group as they burst into loud laughter.

"Pretty Black": "What 'chu laughing 'bout 'Nap,' with your funky mouth smelling like dog shit."

Even Leroy laughed at this.

"Nap": "Your mama mother-fucker."

"Pretty Black": "Your funky mama too."

"Nap"(strongly): "It takes twelve barrels of water to make a steamboat run; it takes an elephant's dick to make your Grandmammy come; she been elephant fucked, camel fucked and hit side the head with your Grandpappy's nuts."

Reese: "Godorr-damn; go on and rap mother-fucker."

Reese began slapping each boy in his hand, giving his positive approval of "Naps" comment. "Pretty Black" in an effort not to be outdone, but directing his verbal play elsewhere stated:

"Pretty Black": "Reese, what you laughing 'bout? You so square, you shit bricked shit."

Frank: "Whoooowee!"

Reese (sounded back): "Square huh, what about your nappy ass hair before it was stewed; that shit was so bad till, when you went to bed at night, it would leave your head and go on the corner and meddle."

The boys slapped each other in the hand and cracked up.

"Pretty Black": "On the streets meddling, bet Dinky didn't offer me no pussy and I turned it down."

Frank: "Rease scared of pussy."

"Pretty Black": "Hell, yeah; the greasy mother rather fuck old ugly, funky cock Sue Willie than get a piece of ass from a decent broad."

Frank: "Godorr-damn! Not Sue Willie."

"Pretty Black": Yeah, ol meat-beating Reese rather screw that cross-eyed, clapsy bitch, who when she cry, tears rip down her ass."

Haywood: "Don't be so mean, Black."

Reese: "Aw shut up, you half-White bastard."

Frank: "Wait, man, Haywood ain't gonna hear much more of that half-White shit; he's a brother too."

Reese: "Brother, my Black ass; that White ass landlord gotta be this mother-fucker's paw."

"Cunny": "Man, you better stop foolin with Haywood; he's turning red."

Haywood: "Fuck yall" (as he withdrew from the "sig" game).

Frank: "Yeah, fuck yall; let's go to the stick hall."

The group left enroute to the billiard hall. (James Maryland, "Signifying at the Outpost," unpublished term paper for the course *Idiom of the Negro Ghettos,* January 1967.)

The above example of sounding is an excellent illustration of the "game" as played by a 15–17-year-old Negro boys, some of whom have already acquired the verbal skill which for them is often the basis for having a high "rep." Ability with words is apparently as highly valued as physical strength. In the sense that the status of one of the participants in the game is diminished if he has to resort to fighting to answer a verbal attack, verbal ability may be even more highly regarded than physical ability.

The relatively high value placed on verbal ability must be clear to most Black boys at early age. Most boys begin their activity in sounding by compiling a repertoire of "one liners." When the game is played the one who has the greatest number of such remarks wins. Here are some examples of "one liners" collected from fifth- and sixth-grade Black boys in Chicago:

Yo mama is so bowlegged, she looks like the bit out of a donut.

Yo mama sent her picture to the lonely hearts club, and they sent it back and said, "We ain't that lonely!"

Your family is so poor the rats and roaches eat lunch out.

Your house is so small the roaches walk single file.

I walked in your house and your family was running around the table. I said, "Why you doin that?" Your mama say, "First one drops, we eat."

Real proficiency in the game comes to only a small percentage of those who play it. These players have the special skill in being able to turn around what their opponents have said and attack them with it. Thus, when someone indifferently said "fuck you" to Concho, his retort was immediate and devastating: "Man, you haven't even kissed me yet."

The "best talkers" from this group often become the successful street-corner, barber shop, and pool hall story tellers who deliver the long, rhymed, witty, narrative stories called "toasts." They are, as Roger D. Abrahams has described, the traditional "men of words" and have become on occasion entertainers such as Dick Gregory and Redd Fox, who are virtuosos at repartee, and preachers, whose verbal power has been traditionally esteemed.

The function of the "dozens" or "sounding" is to borrow status from an opponent through an exercise of verbal power. The opponent feels compelled to regain his status by "sounding" back on the speaker or other group member whom he regards as more vulnerable.

The presence of a group seems to be especially important in controlling the game. First of all, one does not "play" with just anyone since the subject matter is concerned with things that in reality one is quite sensitive about. It is precisely *because* "Pretty Black" has a "Black slick head" that makes him vulnerable to "Cunny's" barb, especially now when the Afro-American "natural" hair style is in vogue. Without the control of the group "sounding" will frequently lead to a fight. This was illustrated by a tragic epilogue concerning Haywood, when Haywood was being "sounded" on in the presence of two girls by his best friend (other members of the group were absent), he refused to tolerate it. He went home, got a rifle, came back and shot and killed his friend. In the classroom from about the fourth grade on fights among Black boys invariably are caused by someone "sounding" on the other person's mother.

Significantly, the subject matter of sounding is changing with the changing self-concept of the Black with regard to those physical characteristics that are characteristically "Negro," and which in the past were vulnerable points in the Black psyche: blackness and "nappy" hair. It ought to be said that for many Blacks, blackness was always highly esteemed and it might be more accurate to regard the present sentiment of the Black community toward skin color as reflecting a shifted attitude for only a *portion* of the Black community. This suggests that "sounding" on someone's light skin color is not new. Nevertheless, one can regard the previously favorable attitude toward light skin color and "good hair" as the prevailing one. "Other things being equal, the more closely a woman approached her White counterpart, the more attractive she was considered to be, by both men and women alike. 'Good hair' (hair that is long and soft) and light skin were the chief criteria." (Elliot Liebow, *Tally's Corner.*)

"The dozens" has been linked to the overall psycho-social growth of the Black male. McCormick has stated that a "single round of a dozen or so exchanges frees more pent-up aggressions than will a dose of sodium pentothal." The fact that one permits a kind of abuse within the rules of the game and within the confines of the group which would otherwise not be tolerated, is filled with psychological import. It seems also important, however, to view its function from the perspective of the nonparticipating members of the group. Its function for them may be to incite and prod individual members of the group to combat for the purpose of energizing the elements, of simply relieving the boredom of just "hanging around" and the malaise of living in a static and restrictive environment.

A summary analysis of the different forms of language behavior which have been discussed above permit the following generalizations:

The prestige norms which influence Black speech behavior are those which have been successful in manipulating and controlling people and situations. The function of all of the forms of language behavior discussed above, with the exception of "running it down," was to project personality, assert oneself, or arouse emotion, frequently with the additional purpose of getting the person to give up or do something which will be of some benefit to the speaker. Only running it down has as its primary function to communicate information and often here too, the personality and style of the speaker in the form of rapping is projected along with the information.

The purpose for which language is used suggests that the speaker views the social situations into which he moves as consisting of a series of transactions which require that he be continually ready to take advantage of a person or situation or defend himself against being victimized. He has absorbed what Horton has called "street rationality." As one of Horton's respondents put it: "The good hustler . . . conditions his mind and must never put his guard too far down, to relax, or he'll be taken."

I have carefully avoided limiting the group within the Black community of whom the language behavior and perspective of their environment is characteristic. While I have no doubt that it is true of those whom are generally called "street people" I am uncertain of the extent to which it is true of a much larger portion of the Black community, especially the male segment. My informants consisted of street people, high school students, and Blacks, who by their occupation as community and youth workers, possess what has been described as a "sharp sense of the streets." Yet it is difficult to find a Black male in the community who has *not* witnessed or participated in "the dozens" or heard of signifying, or rapping, or shucking and jiving at some time during his growing up. It would be equally difficult to imagine a high school student in a Chicago inner-city school not being touched by what is generally regarded as "street culture."

In conclusion, by blending style and verbal power, through rapping, sounding and running it down, the Black in the ghetto establishes his personality; through shucking, gripping and copping a plea, he shows his respect for power; through jiving and signifying he stirs up excitement. With all of the above, he hopes to manipulate and control people and situations to give himself a winning edge.

7

Codifications of reality: Lineal and nonlineal

DOROTHY LEE

Different languages punctuate, categorize, and call attention to various aspects of reality. As a result, individuals from distinct societies learn different codes for representing reality. Language is a clue to these codification differences. From this premise Dorothy Lee shows how the Trobriand language of islanders living in the Solomon Sea area emphasizes the nonlineal aspect of reality, while English calls attention to lineal relationships. This article vividly shows that the structure *of language and communication systems is as important as their content.*

The people of the Trobriand Islands codify, and probably apprehend reality, nonlineally in contrast to our own lineal phrasing. Basic to my investigation of the codification of reality on these two societies, is the assumption that a member of a given society not only codifies experienced reality through the use of the specific language and other patterned behavior characteristics of his culture, but that he actually grasps reality only as it is presented to him in this code. The assumption is not that reality itself is relative; rather, that it is differently punctuated and categorized, or that different aspects of it are noticed by, or presented to the participants of different cultures. If reality itself were not absolute, then true communication of course would be impossible. My own position is that there is an absolute reality, and that communication is possible. If, then, that which the different codes refer to is ultimately the same, a careful study and analysis of a different code and of the culture to which it

From "Lineal and Nonlineal Codifications of Reality," *Psychosomatic Medicine* 12 (May 1950): 89–97. Reprinted by permission of the author and the publisher. This article has appeared under the title, "Codifications of Reality: Lineal and Nonlineal" in Dorothy Lee, *Freedom and Culture* (Englewood Cliffs, N.J.: Prentice-Hall, 1959). The bibliography is omitted.

belongs, should lead us to concepts which are ultimately comprehensible, when translated into our own code. It may even, eventually, lead us to aspects of reality from which our own code excludes us.

It is a corollary of this assumption that the specific phrasing of reality can be discovered through intensive and detailed analysis of any aspect of culture. My own study was begun with an analysis of linguistic formulation, only because it is in language that I happen to be best able to discover my clues. To show how these clues can be discovered and used as guides to the apprehension of reality, as well as to show what I mean by codification, I shall present at first concrete material from the field of language.

That a word is not the reality, not the thing which it represents, has long been a commonplace to all of us. The thing which I hold in my hand as I write, *is* not a pencil; I *call* it a pencil. And it remains the same whether I call it *pencil, molyvi, Bleistift,* or *siwiqoq*. These words are different sound-complexes applied to the same reality; but is the difference merely one of sound-complex? Do they refer to the same *perceived* reality? *Pencil* originally meant little tail; it delimited and named the reality according to form. *Molyvi* means lead and refers to the writing element. *Bleistift* refers both to the form and to the writing-element. *Siwiqoq* means painting-stick and refers to observed function and form. Each culture has phrased the reality differently. To say that *pencil,* for example, applies primarily to form is no idle etymologic statement. When we use this word metaphorically, we refer neither to writing element nor to function, but to form alone; we speak of a pencil of light, or a styptic pencil.

When I used the four words for this object, we all knew what reality was referred to; we knew the meaning of the word. We could visualize the object in my hand, and the words all delimited it in the same way; for example, none of them implied that it was a continuation of my fist. But the student of ethnography often has to deal with words which punctuate reality into different phrasings from the ones with which he is familiar. Let us take, for instance, the words for "brother" and "sister." We go to the islands of Ontong Java to study the kinship system. We ask our informant what he calls his sister and he says *ave;* he calls his brother *kainga*. So we equate *ave* with "sister" and *kainga* with "brother." By way of checking our information we ask the sister what she calls her brother; it turns out that for her, *ave* is "brother," not "sister" as we were led to expect; and that it is her sister whom she calls *kainga*.

The same reality, the same actual kinship is present there as with us; but we have chosen a different aspect for naming. We are prepared to account for this; we say that both cultures name according to what we would call a certain type of blood relationship; but whereas we make reference to absolute sex, they refer to relative sex. Further inquiry, however, discloses that in this, also, we are wrong. Because in our own culture we name relatives according to formal definition and biologic relationship, we have thought that this formulation represents reality; and we have tried to understand the Ontong Javanese relationship terms according to these distinctions which, we believe, are given in nature. But the Ontong Javanese classifies relatives according to a different aspect of reality, differently punctuated. And because of this, he applies *kainga* as well to a wife's sister and a husband's brother; to a man's brother's wife and a woman's sister's husband, as well as to a number of other individuals.

Neither sex nor blood relationship, then, can be basic to this term. The Ontong Javanese name according to their everyday behavior and experience, not according to formal definition. A man shares the ordinary details of his living with his brothers and their wives for a large part of the year; he sleeps in the same large room, he eats with them, he jokes and works around the house with them; the rest of the year he spends with his wife's sisters and their husbands, in the same easy companionship. All these individuals are *kainga* to one another. The *ave,* on the other hand, names a behavior of great strain and propriety; it is based originally upon the relative sex of siblings, yes, but it does not signify biologic fact alone. It names a social relationship, a behavior, an emotional tone. *Ave* can never spend their adult life together, except on rare and temporary occasions. They can never be under the same roof alone together, cannot chat at ease together, cannot refer even distantly to sex in the presence of each other, not even to one's sweetheart or spouse; more than that, everyone else must be circumspect when the *ave* of someone of the group is present. The *ave* relationship also carries special obligations toward a female *ave* and her children. *Kainga* means a relationship of ease, full of shared living, of informality, gaiety; *ave* names one of formality, prohibition, strain.

These two cultures, theirs and our own, have phrased and formulated social reality in completely different ways, and have given their formulation different names. The word is merely the name of this specific cultural phrasing. From this one instance we might formulate the hypothesis — a very tentative one — that among the Ontong Javanese names describe emotive experiences, not observed forms or functions. But we cannot accept this as fact, unless further investigation shows it to be implicit in the rest of their patterned behavior, in their vocabulary and the morphology of their language, in their ritual and their other organized activity.

One more instance, this time from the language of the Wintu Indians of California, will deal with the varying aspect or segmentation of experience which is used as a basis of classification. To begin with, we take the stem *muk.* On the basis of this stem we form the word *mukeda,* which means: "I turned the basket bottom up"; we form *mukuhuru,* which means: "The turtle is moving along"; and we form *mukurumas,* which means: "automobile." Upon what conceivable principle can an automobile be put in the same category as a turtle and a basket? There is such a principle, however, and it operates also when the Wintu calls the activity of laundering, *to make foam continuously.* According to this principle, he uses only one stem, (puq or poq) to form words for all of the following:

puqeda: I just pushed a peg into the ground.
olpuqal: He is sitting on one haunch.
poqorahara: Birds are hopping along.
olpoqoyabe: There are mushrooms growing.
tunpoqoypoqoya: You walk shortskirted, stifflegged ahead of me.

It is difficult for us to discover the common denominator in the different formations from this one stem, or even to believe that there can be one. Yet, when we discover the principle underlying the classification, the categories themselves are understandable. Basic to the classification is the Wintu view of himself as observer; he stays outside the event. He passes no judgment on essence, and where we would have used kinesthetic or participatory experience as the basis of naming, he names as an observer only, for the shape of the activity or the object. The turtle and the automobile can thus naturally be grouped together with the inverted baskets. The mushroom standing on its stem, the fist grasping a peg against the ground, the stiff leg topped by a short skirt or by the body of a bird or of a man resting on a haunch, obviously all belong together in one category. But the progress of a grasshopper cannot be categorized with that of a hopping bird. We, who classify on a different basis, apprehend the hop of the two kinesthetically and see it as basically the same in both cases; but the Wintu see the difference in recurrent shape, which is all-important to them, and so name the two by means of completely different stems. Again, when we discover this principle, it is easy to see that from the observer's point of view laundering is the making of a lot of foam; and to see why, when beer was introduced to the Wintu, it was named *laundry.*

I have discussed at length the diversity of codification of reality in general, because it is the foundation of the specific study which I am about to present. I shall speak of the formulation of experienced reality among the Trobriand Islanders in comparison to our own; I shall speak of the nature of expectancy, of motivation, of satisfaction, as based upon a reality which is differently apprehended and experienced in two different societies; which is, in fact, for each, a different reality. The Trobriand Islanders were studied by the late Bronislaw Malinowski, who has given us the rich and circumstantial material about them which has made this study possible. I have given a detailed presentation of some implications of their language elsewhere; but since it was in their language that I first noticed the absence of lineality, which led me to this study, I shall give here a summary of the implications of the language.

A Trobriand word refers to a self-contained concept. What we consider an attribute of a predicate, is to the Trobriander an ingredient. Where I would say, for example, "A good gardener," or "The gardener is good," the Trobriand word would include both "gardener" and "goodness"; if the gardener loses the goodness, he has lost a defining ingredient, he is something else, and he is named by means of a completely different word. A taytu (a species of yam) contains a certain degree of ripeness, bigness, roundedness, etc.; without one of these defining ingredients, it is something else, perhaps a *bwanawa* or a *yowana.* There are no adjectives in the language; the rare words dealing with qualities are substantivized. The term *to be* does not occur; it is used neither attributively nor existentially, since existence itself is contained; it is an ingredient of being.

Events and objects are self-contained points in another respect; there is a series of beings, but not becoming. There is no temporal connection between objects. The taytu always remains itself; it does not *become* overripe; overripeness is an ingredient of another, a different being. At some point, the taytu *turns into a yowana,* which contains overripeness. And the yowana, overripe as it is, does not put forth shoots, does not *become* a sprouting yowana. When sprouts appear, it ceases to be itself; in its place appears a *silasata.* Neither is there a temporal connection made — or, according to our own premises, perceived — between events; in fact, temporality is meaningless. There are no tenses, no linguistic distinction between past or present. There is no arrangement of activities or events into means and ends, no causal or teleologic relationships. What we consider a causal relationship in a sequence of connected events, is to the Trobriander an ingredient of a patterned whole. He names this ingredient *u'ula.*

There is no automatic relating of any kind in the language. Except for the rarely used verbal it-differents and it-sames, there are no terms of comparison whatever. And we find in an analysis of behavior that the standard for behavior and of evaluation is noncomparative.

These implications of the linguistic material suggest to my mind an absence of axiomatic lineal connection between events or objects in the Trobriand apprehension of reality, and this implication, as I shall attempt to show below, is reinforced in their definition of activity. In our own culture, the line is so basic, that we take it for granted, as given in reality. We see it in visible nature, between material points, and we see it between metaphorical points such as days or acts. It underlies not only our thinking, but also our aesthetic apprehension of the given; it is basic to the emotional climax which has so much value for us, and, in fact, to the meaning of life itself. In our thinking about personality and character, we have taken for granted the presence of the line.

In our academic work, we are constantly acting in terms of an implied line. When we speak of *ap*plying an *at*tribute, for example, we visualize the process as lineal, coming from the outside. If I make a picture of an apple on the board, and want to show that one side is green and the other red I connect these attributes with the pictured apple by means of lines, as a matter of course; how else would I do it? When I organize my data, I *draw* conclusions *from* them. I *trace* a relationship between my facts. I describe a pattern as a *web* of relationships. Look at a lecturer who makes use of gestures; he is constantly making lineal connections in the air. And a teacher with chalk in hand will be drawing lines on the board whether he be a psychologist, a historian, or a paleontologist.

Preoccupation with social facts merely as self-contained facts is mere antiquarianism. In my field, a student of this sort would be an amateur or a dilettante, not an anthropologist. To be an anthropologist, he can arrange his facts in an upward slanting line, in a *unilinear* or *multilinear course* of development; or in *parallel lines* or *converging lines*. Or he may arrange them geographically, with *lines* of diffusion connecting them; or schematically, using *concentric circles*. Or at least, he must indicate what his study *leads to*, what new insights we can *draw from* it. To be accorded status, he must use the guiding line as basic.

The line is found or presupposed in most of our scientific work. It is present in the *induction* and the *deduction* of science and logic. It is present in the philosopher's phrasing of means and ends as lineally connected. Our statistical facts are presented lineally as a *graph* or reduced to a normal *curve*. And all of us, I think, would be lost without our *diagrams*. We *trace* a historical development; we *follow the course* of history and evolution *down* to the present and *up from* the ape; and it is interesting to note, in passing, that whereas both evolution and history are lineal, the first goes up the blackboard, the second goes down.

Our psychologists picture motivation as external, connected with the act through a line, or, more recently, entering the organism through a lineal channel and emerging transformed, again lineally, as response. I have seen lineal pictures of nervous impulses and heartbeats, and with them I have seen pictured lineally a second of time. These were photographs, you will say, of existing fact, of reality; a proof that the line is present in reality. But I am not convinced, perhaps due to my ignorance of mechanics, that we have not created our recording instruments in such a way that they have to picture time and motion, light and sound, heartbeats and nerve impulses lineally, on the unquestioned assumption of the line as axiomatic. The line is omnipresent and inescapable, and so we are incapable of questioning the reality of its presence.

When we see a *line* of trees, or a *circle* of stones, we assume the presence of a connecting line which is not actually visible. And we assume it metaphorically when we follow a *line* of thought, a *course* of action or the *direction* of an argument; when we *bridge* a gap in the conversation, or speak of the *span* of life or of teaching a *course*, or lament our *interrupted career*. We make children's embroidery cards and puzzle cards on this assumption; our performance tests and even our tests for sanity often assume that the line is present in nature and, at most, to be discovered or given visual existence.

But is the line present in reality? Malinowski, writing for members of our culture and using idiom which would be comprehensible to them, described the Trobriand village as follows: "Concentrically with the circular row of yam houses there runs a ring of dwelling huts." He saw, or at any rate, he represented the village as two circles. But in the texts which he recorded, we find that the Trobrianders at no time mention circles or rings or even rows when they refer to their villages. Any word which they use to refer to a village, such as *a* or *this,* is prefixed by the substantival element *kway* which means *bump* or *aggregate of bumps.* This is the element which they use when they refer to a pimple or a bulky rash; or to canoes loaded with yams. In their terms, a village is an aggregate of bumps; are they blind to the circles? Or did Malinowski create the circles himself, out of his cultural axiom?

Again, for us as well as in Malinowski's description of the Trobrianders, which was written necessarily in terms meaningful to us, all effective activity is certainly not a haphazard aggregate of acts, but a lineally planned series of acts leading to an envisioned end. Their gardening with all its specialized activities, both technical and magical, leading to a rich harvest; their *kula* involving the cutting down of trees, the communal dragging of the tree to the beach, the rebuilding or building of large seaworthy canoes, the provisioning, the magical and ceremonial activities involved — surely all these can be carried through only if they are lineally conceived.

But the Trobrianders do not describe their activity lineally; they do no dynamic relating of acts; they do not use even so innocuous a connective as *and.* Here is part of a description of the planting of coconut: "Thou-approach-there coconut thou-bring-here-we-plant-coconut thou-go-thou-plant our coconut. This-here it-emerge sprout. We-push-away this we-push away this-other coconut-husk-fiber together sprout it-sit together root." We who are accustomed to seek lineal continuity, cannot help supplying it as we read this; but the continuity is not given in the

Trobriand text; and all Trobriand speech, according to Malinowski, is "jerky," given in points, not in connecting lines. The only connective I know of in Trobriand is the *pela* which I mentioned above; a kind of preposition which also means "to jump."

I am not maintaining here that the Trobrianders cannot see continuity; rather that lineal connection is not automatically made by them, as a matter of course. At Malinowski's persistent questioning, for example, they did attempt to explain their activities in terms of cause or motivation, by stating possible "results" of uncooperative action. But Malinowski found their answers confused, self-contradictory, inconsistent; their preferred answer was, "It was ordained of old" — pointing to an ingredient value of the act instead of giving an explanation based on lineal connection.

And when they were not trying to find answers to leading questions, the Trobrianders made no such connection in their speech. They assumed, for example, that the validity of a magical spell lay, not in its results, not in proof, but in its very being; in the appropriateness of its inheritance, in its place within the patterned activity, in its being performed by the appropriate person, in its realization of its mythical basis. To seek validity through proof was foreign to their thinking, yet they attempted to do so at the ethnographer's request. I should add here that their names for constellations imply that here they do see lineal figures; I cannot investigate the significance of this, as I have no contextual material. At any rate, I would like to emphasize that, even if the Trobriander does occasionally supply connecting lines between points, his perception and experience do not automatically fall into a lineal framework.

The fact remains that Trobrianders embark on, what is certainly for us, a series of acts which "must require" planning and purposiveness. They engage in acts of gift-giving and gift-receiving which we can certainly see as an exchange of gifts if we want to. When we plot their journeys, we find that they do go from point to point, they do navigate a course, whether they say so or not. Do they merely refrain from giving linguistic expression to something which they actually recognize in nature? On the nonlinguistic level, do they act on an assumption of a lineality which is given no place in their linguistic formulation?

I believe that, where valued activity is concerned, the Trobrianders do not act on an assumption of lineality at any level. There is organization or rather coherence in their acts because Trobriand activity is patterned activity. One act within this pattern brings into existence a preordained cluster of acts. Perhaps one might find a parallel in our culture in the making of a sweater. When I embark on knitting one, the ribbing at the bottom does not *cause* the making of the neckline, nor of the sleeves or the armholes; and it is not part of a lineal series of acts. Rather it is an indispensable part of a patterned activity which includes all these other acts. Again, when I choose a dress pattern, the acts involved in the making of the dress are already present for me. They are embedded in the pattern which I have chosen.

In this same way, I believe, can be seen the Trobriand insistence that though intercourse is a necessary preliminary to conception, it is not the cause of conception. There are a number of acts in the pattern of procreating; one is intercourse, another the entrance of the spirit of a dead Trobriander into the womb. However, there is a further point here. The Trobrianders, when pressed by the ethnographer or teased by the neighboring Dobuans, showed signs of intense embarrassment, giving the impression that they were trying to maintain unquestioningly a stand in which they had to believe. This, I think, is because pattern is truth and value for them; in fact, acts and being derive value from the embedding pattern.

So the question of the perception of a line remains. It is because they find value in pattern that the Trobrianders act according to nonlineal pattern; not because they cannot perceive lineality.

But all Trobriand activity does not contain value; and when it does not, it assumes lineality, and is utterly despicable. For example, the pattern of sexual intercourse includes the giving of a gift from the boy to the girl; but if a boy gives a gift so as to win the girl's favor, he is despised. Again, the kula pattern includes the eventual reception of a gift from the original recipient; the pattern is such that it keeps the acts physically and temporally completely disparate. In spite of this, however, some men are accused of giving gifts as an inducement to their kula partner to give them a specially good kula gift. Such men are labeled with the vile phrase: he barters. But this means that, unvalued and despised, lineal behavior does exist. In fact, there are villages in the interior whose inhabitants live mainly by bartering manufactured articles for yams. The inhabitants of Omarakana, about whom Malinowski's work and this study are mainly concerned, will barter with them, but consider them pariahs.

This is to say that it is probable that the Trobrianders experience reality in nonlineal pattern because this is the valued reality; and that they are capable of experiencing lineally, when value is absent or destroyed. It is not to say, however, that this in itself means that lineality is given, is present in nature, and that pattern is not. Our own insistence on the line, such as lineal causality, for example, is also often based on unquestioned belief or value. To return to the subject of procreation, the husband in our culture, who has long hoped, and tried in vain, to beget children, will nevertheless maintain that intercourse causes conception; perhaps with the same stubbornness and embarrassment which the Trobrianders exhibited when maintaining the opposite.

The line in our culture not only connects, but it moves. And as we think of a line as moving from point to point, connecting one to the other, so we conceive of roads as *running from* locality to locality. A Trobriander does not speak of roads either as connecting two points, or as *running from* point *to* point. His paths are self-contained, named as independent units; they are *to* and *from*, they are *at*. And he himself is *at;* he has no equivalent for our *to* or *from*. There is, for instance, the myth of Tudava, who goes — in our view — from village to village and from island to island planting and offering yams. The Trobriand text puts it this way: "Kitava it-shine village already (i.e., completed) he-is-over. 'I-sail I-go Iwa'; Iwa he-anchor he-go ashore . . . He-sail Digumenu . . . They-drive (him off) . . . he-go Kwaywata." Point after point is enumerated, but his sailing from and to is given as a discrete event. In our view, he is actually following a southeasterly course, more or less; but this is not given as course or line, and no directions are even mentioned. In fact, in the several texts referring to journeyings in the Archipelago, no words occur for the cardinal directions. In sailing, the "following" winds are named according to where they are *at*, the place where they strike the canoe, such as wind-striking-the-outrigger-beam; not according to where they *come from*. Otherwise, we find names for the southwest wind (youyo), and the northwest wind (bombatu), but these are merely substantival names which have nothing to do with direction; names for kinds of wind.

When a member of our society gives an unemotional description of a person, he follows an imaginary line, usually downward: from head to foot, from tip to toe, from hair to chin. The Navaho do the opposite, following a line upward. The Trobriander follows no line, at least none that I can see. "My head boils," says a kula spell; and it goes on to enumerate the parts of the head as follows: nose, occiput, tongue, larynx, speech, mouth. Another spell casting a protective fog, runs as follows: "I befog the hand, I befog the foot, I befog the head, I befog the shoulders . . ." There is a magic formula where we do recognize a line, but it is one which Malinowski did not record verbatim at the time, but which he put down later from memory; and it is not improbable that his memory edited the formula according to the lineality of his culture.

When the Trobriander enumerates the parts of a canoe, he does not follow any recognizable lineal order: "Mist . . . surround me my mast . . . the nose of my canoe . . . my sail . . . my steering oar . . . my canoe-gunwale . . . my canoe-bottom . . . my prow . . . my rib . . . my threading-stick . . . my prow-board . . . my transverse stick . . . my canoe-side."

Malinowski diagrams the garden site as a square piece of land subdivided into squares; the Trobrianders refer to it in the same terms as those which they use in referring to a village — a bulky object or an aggregate of bumps. When the plots in the garden site are apportioned to the gardeners, the named plots are assigned by name, the others by location along each named side of the garden. After this, the inner plots, the "belly" of the garden, are apportioned. Following along a physical rim is a procedure which we find elsewhere also. In a spell naming villages on the main island, there is a long list of villages which lie along the coast northward, then westward around the island, then south. To us, of course, this is lineal order. But we have no indication that the Trobrianders see other than geographical location, point after point, as they move over a physically continuous area; the line as a guide to procedure is not necessarily implied. No terms are used here which might be taken as an implication of continuity; no "along the coast" or "around" or "northward."

When we in our culture deal with events or experiences of the self, we use the line as guide for various reasons, two of which I shall take up here. First, we feel we must arrange events chronologically in a lineal order; how else could our historians discover the causes of a war or a revolution or a defeat? Among the Trobrianders, what corresponds to our history is an aggregate of anecdotes, that is, unconnected points, told without respect to chronological sequence, or development, or causal relationship; with no grammatical distinction made between words referring to past events, or to present or contemplated ones. And in telling an anecdote, they take no care that a temporal sequence should be followed. For instance, they said to Malinowski, "They-eat-taro, they-spew-taro, they-disgusted-taro"; but if time, as we believe, is a moving line, then the revulsion came first in time, the vomiting was the result, coming afterward. Again, they say, "This-here . . . ripes . . . falls-down truly gives-birth . . . sits seed in belly-his"; but certainly the seed is there first, and the birth follows in time, if time is lineal.

Secondly, we arrange events and objects in a sequence which is climactic, in size and intensity, in emotional meaning, or according to some other principle. We often arrange events from earlier to later, not because we are interested in historical causation, but because the present is the climax of our history. But when the Trobriander relates happenings, there is no developmental arrangement, no building up of emotional tone. His stories have no plot, no lineal development, no climax. And when he repeats his garden spell, his list is neither climactic, nor anticlimactic; it sounds merely untidy to us:

> The belly of my garden lifts
> The belly of my garden rises
> The belly of my garden reclines
> The belly of my garden is-a-bushhen's-nest-in-lifting
> The belly of my garden is-an-anthill
> The belly of my garden lifts-bends

The belly of my garden is-an-ironwood-tree-in-lifting
The belly of my garden lies-down
The belly of my garden burgeons.

When the Trobrianders set out on their great ceremonial kula expedition, they follow a preestablished order. First comes the canoe of the Tolab wage, an obscure subclan. Next come the canoes of the great chiefs. But this is not climactic; after the great chiefs come the commoners. The order derives meaning not from lineal sequence, but from correspondence with a present, experienced, meaningful pattern, which is the recreation or realization of the mythical pattern; that which has been ordained of old and is forever. Its meaning does not lie in an item-to-item relationship, but in fitness, in the repetition of an established unit.

An ordering of this sort gives members of our society a certain esthetic dysphoria except when, through deliberate training, we learn to go beyond our cultural expectation; or, when we are too young to have taken on the phrasings of our culture. When we manipulate objects naively, we arrange them on some climactic lineal principle. Think of a college commencement, with the faculty arranged in order of rank or length of tenure or other mark of importance; with the students arranged according to increasing physical height, from shortest to tallest, actually the one absolutely irrelevant principle as regards the completion of their college education, which is the occasion for the celebration. Even when the sophisticated avoid this principle, they are not unconscious of it; they are deliberately avoiding something which is there.

And our arrangement of history, when we ourselves are personally involved, is mainly climactic. My great grandmother sewed by candle light, my grandmother, used a kerosene lamp, my mother did her studying by gaslight, I did it by a naked electric ceiling light, and my children have diffused fluorescent lighting. This is progress; this is the meaningful sequence. To the Trobriander, climax in history is abominable, a denial of all good, since it would imply not only the presence of change, but also that change increases the good; but to him value lies in sameness, in repeated pattern, in the incorporation of all time within the same point. What is good in life is exact identity with all past Trobriand experience, and all mythical experience.

There is no boundary between past Trobriand existence and the present; he can indicate that an action is completed, but this does not mean that the action is past; it may be completed and present or timeless. Where we would say "Many years ago" and use the past tense, the Trobriander will say, "In my father's childhood" and use non-temporal verbs; he places the event situationally, not temporally. Past, present, and future are presented linguistically as the same, are present in his existence, and sameness with what we call the past and with myth, represents value to the Trobriander. Where we see a developmental line, the Trobriander sees a point, at most a swelling in value. Where we find pleasure and satisfaction in moving away from the point, in change as variety or progress, the Trobriander finds it in the repetition of the known, in maintaining the point; that is, in what we call monotony.

Esthetic validity, dignity, and value come to the Trobriander not through arrangement into a climactic line, but rather in the undisturbed incorporation of the events within their original, nonlineal order. The only history which has meaning for him is that which evokes the value of the point, or which, in the repetition, swells the value of the point. For example, every occasion in which a kula object participates becomes an ingredient of its being and swells its value; all these occasions are enumerated with great satisfaction, but the lineal course of the traveling kula object is not important.

As we see our history climactically, so do we plan future experiences climactically, leading up to future satisfaction or meaning. Who but a very young child would think of starting a meal with strawberry shortcake and ending it with spinach? We have come to identify the end of the meal with the height of satisfaction, and we identify semantically the words dessert and reward, only because of the similarity of their position in a climactic line. The Trobriand meal has no dessert, no line, no climax. The special bit, the relish, is eaten *with* the staple food; it is not something to "look *forward* to," while disposing of a meaningless staple.

None of the Trobriand activities is fitted into a climactic line. There is no job, no labor, no drudgery which finds its reward outside the act. All work contains its own satisfaction. We cannot speak of S — R here, as all action contains its own immanent "stimulus." The present is not a means to future satisfaction, but good in itself, as the future is also good in itself; neither better nor worse, neither climactic nor anticlimactic, in fact, not lineally connected nor removed.

It follows that the present is not evaluated in terms of its place within a course of action leading upward to a worthy end. In our culture, we can rarely evaluate the present in itself. I tell you that Sally is selling notions at Woolworth's, but this in itself means nothing. It acquires some meaning when I add that she has recently graduated from Vassar. However, I go on to tell you that she has been assistant editor of *Vogue*, next a nursemaid, a charwoman, a public school teacher. But this is a mere jumble; it makes no sense and has no meaning, because the series leads to nothing. You cannot relate one job to another, and you are unable to see them discretely simply as part of her being. However, I now add that she is gathering material for a book on the working mother. Now all this falls in line, it makes sense in terms of a career. Now her job is good and it makes her happy, because it is part of a planned climactic line leading to more pay, increased recognition, higher rank. There was a story in a magazine about the college girl who fell in love with the milkman one summer; the reader felt tense until it was discovered that this was just a summer job, that it was only a means for the continuation of the man's education in the Columbia Law School. Our evaluation of happiness and unhappiness is bound with this motion along an envisioned line leading to a desired end. In the fulfillment of this course or career — not in the fulfillment of the self as point — do we find value. Our conception of freedom rests on the principle of noninterference with this moving line, noninterruption of the intended course of action.

It is difficult to tell whether climax is given in experience at all, or whether it is always imposed on the given. At a time when progress and evolution were assumed to be implicit in nature, our musicians and writers gave us climactic works. Nowadays, our more reflective art does not present experience climactically. Then, is emotion itself climactic? Climax, for us, evokes "thrill" or "drama." But we have cultures, like the Tikopia, where life is lived, to our perception, on an even emotive plane without thrill or climax. Experiences which "we know to be" climactic, are described without climax by them. For example, they, as well as the Trobrianders, described intercourse as an aggregate of pleasurable experiences. But Malinowski is disturbed by this; he cannot place the erotic kiss in Trobriand experience, since it has no climactic function.

In our culture, childbearing is climactic. Pregnancy is represented by the usual obstetrician as an uncomfortable means to a dramatic end. For most women, all intensity of natural physical experience is nowadays removed from the actual birth itself; but the approach of birth nevertheless is a period of mounting tension, and drama is supplied by the intensive social recognition of the event, the dramatic accumulation of gifts, flowers, telegrams. A pregnancy is not formally announced since, if it does not eventuate in birth, it has failed to achieve its end; and failure to reach the climax brings shame. In its later stages it may be marked with a shower; but the shower looks forward to the birth, it does not celebrate the pregnancy itself. Among the Trobrianders, pregnancy has meaning in itself, as a state of being. At a first pregnancy, there is a long ceremonial involving "preparatory" work on the part of many people, which merely celebrates the pregnancy. It does not anchor the baby, it does not *have as its purpose* a more comfortable time during the pregnancy, it does not *lead to* an easier birth or a healthy baby. It makes the woman's skin white, and makes her be at her most beautiful; yet this *leads* to nothing, since she must not attract men, not even her own husband.

Are we then right in accepting without question the presence of a line in reality? Are we in a position to say with assurance that the Trobrianders are wrong and we are right? Much of our present-day thinking, and much of our evaluation, are based on the premise of the line and of the line as good. Students have been refused admittance to college because the autobiographic sketch accompanying their application showed absence of the line; they lacked purposefulness and ability to plan; they were inadequate as to character as well as intellectually. Our conception of personality formation, our stress on the significance of success and failure and of frustration in general, is based on the axiomatically postulated line. Yet can there by blocking without presupposed lineal motion or effort? If I walk along a path because I like the country, or if it is not important to get to a particular point at a particular time, then the insuperable puddle from the morning's shower is not frustrating; I throw stones into it and watch the ripples, and then choose another path. If the undertaking is of value in itself, a point good in itself, and not because it leads to something, then failure has no symbolic meaning; it merely results in no cake for supper, or less money in the family budget; it is not personally destructive. But failure is devastating in our culture, because it is not failure of the undertaking alone; it is the moving, becoming, lineally conceived self which has failed.

Ethnographers have occasionally remarked that the people whom they studied showed no annoyance when interrupted. Is this an indication of mild temper, or might it be the case that they were not interrupted at all, as there was no expectation of lineal continuity? Such questions are new in anthropology and most ethnographers therefore never thought of recording material which would answer them. However, we do have enough material to make us question the line as basic to all experience; whether it is actually present in given reality or not, it is not always present in experienced reality. We cannot even take it for granted as existing among those members of our society who are not completely or naively steeped in their culture, such as many of our artists, for example. And we should be very careful, in studying other cultures, to avoid the unexamined assumption that their actions are based on the predication of a lineal reality.

8

Cosmetics: The language of bodily adornment

TERENCE S. TURNER

Bodily adornment among the Tchikrin of Brazil includes elaborate painting, earplugs, lip plugs, and various styles of clothing. Terence Turner not only describes these practices, but deciphers their complex code to reveal their meaning. He suggests that body decorations have similar functions in all societies.

Something profound in the nature of man, in his role as a member of a society or culture, seems to be bound up with his universal urge to decorate or transform the surface of his body. We might well ask if the boundaries and appendages of the body carry some universal symbolic significance, and if so, whether their adornment is a way of focusing and expressing this symbolic meaning. In other words, bodily adornment may be a kind of symbolic language. But if it is, how can we decipher its "message"?

The Tchikrin, one of the least-known peoples of the central Brazilian wilderness (a region virtually unpenetrated by Brazilian settlers), are among the world's most exotic body adorners. Their elaborate body painting, their penis sheaths and earplugs, and their spectacular lip plugs raise the question of the symbolic significance of bodily adornment in a uniquely compelling way.

The Tchikrin are the northernmost group of the large Kayapo tribe, a member of the Ge-speaking linguistic family. Their villages are built in a circle around a large central plaza, each house the residence of an ex-

From "Tchikrin: A Central Brazilian Tribe and Its Symbolic Language of Bodily Adornment," *Natural History* 78 (October 1969):50–59, 70. Illustrations are omitted.

tended family. Throughout their lives the women remain in the households of their birth. Men, however, leave their maternal houses at about the age of eight, when they move to the men's house, which is usually built in the center of the plaza. Only after consummating their marriages by fathering a child do men move into their wives' houses.

The pattern of a man's life cycle focuses on his movement from his maternal household, to the men's house, to his wife's household. Before, during, and after these moves, he is classified according to named age grades, each with its distinctive social properties, styles of body painting and hair cutting, and bodily ornaments. There is a separate and rather different system of age grades for women.

Newborn and nursing infants of both sexes are classified in a category whose name means "little ones." They are the most elaborately ornamented Tchikrin of any age. A few days after a baby's birth, its ear lobes — and if it is a boy, its lower lip — are pierced, usually by its father. Cigar-shaped earplugs of reddened wood are inserted in the ear lobes and replaced from time to time with larger ones until the holes in the lobes have become quite large. A narrow dowel or string of beads is also inserted in a boy's lower lip, but this ornament is not enlarged until much later in life. At the same time, the mother crochets cotton bands, reddens them with paint, and fastens them around the infant's wrists, ankles, and knees. When these grow too tight they are cut away and replaced with larger ones.

The cast-off arm and leg bands and the discarded sets of earplugs are saved by the mother in a special pouch, together with the baby's desiccated umbilical cord. The bands and plugs constitute a sort of record of the baby's growth — analogous, in a way, to a modern mother's "baby book." When the baby grows older the father takes its pouch and hangs it on, or buries it at the root of, a hardwood tree in the savanna. This gives the child a magical infusion of strength and well-being, symbolically neutralizing the weakness and vulnerability of its infancy, for hardwood trees are potent sources of strength, endurance, and health in Kayapo ritual symbolism. The red color of the earplugs and cotton bands serves much the same symbolic function — the fostering of growth and strength — for red is associated with health, energy, and vitality.

Body painting is an outstanding feature of the decoration of both male and female babies. Mothers, grandmothers, or other kinswomen, using a stylus made of the center rib of a leaf, draw complex linear patterns over the entire body of the child. Women also paint each other in this complex style, but except for rare ceremonial occasions, they are not allowed to paint men and older boys. Since only women use the stylus method, the men paint each other in a rougher, simpler pattern.

When a boy is weaned, learns to talk well, and can walk easily, which usually happens between the ages of three and four, he "graduates" from the age grade of little ones to that of "boys about to enter the men's house." This transition, like most changes from one major age category to the next, is accompanied by changes in bodily adornment and features of grooming such as hair style. The boy is now stripped of his infantile ornaments (earplugs and cotton arm and leg bands) and his hair is cut short. Boys of this age spend little time with their mothers and sisters; they already form a quasi-independent masculine play group, a precursor of the age sets and societies of the men's house. Their semi-independence of their maternal families and passage out of infancy are expressed not only by doffing their infantile ornaments and long hair but also by the infrequency with which their mothers paint them in the time-consuming linear "stylus" fashion. Boys of this age are far more apt to be painted with broad areas or bands of black and red, applied directly with the hand.

At about the age of eight (the Tchikrin do not reckon age by number of years, but by broad criteria of physical size and maturity) a decisive event occurs in a boy's life. In a brief but solemn ceremony, an unrelated man called a "substitute father" comes to the boy's maternal house, where he sits waiting silently with his wailing father and mother. The substitute father leads him out into the plaza and paints his body solid black. He then takes the boy by the hand into the men's house, which becomes his home.

He is now cut off from the world of family and blood relationships. The painting ritual thus marks the end of childhood for the boy and he enters a new age grade called "the painted ones." From this time on the boy will never again (except for rare ceremonial occasions) be painted by a woman. Henceforth, he will be painted only by other men, in the rough hand style or with a stamp made of a fruit rind that is cut in a simple pattern.

At puberty, boys go through a brief ceremony in which they are given penis sheaths to wear. After this they may replace their beaded lip ornaments with small versions of the mature men's lip plugs. They also let their hair grow long again, in the style of adult men and women.

Hair is associated with sexual powers. Long hair connotes full participation in sexually based relationships. However, since infants as well as mature adults have long hair, it is evident that the Kayapo notion of participation in sexual relations is considerably different and more complex than our own. For the Kayapo, there are two modes of sexual participation. One, like our own culture's conception, consists of the mature individual's active exercise of his sexual powers, above all in the relationship between husband and wife. The other, for which our culture has no counterpart, consists of the infant's passive biological (and social) dependence on the family, a dependence founded upon its parents' procreative sexual relationship. The Kayapo think of an infant before it is weaned more as an extension of its parents' biological being than as an independent individual. It is conceived as still participating in the biological communion with its parents that it enjoyed in the womb. This is understandable in view of the Kayapo notion of pregnancy — that the fetus grows by nursing inside the mother. Birth, therefore, does not fundamentally change the relationship between mother and infant; it merely transfers its locus from inside her body to outside. The father is also involved in this biological connection, for while the child is still in the womb, his semen — like the mother's milk — is thought to nourish the fetus. The birth of the baby terminates this direct physical link with the father, a rupture that renders the father's relation to his newborn child extremely delicate and fraught with danger. In order to minimize this danger, for several days the father abstains from physical exertions or "strong" and "dangerous" acts, such as killing animals, that might otherwise have a deleterious impact on the child's health.

Because weaning marks the end of full physical communion between mother and child, a child's hair is cut at this time. Short hair symbolizes the attenuation of his direct biological connection with others, a connection that is restored when the child grows to physical maturity and is ready to exercise his own sexual powers. The same principle underlies the custom of cutting the hair as a gesture of mourning for the death of a spouse, sibling, or child. The effect of such a kinsman's death is equivalent to weaning, since it suppresses ties, which the Kayapo conceive as based on an intimate biological bond, between the person who has died and the survivor.

A distinction is made between hair of the head and hair of the face and body. Facial hair is customarily plucked as a matter of ordinary grooming of both sexes and all ages. Here again, however, the sexual significance of hair emerges in one of the more stereotyped forms of Kayapo love-play — it is considered to impart a special *frisson* for lovers to pluck a stray eyebrow or eyelash from each other's faces with their teeth.

The Kayapo recognize, in ritual and other ways, the correlation between the development of sexual maturity and the weakening of family ties. They attempt to offset this tendency toward the isolation of the individual from social control by developing alternate forms of communal integration of the individual's developing sexual powers. Public recognition of the individual's steps toward sexual and social maturity is ritually associated with changes in his social status that move him inexorably toward marriage and the founding of his own family.

The penis sheath is the symbolic expression of the social control and regulation of mature male sexual powers. It is bestowed at puberty, and only after the sheath-bestowing ceremony is a youth's hair allowed to grow long again. Sheath and coiffure are thus complementary aspects of the public recognition of the growing boy's biological sexuality and, at the same time, of its integration into the social order.

Penis sheath, lip plug, and long hair symbolize the community's recognition of a boy's physical maturity, but they do not confer on him the right to put his newly recognized powers into practice. He only wins this right by going through the initiation ceremony, which is completely distinct from the penis-sheath rite and centers around the ceremonial "marriage," or betrothal, of the boy. This ritual marriage is not considered binding: it only establishes in principle the boy's ability to have sexual relations and marry any girl he chooses. Going through the initiation ceremony entitles a boy to move up into the age grade of "bachelor youths."

Bachelor youths eventually become engaged in earnest. Engagement, a private arrangement with a girl and her parents, culminates in the girl's pregnancy and the birth of a child. This event marks the climax of the youth's transition from boyhood to mature manhood, and he thereupon passes from the symbolic tutelage of his substitute father, who has presided over the successive stages of the long initiation process. Having founded his own family, he is definitively free of his lingering childhood bonds to his maternal family. He is entitled to move out of the men's house into his wife's house, and simultaneously to graduate to the age grade of mature men, significantly called "fathers." Fathers make up the membership of the men's societies, which meet (but do not reside) in the men's house and conduct the political affairs of the community.

These vital transitions in a man's life are expressed by a final transformation in bodily ornamentation — the replacement of the youth's small lip plug by a saucerlike plate, which may reach a diameter of four inches, or an alternative form, a long cylinder of rock crystal or wood. As an expression of mature manhood, this extraordinary ornament has a complex significance.

One aspect of its symbolism is implicit in the contrast between the lip plug and earplug. Both hearing and speaking have specific social associations for the Kayapo, and these associations relate to each other as complementary passive and active values. Hearing is a passive activity. The word *mari* "hearing" signifies understanding in the passive sense of knowing about something. Hearing in this sense is used in the common idiomatic expression of affirmation of specific relationships. If a man has good relations with his father's side of the family, for example, he says, "I hear them strongly" *(mari taytch)*. Speaking, on the other hand, is perhaps the most fundamental social act of self-assertion, and its assertive connotations are highly elaborated and associated with mature masculinity. Flamboyant oratory is one of the major activities of Kayapo men.

The huge lip plugs of the father's age grade are consciously associated with this flamboyant oral assertiveness. The dynamism and oral aggressiveness of adult male public behavior rests on a foundation of sexual assertiveness: graduation to father status depends on a man's actually siring a child. The fulfillment of male sexual powers in paternity and the resulting integration of men in specific family units are, in other words, what earn men the right to aggressive, oral self-assertion in the men's house. The full-size lip plug, in its double character as the badge of paternity and the symbol of mature male oral aggressiveness, precisely embodies this relationship between the phallic and oral components of adult masculinity, and by the same token, of the family and communal levels of men's social relations.

If paternity is the criterion for communal recognition of male maturity, then infants assume a reciprocal importance as the "objective correlatives" of manhood in both its biological and social aspects (phallic power and family membership). Infants, then, are the passive extensions, or corroborations, of the father's sexual powers and social position as *paterfamilias*. The relation of the infant to its father is in fact analogous to that between hearing (in its Kayapo sense of passive affirmation of social relations) and speaking (considered as social self-assertion). The symbolic complementarity of infantile earplug and paternal lip plug neatly expresses this social complementarity, especially when the phallic connotations of the cigar-shaped earplugs are taken into account. The same considerations explain why women do not wear lip plugs and why neither adult men nor women wear earplugs.

In contrast to the man's pattern of life, for the Tchikrin woman there is no dramatic transformation in social relations involved in biological parenthood. The residence rule dictates that women spend their entire life cycle in the households into which they are born. The contrasts between female and male body decoration reflect the difference in social pattern.

Girls, like boys, dispense with their earplugs and have their hair cut upon weaning. They continue, however, to wear crocheted red cotton arm and leg bands — in recognition of their continuing membership in their parental families — until they are judged ready for childbearing.

At about the age of eight — the same age that a boy leaves home to enter the men's house — a girl is initiated into sexual relations under the aegis of a special ceremonial guardian. This event marks her graduation into the age grade of "given ones." In all probability the name indicates (the Kayapo have no explicit explanation for it) that girls of this age grade are considered to be "bestowed" upon the initiated men of the village for sexual purposes. Given ones are expected to take an active and enthusiastic part in communal dances; dancing in groups during communal rituals is, in fact, their chief collective activity.

The rite that recognizes that a girl has reached the stage of potential motherhood bears many resemblances to the boy's ceremony of induction into the men's house, and has the same purpose of formally dissolving the childhood bond to the parental family. In the girls' ceremony, a "substitute mother" paints the girls' thighs, breasts, and upper arms with broad black stripes, and cuts off their arm and leg bands (the symbols of parental ties). Henceforth, they are known as "black-thighed ones," and are considered ready to consummate their courtships with one of their suitors in marriage by giving birth to a child. Only this event differentiates women in a social sense from their parental families, since it enables them to set up distinct families of their own within the household they share with their parents. Independence from the parental family (established much earlier for boys by their move to the men's house) is the prerequisite for social recognition of their reproductive powers as fully developed, autonomous, and "adult." This recognition, as we have seen, is symbolized for both sexes by long hair. For this reason, a woman is allowed to wear her hair long only upon the birth of her first child.

After attaining black-thighed status, a girl is qualified to join one of the mature women's societies, whose members gather regularly, every few weeks or so, to paint each other. It is interesting that while adult women often use the hand technique of the mature men to paint each other, they may equally well employ the stylus method used by mothers to paint their infants. Men and boys are almost never painted in this style after they leave home for the men's house; the use of it by adult women is another mark of their greater continuity with the social circumstances of childhood.

The typical daily routine of a Tchikrin mother, however, has relatively little place for collective activities. She must nurse her baby and care for her younger children. One of the most frequent maternal chores is delousing, which, interestingly enough, conforms to a sexually asymmetrical pattern partially similar to that of body painting. Women delouse children, other women, and men (usually their husbands), but men do not delouse women.

A woman's day usually includes a trip to her garden or perhaps an expedition to gather firewood, normally cut by women. She is likely to return from either heavily burdened. She must cook for her husband and children (each nuclear family within the household gardens and cooks for itself). The Tchikrin, like other members of the Ge linguistic group, lack pottery. They cook by baking bundles of food wrapped in leaves, in a temporary earth "oven" composed of heated stones, leaves, and earth.

At the end of the day a woman may get a little time to relax with her husband on the family bed, a mat-covered platform of split logs.

Lip plug, earplugs, penis sheath, hair style, cotton leg and arm bands, and body painting make up a symbolic language that expresses a wide range of information about social status, sex, and age. As a language, however, it does more than merely communicate this information from one individual to another: at a deeper level, it establishes a channel of communication *within* the individual between the social and biological aspects of his personality.

The social and psychological "message" of bodily adornment is coded and transmitted on an even more basic level by the colors used in body painting, and the symbolic associations of the parts of the body to which each color is applied. The colors of Tchikrin body painting are red (made from the seeds of the urucú plant), black (made from the juice of the genipa fruit), and, rarely, white (made from white clay), and these are used in determinate ways. Red is always applied on the extremities of the body — the forearms and hands, lower legs and feet, and the face. Black is always used on the trunk and upper parts of the limbs, as well as for the square cheek patches and borders along the shaved area of the forehead. The black face paintings, executed with painstaking care, are often covered immediately after they are finished with a heavy coat of red, which renders them almost invisible. The explanation for this peculiar practice lies in the symbolic values of the colors involved.

Red always connotes energy, health, and "quickness," both in the sense of swiftness and of heightened sensitivity (which the Kayapo conceive of as "quickness" or "lightness" of skin). Black, on the other hand, is associated with transitions between clearly defined states or categories, with "borderline" conditions or regions where normal clear-cut structures of ideas and rules of behavior are "blacked out."

It is interesting that the word for black, *tuk*, also means "dead," and is the adjective used for the zone of land just outside the village, which separates it from the completely wild forest and savanna country. The graveyard and the secluded camps used by groups going through "transitional" rites, such as initiation, are located in this interstitial area. Death itself is conceived of by the Tchikrin as a transitional phase between life and total extinction. The ghosts of the dead live on for one generation in the village of the dead, after which they "die" once more, this time passing into total oblivion.

White, which occurs only in relatively infrequent ceremonial decorations, is associated less with transition than with the pure, "terminal" state of complete transcendence of the normal social world. It is, for example, the color of ghosts. White clay is the food of ghosts, and the villages of the ghosts are always located near outcroppings of white clay or rocks.

Body painting for both ordinary social and ritual occasions seems to be a means of expressing heightened integration and participation in the social order as well as a means of heightening individual biological and psychological powers. Red is applied on the parts of the body most immediately associated with swiftness, agility, and sensory contact with the outside world (feet, hands, and face). This seems logical enough from what we have seen of the symbolic values of the color red. Black is used for the parts of the body most intimately associated with the individual's biological being, his inner self as contrasted with his faculties of relating to the world (the trunk, upper parts of the limbs, and certain areas of the head).

Why should black, which symbolizes the marginal, transitional, or imperfectly integrated aspects of the social order, be thus associated with the individual's presocial (biological) being in those situations where integration into society is being dramatized and reaffirmed?

To answer this question adequately we must start from an understanding of the symbolic significance of the skin in Kayapo culture. The skin, for the Kayapo, is the boundary of the individual on several levels of meaning. In the obvious physical sense, it separates the individual from the external environment, which includes other people. But in a more subtle sense, the skin symbolizes the boundary between two levels of the human personality: the lower level, based on presocial drives emanating from the individual's biological constitution, and the higher level of moral conscience and intellectual consciousness based on cultural principles derived from social sources outside the individual. More simply, this inner, psychological boundary corresponds to the boundary between the physical individual and his society.

The proper balance of relations between the levels of the individual's personality, like proper relations between individuals in society, depends in Kayapo thought on the right sort of communication taking place across these two correlated boundaries. They must be crossed in both directions, for society needs the biological energies of individuals, but it also needs to control them to prevent disruption and chaos. The individual subsists through his biological energies, but he needs the steadying influence of social values, cognitive categories, and moral principles or he will "go berserk" (a recognized condition in Kayapo, known as *aybanh*). Disease, death, the breaking of certain taboos, and going berserk are all conceived as improper forms of eruption of the biological level of existence into the social, orderly level.

The interesting point for our purposes is that all of these "eruptions" are associated with disorders or treatments of the skin: sick people are painted red, dead people either red or black, taboo-breakers get hives or other skin diseases, the skin of berserks becomes alternately overheated and then cold and insensitive, etc. When black, the color associated with transition between the social and asocial worlds, is painted on the skin of the central parts of the body, it expresses the transcendence of the boundary between individual and society and thus reaffirms the mutual integration of the biological individual and the "body social."

It becomes easy to understand, then, why the Tchikrin paint over the black designs of the face with red: They are concerned not so much with esthetic results as with a symbolic statement, in which both colors have complementary "messages" to transmit. The overpainting with red serves to energize, to charge with biological and psychic life-force, the sensory and intelligent part of the person whose socialization has been asserted by the black designs below.

Body painting at this general level of meaning really amounts to the imposition of a second, social "skin" on the naked biological skin of the individual. This second skin of culturally standardized patterns symbolically expresses the "socialization" of the human body — the subordination of the physical aspects of individual existence to common social values and behavior.

It would be misleading to lay too much emphasis on the superficial differences between Tchikrin body adornment and our own culture's elaborate array of clothing and hair styles, makeup, and jewelry. Among the Tchikrin, as among ourselves, the decoration of the surface of the body serves as a symbolic link between the "inner man" and some of his society's most important values.

9

Hair: The long and the short of it

DEXTER K. STRONG

This article deals with the ways in which hair has been defined in Western culture from ancient times to the present. The length of a man's hair carries a message, but the meaning of this has changed over time, becoming entwined with such issues as war and peace, belief and unbelief, suppression and revolt. Dexter Strong sums up the subject by saying, "Hair styles, like the tides, will keep on changing, and life's vital issues will continue to be hopelessly intertwined with what goes on — or does not go on — in the barbershop."

The length of a man's hair and beard has become, in the minds of many, one of the major issues of our time. This fact crept up on me gradually. Schoolmasters such as myself have for years been responsible for seeing to it that the young get their hair cut. A father's determination to keep his son's hair neatly trimmed is legendary, and usually begins early, when he has to overcome Mother's reluctance about that first trip to the barbershop. Currently, however, the subject of long hair and beards is causing more than gentle family arguments. It is a hotter issue between generations than ever before in *my* lifetime, and wherever the topic is discussed it raises blood pressures to alarming levels. It is likely to lead from discussions of style and discipline to frantic condemnations of draft-evasion, homosexuality and LSD.

Even the newspapers fan the flames. Periodically, front pages carry the story of, say, a Stanford coach barring a runner from a track meet, or a principal excluding a long-haired boy from school.

Perhaps reasonable men should be above such a hullaballoo over hair, but my guess is that when any of us first encountered, on Piccadilly

From "Hair: The Long and the Short of It," *Seattle Magazine* 4 (October 1967): 44–48, 59. Reprinted by permission of the publisher and the author. Illustrations and footnotes are omitted.

or on University Way, a six-foot man with hair down to his shoulders, we ourselves had some strong feelings on the subject — feelings that were unlikely to be changed by argument.

If we did react that way, we were normal. Through all of history, men's beards and hair have had such profound significance — superstitious, political, military, religious, social, and psychological — as to set men, from time to time, at each other's throats.[1] Most American males over, say, thirty have their hair trimmed whenever they get around to it, without any fuss, but not a Cavalier — not with those Roundheads breathing down his neck. We all know what Delilah did to Samson. We may never have sworn by the beard of the Prophet, but millions have, and have thought, to boot, that all beardless men were either unbelievers or slaves. Some of us can even remember the passing of the Chinaman's queue with the revolution of 1911. High blood pressure on the subject obviously did not begin with the Beatles.

Take, for example, the war in which David managed to have Uriah killed. The result of the war, David's acquisition of a wife, is far better remembered than what started the war in the first place. In an attempt to reach an understanding with the Ammonites, David had sent his peace emissaries to their new king, Hanun. "Wherefore," according to II Samuel XI, 4, "Hanun took David's servants, and shaved off one half of their beards, and cut off their garments in the middle, even to their buttocks, and sent them away." And note what happened when David heard of this indignity: "The men were greatly ashamed. And the king said, 'Tarry at Jericho until your beards be grown, and then return.'" Apparently the men's lack of pants was a consideration not worth comment. In any case, 33,000 Syrians, hired by the Ammonites, were soon trying to stand off David's hosts led by Joab.

This was no isolated incident. Except when in mourning, the Jews considered shaving, or even trimming the corners of the beard, a sin of the Gentiles, and in some orthodox circles, the beard continues to play an important role today. The Assyrians, too, sported beards — big square ones — and even managed to give them an aggressive forward tilt. The Egyptians, on the other hand, though they used false beards at times, loathed hair, and according to Herodotus, regarded the bearded Greeks as barbarians.

The classical Greeks were bearded, and they pictured most of their gods the same way. Indeed, the beard was so common among the Greeks that Herodotus assumed that the beardless Scythians suffered some dis-

[1] Most of the historical information and quotations in this article come from a hefty volume by Richard Corson, *Fashions in Hair, the First Five Thousand Years* (New York: Hastings House, 1965). Charles Berg's *The Unconscious Significance of Hair* (London: Allen, 1951) is referred to in the text. . . .

ease that made them look like women. There is speculation that the Scythians may even have given rise to the legend of the Amazons.

Certainly the Greeks did not take their beads lightly. Diogenes had a great deal to say on the subject, all of it insulting. When approached by a clean-shaven man one day, Diogenes shouted at him to take off his clothes to prove his sex and refused to say another word to him unless — and until — he did so. Today, anyone choosing to adopt Diogenes's belligerent tactics on University Way would probably find himself shouting not at a hairless man, but at a man with too *much* hair.

Alexander the Great changed everything for the Greeks by requiring his soldiers to shave off their beards, lest, according to one contemporary commentator, the Persians use them as handles. Perhaps he was just reacting against his father, Philip, a believer in beards. According to Plutarch, Philip once appointed a man to a judgeship who was later found to have dyed his hair and beard. The king summarily removed him saying, "I could not think that one that was faithless in his hair could be trusty in his deeds."

The Romans, too, went through cycles of facial hair styles, though they were fairly consistent in wearing the hair of their head short and in brushing it out in all directions from the crown — a style that has frequently been imitated in modern times. Up to about 300 B.C. the Romans were bearded, then they took to beardlessness until the time of Hadrian, who grew a beard to hide some kind of facial disfiguration.

As with other ancient peoples, young Romans were likely to let their hair grow and then to sacrifice the first cuttings to a god. Also obvious among the Romans was a theory of opposites: During periods when shaving was in style, slaves were required to grow beards, but when beards were in fashion, they had to shave on orders of their bearded masters. Similarly, growing a beard in clean-shaven times was a sign of mourning, just as taking off a beard expressed mourning if beards were in style.

The establishment of the Christian church simply added fuel to the flames of dissension, no matter which way the styles were going. The church not only issued meticulous regulations on the shape of the tonsure for priests, but also tried, time and again, to regulate the length of hair and beards for *all* men.

At one point, the church decreed that part of a man's ears and eyes should be visible. Saint Wolstan, when Bishop of Worcester, even stated officially that long hair on men was "highly immoral, criminal and beastly." In the mid-ninth century, the Greek church was beardless, the Roman church, bearded. In Rome a clean face was once mentioned as a grievance in an edict of excommunication. Yet, in 1105, the Bishop of Amiens announced at Christmastime that he would refuse communion to anyone *wearing* a beard.

Mahomet was just as specific, though perhaps more consistent. He dyed his own beard red and instructed his followers to trim theirs in such a way as to differentiate them from the Jews. Slaves in Islam were beardless and so were idolaters. One bard's story of the Crusades — there were folksingers in those days, too — gives Richard Coeur de Lion's recipe for serving up a Saracen's head: Remove the hair "off hed, off berd, and eke off lyppe." This was obviously as cruel a fate as the bard could dream up for a Moslem, even more dreadful than decapitation.

Excitement over hair styles reached a new peak when first long hair, and then wigs, came into fashion in the seventeenth century. Many considered the new style scandalous, and, of course, there were rules against it. The General Court of Massachusetts forbade long hair "if uncomely or prejudical to the common good," and Harvard did not permit its boys "to wear Long Haire, Lockes, Foretops, Curlings, Crispings, Partings, or Powdering of Ye Haire."

In 1653, Thomas Hall, B.D., of Kingsnorton, published a book entitled *The Loathsomeness of Long Haire: or a Treatise Wherein you have the Question stated, many Arguments against it produced, and most material Arguments for it repelled and answered, with the current judgment of Divines both old and new against it. With an Appendix against Painting, Spots, Naked Breasts, etc.* The full title not only makes the author's thesis clear — though he does muddy things up a bit there at the end — but also shows how strongly he feels on the subject.

In his text, the author specifies five ways to tell if a man's hair *is* too long, and No. 4 is most revealing: Hair is too long "when it is scandalous and offensive, when it is so long that the godly are thereby grieved, the weak offended and the wicked hardened." He also strikes a familiar note in his contention that long hair "is the trick of youth and the badge of proud hearts. . . . Indeed it is a foreign trick . . . and therefore unlawful . . . which God condemns."

Hall was no less jaundiced about wigs and stated a man "may not wear the long haire of another, be it of a man, a woman, or it may be of some harlot, who is now in Hell lamenting there the abuse of that excrement." But despite his title and his firm position against long hair and wigs, Thomas Hall was in favor of beards and considered them "a signe of manhood given by God to distinguish the Male from the Female sex." A student of this subject, not to mention a protagonist, has to be able to turn on a dime.

Despite the Reverend Mr. Hall and the divine support he invoked, men stopped wearing beards and started wearing long hair, and they soon took to wigs as well. Pepys tells us of his gradual conversion to the new style. In March of 1663, he tried on two or three wigs at his barber's, but had "no stomach for it." In October, with his wife's help, he selected one and wore it to church the following month, surprised to find that no one "cast their eyes" upon him. By 1665 he had cut off his own hair—periwigs were such a convenience—and in 1667 he records that he bought a new wig for four pounds, ten shillings, "and made a great show."

Once wigs were established, the tumult died down and many predictable things happened. The wigmakers' guild separated from the barber-surgeons' and set up on its own. Peruke-makers petitioned the king to require all adults to wear wigs, but were denied. The ultimate sign of wig acceptance came when men who didn't wear wigs, like George III in his early years and George Washington throughout his adult life, wore their hair to make it *look* as if they did.

Then as now, fathers and sons disagreed sharply on hair styles. Lord Chesterfield, for instance, wrote to his son in 1748:

> I can by no means agree to your cutting off your hair. I am very sure that your headaches do not proceed from thence. . . . Your own hair is at your age an ornament, and a wig, however well made, [is] such a disguise that I will on no account whatever have you cut off your hair. Nature did not give it to you for nothing, still less to cause you the headache. . . .

With the advent of wigs, hair styles became particularly associated with class and calling. Men of law wore the clerical, or tie, peruke; army and navy officers sported a brigadier or possibly a great fox-ear, with a cluster of curls at the temple; men of business were characterized by a full-bottomed, or moderate, tie; elegants, back from Italy, built high toupees on top of a club wig and, along with this total headdress, were called macaronis; and coachmen were said to wear theirs in imitation of the curled hair of a water dog.

Apparently wigs even became a factor in government. Horace Walpole said of Lord Sandwich: "I could have no hope of getting at his ear, for he has put on such a first-rate tie that nothing without the lungs of a boatswain can ever think to penetrate the thickness of his curls." The false-hair fashion, moreover, was responsible for the eighteenth century equivalent of singing commercials. A sign over a shop in London read:

> Oh Absalom! Oh Absalom!
> Oh Absalom! my son,
> If thou hadst worn a periwig,
> Thou hadst not been undone.

And in Paris:

> Passans, contemplex la douleur
> D'Absalom pendu par la nuque;
> Il eut évité ce malheur
> S'il avait porté perruque.

The passing of wigs and long hair caused just as much fuss as their introduction, and while they may not actually have been an issue in the French Revolution, short hair did become fashionable in France in the 1790's. Like the queue in China, the earlier, longer style became associated with the pre-revolutionary regime.

In England and America the change to short hair began about 1783. Though more gradual than in France, it was no less painful. Sometimes the transition was just physically difficult. A well-known, left-profile portrait of John Adams, for example, shows him with a half-wig behind — a kind of tail-piece — to supplement his front hair as it gradually grew out. As late as 1799, Dr. Randolph, Bishop of Oxford, encountered such scandalized opposition when he began to wear his own hair that he reverted to his wig for services of divine worship.

Pigtails came off the British army between 1804 and 1808 by official order, and as far as is known, without incident. But in the U.S. Army, one Lieutenant Colonel, Thomas Butler, refused to obey a similar order of 1801 and clung to his pigtail. For his stubbornness, the army courtmartialed and convicted him, imprisoned him, released him (still with his pigtail on) tried him again — and then let him die, unshorn, of yellow fever before condemning him a second time.

In one profession, the law, the wig stayed on, but not without a fight. Lord Eldon, made Chief Justice of Common Pleas in 1799, did not like his powdered bush wig. Needled by his wife, he asked George III for a special dispensation on account of headaches. King George, with little sympathy for either the baron or baroness, replied tartly: "I will have no innovations in my time" — and made his decision stick.

During the nineteenth century, hair styles did not cause much excitement in either England or America, but there was a lot of fuss about beards and whiskers. The previous century had been one of the few beardless epochs in western history, and the return of these adornments sent blood pressure up to predictable heights.

There had been some advance indications of what would happen when beards returned. In the late eighteenth century, a New Jersey Quaker named Joshua Evans grew a beard. To be sure, he was a bit odd in other ways: He was a vegetarian, wore suits made of undyed wool, and had fundamental objections to the use of leather. It was the beard, though, that aroused his fellow Friends.

One day they visited him in formal delegation, but "left him with a beard on, much as they found him, none having power, or a razor, to cut it off." Foiled in this attempt, his associates took to avoiding him in meeting and denying him a license to travel as a minister. Evans made a spirited defense, and, what's more, he triumphed — *but it took him fourteen years.* He later admitted that his beard was useful in his profession, "many being induced . . . to come to hear me on account of my singular appearance."

The very strength and depth of the anti-beard feeling, and the length of time that Western man had gone beardless actually influenced the return of beards. Certainly the first general crop, those of the French romantics, were symbols of revolt. Young France considered the vast expanse of white cravat then in style a mark of reactionary, classical tastes. Their scorn was profound. Any white linen marked a man as *"un profane, un retardataire, un hottentot, un epicier, un bourgeois, un philistin — pour tout dire en un mot — un classique."* So the young romantics used vast black cravats, or beards, in place of the white expanse.

The same element of revolt does not appear to have accompanied beards back to England and America. Their proponents, drawing with dignity on natural and divine law, on the rules of good health, and on appeals to men's virility, overcame all attacks. As early as 1847, a book appeared entitled *Beard Shaving and the Common Use of the Razor, an Unnatural, Irrational, Unmanly, Ungodly and Fatal Fashion Among Christians.* Some time in the 1850's, an article in the *London Methodist Quarterly Review* expressed concern over the amount of bronchitic infection among ministers of the gospel; this unhappy condition, wrote the author, was attributable to the ministers' disregard of "hygienic law." The cure: Grow a beard to keep your chest warm.

Others wrote not so much with caution as with male bravado:

> Deprive the lion of his mane, the cock of his comb, the peacock of the emerald plumage of his tail, the ram and deer of their horns, and they are not only displeasing to the eye, but they lose much of their power and vigor. . . . Only fashion forces the Englishman to shave off those appendages which give the male countenance the true masculine character indicative of energy, bold daring, and decision.

From the 1860's through the 1890's whiskers and beards were everywhere. This is made clear by Brady's photographs of Civil War generals and pictures of the Presidential cabinets of the 1870's, not to mention the Presidents themselves. Lincoln was clean-shaven during the election of 1860, but grew a beard before his inauguration. Andrew Johnson was clean-shaven — but, of course, he was very nearly impeached. Grant, Hayes, Garfield, and Harrison wore beards, Arthur wore whiskers, and Cleveland a mustache. Even after the beard disappeared in the 1890's, the mustache stayed on with both T. R. and Taft. McKinley was clean-shaven but it was not until Woodrow Wilson that the clean-shaven line was reestablished.

One of the happy aspects of the era was the variety of styles that men evolved in their beards, mustaches, and whiskers. There were Imperials, Dundrearies, and Piccadilly Weepers; there was the Uncle Sam;

Horace Greeley himself wore a Saucer, or Trencher, though out West, where he was pointing; John Muir wore a Nokomis and common men tended to the Square, the Swallowtail or the Miners' beard. There were Mutton Chops and Breakwaters (Disraeli developed a Breakwater); there were Burnsides and Sideburns, Van Dykes, Billees and Goatees, and Horseshoes and Walruses (commonly known as Soupstrainers). Those of us who belong to the gray-flanneled generation can only vaguely grasp what we are missing.

When beards made their exit, beginning in the 1890's, there was almost as much excitement as when they made their entrance fifty years before, largely because the first to adopt the new style were the young English aesthetes. No record exists of what Benjamin Harrison had to say about Oscar Wilde — perhaps this is fortunate — but no doubt he could get as much venom and disgust into a phrase like "that beardless so-and-so" as a 1967 personnel manager can put into "those blankety-blank bearded beatniks."

Harrison, however, lost and the young aesthetes won. By 1903, one writer could state: "I never saw a man wearing a Van Dyke beard who was not selfish, sinister, and pompous as a peacock."

Though beards were *passé* by the turn of the century, the health-and-hair dispute continued. In 1904, *Harper's* carried an article pointing out that mustaches picked up coffee and gravy, but it was the scientists, now deep in the study of germs, who really came charging to the fore. The first official tally was made by a German (naturally), who reported that the average beard contained two million misanthropic microbes. The French approached the subject with more flair. In 1907, a scientist in Paris arranged and carried out a public experiment — medical journals please note. He guided two men, one bearded and one clean-shaven, through the streets and stores of the capital for about an hour. Waiting for them were two young ladies whose lips had been carefully sterilized. The bearded man kissed one young lady, the clean-shaven man the other. Immediately, a sterile brush was passed over each pair of female lips, and then each brush was placed in a separate solution of agar-agar and left for four days.

The results were sensational. The culture from the lips of the girl kissed by the clean-shaven man contained only a few harmless yeast germs, but the other culture, according to the official report, "literally swarmed with malignant microbes, tubercle bacillus, diphtheria and putrefactious germs, minute bits of food, hair from a spider's leg, and other odds and ends."

Science affected men's hair styles for more realistic reasons when the louse was discovered to carry typhus. Soldiers in World War I all had their heads shaved close, and that style has become traditional for the military. Short hair has persisted in civilian life as well, and although a few toothbrush mustaches appeared in the 1920's, not to mention a variety of haircut styles since then among the young (pompadours, crew cuts, butches, Princetons, flattops, and ducktails), the years up to and past World War II have been short-haired, unwhiskered, and beardless.

Now all hell seems to have broken loose again. It is too soon to say whether a new cycle of style is upon us. Certainly hackles and blood pressures are up, and, in the past, these symptoms have often heralded a major change.

What is all the excitement about anyway?

To discover that men have been getting just as excited, off and on, for thousands of years, puts the matter in perspective but hardly answers the question. The Freudians think they have the answer. (Personally, I am inclined to guffaw over some of the more extreme applications of Freudian theory, but I try to restrain myself because I know just enough to concede that the guffaw itself may be highly revealing.)

In his book, *The Unconscious Significance of Hair,* published in 1951, Charles Berg points out that there is plenty of evidence, both clinical and anthropological, to associate hairiness with virility and libidinal development. That the appearance of facial hair coincides with the passage from childhood to manhood is clear enough to me, and I can even follow some of Berg's comments on the folklore of the subject — though I am several laps behind when he gets through with the legend of Rapunzel.

Our attitude toward hair, like all other behavior, says Berg, is an expression of various opposed tensions of the unconscious conflict within us.

> When we attend, preserve or love our hair, we are expressing in displaced form our appreciation of and pleasure in our sexuality. When we remove, cut or control our hair we are giving expression to reaction formations against the . . . libido.

As for beards specifically, Berg considers them either a mark of masculine aggression or an attempt to compensate for unconscious feelings of anonymity. "They may also be," Berg goes on, "a gesture of rebellion against, or emancipation from, the castrating trammels of convention."

If the Freudians are right, then we have a pattern and code-book to help us understand all the bitterness, vituperation, sarcasm, pride, pleasure, shame, and name-calling that have so often accompanied changes in the way men wear their hair and beards.

In a more general way, however, other factors are surely involved. Custom, for one thing is important. If, in our lifetime, shoulder-length hair has been for girls, then shoulder-length hair on boys seems effeminate — despite the certainty that Abraham, Diogenes, D'Artagnan, and George Washington would all have heartily and manfully disagreed.

Our sense of conformity also plays a part. Some of us men probably have grown beards when cruising or camping, but we have always shaved before turning up at church, at the office, or at the Rainier Club. If Jim Owens goes off to the Rose Bowl with a planeload of young men, all of whom are beardless and have their hair neatly trimmed, then this becomes the pattern; and a coach who turns up with a halfback who has grown a beard is bound to feel he has lost face in more senses than one.

More important, we are again in a period when hair styles have increasingly become associated with other, more urgent issues. If some of the vocal demands for a more meaningful and more relevant curriculum come from bearded young men, then we find some of our lifetime assumptions about a liberal education challenged, and beards, by association, themselves become a challenge — perhaps even a threat.

To a strong supporter of the war in Vietnam who sees hairy objectors carrying placards, long hair and beards are for the doves, Freud or no Freud: *What are these damned fringies up to, smoking pot and making a religion out of LSD? By George, these fellows who grow beards and avoid barbers are upsetting everything! Why aren't they out there fighting? What do they mean by taking psychedelic trips and wearing necklaces and telling us how to run the world? Who the hell do they think they are anyway?*

So there we are, right back where we started, confusing hair with war and peace, belief and unbelief, suppression and freedom, traditionalism and revolt. In all our angry uncertainty, though, we may rest quietly assured of this: Hair styles, like the tides, will keep on changing, and life's vital issues will continue to be hopelessly intertwined with what goes on — or does not go on — in the barbershop.

IV

Social structure I: Roles and groups

Man survives by living in organized groups. While these range in size from families to nations, each requires a blueprint for cooperation and predictable interaction. The social structure acts as a map that defines kinds of persons, groups, and behavior appropriate to each. For example, in the university community there are students, faculty, and administrators who interact on the basis of accepted role definitions. Such roles are reciprocal and a change in one leads to a modification in others. The social structure, a necessary ingredient of every society, enables us to anticipate the responses of others and to behave in ways they will judge appropriate.

There are a limited number of principles for ordering roles and groups including kinship, sex, age, residence, occupation, and common interest. The selections that follow demonstrate some of these organizational principles. It is difficult to discuss any aspect of culture without reference to social structure. In every society individuals learn to conform to the rights and duties associated with roles. Language is learned within a particular group, and communication flows along the lines set down by the social structure. The social order provides the framework for economic, religious and political activity.

But the social structure is more than a static pattern. From each individual's perspective, it is a series of roles that are learned, enacted for a time, and often discarded. One moves from child to adult, student to graduate, or single to married status. The experience of changing roles requires adjustment by both the individual and his society. In every culture such transitions are often supported by ceremonies called "rites of passage," as illustrated by the last two articles in this chapter.

10

Primitive kinship

MEYER FORTES

Beginning with the institution of marriage and parenthood, this article traces the nature of the kinship system in general and variations among primitive societies. Detailed descriptions of the Ashanti matrilineal system and the Tallensi patrilineal system are provided, with constant contrasts between these African systems and our own culture. After briefly discussing the importance of kinship terms, Meyer Fortes concludes with a review of several kinship principles formulated by A. R. Radcliffe-Brown.

Ministers, political orators and editorial writers are apt to tell us that the family is the keystone of society. From the biological point of view it would indeed seem to be the ultimate social institution. The conjugal family — husband and wife and their children — gives social expression to the function of human reproduction. Early travelers from our civilization were sometimes shocked because they could find no obvious counterpart of our family among primitive peoples. When they found large communal households, inhabited by men, women, and children having the most bizarre and sometimes downright indecent relationships to one another (in the terminology of our family), they took this as conclusive evidence that these cultures were barbaric.

We have come to know primitive peoples at closer range in recent years. What they have taught us has radically altered our judgment of their family organizations and given us an humbler understanding of our own. Primitive family types vary in their constitution, but they are always precisely structured institutions, embracing the primary loyalty and life

From "Primitive Kinship," *Scientific American* 200 (June 1959): 147–158. Reprinted with permission of the author and the publisher. Illustrations, footnotes, and bibliography are omitted.

activity of their large memberships and enduring from generation to generation. The exact prescription of relationships among members gives each individual a significantly defined connection to a wide circle of his kin. To the individual member, the family's property is the source of livelihood, its ancestors are his gods, its elders his government, and its young men his defense and his support in old age. In simpler cultures (e.g., the Australian aborigines) family and society are actually coterminous: all men are either kinsmen or potential enemies.

We, in contrast, are primarily citizens, not kinsmen. The family is organized anew with each marriage. It must share our allegiance with the many competing claims of our society: the loyalties we owe to the institutions that employ us, to our professional organizations, to political parties, to community and nation. A family of such reduced status and scope is, as a matter of fact, distinctly out of the ordinary as families go. The Hebrew families of the Bible and the Roman *gens* more closely resemble the extended family systems of contemporary primitive cultures than they do our own. Of all the primitive societies I know, the one that most closely resembles ours in isolating the conjugal family as the basic social unit is the Iban, a tribe of headhunters in North Borneo. The vocabulary we employ to describe our kin — our uncles, aunts and cousins — beyond the immediate conjugal family fails to suggest the compelling ties that bind the kinship of peoples other than those of modern European and American civilization. Students of primitive kinship systems have found that they employ a terminology wholly unlike our own: the "classificatory" system, which groups relatives by status rather than sorting out their genetic interrelationships. It appears that all kinship systems obey certain universal principles governing the separation, inner unity, and orderly sequence of generations. Viewed from the vantage point of such understanding, our family appears to be the much-curtailed form of a once far more elaborate and comprehensive organization.

Two "facts of life" necessarily provide the basis of every family: the fact of sexual intercourse is institutionalized in marriage; the fact of parturition is institutionalized in parenthood. Societies differ greatly, however, in which of these institutions they select as the more important. Our society selects marriage: the result is the conjugal family, centered upon a single marital relationship and the children it produces. Most human societies, however, rate parenthood above marriage. This results in the consanguineal family, centered upon a single line of descent.

Biologically our lineal inheritance derives equally from both sides of the family according to Mendelian law. Societies that prize lineage, however, restrict social inheritance either to the maternal or the paternal line.

The social heritage — that is, property, citizenship, office, rank — passes either through the father or through the mother. "Patrilineal" descent (father to son) was the rule in ancient Rome, China and Israel, and occurs in many primitive societies. "Matrilineal" descent (mother's brother to sister's son) is common in Asia, Africa, Oceania, and aboriginal America.

One matrilineal society that flourishes today is the ancient, wealthy and artistic kingdom of Ashanti in Ghana, West Africa. While European mores have made some inroads among the Ashanti, back-country Ashanti villages still keep to their strictly matrilineal ways. Let us consider how such a society works.

First of all, let us note that a matrilineal society is not a matriarchal society: it is not ruled by women. So far as I know there is not, nor has there ever been, such a thing as a genuine matriarchal government. In every preliterate society men, not women, hold the political, legal and economic power; the women usually remain legal minors all their lives, subject to the authority of their menfolk. Primitive peoples usually understand quite well why men, not women, must be the rulers. The women, they say, are incapacitated for warfare and the affairs of state by the necessity of bearing and rearing children. Many peoples, including the Ashanti, believe that women are magically dangerous to men during menstruation and after childbirth.

In describing the Ashanti kinship system I am going to use common English terms (like "aunt" and "cousin") rather than attempt to translate the native terminology. The typical Ashanti household consists of an old woman, her daughters, their children, and one or two of her sons. The old woman, the daughters, and the sons are all married, but where are their spouses? We can suppose that all of these people are on good terms with their husbands and wives; nevertheless they do not form part of the same household with them, because they do not belong to the same clan. The spouses all live nearby, in households belonging to their own clans. The legal head of the household is one of the old woman's sons; he inherited his role from his mother's brother, not his father; he will pass it on to his sister's son, not his own.

Among the Ashanti marriage is governed by strict moral, legal and religious rules. Yet it is clear that the Ashanti find the fact of descent much more important than the fact of marriage. That is why the households are formed by mothers and children rather than by husbands and wives. The lineage group to which the old woman and her children belong is united by the bond of common descent from an ancestress of perhaps the tenth generation before that of the youngest members. Through this ancestress the group traces its descent from an even more remote mythological ancestress: the progenitor of their clan, one of the eight clans into which the Ashanti people is divided.

It is considered a sin and a crime for members of the same Ashanti lineage to have sexual relations; by this token they must look for spouses of independent descent, that is, of a different clan. Since husband and wife commonly reside in separate households, they must live near each other if they are to have a normal marital relationship. More than 80 percent of all marriages occur within the village community. Usually, therefore, one or two lineages of each of the eight clans is found in a village of average size.

The Ashanti rule of matrilineal descent has implications that reach far beyond the domestic household. Every Ashanti is by birth a citizen of the chiefdom to which his maternal lineage belongs. A man or woman can build a house freely on any vacant site in this chiefdom, and can farm any piece of unclaimed soil in the lands that it owns. An individual has no such rights in any other chiefdom. By the rule of matrilineal descent, a man can will no property to his own children; they belong to another household and another clan: his wife's. A man's heirs and successors are his sisters' sons. On his death his property and any position of hereditary rank he may hold pass automatically to his oldest nephew. If he wishes his own sons and daughters to benefit from his property, he must be content to make them gifts during his lifetime. They can accept his gifts only with the consent of his matrilineal heirs and of the elders in his lineage group. In the Ashanti tradition the individual comes under the authority of the mother's brother, not the father. It is the mother's brother whose consent is legally essential for a girl or boy to marry; he is also responsible for any costs that arise from divorce or other suits against them.

How do marriage and parenthood work out in such a system of kinship rules? It is undeniable that the Ashanti have delicate problems of marital adjustment. Both husband and wife must reach a compromise between their primary loyalties to matrilineal kin and their attachment to each other and to their children. When a man marries, he acquires legal rights to his wife's marital fidelity and to domestic services such as the regular provision of his meals. If a wife commits adultery, her husband can claim damages from the other man and apologies and a gift of placation from the wife, even if, as often happens, he does not divorce her. He can and will insist on divorce if his wife neglects her household duties or refuses to sleep with him. The husband is in turn obliged to provide food, clothing, and general care for his wife and children. If he fails in these duties, his wife can divorce him. In fact, divorce is very common among the Ashanti. Usually it is free of acrimony, for it does not involve the splitting of a household.

What an Ashanti man does not acquire by marriage is rights over his wife's reproductive powers, that is, over the children she bears him. These belong to her lineage, as opposed to his. An Ashanti man cannot demand help from his sons, for example in farming or in the payment of a debt, as he can from his sisters' sons. He can punish his nephew, but not his sons. He can order his nieces to marry a man of his choice, but not his daughter.

At the opposite extreme from the Ashanti are the Tallensi, who live nearby in Ghana's remote northern uplands. The Tallensi kinship and marriage system is the mirror image of that of the Ashanti. The Tallensi household is not matrilineal but patrilineal; it consists of a group of men, usually a man and his sons and grandsons, together with their wives and unmarried daughters. The men of this household and others in the immediate neighborhood all share the same patrilineal descent, which they can trace back in the male line to a single male ancestor. Tallensi men share their land, are equally eligible for family offices and join in the worship of ancestral spirits. Like the Ashanti, the Tallensi are "exogamous"; their children must marry members of clans other than their own. Among the Tallensi, however, a woman joins her husband's household on marriage, because he has rights not only to her domestic services and marital fidelity, but also to her children. This is the crucial distinction between matrilineal and patrilineal systems.

Our Western way of reckoning kinship is neither matrilineal nor patrilineal. Rather, it is "bilateral." That is, we consider our mothers' kin to be as closely related to us as our fathers'. Nowadays we follow the same etiquette with both maternal and paternal relatives. Our terminology distinctly reflects the equality of our conjugal family system. Since we rate the conjugal (husband-wife) over the lineal (parent-child) bond, the paternal or maternal orientation of the lineage becomes a matter of indifference. In naming our spouses' relatives we assimilate them to our own: a mother-in-law is a kind of mother, a brother-in-law is a kind of brother, and we treat them accordingly.

Our kinship terminology, like that of the Eskimos and a few other peoples, follows the so-called descriptive system. We have separate labels for each category of our kin, according to their generation, their sex and their linkage to us by descent or marriage. We distinguish our parents ("father" and "mother") from their male siblings ("uncles") and their female siblings ("aunts"). We have different appellations for our own siblings ("brother," "sister") and for our aunts' and uncles' children ("cousins").

Most primitive peoples use the entirely different labels of the classificatory system. This system often strikes Westerners as odd, although it is widespread among the peoples of mankind. Its principle is that in each generation all relatives of the same sex are addressed in the same way, no matter how remote the relationship. A sister and a female first- or second-cousin are all called "sister"; a father, an uncle and more distant male collaterals of their generation are called "father." A woman addresses her nieces and nephews, as well as her own offspring, as "my children." The nieces and nephews, as well as her own children, call her "mother." The Tallensi, the Swazi of South Africa, and many other societies even use words for "father" with a feminine suffix added, to designate the sisters of all the men they address as "father." A Swazi calls his mother's brother a "male mother."

This terminology was recognized for the first time nearly a century ago by a great U.S. anthropologist, Lewis H. Morgan. His *Systems of Consanguinity and Affinity of the Human Family,* published in 1871, founded the modern study of kinship systems. Morgan and his followers believed that classificatory terminology had survived from an extremely primitive stage of social organization, in which a group of sisters would mate promiscuously with a group of brothers and would rear the offspring in common.

By now Morgan's theory of "group marriage" has been completely discredited. Modern anthropology has discovered far more cogent reasons for the existence of classificatory terminology. If a man calls all the male relatives of his generation "brother," it is not because at some remote period the promiscuity of the elder generation made it impossible to tell one's brother from one's cousin. The reason is that such generalized terminology expresses the deep sense of corporate unity in the extended family. A child in such a family knows very well which of the women of the household is his physiological mother. Like children anywhere in the world, he will love his real mother as he loves none of her sisters or female cousins. Yet in the joint family those sisters and cousins share his mother's duties to him, and he must observe the same code of politeness with each of them. If his real mother should die, another of the women he calls "mother" will replace her. The classificatory terminology binds together groups that share status and responsibilities. To people like the Ashanti and Tallensi the word "mother" has a social rather than a biological significance: it defines one rank in a complex family system.

The need to define relationships is crucial in every society, and all kinship systems have evolved in response to this need. We are indebted to A. R. Radcliffe-Brown, the distinguished British anthropologist, for the most satisfactory statement of the underlying principles. The first of these establishes a clear demarcation between successive generations. The elders are not only physiological progenitors of their young; they also protect and nurture them throughout childhood and provide their first training in the crafts, customs, and morals of the tribe. This all-important relationship requires not only love on the part of the parents but also respect on the part of the children. Parental authority is incompatible with complete intimacy. Most societies banish everything sexual from the parent-and-child relationship; the universal taboo on incest between parent and child epitomizes the cleavage between elder and younger generations. Many societies enforce certain "avoidances" that help to maintain social distance between generations. The Tallensi, for example, forbid an eldest son to eat from his father's dish. Some central African tribes carry avoidance to extremes. One tribe, the Nyakyusa, requires fathers and children to live in separate villages. In the matrilineal Ashanti society, on the other hand, it is the uncle to whom children show respect (or at least resentful submission). Ashanti fathers are not figures of authority to their children and need not keep aloof from them. Indeed, the father's lack of authority over his children is compensated for by warm bonds of trust and affection.

Radcliffe-Brown's second principle is the so-called sibling rule of unity and loyalty among the members of a single generation. The unity among siblings (meaning cousins as well as brothers and sisters) is the converse of the first principle of separation between each generation of siblings and the next. Internally, of course, each generation is differentiated by sex and order of birth. Yet the rule generally prevails that siblings share all things on equal terms. Frequently the sibling principle is generalized to include all tribesmen of the same generation. In East and West Africa this is institutionalized in the so-called age-grade system. The pastoral Masai, for example, initiate youths into their lowest "grade" of junior warriors every seven years, two successive grades forming a "generation set." Members of a set are classificatory brothers to each other and are classificatory fathers to the next set. Cattle-keeping and warfare are the tasks of the junior sets, while government is the prerogative of the senior sets.

The third principle of kinship, according to Radcliffe-Brown's scheme, accounts for the orderly succession of the distinct sibling groups in time: this is the rule of "filiation." Most societies, as we have seen, stress this rule more strongly than we do. Filiation is usually traced on strictly matrilineal or patrilineal lines. Occasionally the two modes are combined. In some African tribes the individual inherits land and political offices from his father, and livestock and religious-cult memberships from his mother. The bond of common filiation forms social groups that reach beyond the single household in time as well as space. These groups are often called clans. Frequently they are exogamous; as among the Ashanti and Tallensi, their members may not marry one another but must seek mates from other clans. This establishes "affinal" (in-law) relationships between clans and binds them into a still larger unit: the tribe.

What happens to kinship-based societies when industry, a money economy and Western education impinge on them? Recent investigation shows an increasing breakdown of both patrilineal and matrilineal family systems under such conditions. In their place bilateral systems similar to our own become established. The reasons are obvious. Industry and commerce require the individual to earn wages and to enter legal contracts not as a member of a family but on his own. Western law and education emphasize the responsibilities of individual citizenship and parenthood, as opposed to group citizenship and collective responsibility of kinfolk to children. In his legal and economic roles the individual separates from his kin group. The family constituted by marriage becomes his primary concern. In Africa and elsewhere, as people become industrialized, we are witnessing processes of social evolution analogous to those that shaped the much more limited institution that we call the family.

11

The Nayars and the definition of marriage

E. KATHLEEN GOUGH

After raising the question of a universal definition of marriage, Kathleen Gough describes the marriage system of the Nayar of the Malabar Coast of India, relating it to the caste and lineage system. Different kinds of spouses with their respective rights and duties are discussed. A cross-cultural definition of marriage emerges in the conclusion of the paper.

The problem of a satisfactory definition of marriage has vexed anthropologists for decades and has been raised, but not solved, several times in recent years. Over time it became clear that cohabitation, ritual recognition, definition of sexual rights, or stipulation of domestic services each had too limited a distribution to serve as a criterion for all the unions anthropologists intuitively felt compelled to call "marriage." For good reason therefore the *Notes and Queries* definition of 1951 makes no reference to any of these: "Marriage is a union between a man and a woman such that children born to the woman are recognized legitimate offspring of both parents."[1]

Admirably concise though it is, this definition too raises problems in a number of societies. The Nuer institution of woman-marriage-to-a-woman would be a case in point. Here, both parties to the union are women yet, as Evans-Pritchard[2] has shown, the legal provisions of the union are strictly comparable to those of simple legal marriage between a

From "The Nayars and the Definition of Marriage," *The Journal of the Royal Anthropological Institute of Great Britain and Ireland* 89 (1959): 23–34. Reprinted by permission of the Royal Anthropological Institute of Great Britain and Ireland and of Kathleen Gough Aberle. Notes and bibliographic citations are omitted, and bibliographic information has been transposed into footnotes.

[1] *Notes and Queries in Anthropology*, 6th ed. (London, 1951).

[2] E. E. Evans-Pritchard, *Kinship and Marriage among the Nuer* (Oxford, 1951), pp. 108–109.

man and a woman. Few therefore would question Evans-Pritchard's logic in calling this union a marriage.

The *Notes and Queries* definition contains two criteria: that marriage is a union between one man and one woman, and that it establishes the legitimacy of children. Nuer woman-marriage does not conform to the first criterion but it does to the second. At this point the problem therefore becomes: is a definition feasible which would insist only on the second criterion, that of legitimizing children?

In Europe, Dr. Edmund Leach initiated the most recent chapter in this discussion,[3] and rather than review its whole history it is pertinent for me to take up the argument where he and others have left it. In effect, Dr. Leach answered no to the question posed above. He argued not only against the vagueness of the phrase "legitimate offspring" but also against any use of potential legal paternity as a universal criterion of marriage. He concluded in fact that no definition could be found which would apply to all the institutions which ethnographers commonly refer to as marriage. Instead he named ten classes of rights which frequently occur in connection with what we loosely term marriage, added that "one might perhaps considerably extend this list," and seemed to conclude that since no single one of these rights is invariably established by marriage in every known society, we ought to feel free to call "marriage" any institution which fulfils any one or more of the selected criteria.

There is, surely, a quite simple logical flaw in this argument. For it would mean in effect that every ethnographer might extend at will Dr. Leach's list of marital rights, and in short define marriage in any way he pleased. This may be legitimate in describing a single society. But I would argue that for purposes of cross-cultural comparison, we do need a single, parsimonious definition, simply in order to isolate the phenomenon we wish to study.

In support of his argument against using the legitimizing of children as a universal criterion of marriage, Dr. Leach cited the Nayar case. On the basis of two of my papers on the Nayars,[4] he stated that the Nayars traditionally had "no marriage in the strict (i.e., *Notes and Queries)* sense of the term but only a 'relationship of perpetual affinity' between linked lineages.[5] The woman's children, however they might be begotten, were simply recruits to the woman's own matrilineage." He stated further,

[3] E. R. Leach, "Polyandry, Inheritance, and the Definition of Marriage," *Man* 1955:199.

[4] E. Kathleen Gough, "Changing Kinship Usages in the Setting of Political and Economic Change among the Nayars of Malabar," *The Journal of the Royal Anthropological Institute of Great Britain and Ireland* 82 (1952):71–87, and "The Traditional Lineage and Kinship System of the Nayars," unpublished manuscript in the Haddon Library, Cambridge, 1955.

[5] Gough, "The Traditional Lineage."

"The notion of fatherhood is lacking. The child uses a term of address meaning 'lord' or 'leader' towards *all* its mother's lovers, but the use of this term does not carry with it any connotation of paternity, either legal or biological. On the other hand the notion of affinity is present, as evidenced by the fact that a woman must observe pollution at her ritual husband's death." [6] Later Dr. Leach concludes that "among the matrilineal matrilocal Nayar, as we have seen, right J (to establish a socially significant 'relationship of affinity' between the husband and his wife's brothers) is the only marriage characteristic that is present at all." [7]

This paper has two objectives. It will begin by analyzing traditional Nayar marital institutions and thereby showing that in fact the notion of fatherhood is not lacking and that marriage does serve to establish the legitimacy of children. My analysis will, I hope, not only dispose of a misinterpretation on Dr. Leach's part, but will in general clarify what has always proved a crucial but difficult borderline case for theorists of kinship. The paper will conclude with a new definition of marriage which will again make the status of children born to various types of union critical for decisions as to which of these unions constitute marriage. The ultimate aim is not of course to redefine marriage in a dogmatic way to suit a particular case, for definitions are tools of classification and not aims of research. The aim is to show that there *is* a common element not only in the institutions anthropologists have confidently labelled "marriage" by the *Notes and Queries* definition, but also in some unusual cases to which that definition does not apply. Whether we call the element "marriage" does not much matter provided it is made explicit, but it would probably be convenient to do so.

Nayar marriage in central Kerala

This account will refer to Nayars in the former kingdoms of Calicut, Walluvanad, and Cochin in the center of the Malabar Coast or Kerala. In the northernmost kingdoms (Kolattunad, Kottayam) and probably also in the southernmost kingdom of Travancore, Nayar residence appears to have been avunculocal even before the period of British rule, marriage was optionally polygynous but not polyandrous, and individual men appear to have had definite rights in and obligations to their children. Full information is not available for these northernmost and southernmost kingdoms in the pre-British period. But it seems probable that in the northern kingdoms at least, even the *Notes and Queries* definition of marriage was applicable to the Nayars. It was certainly applicable in the latter half of the nineteenth century for which I have accounts from informants.

My account of marriage in the central kingdoms is a reconstruction

[6] *Ibid.*

[7] Leach, *op. cit.*, p. 183.

of a state of affairs which appears to have been general before 1792 when the British assumed government of the Coast. As I have shown elsewhere Nayar kinship was slowly modified in the nineteenth century and more rapidly in the twentieth. But in remote villages the traditional institutions persisted until towards the end of the nineteenth century and were remembered by a few of my older informants. Their reports are not contradicted and are substantially corroborated by writings of Arab and European travellers of the fifteenth to eighteenth centuries.

In this account I shall use the terms "marriage," "husband," and "wife" without definition. My reasons for doing so will appear later.

In each of the three central kingdoms the Nayar caste was divided into a number of ranked subdivisions characterized by different political functions. Chief of these were (a) the royal lineage, (b) the lineages of chiefs of districts, (c) the lineages of Nayar village headmen and (d) several sub-castes of commoner Nayars. Each of these last either served one of the categories (a) to (c) or else served patrilineal landlord families of Nambudiri Brahmans. I shall deal first with the commoner Nayars of category (d).

There were present in each village some four to seven exogamous matrilineages of a single sub-caste of commoner Nayars. These owed allegiance to the family of the head of the village, which might be a patrilineal Nambudiri family, a Nayar village headman's matrilineage, a branch of the lineage of the chief of the district, or a branch of the royal lineage. The commoners held land on a hereditary feudal-type tenure from the headman's lineage and, in turn, had authority over the village's lower castes of cultivators, artisans, and agricultural serfs. Each retainer lineage tended to comprise some four to eight property-owning units which I call property-groups. The property-group formed a segment of the total lineage and was usually composed of a group of brothers and sisters together with the children and daughters' children of the sisters. The members owned or leased property in common, lived in one house, and were under the legal guardianship of the oldest male *(kāranavan)* of the group. Both the property-group and the lineage were called *taravād.*

Nayar men trained as professional soldiers in village gymnasia, and for part of each year they tended to be absent from the village in wars against neighboring kingdoms or for military exercises at the capitals. Only the *kāranavan,* the women, and the children of the property-group remained permanently in their ancestral homes.

The Nayars of one village or of two adjacent villages formed a neighborhood group (*kara* or *tara*) of some six to ten lineages. Each lineage was linked by hereditary ties of ceremonial cooperation with two or three other lineages of the neighborhood. These linkages were reciprocal but not exclusive, so that a chain of relationships linked all the lineages of the neighborhood. The lineages linked to one's own were called *enangar;* the total neighborhood group, the *enangu.* At least one man and one woman of each linked lineage must be invited to the house of a property-group for the life-crisis rites of its members. Its linked lineages were also concerned if some member of a lineage committed a breach of the religious law of the caste. It was their duty at once to break off relations with the offending lineage and to call a neighborhood assembly to judge and punish the offense. Its linked lineages thus represented the neighborhood group as a whole to the offending lineage and were special guardians of its morality. Sometimes in small neighborhoods the commoner Nayar lineages were all *enangar* to each other, but in larger neighborhoods this was not feasible, for the heads of property-groups would have had too many ceremonial obligations to fulfill.

The linked lineages played their most important role at the pre-puberty marriage rites *(tālikettukalyānam)* of girls. At a convenient time every few years, a lineage held a grand ceremony at which all its girls who had not attained puberty, aged about seven to twelve, were on one day ritually married by men drawn from their linked lineages. The ritual bridegrooms were selected in advance on the advice of the village astrologer at a meeting of the neighborhood assembly. On the day fixed they came in procession to the oldest ancestral house of the host lineage. There, after various ceremonies, each tied a gold ornament *(tāli)* round the neck of his ritual bride. The girls had for three days previously been secluded in an inner room of the house and caused to observe taboos as if they had menstruated. After the *tāli*-tying each couple was secluded in private for three days. I was told that traditionally, if the girl was nearing puberty, sexual relations might take place. This custom began to be omitted in the late nineteenth century, but from some of the literature it appears to have been essential in the sixteenth and seventeenth centuries. At the end of the period of seclusion each couple was purified from the pollution of cohabitation by a ritual bath. In Calicut and Walluvanad each couple in public then tore in two the loin-cloth previously worn by the girl during the "cohabitation" period, as a token of separation. This rite appears to have been omitted in Cochin. In all three kingdoms, however, the ritual husbands left the house after the four days of ceremonies and had no further obligations to their brides. A bride in turn had only one further obligation to her ritual husband: at his death, she and all her children, by whatever biological father, must observe death-pollution for him. Death-pollution was otherwise observed only for matrilineal kin. In Cochin, even if their mother's ritual husband never visited his wife again, her children must refer to him by the kinship term *appan.* Children in the lower, patrilineal castes of this area used this word to refer to the legal father, who was presumed also to be the biological father. In Walluvanad and Calicut I did not hear of this verbal usage and do not know by what term, if any, Nayar children referred to their mother's ritual husband.

The pre-puberty *tāli*-rite was essential for a girl. If she menstruated before it had been performed, she should in theory be expelled from her lineage and caste. In fact, however, my informants told me that in such a case the girl's family would conceal the fact of her maturity until after the rite had been performed. But it was a grave sin to do so and one which would never be publicly admitted.

The *tāli*-rite marked various changes in the social position of a girl. First, it brought her to social maturity. She was now thought to be at least ritually endowed with sexual and procreative functions and was thenceforward accorded the status of a woman. After the rite people addressed her in public by the respectful title *amma* meaning "mother"; and she might take part in the rites of adult women. Second, after the *tāli*-rite a girl must observe all the rules of etiquette associated with incest prohibitions in relation to men of her lineage. She might not touch them, might not sit in their presence, might not speak first to them, and might not be alone in a room with one of them. Third, after the *tāli*-rite and as soon as she became old enough (i.e., shortly before or after puberty), a girl received as visiting husbands a number of men of her sub-caste from outside her lineage, usually but not necessarily from her neighborhood. In addition she might be visited by any Nayar of the higher sub-castes of village headmen, chiefs or royalty, or by a Nambudiri Brahman. All of these relationships were called *sambandham*. Among commoner Nayar women, however, the great majority of unions were with men of commoner sub-caste.

Relations between any Nayar women and a man of *lower* Nayar sub-caste, or between any Nayar woman and a man of one of the lower, non-Nayar castes, were strictly prohibited. If a woman was found guilty of such a relationship her lineage's *enangar* carried the matter to the neighborhood assembly. This temporarily excommunicated the woman's property-group until justice had been done. In the nineteenth century and early this century the property-group was reaccepted into caste only after its *kāranavan* had dismissed the woman from her household and caste, never to return. In pre-British times a woman so dismissed became the property of the king or chief and might be sold into slavery with foreign traders. Alternatively, however, the men of her property-group had the right, sometimes exercised, to kill both the woman and her lover and thus preserve the good name of their lineage.

After the ritual marriage the bridegroom need have no further contact with his ritual wife. If both parties were willing, however, he might enter into a sexual relationship with his ritual bride about the time of her puberty. But he had no priority over other men of the neighborhood group. There is some uncertainty as to the number of visiting husbands a woman might have at one time. Writers of the sixteenth and seventeenth centuries report that a woman usually had some three to eight regular husbands but might receive other men of her own or a higher caste at will. Hamilton in 1727 stated that a woman might have as husbands "twelve but no more at one time." [8] As late as 1807 Buchanan reported that Nayar women vied with each other as to the number of lovers they could obtain.[9] A few of my older informants could remember women who had had three or four current husbands, although plural unions were being frowned upon and had almost died out by the end of the last century. There appears to have been no limit to the number of wives of appropriate sub-caste whom a Nayar might visit concurrently. It seems, therefore, that a woman customarily had a small but not a fixed number of husbands from within her neighborhood, that relationships with these men might be of long standing, but that the woman was also free to receive casual visitors of appropriate sub-caste who passed through her neighborhood in the course of military operations.

A husband visited his wife after supper at night and left before breakfast next morning. He placed his weapons at the door of his wife's room and if others came later they were free to sleep on the verandah of the woman's house. Either party to a union might terminate it at any time without formality. A passing guest recompensed a woman with a small cash gift at each visit. But a more regular husband from within the neighborhood had certain customary obligations. At the start of the union it was common although not essential for him to present the woman with a cloth of the kind worn as a skirt. Later he was expected to make small personal gifts to her at the three main festivals of the year. These gifts included a loin-cloth, betel-leaves and areca-nuts for chewing, hair-oil and bathing-oil, and certain vegetables. Failure on the part of a husband to make such a gift was a tacit sign that he had ended the relationship. Most important, however, when a woman became pregnant it was essential for one or more men of appropriate sub-caste to acknowledge probable paternity. This they did by providing a fee of a cloth and some vegetables to the low-caste midwife who attended the woman in childbirth. If no man of suitable caste would consent to make this gift, it was assumed that the woman had had relations with a man of lower caste or with a Christian or a Muslim. She must then be either expelled from her lineage and caste or killed by her matrilineal kinsmen. I am uncertain of the precise fate of the child in such a case, but there is no doubt at all that he could not be ac-

[8] Alexander Hamilton, *A New Account of the East Indies*, 2 vols. (Edinburgh, 1727), I:310.

[9] Francis (Hamilton) Buchanan, *A Journey from Madras through Mysore, Canara and Malabar*, 3 vols. (London, 1807), I:411.

cepted as a member of his lineage and caste. I do not know whether he was killed or became a slave; almost certainly, he must have shared the fate of his mother. Even as late as 1949, over a hundred and fifty years after the establishment of British rule, a Nayar girl who became pregnant before the modern marriage ceremony was regarded as acting within the canons of traditional religious law if she could simply find a Nayar of suitable sub-caste to pay her delivery expenses. But if no Nayar would consent to this she ran the danger of total ostracism, with her child, by the village community. I heard of several cases in which such a girl was driven from her home by her *kāranvan* at the command of the sub-caste assembly. Her natal kinsmen then performed funeral rites for her as if she had died. In each case the girl took refuge in a town before or shortly after her child was born.

Although he made regular gifts to her at festivals, in no sense of the term did a man maintain his wife. Her food and regular clothing she obtained from her matrilineal group. The gifts of a woman's husbands were personal luxuries which pertained to her role as a sexual partner — extra clothing, articles of toilet, betel, and areca-nut the giving of which is associated with courtship, and the expenses of the actual delivery, not, be it noted, of the maintenance of either mother or child. The gifts continued to be made at festivals only while the relationship lasted. No man had obligations to a wife of the past.

In these circumstances the exact biological fatherhood of a child was often uncertain, although, of course, paternity was presumed to lie with the man or among the men who had paid the delivery expenses. But even when biological paternity was known with reasonable certainty, the genitor had no economic, social, legal, or ritual rights in nor obligations to his children after he had once paid the fees of their births. Their guardianship, care, and discipline were entirely the concern of their matrilineal kinsfolk headed by their *kāranavan*. All the children of a woman called all her current husbands by the Sanskrit word *acchan* meaning "lord." They did not extend kinship terms at all to the matrilineal kin of these men. Neither the wife nor her children observed pollution at the death of a visiting husband who was not also the ritual husband of the wife.

In most matrilineal systems with settled agriculture and localized matrilineal groups, durable links are provided between these groups by the interpersonal relationships of marriage, affinity, and fatherhood. The husbands, affines, fathers, and patrilateral kin of members of the matrilineal group have customary obligations to and rights in them which over time serve to mitigate conflicts between the separate matrilineal groups. The Nayars had no such durable institutionalized interpersonal links. This does not mean that men did not sometimes form strong emotional attachments to particular wives and their children. My information indicates that they did. I know for example that if a man showed particular fondness for a wife, his wife's matrilineal kin were likely to suspect the husband's matrilineal kin of hiring sorcerers against them. For the husband's matrilineal kin would be likely to fear that the husband might secretly convey to his wife gifts and cash which belonged rightfully to his matrilineal kin. This suspicion was especially rife if the husband was a *kāranavan* who controlled extensive property. Informal emotional attachments did therefore exist between individuals of different lineages. But what I wish to indicate is that among the Nayars, these interpersonal affinal and patrilateral links were not invested with customary legal, economic, or ceremonial functions of a kind which would periodically bring members of different lineages together in mandatory forms of cooperation. Four special kinship terms did apparently exist for use in relation to affines acquired through the *sambandham* relationship, although, as I have said, there were no patrilateral terms for kin other than the mother's husbands. All men and women currently engaged in *sambandham* unions with members of ego's property group, and all members of the property-groups of these individuals, were collectively referred to as *bandhukkal* ("joined ones"). A current wife of ego's mother's brother was addressed and referred to as *ammāyi,* and a wife of the elder brother as *jyeshtati amma* (literally "elder-sister-mother"). Finally, the own brother and the *sambandham* husband of a woman employed the reciprocal term *aliyan* to refer to each other but used no term of address. All the current *bandhukkal* of a property-group were invited to household feasts, but as individual affines they had no ceremonial or economic obligations and were not obliged to attend. As representatives of *enangar* lineages, however, some of these same individuals might be obliged to attend feasts and to fulfill ceremonial obligations *as enangar.* But as particular affines they had no obligations. In place, therefore, of institutionalized interpersonal patrilateral and affinal links, the Nayars had the hereditary institution of linked lineages. Whether or not, at a particular time, sexual relationships existed between individuals of linked lineages, the linked lineages must fulfill their obligations at household ceremonies and give neighborly help in such emergencies as birth and death. In the patrilineal and double unilineal castes of Kerala precisely the same obligations are fulfilled by the matrilateral kin and affines of individual members of the patrilineal group. The linked lineages of the Nayars must therefore, I think, be regarded as having a relationship of "perpetual affinity," which carried the more formal functions of affinity and persisted through the making and breaking of individual sexual ties.

In view of these facts, it is convenient to mention here that Dr. Leach's statement that Nayar marriage served "to establish a socially significant relationship between the husband and his wife's brothers" is not, strictly speaking, correct. The *sambandham* union did not establish "a socially significant relationship" between brothers-in-law, for in spite of the reciprocal kinship term these persons had no institutionalized obligations to one another by virtue of the particular *sambandham* tie. Further, the *tāli*-rite did not *establish* a relationship between the ritual husband and the brothers of his ritual bride. The ceremony set up no special obligations between these persons; it was merely that their lineages were, hereditarily, *enangar*, both before and after any particular *tāli*-rite. What the rite did *establish* was a ritual relationship between the *tāli*-tier and his ritual bride, and, as I shall try to show later, a relationship of group-marriage between the bride and all men of her sub-caste outside her lineage. But a particular *tāli*-rite in no way modified the hereditary relationships between male *enangar*. It is for this reason that I call the *enangar* relationship one of "perpetual affinity" *between lineages*, which, though it carried the ceremonial functions of affinity, persisted irrespective of particular *sambandhams* and *tāli*-rites.

The Nayars of this area were thus highly unusual. For they had a kinship system in which the elementary family of father, mother, and children was not institutionalized as a legal, productive, distributive, residential, socializing, or consumption unit. Until recent years, some writers have thought that at least as a unit for some degree of cooperation in economic production and distribution, the elementary family was universal. This view has been put forward most forcibly by Murdock.[10] Radcliffe-Brown, however, was one of the earliest anthropologists to observe that if the written accounts of the Nayars were accurate, the elementary family was not institutionalized among them.[11] My research corroborates his findings.

I turn briefly to marital institutions among the higher Nayar subcastes of village headmen, district chiefs, and royalty. At various times during the pre-British period these lineages were accorded political office and set themselves up as of higher ritual rank than the commoner Nayars. The ritual ranking between these major aristocratic subdivisions was fairly stable, but the mutual ranking of lineages within each subdivision was in dispute. Most village headmen acknowledged the ritual superiority of district chiefs, and most chiefs, of the royal lineage. But some village headmen disputed among themselves for ritual precedence and so did many chiefs. As a result, each of these aristocratic lineages tended to set itself up as a separate sub-caste, acknowledging ritual superiors and inferiors but acknowledging no peers. In the course of time, moreover, following the vicissitudes of political fortune, such lineages could rise or fall

[10] G. P. Murdock, *Social Structure* (New York, 1949), chap. I.

[11] A. R. Radcliffe-Brown and D. Forde, eds., *African Systems of Kinship and Marriage* (Oxford, 1950), pp. 73ff.

in the ritual hierarchy. It was in these lineages therefore that hypergamous unions became most highly institutionalized, for most of these lineages refused to exchange spouses on equal terms. Instead, most of them married all their women upwards and all their men downwards. Women of village headman's lineages entered *sambandham* unions with chiefly, royal, or Nambudiri Brahman men. Men of these lineages had unions with commoner Nayar women. Chiefly women had unions with royals or Nambudiris; chiefly men, with the women of village headmen's or commoner Nayar lineages. Royal women for the most part had unions with Nambudiri Brahmans of the highest rank. A few, especially in Calicut, however, had unions with men of older and ritually higher ranking royal lineages which had through conquest become politically subordinate to their own. Among Nambudiri Brahmans, only eldest sons were permitted to marry Nambudiri women and beget children for their own families. Younger sons of Nambudiri households might have *sambandham* unions with Nayar women of any sub-caste.

In all these hypergamous unions the visiting husband owed the same periodic gifts to his wife as in the case of equal unions between persons of the same commoner sub-caste. The husband in a hypergamous union was also held responsible for payment of delivery expenses at the birth of a child to his wife. Hypergamous unions differed from "equal" unions in that in the former, the husband, being of higher ritual rank, might not eat in the house of his wife. The husband was also prohibited from touching his wife, her children, or her other kinsfolk during the daytime while he was in a state of ritual purity. Finally, although children called their mother's higher caste husband by the term *acchan* plus the caste title, Nayars as a whole were not permitted to use affinal terms toward the Nambudiri husbands of their womenfolk, nor did Nambudiris address or refer to their Nayar wives' brothers as affines. Nayars insist however that a *sambandham* union with a Nambudiri Brahman was of the same character as a *sambandham* union with a Nayar of equal sub-caste. It seems that from the legal point of view we must also judge it to be so, since the Brahman husband, like the Nayar, was responsible for payments at the birth of a child to his Nayar wife. During my fieldwork, the three Nambudiri Brahmans whom I was able to question closely on this subject told me that from *their* point of view only marriage to a Nambudiri woman with Vedic rites could be regarded as true marriage and that *sambandham* unions with Nayar women were a kind of concubinage. There seems to me no reason why we should not regard these latter unions as concubinage from the point of view of the Brahmans and (since they fulfilled the conditions of Nayar marriage) marriage from the point of view of the Nayars. This seems to me, in fact, the only possible interpretation, since the Brahmans are patrilineal and the child of a Brahman-Nayar union is not legitimized into the Brahman caste. The contrast from the Brahman point of view appears most sharply in the case of an eldest son, who may marry one or more Nambudiri women with Vedic rites and may also have liaisons with one or more Nayar women. The Brahman wife's children are of course fully legitimized into the Brahman caste from birth. But the Nayar wife and her children traditionally had no rights of patrilineal descent of inheritance whatsoever, might not enter the kitchen of the Brahman house, and might not touch its inhabitants.

Consistently with the difference in direction of *sambandham* unions, the *enangar* institution in these aristocratic Nayar lineages differed somewhat from that in the commoner sub-castes. In general, an aristocratic Nayar lineage had as *enangar* two or more lineages of a sub-caste higher than itself from which its women were wont to draw husbands in the *sambandham* relationship. The linked lineage relationship was in these cases not reciprocal. A chiefly lineage might act as *enangar* for the lineages of one or two village headmen, but had as its own *enangar* one or two chiefly or royal lineages of higher rank than itself. Nambudiri Brahman lineages acted as *enangar* for the highest ranks of chiefs and royalty. In this case too the aristocratic Nayar lineage had of course no reciprocal ritual obligations towards the Brahman families with which it was linked. The functions of these aristocratic *enangar* were, as far as I can detect, the same as in the case of commoner Nayars. In particular, men of the higher ranking *enangar* lineages tied the *tāli* at the pre-puberty marriage of aristocratic girls — appropriately, for it was from these and other such higher ranking lineages that the girls would later draw visiting husbands. Plural unions were customary in these aristocratic lineages as among commoner Nayars. Obviously, however, the choice of husbands became more and more restricted as one ascended the scale of ranked sub-castes, and at the top of the Nayar hierarchy it was restricted to Nambudiri Brahmans.

I turn now to my interpretation of Nayar marital institutions. To accomplish this it is necessary to classify the rights and obligations obtaining between "spouses" and between "fathers" and their "children." These fall into two categories: those of the *tāli*-rite and those of the *sambandham* union. In relations between spouses of the *tāli*-rite, the important rights are those of the woman. The ritual husband had, it is true, apparently at one time the right to deflower his bride. But the accounts of many writers indicate that this right was not eagerly sought, that in fact it was viewed with repugnance and performed with reluctance. The ritual husband also had the right that his ritual wife should mourn his death. But we may assume that this right had more significance for the wife than for the husband, for it was not attended by offerings to the departed spirit. These could be performed only by matrilineal kin. The ritual bride's rights were complementary to her husband's, but for her they were of supreme importance. She had, first, the right to *have* a ritual husband of her own or a superior sub-caste before she attained maturity. Her life depended on this, for if she was not ritually married before puberty she was liable to excommunication and might possibly be put to death. She held this claim against her sub-caste as a whole exclusive of her lineage, or (in the case of aristocratic lineages) against a higher sub-caste. This group must, through the institution of the linked lineages, provide her with a ritual husband of correct rank and thus bring her to maturity in honour instead of in shame. It was the duty of her lineage kinsmen to see to it that some representative from their linked lineages fulfilled this right. The ritual wife's second right was that of observing pollution at the death of her ritual husband. I interpret this as a mark of proof that she had once been married in the correct manner and that this ritual relationship had retained significance for *her* throughout her ritual husband's life.

The *tāli*-tier had no rights in his ritual wife's children except that they should observe pollution at his death. From the child's point of view, however, his mother's ritual husband must have been a figure of great symbolic significance. For a child whose mother had no ritual husband could not acquire membership in his caste and lineage at all. The birth of a child before his mother's *tāli*-rite was absolutely forbidden and, in the nature of the case, can scarcely ever have happened. If it did occur, mother and child must certainly have been expelled and were most probably killed. The child's observance of pollution for his mother's ritual husband — like the use of the kinship term *appan* in Cochin — was a formal recognition that, for ritual purposes, he had been "fathered" by a man of appropriate caste.

Turning to the *sambandham* union, it seems clear that the husband had no exclusive rights in his wife. He had only, in common with other men, sexual privileges which the wife might withdraw at any time. Again it is the wife's rights which are important. The wife had the right to gifts from her husband at festivals, gifts of little economic value but of high prestige value, for they established her as a woman well-favored by men. But most significant was the woman's right to have her delivery expenses paid by one or more husbands of appropriate caste, that is, to have it openly acknowledged that her child had as biological father a man of required ritual rank. Her matrilineal kinsmen could if necessary press for the fulfillment of this right in a public assembly of the neighborhood: in cases of doubtful paternity any man who had been currently visiting the woman could be forced by the assembly to pay her delivery expenses. But if no man of appropriate rank could be cited as potential father, woman and child were expelled from their lineage and caste.

The *sambandham* father had no rights in his wife's children. Here again, however, the child had one right in his possible biological fathers:

that one or more of them should pay the expenses associated with his birth, and thus entitle him to enter the world as a member of his lineage and caste.

It is clear therefore that although the elementary family of one father, one mother and their children was not institutionalized as a legal, residential, or economic unit, and although individual men had no significant rights in their particular wives or children, the Nayars did institutionalize the concepts of marriage and of paternity, and gave ritual and legal recognition to both. It is here that I must contradict Dr. Leach's interpretation of the situation, for it is not true that "the notion of fatherhood is lacking" nor is it true that "a woman's children, however they might be begotten, were simply recruits to the woman's matrilineage." [12] For unless his mother was ritually married by a man of appropriate caste and, unless his biological paternity was vouched for by one or more men of appropriate caste, a child could never enter his caste or lineage at all. As I pointed out in both the papers quoted by Dr. Leach, the Nayars were aware of the physiological function of the male in procreation and attached significance to it, for they expected a child to look like his genitor. Like all the higher Hindu castes of India, they based their belief in the moral rightness of the caste system in part upon a racist ideology which involved the inheritance of physical, intellectual, and moral qualities by a child from both of its natural parents, and which held that the higher castes were, by virtue of their heredity, superior to the lower castes. It was ostensibly for this reason that the Nayars forbade with horror sexual contacts between a Nayar woman and a man of lower caste, and that they expelled or put to death women guilty of such contacts. This racist ideology also provided a motive for hypergamous unions, for Nayars of aristocratic lineages boasted of the superior qualities they derived from royal and Brahmanical fatherhood.

Moreover, although individual men had no significant customary rights in their wives and children, marriage and paternity were probably significant factors in political integration. For hypergamous unions bound together the higher sub-castes of the political and religious hierarchies. Multiple sexual ties, as well as the *enangar* relationship, linked office-bearing lineages to each other and to their retainers in a complicated manner. And Nayar men phrased their loyalty to higher ranking military leaders, rulers, and Brahmans in terms of a debt owed to benevolent paternal figures whose forebears had collectively fathered them and whose blood they were proud to share. The generalized concept of fatherhood thus commanded the Nayar soldier's allegiance to his wider caste unit, to the rulers of his village, chiefdom, and kingdom and to his religious

[12] Leach, *op. cit.*, p. 183.

authorities. It was associated with tender loyalty and with fortitude in war.

I cannot entirely blame Dr. Leach for underestimating the significance of Nayar paternity on the basis of his reading of my earlier papers. For in those papers I was concerned to emphasize the lack of rights of individual men in their spouses and children. It is true that in 1952 I wrote: "Marriage . . . was the slenderest of ties, while as a social concept fatherhood scarcely existed." [13] I had not then realized the fundamental necessity to a Nayar of having both a ritual and a biological father of appropriate caste. Moreover I myself confused the issue by referring to the *sambandham* partners as "husbands" and "wives" in my first paper [14] and as "lovers" and "mistresses" in my second.[15] For it was not until some time after I read Dr. Leach's paper that I decided to classify Nayar unions unequivocally as marriage and arrived at a definition of marriage which would include the Nayar case. In my own defense I must, however, note that in my paper of 1955 I mentioned that children must observe death pollution for their mother's ritual husband, and that in Cochin they used the kinship term a*ppan* for this ritual father. In both papers quoted by Dr. Leach, finally, I noted that sexual relations were forbidden between a Nayar woman and a man of lower caste or sub-caste, and that the current *sambandham* husbands of a woman must pay her delivery expenses.

I regard Nayar unions as a form of marriage for two reasons. One is that although plural unions were customary, mating was not promiscuous. Sexual relations were forbidden between members of the same lineage on pain of death. It was also forbidden for two men of the same property-group wittingly to have relations with one woman, or for two women of the same property-group to have relations with one man. (This rule of course automatically excluded relations between a man and his biological daughter.) Further, relations were absolutely prohibited between a Nayar woman and a man of lower sub-caste or caste. These prohibitions are directly connected with my second and more important reason for regarding these unions as marriage, namely that the concept of legally established paternity *was* of fundamental significance in establishing a child as a member of his lineage and caste.

Granted that Nayar unions constituted a form of marriage, we must I think classify them as a clear case of group-marriage. This was the interpretation to which I inclined in 1952 [16] and it is, I now think, the only interpretation which makes sense of the descriptive material I have pre-

[13] Gough, "Changing Kinship Usages," p. 73.
[14] *Ibid.*
[15] Gough, "The Traditional Lineage."
[16] Gough, "Changing Kinship Usages," p. 73.

sented. The *tāli*-rite, as I see it, initiated for each individual Nayar girl a state of marriage to a collectivity of men of appropriate caste. First, the rite ceremonially endowed the girl with sexual and procreative functions. (The mock menstrual seclusion before the rite is relevant to this, as is the actual defloration.) Second, the woman's natal kinsmen surrendered the newly acquired rights in her sexuality, though not in her procreative functions, to a male representative from outside her lineage. This appears in that rules of etiquette associated with incest prohibitions came into force from this date. Third, rights in the woman's sexuality were received by her *enangan* as representative of the men of his sub-caste as a whole. This appears in that the individual *enangan,* as a special sexual partner, was dismissed at the end of the ceremonies and might approach the woman again only as one among a series of equal husbands. In the commoner sub-castes the *enangan* was of the same sub-caste as the woman, and through him as representative sexual rights in the woman were conferred on all men of her sub-caste as a collectivity. They were also in fact extended to any man of higher sub-caste who might favor her with his attentions. In aristocratic lineages the ritual husband was of a sub-caste higher than the woman's, and through him, as representative, sexual rights in the woman were conferred upon all men of higher sub-caste as a collectivity. Fourth, the *tāli*-rite, by providing the woman with a ritual husband who (in my view) symbolized all the men of his sub-caste with whom the woman might later have relationships, also provided her children with a ritual father who symbolized the correctness of their paternity. The children acknowledged their debt to him by mourning at his death.

The later *sambandham* unions, by this interpretation, involved the claiming of sexual privileges by men all of whom were potential husbands by virtue of their membership in a sub-caste. The husbands had, however, no individually exclusive rights and could be dismissed at the woman's wish. Their duties as members of their caste were to provide the woman and her lineage with children and to acknowledge their potential biological paternity through birth-payments which legitimized the woman's child.

THE DEFINITION OF MARRIAGE

I have called the Nayar unions marriage because they involved the concept of legal paternity. It is clear however that such a form of group marriage will not fit the *Notes and Queries* definition of "a union between *a* man and *a* woman such that children born to the woman are recognized legitimate offspring of both parents" (my italics). For legitimacy in the case of the Nayar child required both a ritual father and a "legalized genitor" of appropriate rank, and indeed a child might have more than one "legal genitor" if two or more men had jointly paid the expenses of his birth.

As a tentative move toward a new definition which will have cross-cultural validity and will fit the Nayar and several other unusual cases, I suggest the following: "Marriage is a relationship established between a woman and one or more other persons, which provides that a child born to the woman under circumstances not prohibited by the rules of the relationship, is accorded full birth-status rights common to normal members of his society or social stratum."

A few footnotes to this definition may help to vindicate its inevitably clumsy phraseology. "One or more persons" (in place of "a man") will bring into the definition both group-marriage of the Nayar type and also true fraternal polyandry. It also brings within the definition such unusual types as woman-marriage-to-a-woman. "Under circumstances not prohibited by the rules of the relationship" would bring into the definition various problematic cases. It is possible for example that there are patrilineal societies in which a husband may legally repudiate a child illicitly begotten upon his wife by another man, without divorcing the wife herself. In this case the previous establishment of the marriage would *not* ensure full birth-status rights to the child, for the rules of the marriage relationship would have been broken through the circumstances which led to his birth. "Full birth-status rights common to all normal members . . ." is a compressed reference to all the social relationships, property-rights, etc., which a child acquires at birth by virtue of his legitimacy, whether through the father or through the mother. For patrilineal societies the phrase "full birth-status rights" will include the right which a child acquires in his *pater* as a person and in his *pater's* group. It will include, that is to say, the legitimization of fatherhood, or more precisely, of "father-sonhood." The phrase is, however, broader than any concept of specific rights in a particular father. It will therefore take care of a case like the Nayar in which all rights are acquired *through* the mother but in which a relationship must be established between the mother and one or more other persons in order for these matrilineal rights to be ratified. Such a process may be called the legitimization of motherhood, or more precisely of "mother-sonhood." Moreover "full birth-status rights" is, I think, not only broader but more precise than "recognized legitimate offspring," to the vagueness of which Dr. Leach took exception. The inclusion of "society or social stratum" makes allowances for class or caste systems in which birth-status rights vary between strata. The case of the Nayars, who are a matrilineal caste in a predominantly patrilineal society, is an obvious example of this.

It should also perhaps be pointed out that this definition does not state that full birth-status rights cannot be acquired by a child except through the marriage of its mother, but only that marriage provides for the acquisition of these rights. The definition does not therefore exclude societies like the Nuer in which a man may legitimize the child of an unmarried woman upon payment of a legitimization fee, without becoming married to the mother.[17]

Prince Peter has objected to the *Notes and Queries* definition and, by implication, to any definition which would make the legitimization of children through the mother's relationship to another party the distinctive characteristic of marriage.[18] His reason for objecting is that in some societies like the Toda, "marriage and legitimacy of the children can be looked upon as two different and separate concepts, and it may be necessary to go through a ceremony of legitimization of the offspring (the Toda *pursütpimi* ceremony) in order to establish who is the legal father, because marriage rites are insufficient in themselves to do this."

However, it seems from Rivers's account that precisely what distinguishes the Toda institution which Prince Peter translates as "marriage" *(mokh-vatt)* from that which he translates as "concubinage" *(mokhthoditi)* [19] is that a "husband" holds the right to legitimize some or all of his "wife's" children by the *pursütpimi* ceremony, whereas a lover in the *mokhthoditi* union, being of a different endogamous group from the woman, does not hold this right.[20] A husband acquires the right to perform the *pursütpimi* ceremony, it seems, by virtue of arranged marriage to an infant or through payment of cattle to a former husband or to a group of former husbands of the wife. The Toda marriage union at its inception does therefore provide that a child born to the woman (under circumstances not prohibited by the rules of the relationship) *must be* legitimized before his birth; the *pursütpimi* ceremony confirms his legitimacy by attaching him to a particular father and giving him rights in the father's patrilineal group. In the Toda case again therefore the concept of legal paternity is *the* distinguishing characteristic of marriage, even though the individual husband, because of polyandry, may be permitted to legitimize only some and not all of the children born to his wife. The Toda case therefore fits my definition, whether we regard the *pursütpimi* ceremony as the final one of a sequence of marriage rites, or as a legitimizing act which, under circumstances not prohibited by the rules of the relationship, one or another of the woman's husbands is legally obliged to fulfill.

I do not argue that all societies must necessarily be found to have

[17] Evans-Pritchard, *op. cit.*, pp. 21, 26.

[18] H.R.H. Prince Peter of Greece and Denmark, "For a New Definition of Marriage," *Man* 1956:46.

[19] Prince Peter, *op. cit.*, 1957:35.

[20] W. H. R. Rivers, *The Todas* (London, 1906), p. 526.

marriage by my definition. There may yet turn out to be whole societies — or more probably whole social strata — in which children acquire no birth-status rights except through their mother, by the simple fact of birth. It is possible for example that some slave populations do not have marriage in this sense of the term. What I do wish to suggest however is that for most if not all the societies for which we now have information, including the Nayar, marriage as I have defined it is a significant relationship, distinguished by the people themselves from all other kinds of relationships. My definition should therefore enable us to isolate marriage as a cross-cultural phenomenon, and from there to proceed to the more exciting task: that of investigating the differential circumstances under which marriage becomes invested with various other kinds of rights and obligations. Some of the most important of these Dr. Leach has already listed for us.

12

Sororities and the husband game

JOHN FINLEY SCOTT

In every society, there are norms governing marriage. In American society, as in many others, class differences are maintained by our marriage rules. The structure and function of the university sorority are analyzed by John Finley Scott for their effect upon class structure.

> Marriages, like births, deaths, or initiations at puberty, are rearrangements of structure that are constantly recurring in any society; they are moments of the continuing social process regulated by custom; there are institutionalized ways of dealing with such events. — A. R. Radcliffe-Brown, *African Systems of Kinship and Marriage.*

In many simple societies, the "institutionalized ways" of controlling marriage run to diverse schemes and devices. Often they include special living quarters designed to make it easy for marriageable girls to attract a husband: the Bontok people of the Philippines keep their girls in a special house, called the *olag,* where lovers call, sex play is free, and marriage is supposed to result. The Ekoi of Nigeria, who like their women fat, send them away to be specially fattened for marriage. Other peoples, such as the Yao of central Africa and the aborigines of the Canary Islands, send their daughters away to "convents" where old women teach them the special skills and mysteries that a young wife needs to know.

Accounts of such practices have long been a standard topic of anthropology lectures in universities, for their exotic appeal keeps the students, large numbers of whom are sorority girls, interested and alert. The control of marriage in simple societies strikes these girls as quite different

From "Sororities and the Husband Game," *Trans*-action 2 (September–October 1965):10–14. Illustrations and glossary are omitted.

from the freedom that they believe prevails in America. This is ironic, for the American college sorority is a pretty good counterpart in complex societies of the fatting houses and convents of the primitives.

Whatever system they use, parents in all societies have more in mind than just getting their daughters married; they want them married to the *right* man. The criteria for defining the right man vary tremendously, but virtually all parents view some potential mates with approval, some with disapproval, and some with downright horror. Many ethnic groups, including many in America, are *endogamous,* that is, they desire marriage of their young only to those within the group. In *shtetl* society, the Jewish villages of eastern Europe, marriages were arranged by a *shatchen,* a matchmaker, who paired off the girls and boys with due regard to the status, family connections, wealth, and personal attractions of the participants. But this society was strictly endogamous — only marriage within the group was allowed. Another rule of endogamy relates to social rank or class, for most parents are anxious that their children marry at least at the same level as themselves. Often they hope the children, and especially the daughters, will marry at a higher level. Parents of the *shtetl,* for example, valued *hypergamy* — the marriage of daughters to a man of higher status — and a father who could afford it would offer substantial sums to acquire a scholarly husband (the most highly prized kind) for his daughter.

The marriage problem, from the point of view of parents and of various ethnic groups and social classes, is always one of making sure that girls are available for marriage with the right man while at the same time guarding against marriage with the wrong man.

The university convent

The American middle class has a particular place where it sends its daughters so they will be easily accessible to the boys — the college campus. Even for the families who worry about the bad habits a nice girl can pick up at college, it has become so much a symbol of middle-class status that the risk must be taken, the girl must be sent. American middle-class society has created an institution on the campus that, like the fatting house, makes the girls more attractive; like the Canary Island convent, teaches skills that middle-class wives need to know; like the *shtetl,* provides matchmakers; and without going so far as to buy husbands of high rank, manages to dissuade the girls from making alliances with lower-class boys. That institution is the college sorority.

A sorority is a private association which provides separate dormitory facilities with a distinctive Greek letter name for selected female college students. Membership is by invitation only, and requires recommendation by former members. Sororities are not simply the feminine counterpart of the college fraternity. They differ from fraternities because marriage is a more important determinant of social position for women than for men in American society, and because standards of conduct associated with marriage correspondingly bear stronger sanctions for women than for men. Sororities have much more "alumnae" involvement than fraternities, and fraternities adapt to local conditions and different living arrangements better than sororities. The college-age sorority "actives" decide only the minor details involved in recruitment, membership, and activities; parent-age alumnae control the important choices. The prototypical sorority is not the servant of youthful interests; on the contrary, it is an organized agency for controlling those interests. Through the sorority, the elders of family, class, ethnic, and religious communities can continue to exert remote control over the marital arrangements of their young girls.

The need for remote control arises from the nature of the educational system in an industrial society. In simple societies, where children are taught the culture at home, the family controls the socialization of children almost completely. In more complex societies, education becomes the province of special agents and competes with the family. The conflict between the family and outside agencies increases as children move through the educational system and is sharpest when the children reach college age. College curricula are even more challenging to family value systems than high school courses, and children frequently go away to college, out of reach of direct family influence. Sometimes a family can find a college that does not challenge family values in any way: devout Catholic parents can send their daughters to Catholic colleges; parents who want to be sure that daughter meets only "Ivy League" men can send her to one of the "Seven Sisters" — the women's equivalent of the Ivy League, made up of Radcliffe, Barnard, Smith, Vassar, Wellesley, Mt. Holyoke, and Bryn Mawr — if she can get in.

The solution of controlled admissions is applicable only to a small proportion of college-age girls, however. There are nowhere near the number of separate, sectarian colleges in the country that would be needed to segregate all the college-age girls safely, each with her own kind. Private colleges catering mostly to a specific class can still preserve a girl from meeting her social or economic inferiors, but the fees at such places are steep. It costs more to maintain a girl in the Vassar dormitories than to pay her sorority bills at a land-grant school. And even if her family is willing to pay the fees, the academic pace at the elite schools is much too fast for most girls. Most college girls attend large, tax-supported universities where the tuition is relatively low and where admissions policies let in students from many strata and diverse ethnic backgrounds. It is on the campuses of the free, open, and competitive state universities of the country that the sorority system flourishes.

When a family lets its daughter loose on a large campus with a heterogenous population, there are opportunities to be met and dangers to guard against. The great opportunity is to meet a good man to marry, at the age when the girls are most attractive and the men most amenable. For the girls, the pressure of time is urgent; though they are often told otherwise, their attractions are in fact primarily physical, and they fade with time. One need only compare the relative handicaps in the marital sweepstakes of a thirty-eight-year-old single male lawyer and a single, female teacher of the same age to realize the urgency of the quest.

The great danger of the public campus is that young girls, however properly reared, are likely to fall in love, and — in our middle-class society at least — love leads to marriage. Love is a potentially random factor, with no regard for class boundaries. There seems to be no good way of preventing young girls from falling in love. The only practical way to control love is to control the type of men the girl is likely to encounter; she cannot fall dangerously in love with a man she has never met. Since kinship groups are unable to keep "undesirable" boys off the public campus entirely, they have to settle for control of counter-institutions within the university. An effective counter-institution will protect a girl from the corroding influences of the university environment.

There are roughly three basic functions which a sorority can perform in the interest of kinship groups:

It can ward off the wrong kind of men.
It can facilitate moving-up for middle-status girls.
It can solve the "Brahmin problem" — the difficulty of proper marriage that afflicts high-status girls.

Kinship groups define the "wrong kind of man" in a variety of ways. Those who use an ethnic definition support sororities that draw an ethnic membership line; the best examples are the Jewish sororities, because among all the ethnic groups with endogamous standards (in America at any rate), only the Jews so far have sent large numbers of daughters away to college. But endogamy along class lines is even more pervasive. It is the most basic mission of the sorority to prevent a girl from marrying out of her group (exogamy) or beneath her class (hypogamy). As one of the founders of a national sorority artlessly put it in an essay titled "The Mission of the Sorority":

> There is a danger, and a very grave danger, that four years' residence in a dormitory will tend to destroy right ideals of home life and substi-

> tute in their stead a belief in the freedom that comes from community living . . . culture, broad, liberalizing, humanizing culture, we cannot get too much of, unless while acquiring it we are weaned from home and friends, from ties of blood and kindred.

A sorority discourages this dangerous weaning process by introducing the sisters only to selected boys; each sorority, for example, has dating relations with one or more fraternities, matched rather nicely to the sorority on the basis of ethnicity and/or class. (A particular sorority, for example, will have dating arrangements not with all the fraternities on campus, but only with those whose brothers are a class-match for their sisters.) The sorority's frantically busy schedule of parties, teas, meetings, skits, and exchanges keep the sisters so occupied that they have neither time nor opportunity to meet men outside the channels the sorority provides.

Marrying up

The second sorority function, that of facilitating hypergamy, is probably even more of an attraction to parents than the simpler preservation of endogamy. American society is not so much oriented to the preservation of the *status quo* as to the pursuit of upward mobility.

In industrial societies, children are taught that if they study hard they can get the kind of job that entitles them to a place in the higher ranks. This incentive actually is appropriate only for boys, but the emphasis on using the most efficient available means to enter the higher levels will not be lost on the girls. And the most efficient means for a girl — marriage — is particularly attractive because it requires so much less effort than the mobility through hard work that is open to boys. To the extent that we do socialize the sexes in different ways, we are more likely to train daughters in the ways of attracting men than to motivate them to do hard, competitive work. The difference in motivation holds even if the girls have the intelligence and talent required for status climbing on their own. For lower-class girls on the make, membership in a sorority can greatly improve the chances of meeting (and subsequently marrying) higher-status boys.

Now we come to the third function of the sorority — solving the Brahmin problem. The fact that hypergamy is encouraged in our society creates difficulties for girls whose parents are already in the upper strata. In a hypergamous system, high status *men* have a strong advantage; they can offer their status to a prospective bride as part of the marriage bargain, and the advantages of high status are often sufficient to offset many personal drawbacks. But a *woman's* high status has very little exchange value because she does not confer it on her husband.

This difficulty of high status women in a hypergamous society we may call the Brahmin problem. Girls of Brahmin caste in India and Southern white women of good family have the problem in common. In order to avoid the horrors of hypogamy, high status women must compete for high status men against women from all classes. Furthermore, high status women are handicapped in their battle by a certain type of vanity engendered by their class. They expect their wooers to court them in the style to which their fathers have accustomed them; this usually involves more formal dating, gift-giving, escorting, taxiing, etc., than many college swains can afford. If upperstratum men are allowed to find out that the favors of lower class women are available for a much smaller investment of time, money, and emotion, they may well refuse to court upper-status girls.

In theory, there are all kinds of ways for upper-stratum families to deal with surplus daughters. They can strangle them at birth (female infanticide); they can marry several to each available male (polygyny); they can offer money to any suitable male willing to take one off their hands (dowries, groom-service fees). All these solutions have in fact been used in one society or another, but for various reasons none is acceptable in our society. Spinsterhood still works, but marriage is so popular and so well rewarded that everybody hopes to avoid staying single.

The industrial solution to the Brahmin problem is to corner the market, or more specifically to shunt the eligible bachelors into a special marriage market where the upper stratum women are in complete control of the bride-supply. The best place to set up this protected marriage-market is where many suitable men can be found at the age when they are most willing to marry — in short, the college campus. The kind of male collegians who can be shunted more readily into the specialized marriage-market that sororities run, are those who are somewhat uncertain of their own status and who aspire to move into higher strata. These boys are anxious to bolster a shaky self-image by dating obviously high-class sorority girls. The fraternities are full of them.

How does a sorority go about fulfilling its three functions? The first item of business is making sure that the girls join. This is not as simple as it seems, because the values that sororities maintain are more important to the older generation than to the college-age girls. Although the sorority image is one of membership denied to the "wrong kind" of girls, it is also true that sororities have quite a problem of recruiting the "right kind." Some are pressured into pledging by their parents. Many are recruited straight out of high school, before they know much about what really goes on at college. High school recruiters present sorority life to potential rushees as one of unending gaiety; life outside the sorority is painted as bleak and dateless.

A membership composed of the "right kind" of girls is produced by the requirement that each pledge must have the recommendation of, in most cases, two or more alumnae of the sorority. Membership is often passed on from mother to daughter — this is the "legacy," whom sorority actives have to invite whether they like her or not. The sort of headstrong, innovative, or "sassy" girl who is likely to organize a campaign inside the sorority against prevailing standards is unlikely to receive alumnae recommendations. This is why sorority girls are so complacent about alumnae dominance, and why professors find them so bland and uninteresting as students. Alumnae dominance extends beyond recruitment, into the daily life of the house. Rules, regulations, and policy explanations come to the house from the national association. National headquarters is given to explaining unpopular policy by an available strategem; a favorite device (not limited to the sorority) is to interpret all nonconformity as sexual, so that the girl who rebels against wearing girdle, high heels, and stockings to dinner two or three times a week stands implicitly accused of promiscuity. This sort of argument, based on the shrewdness of many generations, shames into conformity many a girl who otherwise might rebel against the code imposed by her elders. The actives in positions of control (house manager, pledge trainer, or captain) are themselves closely supervised by alumnae. Once the right girls are initiated, the organization has mechanisms that make it very difficult for a girl to withdraw. Withdrawal can mean difficulty in finding alternative living quarters, loss of prepaid room and board fees, and stigmatization.

Sororities keep their members, and particularly their flighty pledges, in line primarily by filling up all their time with house activities. Pledges are required to study at the house, and they build the big papier-mache floats (in collaboration with selected fraternity boys) that are a traditional display of "Greek Row" for the homecoming game. Time is encompassed completely; activities are planned long in advance, and there is almost no energy or time available for meeting inappropriate men.

The girls are taught — if they do not already know — the behavior appropriate to the upper strata. They learn how to dress with expensive restraint, how to make appropriate conversation, how to drink like a lady. There is some variety here among sororities of different rank; members of sororities at the bottom of the social ladder prove their gentility by rigid conformity in dress and manner to the stereotype of the sorority girl, while members of top houses feel socially secure even when casually dressed. If you are born rich you can afford to wear Levi's and sweatshirts.

Preliminary events

The sorority facilitates dating mainly by exchanging parties, picnics, and other frolics with the fraternities in its set. But to augment this the "fixer-uppers" (the American counterpart of the *shatchen*) arrange dates with selected boys; their efforts raise the sorority dating rate above the independent level by removing most of the inconvenience and anxiety from the contracting of dates.

Dating, in itself, is not sufficient to accomplish the sorority's purposes. Dating must lead to pinning, pinning to engagement, engagement to marriage. In sorority culture, all dating is viewed as a movement toward marriage. Casual, spontaneous dating is frowned upon; formal courtship is still encouraged. Sorority ritual reinforces the progression from dating to marriage. At the vital point in the process, where dating must be turned into engagement, the sorority shores up the structure by the pinning ritual, performed after dinner in the presence of all the sorority sisters (who are required to stay for the ceremony) and attended, in its classic form, by a choir of fraternity boys singing outside. The commitment is so public that it is difficult for either partner to withdraw. Since engagement is already heavily reinforced outside the sorority, pinning ceremonies are more elaborate than engagements.

The social columns of college newspapers faithfully record the successes of the sorority system as it stands today. Sorority girls get engaged faster than "independents," and they appear to be marrying more highly ranked men. But what predictions can we make about the system's future?

All social institutions change from time to time, in response to changing conditions. In the mountain villages of the Philippines, the steady attacks of school and mission on the immorality of the *olag* have almost demolished it. Sororities, too, are affected by changes in the surrounding environment. Originally they were places where the few female college students took refuge from the jeers and catcalls of men who thought that nice girls didn't belong on campus. They assumed their present, endogamy-conserving form with the flourishing of the great land-grant universities in the first half of this century.

On the brink

The question about the future of the sorority system is whether it can adapt to the most recent changes in the forms of higher education. At present, neither fraternities nor sororities are in the pink of health. On some campuses there are chapter houses which have been reduced to taking in nonaffiliated boarders to pay the costs of running the property. New sorority chapters are formed, for the most part, on new or low-prestige campuses (where status-anxiety is rife); at schools of high prestige fewer girls rush each year and the weaker houses are disbanding.

University administrations are no longer as hospitable to the Greeks as they once were. Most are building extensive dormitories that compete effectively with the housing offered by sororities; many have adopted regulations intended to minimize the influence of the Greeks on campus activities. The campus environment is changing rapidly: academic standards are rising, admission is increasingly competitive and both male and female students are more interested in academic achievement; the proportion of graduate students seriously training for a profession is increasing; campus culture is often so obviously pluralist that the Greek claim to monopolize social activity is unconvincing.

The sorority as it currently stands is ill-adapted to cope with the new surroundings. Sorority houses were built to provide a setting for lawn parties, dances, and dress-up occasions, and not to facilitate study; crowding and noise are severe, and most forms of privacy do not exist. The sorority songs that have to be gone through at rushing and chapter meetings today all seem to have been written in 1915 and are mortifying to sing today. The arcane rituals, so fascinating to high school girls, grow tedious and sophomoric to college seniors.

But the worst blow of all to the sorority system comes from the effect of increased academic pressure on the dating habits of college men. A student competing for grades in a professional school, or even in a difficult undergraduate major, simply has not the time (as he might have had in, say, 1925) to get involved in the sorority forms of courtship. Since these days almost all the "right kind" of men *are* involved in demanding training, the traditions of the sorority are becoming actually inimical to hypergamous marriage. Increasingly, then, sororities do not solve the Brahmin problem but make it worse.

One can imagine a sorority designed to facilitate marriage to men who have no time for elaborate courtship. In such a sorority, the girls — to start with small matters — would improve their telephone arrangements, for the fraternity boy in quest of a date today must call several times to get through the busy signals, interminable paging, and lost messages to the girl he wants. They might arrange a private line with prompt answering and faithfully recorded messages, with an unlisted number given only to busy male students with a promising future. They would even accept dates for the same night as the invitation, rather than, as at present, necessarily five to ten days in advance, for the only thing a first-year law student can schedule that far ahead nowadays is his studies. Emphasis on fraternity boys would have to go, for living in a fraternity and pursuing a promising (and therefore competitive) major field of study are rapidly becoming mutually exclusive. The big formal dances would go (the fraternity boys dislike them now); the football floats would go; the pushcart races would go. The girls would reach the hearts of their men not through helping them wash their sports cars but through typing their term papers.

But it is inconceivable that the proud traditions of the sororities that compose the National Panhellenic Council could ever be bent to fit the new design. Their structure is too fixed to fit the changing college and their function is rapidly being lost. The sorority cannot sustain itself on students alone. When parents learn that membership does not benefit their daughters, the sorority as we know it will pass into history.

13

Age groups and role change in Africa

ROBERT A. LEVINE
BARBARA B. LEVINE

Age groups are a common feature of most societies, including our own. Here, Robert and Barbara Levine describe the changes that must occur for a Gusii boy to move from childhood to the world of adult males. Age as an organizing factor in society becomes clear in the discussion of the structure and function of the rite of passage the boys experience.

At the age of eight or nine, when Nyansongo girls are being initiated into womanhood, the boys are still mere children who have not yet begun to aspire to adult status. Many of them are still timidly experimenting with the frightening prospect of sleeping outside the mother's house, and neither they nor their fathers and brothers will consider them even slightly ready to graduate from being "little boys" (*abaisia,* sing. *omoisia*) to "circumcised men" or "warriors" (*abamura,* sing. *omomura*).

The uncircumcised boy of eight to twelve is usually the chief herder of cattle in the family and sometimes one of the major behavior problems as well. Unlike the girl, in the preinitiation period, he is not being progressively introduced to the kind of life and tasks which he will have as an adult; rather, he has a distinct way of life that does not prepare him for the future. Three problems can develop during this period, involving (1) dependency on the mother, (2) irresponsibility, and (3) aggressive and sexual offenses.

Although he has begun sleeping outside his mother's house, the uncircumcised boy does not ordinarily do so every night but only when his father sleeps with his mother. For the sons of monogamists this may be every night, while for sons of polygymists, widows, and men who are working outside of the district, it may be less frequent. Even so, if there are circumcised brothers sleeping in their separate hut, the boy may be persuaded to sleep out with them rather than with his mother at every opportunity. Of the children studied, sons of widows were found sleeping outside the mother's house at the latest age, nine to ten, and one of them was reported to be so terrified by noises when he first tried it that he ran back crying to his mother during the night. Even when the boy is accustomed to sleeping away from the mother regularly, he is comforted by the knowledge that he can return to sleep occasionally if he wants to, and he may sit near the mother in her cooking place in the daytime and beg food, money, and permission to go places. Ordinarily the mother does little to discourage this; indeed, the boy of this age is clever at so manipulating his mother's behavior as to be rewarded for his dependence. It should be noted that this close relationship with the mother, particularly in the case of boys who do not have cattle to herd, may involve the boy's learning and practicing the most typically feminine chores, namely, grinding and cooking. All of this may be disturbing to the father, older brother, or whatever adult male is closest to the family. Even the possible sexual connotations of the boy's closeness to his mother are explicitly thought of. Nyansongo men claimed that in days of old when all of a boy's circumcised brothers were living away in cattle-villages, boys remained sexually innocent until a later age. The abolition of the cattle-villages and the presence of older boys at home are the cause, they claim, of the lowering of the age of circumcision because boys gain sexual sophistication at a younger age and have to be moved away from their mothers earlier. Whether or not this historical explanation is true, there can be no doubt that a father feels it is improper for a boy of ten, whom he knows to have some sexual knowledge, to be in such a close relationship with his mother, especially sleeping near her and sitting with her while she squats to cook in the house. In the context of the customary avoidance between mother and adult son, such dependency is viewed as fraught with sexual overtones. This is one reason why the father feels it would be good for the boy to be circumcised and initiated into adult status.

Another aspect of the boy's behavior which presents a problem to his parents is his irresponsibility. Although he is in charge of herding cattle, sheep, and goats, the boy's adventurous spirit takes him off hunting birds, fishing, and climbing trees with the other boys of the same age. Sometimes he leaves the cattle in the care of a younger brother who may not be capable of handling them; sometimes he goes off without making any provision for their care. Eventually, the cows do some damage; there is a law suit, and the boy is punished by his father, but usually he continues to find ways of evading his duty to the herds. Mothers find that boys of ten to twelve disobey them, refuse to do assigned tasks, disappear when called for, go long distances from home and return erratically. In some of the most extreme cases, the boys take to stealing and become serious threats to neighborhood property. Some mothers say they will not beat boys of this age for fear of retaliation; food deprivation is typically used by mothers under such circumstances. But the father, if he is present, may be increasingly called on to discipline the boy, and this may be another reason for his wanting his son to be circumcised.

A third problem presented by an uncircumcised boy to his parents is his aggressive and sexual behavior. As the oldest sibling in his herding group, he is liable to bully and terrorize the younger ones to a point which parents consider reprehensible. An even more certain source of trouble is in his relations with younger girls who are already initiated. An initiated girl expects to be treated like a woman, and especially by uninitiated boys. But a ten-year-old boy is not prepared to accept a nine-year-old girl as worthy of respect. If the younger initiated girl is his sister, he may continue to order her about and to insult her as he did before. She will report this to the parents, who scold him for insulting his initiated sister. If the girl is not a sister, the boy may wish to engage in sex play with her as he did sporadically in the bush before her initiation. Now, however, she spurns him as a little boy, and he is so infuriated that he beats her or shoots at her with a slingshot. Girls invariably report such attacks, and their mothers come raging to the parents of the boy about it. The boy is often beaten and scolded by the father for such behavior, but it is considered more effective to get him circumcised so that he will not continue in an inferior status to younger girls. The boys who postponed their circumcision for several years were the greatest behavior problems for their parents; they were noticeably more disobedient, disrespectful, and overdependent on their mothers than other boys of the same age, and one of them was frequently accused by adults of sexual and aggressive offenses as well as theft of small articles.

The majority of boys are eager to be initiated and to become big men who can go away to work on the tea plantations or begin school. Like girls, they do not want to be left behind by their agemates when the latter are circumcised. Boys are more impressed by the awesome kinship duties of adulthood than girls; they seem to realize initiation means giving up dependence on mother and the relatively reckless, mischievous life of the pastures, and they are somewhat frightened. Furthermore, they know that male initiates are subjected to painful hazing as well as the circumcision operation, and this adds to their apprehensiveness. In spite of these fears, the average boy comes to want to be initiated spontaneously. He proves that he "has sense" not only by continuous sleeping in the children's house but also by wearing shorts to show he is developing a proper sense of modesty, and sometimes by doing agricultural work to indicate seriousness of purpose. The extent to which the father pretends to be skeptical about the boy's fitness in order to spur him on, or coaxes him toward initiation, depends on whether the boy is eager for it; in which case the father would be skeptical, or reluctant, requiring coaxing.

Before the day when the other boys in the community are going to the circumciser, a boy who wants to be initiated must choose his sponsor from among the initiated but unmarried boys who are of the same generation but who are not actual brothers. The sponsor is in charge of one or several novices during their seclusion and is assisted by a second boy whom he appoints. The novices shave their heads the day before and sleep at the hut of an initiated boy, not necessarily the sponsor or his assistant, who will escort them to the circumciser. Several escorts of the same age sleep there.

They rise in the middle of the night, for it is customary to reach the circumciser before dawn. The older boys may treat the novice roughly and, as a final test, try to frighten him with stories of the pain and how bad it is to be a coward. If the boy persists without crying, he bathes in the cold water of a stream and proceeds naked toward the house of the circumciser, about two miles from Nyansongo. The older boys buffet and shout at the novices along the way. Parents and classificatory fathers may not attend a boy's initiation, but brothers, classificatory brothers, and unrelated women who happen to be nearby may witness it. The boy is led to a special tree, and he stands back to the tree and arms above his head against the tree in readiness for the operation. In contrast to the girls, who are held tightly for their clitoridectomy, boys have to face circumcision on their feet and unsupported by another person. The circumciser kneels before the boy to perform the operation, and the older boys and men, standing behind the circumciser, aim spears and clubs at the boy's head, shouting continuously throughout the operation that he will be killed if he moves or shows signs of pain. A number of boys interviewed before circumcision expressed the conviction that they would be killed if they cried or tried to escape. The boys who were observed did not move during the operation; they looked up into space or at the men threatening them with spears with expressionless faces. After the quick operation, the boy is led away with his newly circumcised agemates, holding the penis (to prevent bleeding) with one hand and carrying a branch of a bush (*ekerundu*) used in many rituals as a fertility symbol.

In the afternoon the novices are led into seclusion by classificatory brothers who sing the *esimbore* for male initiation, with the words:

> Uncircumcised little boys have had pain!
> The circumciser has taken our penis;
> He has made you a spear and a hard shield.

Fight the Kipsigis, fight the Kipsigis!
Fight the Abatende, fight the Abatende!
Uncircumcised little boys have had pain!
Mother's clitoris, mother's clitoris;
Mother's pubic hair, mother's pubic hair.
Uncircumcised little boys copulate with mother!
Uncircumcised little boys have had pain.

The next to last line is interpreted as referring to the fact that before circumcision a boy's mother could touch his penis and sleep in the same house. The men singing this song are much more sedate than their counterparts in female initiation; they simply march slowly. Furthermore, unlike their female counterparts, the men affected by Christianity are embarrassed by the obscene lyrics and even sing bowdlerized versions on some occasions.

Mothers and other related women are unable to see the novices, for the latter are shielded by blankets and the crowd of singing men. The women express their jubilation by trilling and running about lifting their skirts immodestly. The whole affair is much less elaborate and lively than the girls' leading-in ceremony. Unlike girls, who are secluded in their mothers' houses, male novices are led into a newly built house which two or three of them will share during seclusion. There is considerable ritual paraphernalia associated with seclusion and the postcircumcision rites of initiation; bull-roarers, a fire that must not be allowed to go out, a particular kind of grass (*esuguta*) stuck into the floor of the hut, which must not be allowed to wither. The mothers of the novices prepare food and send it to them, but no one else may eat the leftovers. Much food is needed for the novices "to heal their wounds." Boys of different seclusion huts meet each other outside, primarily for hunting. Until about ten years ago, they would steal chickens from homesteads in the neighborhood without reproach, but now the fathers of novices who do so are faced with lawsuits and the practice has virtually died out. Married persons are barred from entering the seclusion hut, although others may come and go freely. In or out of the hut, however, the novice must not be seen by classificatory parents. He carries ashes with him outside to throw up as a warning when persons of the parents' generation inadvertently approach. There must be no fighting among the novices in the seclusion; a sacrifice would have to be performed if an outbreak occurred. The boy's life in seclusion is generally an enjoyable one, although he must carefully follow ritual prohibitions on dressing, bathing, and licking his lips as well as rules limiting social intercourse.

Hazing by other boys is an essential feature of the seclusion period, although it is not so severe as that found in many other East and South African societies. On the third night after circumcision, an indoor event known as *esubo* is conducted by the older boys. The novices are forced to eat a number of caustic and nauseating substances which the older boys tell them are delicious foods. Refusal to eat brings a beating. They are threatened with being eaten by an animal called *enyabububu* and are then shown that the noises attributed to the animal are made by a bull-roarer. Another bull-roarer is used outside the hut, with an announcement for the benefit of women and children that a great beast is swallowing the novices. Soon after, the older boys announce that the beast has vomited them up again. Toward the end of the night, the novices are beaten with nettles, made to pull up pegs near a fire with their teeth, and have their fingers twisted in long bows. Although formalized hazing occurs on this one night only, older boys can come and torment the novice throughout the initiation period. They may tell a novice to call for his mother, then beat him when he does so, telling him he's a man now and shouldn't need to call her. Sometimes they explicitly warn him against further familiarity with mother and stress the keeping of initiation rituals secret from women. Direct instruction rarely goes further than this, but there can be no doubt that the novice understands the moral lessons presented to him in this manner. All boys are aware of the respect and avoidance rules of adult status long before their initiation, and hazing helps to make them realize that the rules now apply to them.

Traditional ceremonies of emergence from seclusion involve several cycles of cleansing, blessing, anointing, and feasting. Most significant is the anointing of the boy's forehead with white earth by the father, who promises to "respect" the boy (i.e., to refrain from beating him) and commands the initiate to respect him in turn. Underlying this ritual is the assumption that, morally, the boy is now a finished product. Having learned the correct rules of behavior through the instruction and chastisement of his parents, he is thought to have no further need of the physical punishment used as a teaching method for children. In our opinion, the majority of Nyansongo boys accept the moral trust of their fathers with great solemnity. Fathers whose sons were particularly delinquent in their pre-initiation behavior entertain the hope that initiation will have made them "sensible" enough to behave properly when put on their own, although there is some cynicism about this under contemporary circumstances.

The difference between boys' and girls' initiation sheds some light on the meaning and function of the male rite. The girl is accompanied to the genital operation by her mother and secluded in her mother's house; the boy is kept apart from his parents from the time of his leaving the house to be circumcised to his emergence several weeks later. The girl is held down during the genital operation, while the boy must stand to face the knife alone. The girl is confined to her mother's house during seclusion; the boy's seclusion in a special house involves going out to meet others for adventures in hunting and theft. In short, initiation encourages boys to be self-reliant, to do without parental support, to endure hardship unflinchingly, to cooperate with related agemates, and to venture forth with weapons. There is no such encouragement for girls, and this is congruent with the fact that the girl leaves her mother's house, not at initiation but at marriage, five or six years later, when she will be transformed from *enyaroka,* "a circumcised thing," to *omosubaati,* a young married woman. Initiation, however, is the only formal change of residence and status for the young male, who moves permanently from his mother's house to his own hut nearby and becomes *omomura,* "young man," which he continues to be after marriage, until his son is circumcised and he becomes *omogaka,* "elder." The emphasis in female initiation is on sexual stimulation, while in male initiation, sexual avoidance and respect for parents are stressed. In augmenting and manipulating her sexual attractiveness in postinitiation years, the girl becomes increasingly inconsiderate of her parents' wishes and commands. The initiated boy, however, is more respectful and obedient than he was as the footloose roughneck of the pastures. While they are not pleased with the girl's misbehavior during adolescence, parents do not consider it unnatural nor try to correct it more than is necessary to assure a legitimate marriage. "If she is bad, let her husband beat her," Nyansongo adults say of the unmarried girl, adding that once she is initiated it is not the place of the parents to punish her. The boy's behavior continues to be the concern of his parents, for he never moves away from their homestead, and physical punishment by the father is replaced by economic and supernatural sanctions after his initiation. The parental concept of initiation as a moral finishing school for boys and the lack of such a concept for girls thus appears to be related to the patrilocality of Nyansongo marriage.

After initiation, the boy assumes adult responsibilities. In the past he joined other warriors in the cattle-villages for defense of the herds and raiding other groups. Nowadays, after a few years he usually goes off to work on the tea plantations or in the city. When he is home he helps his father build houses and mend fences, and occasionally he supervises the herding of his uncircumcised brothers. Living in a separate hut within the homestead, he eats food cooked by his mother and brought to him by younger children. His relations with his mother become more distant although still affectionate. In the past it was mandatory for a boy to give his mother a goat before entering her house after initiation, but this custom is rarely practiced nowadays. In any event, he may not enter the cooking and sleeping area of her house and must avoid obscene language or any mention of sex in her presence. His sex life is now private as far as his parents are concerned. They make no mention of the girls he brings to his house, and no longer punish him for participation in sexual relations. His father expects great deference and obedience from him when he is home and financial contributions when he is working away from home.

While young initiated boys usually have stiff, formal relations with their parents, they tend to spend a good deal of their time with boys of the same age, usually from the same neighborhood or community. If they were circumcised in the same year, regardless of whether or not they shared a seclusion hut, such boys are *abakiare* (sing. *omokiare*), "pals," and this means they can hurl obscene insults at each other and deride each other without offense being taken. In a sense, the pal relationship is the mirror image of the father-son relationship; all conditions are reversed. Whereas the son is bound to his father by kinship and economic obligations, nothing ties him to his pal except shared ephemeral interests. While he must respect his father, he can jokingly but sharply insult his pal. Sex is a forbidden topic for discussion with the father but is foremost with the pal. Pals cooperate in seducing girls together in their youth, but the permanence of their relationship depends on their actual kin and residential relationships to each other. Regardless of whether the specific relationship is continued, the pattern of contrast between intergenerational relations and peer relations becomes solidified in the postinitiation period and perpetuated throughout the life of the Nyansongo male.

14

Rebirth in the airborne

MELFORD S. WEISS

The structural criteria of special purpose *(military),* sex *(male), and* age *(adult), all emerge from this study of induction into the airborne. Melford Weiss describes the rituals one must go through in order to move from civilian status to that of paratrooper. The training period includes elements of superstition, magic, and ceremony, and is compared to similar rites in non-Western cultures.*

When an American paratrooper first learns to jump, he does more than step out of an airplane. He steps into a new way of life. Furthermore, his training even takes note of this major transition in his life in a formal ceremonial manner. This training period — marked by pomp and circumstance, superstition and ritual — is what anthropologists refer to as a *rite of passage.*

Rites of passage are universal features of complex as well as simple societies. They mark critical changes in man's life cycle, such as birth, death, and initiation. The paratrooper training program can best be understood as an initiation, a form of entry into an elite group. The process is interwoven with magical and symbolic ritual practices. In one training unit, for example, each time the trainees enter the airplane, the jumpmaster draws a line on the ground in front of the entrance hatch with the toe of his boot. Each prospective jumper then stomps upon the line before entering the airplane in order to ensure a safe landing. Whether or not they actually believe in the practice (many do not) is of decidedly less importance than the fact that this ritual serves to bind the group together.

From "Rebirth in the Airborne," *Trans*-action 4 (May 1967): 23–26. Illustrations and bibliography are omitted.

A paratrooper's training ends in a ceremonial climax. At the close of training it is customary in some military units to reenact the jumping procedure in a fashion symbolic of rebirth. Newly qualified paratroopers are invited to a "prop blast" at the noncommissioned officers' club. There a wooden model of an airplane has been hastily rigged. The new initiates line up in jump formation inside the plane. They jump and land facing the jumpmaster, their instructor. He hands each a loving cup full of "blast juice." This must be quaffed within the count of "1000, 2000, 3000," the time between an actual jump from a plane and the opening of the chute. Failure to drain it to the dregs within the allotted span is called a "malfunction," the term for chute failure. The process must be repeated, perhaps three or four times, till success is achieved. Then the initiate is ritually one with his fellows.

Initiation rites

Rites of passage vary in different cultures, but according to Arnold Van Gennep a typical rite has three stages:

— *separation* from the former group or state;
— *transition* to the new;
— and, finally, *incorporation*.

In birth and death rites, for example, separation is emphasized most: "The Lord giveth, the Lord has taken away." In the case of paratrooper training the transitional phase is most important. The paratrooper rite described here is a composite of training programs of many groups from World War II to the present time.

The paratrooper school is inside a compound surrounded by barbed wire and guarded by sentries. In this compound the trainee is fed, trained, and occasionally entertained. He is allowed to go out in the evening but usually does so in the company of other troopers. Fraternization with the nonparatrooper world is not encouraged, but separation from the former civilian environment is only partial.

The transitional phase usually lasts three weeks. During the last week the candidate makes five practice jumps which mark stages in his progress toward final acceptance. Not all the jumps are equally important — the first and fifth are most significant.

Paratrooper training is officially a secular affair. But certain superstitious practices which are interwoven show that, in the broadest sense, it is also a religious rite. From the beginning of the transition period the trainees are subjected to continuous periods of anxiety. Since they are all volunteers with a strong emotional investment in success, these stresses serve to bind them more closely to one another and to the group they seek to enter. So do the "magical" devices they learn to use to relieve anxiety. These include the wearing of charms and fetishes, such as a girl friend's picture above the heart, a pair of sweat socks worn on a previous successful jump, or a replica of the "trooper wings" placed inside a boot.

Use of "sympathetic magic" is fostered by the paratrooper mythology to which the trainee is exposed during this stage. The following examples of paratrooper tales illustrate elements of both *mana* (a spiritual force independent of persons or spirits which explains success, excellence, and potency when these qualities are not otherwise explainable) and *taboo* (a prohibition based upon the assumption that disastrous consequences can be averted if certain acts are not performed):

> He was a jinx and was always present at any accident. I would never jump with him in my line. I once touched him before I was about to jump and pretended to be sick in order to avoid jumping that day. Nobody laughed at me when I told them the real reason.
>
> A master jumper told this story: "When I was a youngster, I felt that should I ever lose my original set of wings I could never jump again. They had a natural magic about them which protected me. When I went home I put them in the bottom drawer of my mother's dresser. I knew they would be safe there!"
>
> Legend maintains that the paratrooper compound is off limits, and one myth relates the unhappy story of the intoxicated soldier from another unit who tried to sneak into the compound and was found next morning with his face severely scratched. The soldier claimed that he was attacked by a small bird and then passed out. But paratroopers claim that the bird was in fact the "screaming eagle," the totemic symbol of the 101st Airborne Division.

During the transition period myth and magic help the trainee to identify with paratroopers in general and share their *esprit de corps*. This becomes a formidable force as airborne units are made up entirely of volunteers. Thus a man becomes a paratrooper by choice and remains one all his military life unless he disobeys a direct order to jump. As in the case of other select military units, paratroopers are bound to one another by pride in a common history and system of training. They consider themselves superior to all other such groups — not only in their military virtues, but in their vices as well. A paratrooper is supposed to be able to outdrink, outbrawl, and outwhore any other member of the armed forces.

THE JUMPOUT DROPOUT

Systems of initiation depend for their success upon how much the candidate wants to belong to the group. Sometimes, in the case of paratrooper training, he may not want to badly enough. A young man may decide he does not care to spend his active life plunging out of airplanes with nothing but the silkworm's art for support. Since all trainees are volunteers, this is technically no disgrace. All he has to do is request reassignment.

But because of the problem of preserving group morale the dropout is usually eliminated with almost indecent haste. Many instructors feel that to let him hang around will spread the "rot," and other failures or jumping accidents may result. When a would-be dropout says he wants out at the end of a training day, he is more than likely to be called to the orderly room during the next morning's formation. By the time the other trainees return from their midday meal he will have left the training area forever, usually to spend a month's KP duty in some nonelite holding company. For example one dropout said:

> I was scared and I knew it. I dared not let the others know, but I did not think I could hide it very long. We were listening to a master jumper telling us about his first jump and my stomach got queasy and I was sick. I told my sergeant I wanted out. I left the very next day.

If a trainee should quit during the training day, particularly with a public fuss, more brusque tactics may be used. One would-be paratrooper reports:

> I was fed up with this bastard. I made a scene and cursed the Army and shouted that you can shove the paratroopers. I yelled, "I quit." My training NCO rapidly approached me, ripped the patch from my shoulder, and cut the laces of my jump boots.

In some primitive societies those who fail the tests of manhood may be killed outright. The ripping of the patch and the cutting of the laces serves the same function symbolically. It signifies the separation of the dropout from his companions and thus binds the group more closely together, as does the knowledge that the failure is headed for KP or some other nonstatus duty.

As noted before, the transitional phase of paratrooper training has substages. These occur mainly after the first and fifth (last) practice jump. After the first there is no ceremony, but there is a change in the relationship between the trainees and the seasoned paratroopers. As soon as the jumping experience has been shared, the trainee begins to be treated with at least a modicum of respect by his instructors. Conversation in the barracks becomes less guarded. Before any mention of "spilling silk" or "flying a streamer" was avoided. Now jokes about jumping accidents and chute failures are freely bandied about.

The fifth jump is marked by a definite ritual. After the first four the trainee rolls his own chute. After the last he hands it to the platoon sergeant, who rolls it for him and places it in the supply truck. Then the NCO shakes his pupil's hand, congratulates him, and in some cases invites him to use his, the sergeant's, given name. This reversal of roles marks acceptance into the group. The same evening this is confirmed at a party at the enlisted men's club, usually off limits to officers. The paratroopers-to-be, including officer candidates, are invited to join in the drinking and usually do.

The whole transitional period in paratrooper training closely parallels initiation rites in both Western and non-Western societies. During this stage the initiate learns the formulas, gestures, and chants of the brotherhood. These include a paratrooper prayer and a paratrooper song. The latter is a gruesome chant in which the paratrooper verbalizes, jokingly, his fear of sudden and gory death. It is sung to the tune of "The Battle Hymn of the Republic":

Is everybody ready? cried the Sergeant, looking up.
Our hero feebly answered yes, as they stood him up.
He leapt right out into the blast, his static line unhooked.
O he ain't gonna jump no more!

There was blood upon the risers, there were brains upon the chute,
His intestines were a dangling from his paratrooper boots;
They picked him up still in his chute and poured him from his boots;
O he ain't gonna jump no more!

CHORUS: Glory gory what a helluva way to die!
Glory gory what a helluva way to die!
Glory gory what a helluva way to die!
Oh he ain't gonna jump no more!

Wings and a three-day pass

After transition comes incorporation in two stages — an official ceremony and the unofficial "prop blast" described earlier. The official ceremony is a colorful affair in the tradition of most military rituals. It marks the end of the rigorous training and is a welcome climax to weeks of agonizing tension. It takes place the day after the final (fifth) practice jump. The men in the training unit line up in alphabetical order; uniforms are smartly pressed, faces agonizingly clean shaven, and hair close cropped. They stand at attention while the post band plays the national anthem, followed by "Ruffles and Flourishes." The division flag flies just beneath Old Glory.

The men bow their heads as the post chaplain reads from the Bible. After a congratulatory speech the training commandant presents each man with his diploma. The division commandant passes through the ranks, reviews the troops, and pins "wings" to each man's chest. The chaplain delivers the closing benediction. The band continues to play military music as the men now assemble by training platoon and proudly march by the reviewing stand. As the soldiers reach the stand, they are saluted by the senior officers, and the new troopers return the salute. The men are then dismissed and given a three-day pass.

Many features of this ceremony have symbolic significance. The new paratrooper is being initiated into a special brotherhood within the military forces of an American, predominantly Christian, society. The chaplain's benediction gives the ceremony "divine sanction" and links it, however tenuously, with the prevailing Christian religion. The "American heritage" is reflected by the American flag and the national anthem. The polished boots, clean shaves, and close haircuts set up the image of the "clean-cut, all-American boy." The rest of the rite is military, with calculated differences. The marching, the salute, the respect for rank, and the three-day pass remind the paratrooper that he is a member of the armed forces. But the jump-school graduation certificate and the "wings" belong only to paratroopers and serve as permanent marks of that status.

The brotherhood of all troopers is symbolized by the formation itself. While the platoon is the standard military unit, on this one day the men line up in alphabetical order. This wipes out platoon distinctions and incorporates all the men in a pan-paratrooper sodality. Being saluted first by their superiors, against military protocol, shows the "troopers" that they now occupy a coveted status in the military.

Although the training NCO's are not required to attend, they are present throughout the ceremony. At the close they rush to congratulate the new members and welcome them into the brotherhood. The new status of the members has now been recognized and sanctioned by military society. With the evening's "prop blast" and its symbolic reenactment of the jumping process, the rite of passage is complete. The initiate is now wholly separated from his past life and "reborn" into a new, select brotherhood and a new way of life.

V

Social structure II: Inequality

In every society the place a person occupies in the social structure is evaluated. It is difficult, if not impossible, to encounter different kinds of people without appraising their social worth, for example, the roles of student, garbage collector, judge, mental patient, prostitute, senator, mortician, policeman. Whatever the content of these different social identities, the fact is that we attach differential social worth to each. Underlying their relative value is some criterion *that becomes the principle of each particular system of inequality. Among some New Guinea natives, a man's worth is based on the number of pigs he can maintain. The Kwakiutl determined social worth in terms of birth order, and the eldest son was always of higher rank than his younger brothers. The variety of criteria used to evaluate and rank members of a society is vast: age, sex, birth order, wealth, religious purity, locality, and number of pigs or cars or wives are only a few.*

Many of these criteria for inequality are also discussed in other chapters, but this one includes several selected because of their immense importance in our own society. A cultural perspective on these principles of inequality is especially important. Race, sex, and poverty are among the most widely used markers of so-

cial worth. However, each of these is symbolically defined — a fact that leads to wide variation in their meaning from one society to another.

15

The color of race

JULIAN PITT-RIVERS

Although skin color is employed as a criterion for evaluation, the extent of its use varies from one culture to another. In this article, Julian Pitt-Rivers describes a fundamental difference between the North and the South American views of race: North American racial inequality is based on skin color, while Latins use a variety of criteria. The author shows the consequences for culture change in each evaluation system.

Among its many *fiestas*, the Hispanic world celebrates one with the name of "El día de la raza" (which is what is called Columbus Day in the United States). Why it should be so called remains something of an enigma. It was inaugurated in Spain in 1917 to encourage friendship with Latin America, but its name has been changed there to "El día de la Hispanidad" — in the cause, more suitable to present times, of extolling Spanish culture rather than Spanish genes. The old name still remains, however, in Mexico and in other countries. The *fiesta* might, more consequentially, have been called "The Day of Race Relations" rather than of "The Race," for it celebrates the day on which they may be said to have commenced.

For the Spaniards, the celebration evokes the age, long since eclipsed, when they conquered half the world; it pays tribute to the egregious stamina of their ancestors. But Mexicans tend to think it refers to the Aztec race; the Monumento a la Raza in Mexico City is composed of a pyramid surmounted by an Aztec eagle. In other countries, some people think it refers to the Spanish race, but it seldom evokes for anyone the name of Columbus, whose race remains a matter of dispute to this day.

From "Race, Color, and Class in Central America and the Andes," *Daedalus* 96 (Spring 1967): 542–559. Reprinted by permission of the publisher and the author from *Daedalus*, Journal of the American Academy of Arts and Sciences, Boston, Massachusetts. Many footnotes are omitted.

Quite apart from the mysteries surrounding The Day of the Race, the concept of *race* itself is unclear in Latin America. My concern here is not with what anthropologists mean by *race,* but only with what the people of Latin America think the word means when they encounter it in their daily speech. By minimal definition, it refers to a group of people who are felt to be somehow similar in their essential nature. El Día de la Raza is above all a patriotic *fiesta;* it expresses national unity, the common nature of the whole nation. As such, it is certainly worth celebrating, especially in countries where racial differences pose such grave moral and social problems on other days of the year. It is in keeping with this interpretation that the *fiesta* should be a comparatively modern innovation coinciding with the growth of national and social consciousness.

The word *race* is, of course, also used to mark differences of ethnic identity within the nation. Sometimes awareness of any implication of heredity is so slight that a man can think of himself as belonging to a race different from that of his parents. The word clearly owes little to physical anthropology but refers, however it may be defined, to the ways in which people are classified in daily life. What are called race relations are, in fact, always questions of social structure.

Ethnic classification is the end product of the most elusive social processes that endow not only words but feelings and perceptions with a special significance. The varied definitions of *race* have no more in common than the fact that they say something about the essential and indelible nature of people. Hence, for all its ambiguities, the notion of race possesses a prime claim upon the solidarities that bind men into social and political alliance.

Approaches to the study of race relations have varied considerably. Certain theories constructed out of the commonplaces of the traditional popular idiom attribute culture to "blood." Moral qualities, like psychological characteristics and intellectual aptitudes, are thought to derive from heredity, since the "blood" is what is inherited. The social order depends, by implication, upon genetic transmission, since the capacities and the character that fit people for a particular status are acquired by birth.

This view leads to the conclusion that social status should be hereditary and derive from the nature of persons. The system works well enough because the totality of a person's descent is not only hard to know in a genetically homogeneous population, but also quite easily falsified. Birth produces the expectation of excellence. Recognized excellence demonstrates the presence of distinguished forebears who may not have previously been claimed. "Blood will out!" In operation the system confirms its premises. Thanks to its flexibility, the facts can be made to fit; the reality of social mobility can be reconciled with a belief in the determinism of birth.

Where descent can be inferred from appearance, such a theory finds itself constricted. Plebian origins do not "show"; colored origins do. Putative descent can no longer be invoked to validate the reality established by the social process, but the real ancestors come to light in the phenotype. "Bad blood" explains moral and intellectual defects, but in those who show visible signs of having it, these can be expected in advance. Moral qualities are no longer inferred from status; rather, status is accorded on the basis of physical qualities that can be seen, and these, then, determine the nature of persons. Birth decides not merely opportunity but fate. In a homogeneous society the possession of a prestigious ancestor entitles a man to claim status. Once blood is a matter of ethnic distinction, however, its purity becomes the subject of concern. The attribution of an impure ancestor destroys status. Blood exchanges a positive for a negative significance. Preoccupations with "purity of descent" take on a racial connotation and bring an adverse value to miscegenation (a word which by the unhappy fortuity of its spelling becomes misconstrued today to imply that racial prejudices have a scientific background). The result is a color bar, prohibiting social mobility and enforcing ethnic endogamy.

When blood is considered the determinant of culture, racial differences between peoples can be used to explain all else, even military and political fortunes. Purity of blood becomes the key to national success. The most distinguished literary expression of such ideas is that of Gobineau. By zeal and industry rather than by any great originality of mind, he succeeded in elevating the social prejudices of a petty noble of the mid-nineteenth century to the status of a philosophy of history. If Gobineau committed what Claude Lévi-Strauss has called the "original sin" of anthropology,[1] later anthropologists have committed other less spectacular sins in their attempts to grapple with the problems of race relations — or, more often, they have sinned by default in not attempting to grapple with them at all.

The "diffusionist" theory offered such an evasion. Viewing race relations in terms of culture contact, this theory concentrated upon establishing the origin of the cultural traits of different peoples to the neglect of their present social function. The preoccupation with the transmission of culture between different ethnic groups, rather than with reciprocal modes of behavior, left this branch of anthropology with little to say about the problems of race relations. This is particularly important in Latin America, where in the past a great many anthropologists have devoted their labors to the discovery of the cultures of pre-Hispanic times on the assumption that they have been preserved among the Indians of the present. This archaeological orientation has meant that, until recently, in spite of

[1] Claude Lévi-Strauss, *Race et Histoire* (Paris, 1952), p. 5.

the quantity of professional work done in Latin America, few accounts have been concerned with race relations as such. Concentrating on the passage of cultural traits rather than on the social structure through which these traits passed, the anthropologists tended to deal with only one side of the ethnic division and touched only incidentally its relationship to the other.

The Marxist interpretation of race relations has been of the greatest importance in stressing their economic aspects and in giving them a dynamic dimension. It has clarified in particular the stages of colonial development. But if the proponents of the "acculturation theory" have neglected the society within which acculturation took place, the Marxist sociologists have tended to neglect the significance of culture by treating race relations simply as a special instance of class relations carried over into a colonial setting.

The same reproach cannot be leveled at the American urban sociologists whose awareness of the factor of culture and whose feeling for its nuances have brought a high level of excellence to their ethnography. But, as Professor Everett Hughes pointed out a dozen years ago (and it is still true), they have been inclined to conduct their analysis within the framework of their own values and reformist desires. For want of a comparative field of reference, they have tended to overlook the wider significance of their data.

Studies of race relations by political thinkers have seldom given sufficient weight to the course of feeling that lies behind political events or to the dynamics of a changing consciousness and the formation of fresh solidarities. Politics has been called the science of the possible. Time and again it has turned out to be, where racial issues were concerned, the science of what was once possible but is so no longer.

A study that straddles the frontiers of established disciplines requires consideration from such varied viewpoints. It must above all achieve a synthesis of the cultural and the social aspects. The detail of the ethnography must be integrated in an overview of race relations in space and time. The preliminary condition of such an enterprise is a clear description of the systems of ethnic classification at the local level and a recognition of their social significance. Charles Wagley was making this point when he coined the phrase "social race." [2] He went on to point to the importance of knowing how the terminology varies, for this matter is filled with confusion. Not only do the words used vary from area to area

[2] Charles Wagley, "On the Concept of Social Race in the Americas," *Actas del 33 Congreso Internacional de Americanistas* (San José, 1959). Reprinted in Dwight B. Heath and Richard N. Adams, eds., *Contemporary Cultures and Societies of Latin America* (New York, 1965).

and from class to class, but the conceptions to which they correspond also change, and the criteria on which the system of classification is based vary in relevance. It is difficult to say what is an Indian, but it is scarcely easier to say what is a Negro.

Terminological inconsistencies complicate from the outset discussion of race relations in Latin America. Indeed, there is not even agreement as to whether or not a "problem" of race relations exists in Latin America. The nationals of these countries often deny the existence of racial discrimination. They claim from this fact a virtue that makes them, despite their supposed economic and technological underdevelopment, the moral superiors of their northern neighbor, whose "inhumanity" toward colored people they deplore. Moreover, this opinion is held not only by Latin Americans themselves, but by outside observers, the most eminent of whom is Professor Arnold Toynbee, who speaks of the Latin American's freedom from race prejudice.

This point of view, in many cases a way of expressing criticism of the United States, is also held by many patriotic American citizens, including especially some who are "colored" and whose testimony, if firsthand, might be thought to suffice. Nevertheless, it is not by any means held universally and is sometimes regarded as a myth. Certain critics, both national and foreign, maintain that race is as important in Latin as in North America, once it is admitted that in addition to differences in the form discrimination takes, there is a major difference: The race that is penalized is the Indian rather than the Negro. Neither of these points of view appears correct. Both are confused as to the nature of the question. Yet by examining the observations upon which they are based and how they have come to hold sway, one can understand better the role ethnic distinctiveness plays in ordering the society of Latin America.

"Segregation" as it is found in the United States does not exist in Latin America. "Color" in the North American sense is not the basis of a classification into two statuses to which differential rights attach. Segregated schools, public facilities, transport, or restaurants do not exist in Latin America. The Negro is not formally distinguished at any point. While many institutions are devoted specifically to the Indians, the definition of Indian in this regard is not based on physical criteria. Moreover, neither color nor phenotype has sufficed in the past to debar men from prominence in the national life, as the long list of Negroid or Indian-looking men of eminence in Latin American history shows.

Intermarriage is not regarded with horror. Among the upper classes and in many places among the population generally, it is, however, considered denigrating to marry someone much darker than oneself. This is so, for example, in Barranquilla, Colombia, where the greater part of the population is more or less Negroid. The idea of physical contact with darker races is nowhere considered shocking, nor is it regarded as polluting by the whites. Dark-skinned people are thought to be more sensual and therefore more desirable sexually. This is not the expression of a neurotic fear of sexual insufficiency but an accepted and openly stated commonplace. Pale-skinned people of both sexes are thought to be more frigid and proud, and less warmhearted. Mistresses tend, consequently, to be more swarthy than wives, whose pale skin indicates social superiority.

The immense majority of the population from Mexico to Bolivia are well aware of their mixed ancestry. "A touch of the tarbrush" can, therefore, never mean total social disqualification. "We are all half-castes," Mexicans commonly remark, pointing to their forearm to show the color of their skin. Still, they sometimes go on to stress that only a small percentage of their blood is Indian. National unity demands that to be truly Mexican they must have some Indian blood, but social aspirations require that they should not have too much. Color is a matter of degree, not the basis of a division into black and white.

In consequence, physical characteristics cannot be said to be socially insignificant; their significance is only different. Physical traits never account for more than part of the image that individuals present. These images are perceived in terms of what they can be contrasted with; there is no color problem where the population is homogeneous in color, whatever that color may be. Social distinctions must then be made according to other criteria. From one place to another, in greater or lesser degree, physical traits are qualified by cultural and economic indicators in order to produce that total image which accords a social identity.

Arnulfo Arias, a former president of Panama known for his "racist" policy, is credited with the proposal to exterminate the Negroes. In a country whose capital city is predominantly Negro, he nevertheless retained sufficient popularity to be a close runner-up in the presidential elections of 1964. This is no longer curious when one realizes that the term *Negro* refers only to the population of Jamaican origins. Imported for the construction of the canal, these people have retained their English tongue and their Protestant faith. Language and religion are the significant qualifiers of color in the definition of *Negro* in Panama.

In Barranquilla, Colombia, color is qualified by other social factors, and the term *Negro* confined to the slum-dwellers of the city. In the modern housing developments where no one is to be seen who would not qualify as a Negro in the United States, one may be told: "Only white people live here." The definition of *Negro* varies from place to place and, of course, from class to class. A man may be defined as Negro in one place, but simply as *moreno, trigueño, canela,* or even white in another.

A man who would be considered Negro in the United States might, by traveling to Mexico, become *moreno* or *prieto,* then *canela* or *trigueño* in Panama, and end up in Barranquilla white. The definition of *Indian* presents a comparable problem once the word no longer refers to a member of an Indian community. Different places and classes use different criteria.

Skin color is merely one of the indices among physical traits that contribute to a person's total image. It is not necessarily more significant than hair type or shape of eye. The relative evaluation of different physical traits varies. The Reichel-Dolmatoffs record of a village in Northern Colombia:

> Distinctions are made mainly according to the nature of the hair and of the eyes and to a certain degree according to stature. Skin color, the shape of the lips or nose, or other similar traits are hardly taken into account. In this way, a person with predominantly Negroid features, but with long and wavy hair is often considered a "Spaniard." On the other hand, an individual with predominantly Caucasoid features and a light skin, but with straight black hair, slightly oblique eyes and of small stature, is considered an "Indian." [3]

The social structure is divided, primarily according to place of residence, into two segments — Spanish and Indian. This dichotomy, while employing a strictness which the Reichel-Dolmatoffs regard as exceptional in Colombia, allows no place for the category "Negro."

The system of classification makes what it will of the objective reality of the phenotype. The forces of the social structure utilize the raw material of phenotypical distinctions, building out of it the social statuses into which people are classified.

It has sometimes been said that the difference between Anglo and Latin America is that in the former anyone who has a drop of Negro blood is a Negro, whereas in the latter anyone who has white blood is a white. The first statement is approximately true, but the second is emphatically not so. The concept of "blood" is fundamentally different in the two and has, in the past, varied from one century to another.

In Latin America, a person with nonwhite physical traits may be classed as white socially. A trace of European physique is, however, quite insufficient in itself to class a person as white. Although Indians with pale skin and European traits or gray hair may be found sporadically throughout Latin America, they are considered to be no less Indian on this account. In any market in the Andes one or two can usually be seen, and the *indio gringo* ("fair-skinned" or "blond" Indian) is a recognized

[3] G. and A. Reichel-Dolmatoff, *The People of Aritama* (Chicago, 1961), p. 138.

type in parts of northern Peru. There is nothing anomalous in this description. "Indian" is not, in the first place, a physical type but a social status. The Indian is distinguished not by genetic inheritance but by birth in, and therefore membership of, an Indian community and by possession of that community's culture. This is all that is needed for the definition of an Indian, though Indians normally look "Indian." The word *Indian* has, therefore, come to mean "of Indian descent"; it is used of persons who no longer occupy Indian status, but whose physical resemblance to the Indians implies descent from them. Since Indians are the "lowest" or least "civilized" element of the population, the word in this sense means "low class." It can also be used to mean "savage," or "uncivilized," or "bad" in a purely figurative way — equivalent, say, to that of *canaille* in French. *Negro,* on the other hand, denotes a physical type that commonly carries with it the general implication of low class, but culture is usually quite subsidiary to the definition.

Racial status in the United States, defined in terms of "blood" and identified purely by physical appearance, divides the population into two halves within which two parallel systems of class differentiation are recognized. In Latin America, appearance is merely one indicator of social position. It is never sufficient in itself to determine how an individual should be classed. The discrimination imposed on the basis of "color" in the United States has sometimes been called a "caste" system and has been contrasted with class systems. This distinction is impossible in Latin America where color is an ingredient of total social position, not the criterion for distinguishing two racial "castes." A policy of segregation on the basis of color would, therefore, be not merely repugnant to Latin Americans but literally impossible.

Even in Panama where the bulk of the urban population is Negro and the "oligarchy," as the traditional upper class is called, entirely European, the notion of segregation is repulsive. A member of the Panamanian upper class concluded a bitter criticism of discrimination in the United States with the remark: "After all, it's a matter of luck whether one is born black or white." It remained to be added, of course, that in Panama it is nevertheless bad luck to be born black and good luck to be born white.

At the time of the race riots in Oxford, Mississippi, Hector Velarde, a distinguished critic, took the occasion to deplore racial discrimination in the United States in an article in a Peruvian newspaper. Why can the North Americans not learn from us the virtue of racial tolerance? he asked. He went on to illustrate his argument with the usage of the word *negrita* as a term of affection. *Negrita de mi alma* was an expression used toward a sweetheart, he said. Indeed he did not exaggerate, for *negrita* and *negra* are both forms of address that imply a certain intimacy or informality (as a diminutive the former carries the implication of a potential sexual interest the latter lacks). Velarde did not mention the Indians (who are very much more numerous in Peru than the Negroes). If he had, it would not have helped his thesis since *Indian* is never used in an equivalent fashion, though *cholo* ("civilized Indian") and *zambo* ("half-caste") are both used as terms of affection among comrades.

The implication of racial equality that he drew from his examples invites precision. Such terms do not find their way into such a context because they are flattering in formal usage, but precisely because they are not. Intimacy is opposed to respect; because these terms are disrespectful, they are used to establish or stress a relationship in which no respect is due. The word *nigger* is used in this way among Negroes in the United States, but only among Negroes. Color has, in fact, the same kind of class connotation in the Negro community as in Latin America: Pale-skinned means upper class. Hence *nigger*, in this context dark-skinned or lower class, implies a relationship that is free of the obligation of mutual respect. Velarde's example, consequently, shows that color is an indicator of class, not a criterion of caste.

Those who find no racial discrimination in Latin America take the United States as their model. They point out, correctly, that there is no color bar and that race riots do not occur. (Indian risings are a matter they do not consider.) On the other hand, those who do find racial discrimination in Latin America are concerned with the fact that there exist high degrees of social differentiation that are habitually associated with physical traits and frequently expressed in the idiom of "race." They justify their view by the racial overtones given to social distinctions. In Latin America, these critics are commonly persons of left-wing sympathy who see racial discrimination as a bulwark of class distinction and, evading all nuances, they equate the two. Taking more easily to the emotive aspects of Marxism than to its dialectic, these would-be Marxists end by finding themselves as far from reality as those colonial legislators who once attempted so vainly to control the legal status of individuals on the basis of their descent. Because there is no color bar but rather a color scale that contributes only partially to the definition of status, they are pushed to an implied definition of race that is worthy of Gobineau. They speak of "racial hypocrisy" to explain why certain people claim a "racial" status to which their phenotype would not entitle them if "race" were really a matter of genes. This "false race-consciousness" is false only by the standards of a theory that would obliterate the historical evolution of the past four hundred years. History may validate these theorists if the Chinese interpretation of Marxist-Leninism acquires authority, and the class struggle, transposed to the international plane, becomes a matter of race.

The contrary opinion is usually held by persons of right-wing views. They regard class distinctions as either unobjectionable, insignificant, or at least inevitable. Once they can cite examples of people of upper-class status who show marked traces of non-European descent, they are satisfied that there is no racial discrimination in their country. (This conviction accords with the liberality of their nature and the official creed of their nation.) They are content that there is no problem if there is no "discrimination" as in the United States.

In the first case, the distinctiveness of class and color must be denied; in the second, the association between the two. The first theory ignores the individual instance; only the statistical aspect counts. The exception is evaded lest it disprove the rule. The second theory takes as significant only the chosen individual instance, overlooking the existence of a statistical norm. Indeed, no one is boycotted on account of his phenotype if his class standing is secured by the other criteria that define high status. In such a case, infrequent as it may be in Panama, color may properly be said to be a matter of luck in the sense that it is a contingency that carries little of the weight of social definition. Economic power, culture, and community are what count.

The disapproval that Latin American visitors to the United States feel of the segregation they find there is not unconnected with the disrespectful attitude they are likely to inspire as Spanish speakers. They know that as Hispanics they are judged socially inferior in many places. Visitors from the United States, on the other hand, are often highly critical of the treatment the Indians of Latin America receive. This strikes them as much more reprehensible than the treatment of the Negroes in their own country, who have indeed much greater opportunities to improve their economic position and who, as domestic servants, are treated with more courtesy and consideration by their employers than the Indians of Latin America — a fact not unconnected with the shortage of domestic servants in the United States. Moreover, the treatment of Indians appears all the less justifiable to these visitors because Indians are not the object of discrimination throughout the greater part of North America.

Thus, comfortably blinkered by the assumptions of their own culture, each nation sees the mite in the other's eye.

In the United States one does sometimes find strong sentiments of hostility toward Indians in areas surrounding their communities; the same is sometimes true in Latin America of the Negroes (however they happen to be defined there). If Indians are not generally subject to discrimination in the United States nor Negroes in Latin America, it is in the first place due to their numerical weakness. In both countries, they pose local, not national, problems. There is roughly one Indian to fifty Negroes in the

United States; in Latin America, the inverse disproportion would be greater even if one were to include only those recognized as Negro. Such comparison can be taken no further than this, however, since the nature of social distinctions is different in the two lands.

The Indian's predicament in Latin America can be likened to that of the Negro in the United States in only one way: Both provide a major national problem at the present time. There the resemblance stops. Not only is the nature of race relations fundamentally different in the societies that evolved from the English and Spanish colonies, but Indians and Negroes are different in their physical appearance and cultural origins. They are different above all in their place within the structure of the two societies, and have been so from the very beginning of colonial times. The Indians were the original inhabitants of the land; their incorporation or their refusal to be incorporated into colonial society hinged on the existence of Indian communities with a separate culture and a separate identity. The Negroes came in servile status and were marketed as chattel to the industrialized producers of sugar and metals. Cut off from their fellows, they soon lost their language and their original culture and became an integral part of colonial society.

The Negro's status was within colonial society. The Indian's was not. To the extent that the Indian abandoned his Indian community and changed his culture, he lost his Indian identity. While the status of Negro refers to phenotype and attaches to individuals, Indian status refers to culture and attaches to a collectivity. One might speak of individual versus collective status, with all that these imply in terms of social structure. Consequently, while phenotypical differences are irrelevant to the definition of the Indian — hence the *indio gringo* — they have importance in according an individual status once he becomes "civilized." They establish a presumption as to descent, and this is an ingredient of class status. Paradoxically, the genetic background is important only in social distinctions between persons who are recognized as belonging to the same "non-Indian" race; not in the distinction between them and the Indians. "Race" is a matter of culture and community, not of genes, though class is connected with genes.

The problems of race relations in North America and Latin America are, therefore, fundamentally different. One concerns the assimilation of all ethnic groups into a single society; the other, the status distinction between persons who have been assimilated for hundreds of years but who are still distinguished socially by their appearance. The two are comparable only at the highest level of abstraction. One may wonder, therefore, whether the word *caste,* which is so often used in reference to the status distinction between Indians and *mestizos* (or *ladinos*) in Latin American society is not something of a misnomer. It carries quite different implications in Latin as opposed to North America. It would appear that it comes into the sociological literature about Latin America on the basis of several different and all equally false assumptions which will be dealt with elsewhere.

While the value of color is somewhat similar within the Negro community of the United States and the Hispanic section of Latin America, the Negro community is separated by a *caste* distinction from a socially superior element defined by phenotype; the Hispanic population of Latin America is distinguished by language and customs, beliefs and values and habitat from an element it regards as inferior, which does not participate in the same social system and, for the most part, far from wishing to be integrated into it, desires only to be rid of the *mestizos* physically. For this reason, the aims of Indian rebellions are the opposite of the aims of race riots. The former would like to separate once and for all the two ethnic elements; the latter are inspired by the resentment at the existence of a separation. Indians rebel to drive the intruders out of the countryside; Negroes riot in towns when they are not accorded full civic privileges.

The ethnic statuses of modern Latin America vary in number from the simple division into Indian and *mestizo* found in Mexico north of the Isthmus to the four tiers of highland Peru which include *cholos* and *blancos: (indio, cholo, mestizo, blanco)*. These "social races" have much in common with the class distinctions of stratified societies. Woodrow Borah has even maintained that the ethnic distinction in Mexico is no more in essence than a matter of social class. This view raises a further problem in those areas where a regional ethnic consciousness emerges, for example among the Tlascalans, Isthmus Zapotecs, and the wealthy, educated Indians of Quetzaltenango in Guatemala.

Admitting that the class structure of Latin America carries ethnic overtones, how is this structure affected by class differences being thought about largely in the idiom of "race"? Such a view implies that classes are different in their essential nature. If the concept of "social race" teaches us to think about race in terms of social structure, we should also have a concept of "ethnic class" to remind us that class systems no longer function in the same way once class has phenotypical associations. Processes of selection come into operation that cannot exist in a homogeneous population however it is stratified.

This observation leads to a conclusion that does not altogether accord with that of Professor Wagley who states: "At least, theoretically, it is only a question of time until such populations may be entirely classed as mestizo by social race and social differentiation will be entirely in terms of socioeconomic classes." [4]

[4] Wagley, "On the Concept of Social Race in the Americas," p. 540.

In terms of his thesis continued racial intermixture produces in Latin America, unlike North America, a blurring of the distinctions among different "social races." This would be true enough, if time could be trusted to produce phenotypical homogeneity, but it ceases to be so once one introduces the notion of selection into the theory. The absence of a bar on intermarriage does not necessarily produce homogeneity.

Distinctions of status are not always exhibited in the same ways. The castes of India are held apart by prohibitions on physical contact and commensality, and by endogamy. Feudal Europe accorded no importance to the first two and little to the third. The division of labor implied by any social distinction can bring people into either direct cooperation or segregation, depending upon the range of their ties and the basis of their "complementarity." If their status difference is assured in one way, it may prove indifferent to any other basis of distinction. For this reason the intimacy to which servants were admitted by their masters was greater in an earlier age when social distinctions were more clear-cut.

Physical differences can never be obliterated, but whether they, rather than cultural or social differences, are regarded as significant is a matter each social system decides for itself. It is for this reason that the value accorded to physical appearance varies so greatly from place to place and class to class in Latin America. But the significance of phenotype also varies greatly according to context. Political or commercial alliances are not the same as alliances through marriage. Their products are of a different order. Profits are colorless, children are not. Hence, phenotype may not matter in commercial dealings, but it is never more important than in marriage.

In Latin America today the grandchildren of a rich man who looks Indian or Negroid always appear much more European than he is himself. Color is an ingredient, not a determinant of class. It can, therefore, be traded for the other ingredients. It is not something that can be altered in the individual's life, but it is something that can be put right in the next generation. For this reason, the wives of the well-to-do tend to look more European than their husbands. In the lower classes, paler children are sometimes favored at the expense of their more swarthy siblings; their potential for social mobility is greater.

Individual motivations are ordered to produce conformity with an ideal image of ethnic class. This tends to reinforce the original image. Moreover, demographical factors reinforce this conformity in other ways — through the immigration of Europeans into Latin America and the existence of a pool of unassimilated Indians on the land. Indians are constantly abandoning their Indian identity and becoming integrated into the nation. This process is not unconnected with the current flight to the cities, for you lose Indian status once you settle in the city. The result is a continual influx of persons of mainly Indian physique into the proletariat. At the same time, the immigration of Europeans into these countries has been very considerable in the last two decades, and these Europeans have almost all been absorbed into the upper classes. For demographic reasons, the correlation between class and color is increasing rather than diminishing.

Moreover, the significance of this correlation is also increasing under modern conditions. (It would be rash to say that it will go on increasing in the future, for the structure itself may well change to offset this effect.) The expansion of the open society at the expense of the local community changes the criteria whereby people are defined socially. Where known descent establishes status, color may carry little of the weight of social definition, but the descent must be known. It must be known whose child you are if you are to inherit the status of your father. If you have exchanged your local community for the big city, your descent becomes a matter of conjecture; you can no longer be respected because of your birth despite your Indian features. If you look Indian, it will be concluded that you were born of Indian parents. Thus, in the open society, appearances take over the function of descent in allocating social status. In a world in flux, the fact that appearance cannot be dissimulated recommends it above all other indicators. Clothing, speech, and culture are losing force as indicators of status in the context of expanding cities, but color is becoming ever more crucial.

Although these same conditions might create an increase in social mobility that would tend to reduce the phenotypical correlation of class, it appears that the opposite is happening today. If the classification into social races is losing its precision, the ethnic aspect of class is coming to have increased importance. The social structure is changing and with it the criteria of social classification. Under modern industrial conditions, much of Latin America is moving from the systems of social race that flourished in the communities of yesterday to a system of ethnic class adapted to the requirements of the open society of tomorrow.

16

Male and female: The doctor-nurse game

LEONARD I. STEIN

The preceding article by Pitt-Rivers focused on physical appearance as a basic criterion people use to classify each other and assign social worth. This article relates the characteristics of sex and occupational role to inequality. Leonard Stein describes the game played between doctor and nurse in American hospitals, the object of which is for the nurse to transmit recommendations for the treatment of patients to the doctor without appearing to challenge his authority as a male and a physician. Employing rules of behavior defined for this purpose in American culture, the nurse must be indirect and deferential as she advises on treatment, while the doctor must be positive and accepting. If either breaks the rules, interaction becomes strained, and effective working relations in the hospital break down.

The relationship between the doctor and the nurse is a very special one. There are few professions where the degree of mutual respect and cooperation between co-workers is as intense as that between the doctor and nurse. Superficially, the stereotype of this relationship has been dramatized in many novels and television serials. When, however, it is observed carefully in an interactional framework, the relationship takes on a new dimension and has a special quality which fits a game model. The underlying attitudes which demand that this game be played are unfortunate. These attitudes create serious obstacles in the path of meaningful communications between physicians and nonmedical professional groups.

The physician traditionally and appropriately has total responsibility for making the decisions regarding the management of his patients'

From "The Doctor-Nurse Game," *Archives of General Psychiatry* 16 (June 1967): 699–703. Reprinted by permission of the publisher and the author.

treatment. To guide his decisions he considers data gleaned from several sources. He acquires a complete medical history, performs a thorough physical examination, interprets laboratory findings, and at times, obtains recommendations from physician-consultants. Another important factor in his decision-making are the recommendations he receives from the nurse. The interaction between doctor and nurse through which these recommendations are communicated and received is unique and interesting.

THE GAME

One rarely hears a nurse say, "Doctor I would recommend that you order a retention enema for Mrs. Brown." A physician, upon hearing a recommendation of that nature, would gape in amazement at the effrontery of the nurse. The nurse, upon hearing the statement, would look over her shoulder to see who said it, hardly believing the words actually came from her own mouth. Nevertheless, if one observes closely, nurses make recommendations of more import every hour and physicians willingly and respectfully consider them. If the nurse is to make a suggestion without appearing insolent and the doctor is to seriously consider that suggestion, their interaction must not violate the rules of the game.

Object of the game. The object of the game is as follows: the nurse is to be bold, have initiative, and be responsible for making significant recommendations, while at the same time she must appear passive. This must be done in such a manner so as to make her recommendations appear to be initiated by the physician.

Both participants must be acutely sensitive to each other's nonverbal and cryptic verbal communications. A slight lowering of the head, a minor shifting of position in the chair, or a seemingly nonrelevant comment concerning an event which occurred eight months ago must be interpreted as a powerful message. The game requires the nimbleness of a high wire acrobat, and if either participant slips the game can be shattered; the penalties for frequent failure are apt to be severe.

Rules of the game. The cardinal rule of the game is that open disagreement between the players must be avoided at all costs. Thus, the nurse must communicate her recommendations without appearing to be making a recommendation statement. The physician, in requesting a recommendation from a nurse, must do so without appearing to be asking for it. Utilization of this technique keeps anyone from committing themselves to a position before a sub rosa agreement on that position has already been established. In that way open disagreement is avoided. The greater the significance of the recommendation, the more subtly the game must be played.

To convey a subtle example of the game with all its nuances would require the talents of a literary artist. Lacking these talents, let me give you the following example which is unsubtle, but happens frequently. The medical resident on hospital call is awakened by telephone at 1:00 A.M. because a patient on a ward, not his own, has not been able to fall asleep. Dr. Jones answers the telephone and the dialogue goes like this:

This is Dr. Jones.

(An open and direct communication.)

Dr. Jones, this is Miss Smith on 2W — Mrs. Brown, who learned today of her father's death, is unable to fall asleep.

(This message has two levels. Openly, it describes a set of circumstances, a woman who is unable to sleep and who that morning received word of her father's death. Less openly, but just as directly, it is a diagnostic and recommendation statement; i.e., Mrs. Brown is unable to sleep because of her grief, and she should be given a sedative. Dr. Jones, accepting the diagnostic statement and replying to the recommendation statement, answers.)

What sleeping medication has been helpful to Mrs. Brown in the past?

(Dr. Jones, not knowing the patient, is asking for a recommendation from the nurse, who does know the patient, about what sleeping medication should be prescribed. Note, however, his question does not appear to be asking her for a recommendation. Miss Smith replies.)

Pentobarbital mg 100 was quite effective night before last.

(A disguised recommendation statement. Dr. Jones replies with a note of authority in his voice.)

Pentobarbital mg 100 before bedtime as needed for sleep; got it?

(Miss Smith ends the conversation with the tone of a grateful supplicant.)

Yes, I have, and thank you very much doctor.

The above is an example of a successfully played doctor-nurse game. The nurse made appropriate recommendations which were accepted by the physician and were helpful to the patient. The game was successful because the cardinal rule was not violated. The nurse was able to make her recommendation without appearing to, and the physician was able to ask for recommendations without conspicuously asking for them.

The scoring system. Inherent in any game are penalties and rewards for the players. In game theory, the doctor-nurse game fits the nonzero sum game model. It is not like chess, where the players compete with each other and whatever one player loses the other wins. Rather, it is the kind of game in which the rewards and punishments are shared by both players. If they play the game successfully they both win rewards, and if they are unskilled and the game is played badly, they both suffer the penalty.

The most obvious reward from the well-played game is a doctor-nurse team that operates efficiently. The physician is able to utilize the nurse as a valuable consultant, and the nurse gains self-esteem and professional satisfaction from her job. The less obvious rewards are no less important. A successful game creates a doctor-nurse alliance; through this alliance the physician gains the respect and admiration of the nursing service. He can be confident that his nursing staff will smooth the path for getting his work done. His charts will be organized and waiting for him when he arrives, the ruffled feathers of patients and relatives will have been smoothed down, and his pet routines will be happily followed, and he will be helped in a thousand and one other ways.

The doctor-nurse alliance sheds its light on the nurse as well. She gains a reputation for being a "damn good nurse." She is respected by everyone and appropriately enjoys her position. When physicians discuss the nursing staff it would not be unusual for her name to be mentioned with respect and admiration. Their esteem for a good nurse is no less than their esteem for a good doctor.

The penalties for a game failure, on the other hand, can be severe. The physician who is an unskilled gamesman and fails to recognize the nurses' subtle recommendation messages is tolerated as a "clod." If, however, he interprets these messages as insolence and strongly indicates he does not wish to tolerate suggestions from nurses, he creates a rocky path for his travels. The old truism "If the nurse is your ally you've got it made, and if she has it in for you, be prepared for misery" takes on life-sized proportions. He receives three times as many phone calls after midnight than his colleagues. Nurses will not accept his telephone orders because "telephone orders are against the rules." Somehow, this rule gets suspended for the skilled players. Soon he becomes like Joe Bfstplk in the "Li'l Abner" comic strip. No matter where he goes, a black cloud constantly hovers over his head.

The unskilled gamesman nurse also pays heavily. The nurse who does not view her role as that of consultant, and therefore does not attempt to communicate recommendations, is perceived as a dullard and is mercifully allowed to fade into the woodwork.

The nurse who does see herself as a consultant but refuses to follow the rules of the game in making her recommendations has hell to pay. The outspoken nurse is labeled a "bitch" by the surgeon. The psychiatrist describes her as unconsciously suffering from penis envy and her behavior is the acting out of her hostility towards men. Loosely translated, the psychiatrist is saying she is a bitch. The employment of the unbright outspoken nurse is soon terminated. The outspoken bright nurse whose recommendations are worthwhile remains employed. She is, however, constantly reminded in a hundred ways that she is not loved.

Genesis of the game

To understand how the game evolved, we must comprehend the nature of the doctors' and nurses' training which shaped the attitudes necessary for the game.

Medical student training. The medical student in his freshman year studies as if possessed. In the anatomy class he learns every groove and prominence on the bones of the skeleton as if life depended on it. As a matter of fact, he literally believes just that. He not infrequently says, "I've got to learn it exactly; a life may depend on me knowing that." A consequence of this attitude, which is carefully nurtured throughout medical school, is the development of a phobia: the overdetermined fear of making a mistake. The development of this fear is quite understandable. The burden the physician must carry is at times almost unbearable. He feels responsible in a very personal way for the lives of his patients. When a man dies leaving young children and a widow, the doctor carries some of her grief and despair inside himself; and when a child dies, some of him dies too. He sees himself as a warrior against death and disease. When he loses a battle, through no fault of his own, he nevertheless feels pangs of guilt, and he relentlessly searches himself to see if there might have been a way to alter the outcome. For the physician a mistake leading to a serious consequence is intolerable, and any mistake reminds him of his vulnerability. There is little wonder that he becomes phobic. The classical way in which phobias are managed is to avoid the source of the fear. Since it is impossible to avoid making some mistakes in an active practice of medicine, a substitute defensive maneuver is employed. The physician develops the belief that he is omnipotent and omniscient, and therefore incapable of making mistakes. This belief allows the phobic physician to actively engage in his practice rather than avoid it. The fear of committing an error in a critical field like medicine is unavoidable and appropriately realistic. The physician, however, must learn to live with the fear rather than handle it defensively through a posture of omnipotence. This defense markedly interferes with his interpersonal professional relationships.

Physicians, of course, deny feelings of omnipotence. The evidence, however, renders their denials to whispers in the wind. The slightest mistake inflicts a large narcissistic wound. Depending on his underlying personality structure the physician may obsess for days about it, quickly rationalize it away, or deny it. The guilt produced is unusually exaggerated and the incident is handled defensively. The ways in which physicians enhance and support each other's defenses when an error is made could be the topic of another paper. The feeling of omnipotence become generalized to other areas of his life. A report of the Federal Aviation

Agency (FAA), as quoted in *Time Magazine* (August 5, 1966), states that in 1964 and 1965 physicians had a fatal-accident rate four times as high as the average for all other private pilots. Major causes of the high death rate were risk-taking attitudes and judgments. Almost all of the accidents occurred on pleasure trips, and were therefore not necessary risks to get to a patient needing emergency care. The trouble, suggested an FAA official, is that too many doctors fly with "the feeling that they are omnipotent." Thus, the extremes to which the physician may go in preserving his self-concept of omnipotence may threaten his own life. This overdetermined preservation of omnipotence is indicative of its brittleness and its underlying foundation of fear or failure.

The physician finds himself trapped in a paradox. He fervently wants to give his patient the best possible medical care, and being open to the nurses' recommendations helps him accomplish this. On the other hand, accepting advice from nonphysicians is highly threatening to his omnipotence. The solution for the paradox is to receive sub rosa recommendations and make them appear to be initiated by himself. In short, he must learn to play the doctor-nurse game.

Some physicians never learn to play the game. Most learn in their internship, and a perceptive few learn during their clerkships in medical school. Medical students frequently complain that the nursing staff treats them as if they had just completed a junior Red Cross first-aid class instead of two years of intensive medical training. Interviewing nurses in a training hospital sheds considerable light on this phenomenon. In their words they said,

> A few students just seem to be with it, they are able to understand what you are trying to tell them, and they are a pleasure to work with; most, however, pretend to know everything and refuse to listen to anything we have to say and I guess we do give them a rough time.

In essence, they are saying that those students who quickly learn the game are rewarded, and those that do not are punished.

Most physicians learn to play the game after they have weathered a few experiences like the one described below. On the first day of his internship, the physician and nurse were making rounds. They stopped at the bed of a fifty-two-year-old woman who, after complimenting the young doctor on his appearance, complained to him of her problem with constipation. After several minutes of listening to her detailed description of peculiar diets, family home remedies, and special exercises that have helped her constipation in the past, the nurse politely interrupted the patient. She told her the doctor would take care of the problem and that he had to move on because there were other patients waiting to see him. The young doctor gave the nurse a stern look, turned toward the patient, and kindly told her he would order an enema for her that very afternoon. As they left the bedside, the nurse told him the patient has had a normal bowel movement every day for the past week and that in the twenty-three days the patient has been in the hospital she has never once passed up an opportunity to complain of her constipation. She quickly added that *if* the doctor wanted to order an enema, the patient would certainly receive one. After hearing this report the intern's mouth fell open and the wheels began turning in his head. He remembered the nurse's comment to the patient that "the doctor had to move on," and it occurred to him that perhaps she was really giving him a message. This experience and a few more like it, and the young doctor learns to listen for the subtle recommendations the nurses make.

Nursing student training. Unlike the medical student who usually learns to play the game after he finishes medical school, the nursing student begins to learn it early in her training. Throughout her education she is trained to play the doctor-nurse game.

Student nurses are taught how to relate to physicians. They are told he has infinitely more knowledge than they, and thus he should be shown the utmost respect. In addition, it was not many years ago when nurses were instructed to stand whenever a physician entered a room. When he would come in for a conference the nurse was expected to offer him her chair, and when both entered a room the nurse would open the door for him and allow him to enter first. Although these practices are no longer rigidly adhered to, the premise upon which they were based is still promulgated. One nurse described that premise as, "He's God almighty and your job is to wait on him."

To inculcate subservience and inhibit deviancy, nursing schools, for the most part, are tightly run, disciplined institutions. Certainly there is great variation among nursing schools, and there is little question that the trend is toward giving students more autonomy. However, in too many schools this trend has not gone far enough, and the climate remains restrictive. The student's schedule is firmly controlled and there is very little free time. Classroom hours, study hours, mealtime, and bedtime with lights out are rigidly enforced. In some schools meaningless chores are assigned, such as cleaning bedsprings with cotton applicators. The relationship between student and instructor continues this military flavor. Often their relationship is more like that between recruit and drill sergeant than between student and teacher. Open dialogue is inhibited by attitudes of strict black and white, with few, if any, shades of gray. Straying from the rigidly outlined path is sure to result in disciplinary action.

The inevitable result of these practices is to instill in the student nurse a fear of independent action. This inhibition of independent action is most marked when relating to physicians. One of the students' greatest fears is making a blunder while assisting a physician and being publicly ridiculed by him. This is really more a reflection of the nature of their training than the prevalence of abusive physicians. The fear of being humiliated for a blunder while assisting in a procedure is generalized to the fear of humiliation for making any independent act in relating to a physician, especially the act of making a direct recommendation. Every nurse interviewed felt that making a suggestion to a physician was equivalent to insulting and belittling him. It was tantamount to questioning his medical knowledge and insinuating he did not know his business. In light of her image of the physician as an omniscient and punitive figure, the questioning of his knowledge would be unthinkable.

The student, however, is also given messages quite contrary to the ones described above. She is continually told that she is an invaluable aid to the physician in the treatment of the patient. She is told that she must help him in every way possible, and she is imbued with a strong sense of responsibility for the care of her patient. Thus she, like the physician, is caught in a paradox. The first set of messages implies that the physician is omniscient and that any recommendation she might make would be insulting to him and leave her open to ridicule. The second set of messages implies that she is an important asset to him, has much to contribute, and is duty-bound to make those contributions. Thus, when her good sense tells her a recommendation would be helpful to him she is not allowed to communicate it directly, nor is she allowed not to communicate it. The way out of the bind is to use the doctor-nurse game and communicate the recommendation without appearing to do so.

Forces preserving the game

Upon observing the indirect interactional system which is the heart of the doctor-nurse game, one must ask the question, "Why does this inefficient mode of communication continue to exist?" The forces mitigating against change are powerful.

Rewards and punishments. The doctor-nurse game has a powerful innate self-perpetuating force — its system of rewards and punishments. One potent method of shaping behavior is to reward one set of behavioral patterns and to punish patterns which deviate from it. As described earlier, the rewards given for a well-played game and the punishments meted out to unskilled players are impressive. This system alone would be sufficient to keep the game flourishing. The game, however, has additional forces.

The strength of the set. It is well recognized that sets are hard to break. A powerful attitudinal set is the nurse's perception that making a suggestion to a physician is equivalent to insulting and belittling him. An example of where attempts are regularly made to break this set is seen on psychiatric treatment wards operating on a therapeutic community model. This model requires open and direct communication between members of the team. Psychiatrists working in these settings expend a great deal of energy in urging for and rewarding openness before direct patterns of communication become established. The rigidity of the resistance to break this set is impressive. If the physician himself is a prisoner of a set and therefore does not actively try to destroy it, change is near impossible.

The need for leadership. Lack of leadership and structure in any organization produces anxiety in its members. As the importance of the organization's mission increases, the demand by its members for leadership commensurately increases. In our culture human life is near the top of our hierarchy of values, and organizations which deal with human lives, such as law and medicine, are very rigidly structured. Certainly some of this is necessary for the systematic management of the task. The excessive degree of rigidity, however, is demanded by its members for their own psychic comfort rather than for its utility in efficiently carrying out its mission. The game lends support to this thesis. Indirect communication is an inefficient mode of transmitting information. However, it effectively supports and protects a rigid organizational structure with the physician in clear authority. Maintaining an omnipotent leader provides the other members with a great sense of security.

Sexual roles. Another influence perpetuating the doctor-nurse game is the sexual identity of the players. Doctors are predominately men and nurses are almost exclusively women. There are elements of the game which reinforce the stereotyped roles of male dominance and female passivity. Some nursing instructors explicitly tell their students that their femininity is an important asset to be used when relating to physicians.

The community

The doctor and nurse have a shared history and thus have been able to work out their game so that it operates more efficiently than one would expect in an indirect system. Major difficulty arises, however, when the physician works closely with other disciplines which are not normally considered part of the medical sphere. With expanding medical horizons encompassing cooperation with sociologists, engineers, anthropologists, computer analysts, etc., continued expectation of a doctor-nurselike interaction by the physician is disastrous. The sociologist, for example, is not willing to play that kind of game. When his direct communications are rebuffed the relationship breaks down.

The major disadvantage of a doctor-nurselike game is its inhibitory effect on open dialogue which is stifling and anti-intellectual. The game is basically a transactional neurosis, and both professions would enhance themselves by taking steps to change the attitudes which breed the game. . . .

17

Stereotypes: Explaining people who are different

OZZIE G. SIMMONS

Inequality and accompanying social distance leads to the formation of different group identities. This article by Ozzie Simmons is concerned with the principal assumptions and expectations that Anglo- and Mexican-Americans have of one another in a South Texas town: how they see each other; the extent to which these pictures are realistic; and the implications of their intergroup relations and cultural differences for fulfillment of their mutual expectations. The Anglo-Americans hold the superior position and possess stereotypes of themselves and Mexican-Americans that support their status. Mexican-Americans seek equality with Anglos, but on terms that preserve what they feel is best in Mexican culture.

A number of psychological and sociological studies have treated ethnic and racial stereotypes as they appear publicly in the mass media and also as held privately by individuals. The present paper is based on data collected for a study of a number of aspects of the relations between Anglo-Americans and Mexican-Americans in a South Texas community, and is concerned with the principal assumptions and expectations that Anglo- and Mexican-Americans hold of one another; how they see each other; the extent to which these pictures are realistic; and the implications of their mutual expectations.

From "The Mutual Images and Expectations of Anglo-Americans and Mexican-Americans," *Daedalus* 90 (Spring 1961): 286–299. Reprinted by permission of the publisher and the author from *Daedalus*, Journal of the American Academy of Arts and Sciences, Boston, Massachusetts. Most of the references are omitted.

THE COMMUNITY

The community studied (here called "Border City") is in South Texas, about 250 miles south of San Antonio. Driving south from San Antonio, one passes over vast expanses of brushland and grazing country, then suddenly comes upon acres of citrus groves, farmlands rich with vegetables and cotton, and long rows of palm trees. This is the "Magic Valley," an oasis in the semidesert region of South Texas. The Missouri Pacific Railroad (paralleled by Highway 83, locally called "The longest street in the world") bisects twelve major towns and cities of the Lower Rio Grande Valley between Brownsville, near the Gulf of Mexico, and Rio Grande City, 103 miles to the west.

Border City is neither the largest nor the smallest of these cities, and is physically and culturally much like the rest. Its first building was constructed in 1905. By 1920 it had 5,331 inhabitants, and at the time of our study these had increased to an estimated 17,500. The completion of the St. Louis, Brownsville, and Mexico Railroad in 1904 considerably facilitated Anglo-American immigration to the Valley. Before this the Valley had been inhabited largely by Mexican ranchers, who maintained large haciendas in the traditional Mexican style based on peonage. Most of these haciendas are now divided into large or small tracts that are owned by Anglo-Americans, who obtained them through purchase or less legitimate means. The position of the old Mexican-American landowning families has steadily deteriorated, and today these families, with a few exceptions, are completely overshadowed by the Anglo-Americans, who have taken over their social and economic position in the community.

The Anglo-American immigration into the Valley was paralleled by that of the Mexicans from across the border, who were attracted by the seemingly greater opportunities for farm labor created by the introduction of irrigation and the subsequent agricultural expansion. Actually, there had been a small but steady flow of Mexican immigration into South Texas that long antedated the Anglo-American immigration. At present, Mexican-Americans probably constitute about two-fifths of the total population of the Valley.

In Border City, Mexican-Americans comprise about 56 percent of the population. The southwestern part of the city, adjoining and sometimes infiltrating the business and industrial areas, is variously referred to as "Mexiquita," "Mexican-town," and "Little Mexico" by the city's Anglo-Americans, and as the *colonia* by the Mexican-Americans. With few exceptions, the *colonia* is inhabited only by Mexican-Americans, most of whom live in close proximity to one another in indifferently constructed houses on tiny lots. The north side of the city, which lies across the railroad tracks, is inhabited almost completely by Anglo-Americans. Its appearance is in sharp contrast to that of the *colonia* in that it is strictly residential and displays much better housing.

In the occupational hierarchy of Border City, the top level (the growers, packers, canners, businessmen, and professionals) is overwhelmingly Anglo-American. In the middle group (the white-collar occupations) Mexicans are prominent only where their bilingualism makes them useful, for example, as clerks and salesmen. The bottom level (farm laborers, shed and cannery workers, and domestic servants) is overwhelmingly Mexican-American.

These conditions result from a number of factors, some quite distinct from the reception accorded Mexican-Americans by Anglo-Americans. Many Mexican-Americans are still recent immigrants and are thus relatively unfamiliar with Anglo-American culture and urban living, or else persist in their tendency to live apart and maintain their own institutions whenever possible. Among their disadvantages, however, the negative attitudes and discriminatory practices of the Anglo-American group must be counted. It is only fair to say, with the late Ruth Tuck, that much of what Mexican-Americans have suffered at Anglo-American hands has not been perpetrated deliberately but through indifference, that it has been done not with the fist but with the elbow. The average social and economic status of the Mexican-American group has been improving, and many are moving upward. This is partly owing to increasing acceptance by the Anglo-American group, but chiefly to the efforts of the Mexican-Americans themselves.

Anglo-American assumptions and expectations

Robert Lynd writes of the dualism in the principal assumptions that guide Americans in conducting their everyday life and identifies the attempt to "live by contrasting rules of the game" as a characteristic aspect of our culture.[1] This pattern of moral compromise, symptomatic of what is likely to be only vaguely a conscious moral conflict, is evident in Anglo-American assumptions and expectations with regard to Mexican-Americans, which appear both in the moral principles that define what intergroup relations ought to be, and in the popular notions held by Anglo-Americans as to what Mexican-Americans are "really" like. In the first case there is a response to the "American creed," which embodies ideals of the essential dignity of the individual and of certain inalienable rights to freedom, justice, and equal opportunity. Accordingly, Anglo-Americans believe that Mexican-Americans must be accorded full acceptance and equal status in the larger society. When their orientation to these ideals is uppermost, Anglo-Americans believe that the assimilation

[1] Robert S. Lynd, *Knowledge for What?* (Princeton: Princeton University Press, 1948).

of Mexican-Americans is only a matter of time, contingent solely on the full incorporation of Anglo-American values and ways of life.

These expectations regarding the assimilation of the Mexican are most clearly expressed in the notion of the "high type" of Mexican. It is based on three criteria: occupational achievement and wealth (the Anglo-American's own principal criteria of status) and command of Anglo-American ways. Mexican-Americans who can so qualify are acceptable for membership in the service clubs and a few other Anglo-American organizations and for limited social intercourse. They may even intermarry without being penalized or ostracized. Both in their achievements in business and agriculture and in wealth, they compare favorably with middle-class Anglo-Americans, and they manifest a high command of the latter's ways. This view of the "high type" of Mexican reflects the Anglo-American assumption that Mexicans are assimilable; it does not necessarily insure a full acceptance of even the "high type" of Mexican or that his acceptance will be consistent.

The assumption that Mexican-Americans will be ultimately assimilated was not uniformly shared by all the Anglo-Americans who were our informants in Border City. Regardless of whether they expressed adherence to this ideal, however, most Anglo-Americans expressed the contrasting assumption that Mexican-Americans are essentially inferior. Thus the same people may hold assumptions and expectations that are contradictory, although expressed at different times and in different situations. As in the case of their adherence to the ideal of assimilability, not all Anglo-Americans hold the same assumptions and expectations with respect to the inferiority of Mexican-Americans; and even those who agree vary in the intensity of their beliefs. Some do not believe in the Mexican's inferiority at all; some are relatively moderate or sceptical, while others express extreme views with considerable emotional intensity.

Despite this variation, the Anglo-Americans' principal assumptions and expectations emphasize the Mexicans' presumed inferiority. In its most characteristic pattern, such inferiority is held to be self-evident. As one Anglo-American woman put it, "Mexicans are inferior because they are so typically and naturally Mexican." Since they are so obviously inferior, their present subordinate status is appropriate and is really their own fault. There is a ready identification between Mexicans and menial labor, buttressed by an image of the Mexican worker as improvident, undependable, irresponsible, childlike, and indolent. If Mexicans are fit for only the humblest labor, there is nothing abnormal about the fact that most Mexican workers are at the bottom of the occupational pyramid, and the fact that most Mexicans are unskilled workers is sufficient proof that they belong in that category.

Associated with the assumption of Mexican inferiority is that of the homogeneity of this group — that is, all Mexicans are alike. Anglo-Americans may classify Mexicans as being of "high type" and "low type" and at the same time maintain that "a Mexican is a Mexican." Both notions serve a purpose, depending on the situation. The assumption that all Mexicans are alike buttresses the assumption of inferiority by making it convenient to ignore the fact of the existence of a substantial number of Mexican-Americans who represent all levels of business and professional achievement. Such people are considered exceptions to the rule.

Anglo-American images of Mexican-Americans

To employ Gordon Allport's definition, a stereotype is an exaggerated belief associated with a category, and its function is to justify conduct in relation to that category.[2] Some of the Anglo-American images of the Mexican have no ascertainable basis in fact, while others have at least a kernel of truth. Although some components of these images derive from behavior patterns that are characteristic of some Mexican-Americans in some situations, few if any of the popular generalizations about them are valid as stated, and none is demonstrably true of all. Some of the images of Mexican-Americans are specific to a particular area of intergroup relations, such as the image of the Mexican-American's attributes as a worker. Another is specific to politics and describes Mexicans as ready to give their votes to whoever will pay for them or provide free barbecues and beer. Let us consider a few of the stereotypical beliefs that are widely used on general principles to justify Anglo-American practices of exclusion and subordination.

One such general belief accuses Mexican-Americans of being unclean. The examples given of this supposed characteristic most frequently refer to a lack of personal cleanliness and environmental hygiene and to a high incidence of skin ailments ascribed to a lack of hygienic practices. Indeed, there are few immigrant groups, regardless of their ethnic background, to whom this defect has not been attributed by the host society, as well as others prominent in stereotypes of the Mexican. It has often been observed that for middle-class Americans cleanliness is not simply a matter of keeping clean but is also an index to the morals and virtues of the individual. It is largely true that Mexicans tend to be much more casual in hygienic practices than Anglo-Americans. Moreover, their labor in the field, the packing sheds, and the towns is rarely clean work, and it is possible that many Anglo-Americans base their conclusions on what they observe in such situations. There is no evidence of a higher incidence of skin ailments among Mexicans than among Anglo-Americans. The belief that Mexicans are unclean is useful for rationalizing the Anglo-American

[2] Gordon W. Allport, *The Nature of Prejudice* (Cambridge: Addison-Wesley Publishing Company, 1954).

practice of excluding Mexicans from any situation that involves close or allegedly close contact with Anglo-Americans, as in residence, and the common use of swimming pools and other recreational facilities.

Drunkenness and criminality are a pair of traits that have appeared regularly in the sterotypes applied to immigrant groups. They have a prominent place in Anglo-American images of Mexicans. If Mexicans are inveterate drunkards and have criminal tendencies, a justification is provided for excluding them from full participation in the life of the community. It is true that drinking is a popular activity among Mexican Americans and that total abstinence is rare, except among some Protestant Mexican-Americans. Drinking varies, however, from the occasional consumption of a bottle of beer to the heavy drinking of more potent beverages, so that the frequency of drinking and drunkenness is far from being evenly distributed among Mexican-Americans. Acually, this pattern is equally applicable to the Anglo-American group. The ample patronage of bars in the Anglo-American part of Border City, and the drinking behavior exhibited by Anglo-Americans when they cross the river to Mexico indicate that Mexicans have no monopoly on drinking or drunkenness. It is true that the number of arrests for drunkenness in Border City is greater among Mexicans, but this is probably because Mexicans are more vulnerable to arrest. The court records in Border City show little difference in the contributions made to delinquency and crime by Anglo- and Mexican-Americans.

Another cluster of images in the Anglo-American stereotype portrays Mexican-Americans as deceitful and of a "low" morality, as mysterious, unpredictable, and hostile to Anglo-Americans. It is quite possible that Mexicans resort to a number of devices in their relations with Anglo-Americans, particularly in relations with employers, to compensate for their disadvantages, which may be construed by Anglo-Americans as evidence of deceitfulness. The whole nature of the dominant-subordinate relationship does not make for frankness on the part of Mexicans or encourage them to face up directly to Anglo-Americans in most intergroup contacts. As to the charge of immorality, one need only recognize the strong sense of loyalty and obligation that Mexicans feel in their familial and interpersonal relations to know that the charge is baseless. The claim that Mexicans are mysterious and deceitful may in part reflect Anglo-American reactions to actual differences in culture and personality, but like the other beliefs considered here, is highly exaggerated. The imputation of hostility to Mexicans, which is manifested in a reluctance to enter the *colonia*, particularly at night, may have its kernel of truth, but appears to be largely a projection of the Anglo-American's own feelings.

All three of these images can serve to justify exclusion and discrimination: if Mexicans are deceitful and immoral, they do not have to be accorded equal status and justice; if they are mysterious and unpredictable, there is no point in treating them as one would a fellow Anglo-American; and if they are hostile and dangerous, it is best that they live apart in colonies of their own.

Not all Anglo-American images of the Mexican are unfavorable. Among those usually meant to be complimentary are the beliefs that all Mexicans are musical and always ready for a fiesta, that they are very "romantic" rather than "realistic" (which may have unfavorable overtones as well), and that they love flowers and can grow them under the most adverse conditions. Although each of these beliefs may have a modicum of truth, it may be noted that they tend to reinforce Anglo-American images of Mexicans as childlike and irresponsible, and thus they support the notion that Mexicans are capable only of subordinate status.

Mexican-American assumptions, expectations, and images

Mexican-Americans are as likely to hold contradictory assumptions and distorted images as are Anglo-Americans. Their principal assumptions, however, must reflect those of Anglo-Americans — that is, Mexicans must take into account the Anglo-Americans' conflict as to their potential equality and present inferiority, since they are the object of such imputations. Similarly, their images of Anglo-Americans are not derived wholly independently, but to some extent must reflect their own subordinate status. Consequently, their stereotypes of Anglo-Americans are much less elaborate, in part because Mexicans feel no need of justifying the present intergroup relation, in part because the very nature of their dependent position forces them to view the relation more realistically than Anglo-Americans do. For the same reasons, they need not hold to their beliefs about Anglo-Americans with the rigidity and intensity so often characteristic of the latter.

Any discussion of these assumptions and expectations requires some mention of the class distinctions within the Mexican-American group. Its middle class, though small as compared with the lower class, is powerful within the group and performs the critical role of intermediary in negotiations with the Anglo-American group. Middle-class status is based on education and occupation, family background, readiness to serve the interests of the group, on wealth, and the degree of acculturation, or command of Anglo-American ways. Anglo-Americans recognize Mexican class distinctions (although not very accurately) in their notions of the "high type" and "low type" of Mexicans.

In general, lower-class Mexicans do not regard the disabilities of their status as being nearly as severe as do middle-class Mexican-Americans. This is primarily a reflection of the insulation between the Anglo-American world and that of the Mexican lower class. Most Mexicans, regardless of class, are keenly aware of Anglo-American attitudes and practices with regard to their group, but lower-class Mexicans do not conceive of participation in the larger society as necessary nor do they regard Anglo-American practices of exclusion as affecting them directly. Their principal reaction has been to maintain their isolation, and thus they have not been particularly concerned with improving their status by acquiring Anglo-American ways, a course more characteristic of the middle-class Mexican.

Mexican-American assumptions and expectations regarding Anglo-Americans must be qualified, then, as being more characteristic of middle- than of lower-class Mexican-Americans. Mexicans, like Anglo-Americans, are subject to conflicts in their ideals, not only because of irrational thinking on their part but also because of Anglo-American inconsistencies between ideal and practice. As for ideals expressing democratic values, Mexican expectations are for obvious reasons the counterpart of the Anglo-Americans' — that Mexican-Americans should be accorded full acceptance and equal opportunity. They feel a considerable ambivalence, however, as to the Anglo-American expectation that the only way to achieve this goal is by a full incorporation of Anglo-American values and ways of life, for this implies the ultimate loss of their cultural identity as Mexicans. On the one hand, they favor the acquisition of Anglo-American culture and the eventual remaking of the Mexican in the Anglo-American image; but on the other hand, they are not so sure that Anglo-American acceptance is worth such a price. When they are concerned with this dilemma, Mexicans advocate a fusion with Anglo-American culture in which the "best" of the Mexican ways, as they view it, would be retained along with the incorporation of the "best" of the Anglo-American ways, rather than a one-sided exchange in which all that is distinctively Mexican would be lost.

A few examples will illustrate the point of view expressed in the phrase, "the best of both ways." A premium is placed on speaking good, unaccented English, but the retention of good Spanish is valued just as highly as "a mark of culture that should not be abandoned." Similarly, there is an emphasis on the incorporation of behavior patterns that are considered characteristically Anglo-American and that will promote "getting ahead," but not to the point at which the drive for power and wealth would become completely dominant, as is believed to be the case with Anglo-Americans.

Mexican ambivalence about becoming Anglo-American or achieving a fusion of the "best" of both cultures is compounded by their ambivalence about another issue, that of equality versus inferiority. That Anglo-Americans are dominant in the society and seem to monopolize its accomplishments and rewards leads Mexicans at times to draw the same conclusion that Anglo-Americans do, namely, that Mexicans are inferior.

This questioning of their own sense of worth exists in all classes of the Mexican-American group, although with varying intensity, and plays a substantial part in every adjustment to intergroup relations. There is a pronounced tendency to concede the superiority of Anglo-American ways and consequently to define Mexican ways as undesirable, inferior, and disreputable. The tendency to believe in his own inferiority is counterbalanced, however, by the Mexican's fierce racial pride, which sets the tone of Mexican demands and strivings for equal status, even though these may slip into feelings of inferiority.

The images Mexicans have of Anglo-Americans may not be so elaborate or so emotionally charged as the images that Anglo-Americans have of Mexicans, but they are nevertheless stereotypes, over-generalized, and exaggerated, although used primarily for defensive rather than justificatory purposes. Mexican images of Anglo-Americans are sometimes favorable, particularly when they identify such traits as initiative, ambition, and industriousness as being peculiarly Anglo-American. Unfavorable images are prominent, however, and, although they may be hostile, they never impute inferiority to Anglo-Americans. Most of the Mexican stereotypes evaluate Anglo-Americans on the basis of their attitudes toward Mexican-Americans. For example, one such classification provides a twofold typology. The first type, the "majority," includes those who are cold, unkind, mercenary, and exploitative. The second type, the "minority," consists of those who are friendly, warm, just, and unprejudiced. For the most part, Mexican images of Anglo-Americans reflect the latter's patterns of exclusion and assumptions of superiority, as experienced by Mexican-Americans. Thus Anglo-Americans are pictured as stolid, phlegmatic, cold-hearted, and distant. They are also said to be braggarts, conceited, inconstant, and insincere.

Intergroup relations, mutual expectations, and cultural differences

A number of students of intergroup relations assert that research in this area has yet to demonstrate any relation between stereotypical beliefs and intergroup behavior; indeed, some insist that under certain conditions ethnic attitudes and discrimination can vary independently. Arnold M. Rose, for example, concludes that "from a heuristic standpoint it may be desirable to assume that patterns of intergroup relations, on the one hand, and attitudes of prejudice and stereotyping, on the other hand, are fairly unrelated phenomena although they have reciprocal influences on each other. . . ."[3] In the present study, no systematic attempt was made to investigate the relation between the stereotypical beliefs of particular individuals and their actual intergroup behavior; but the study did yield much

[3] Arnold M. Rose, "Intergroup Relations vs. Prejudice: Pertinent Theory for the Study of Social Change," *Social Problems* 4 (1956): 173–176.

evidence that both images which justify group separatism and separateness itself are characteristic aspects of intergroup relations in Border City. One of the principal findings is that in those situations in which contact between Anglo-Americans and Mexicans is voluntary (such as residence, education, recreation, religious worship, and social intercourse) the characteristic pattern is separateness rather than common participation. Wherever intergroup contact is necessary, as in occupational activities and the performance of commercial and professional services, it is held to the minimum sufficient to accomplish the purpose of the contact. The extent of this separateness is not constant for all members of the two groups, since it tends to be less severe between Anglo-Americans and those Mexicans they define as of a "high type." Nevertheless, the evidence reveals a high degree of compatibility between beliefs and practices in Border City's intergroup relations, although the data have nothing to offer for the identification of direct relationships.

In any case, the separateness that characterizes intergroup relations cannot be attributed solely to the exclusion practices of the Anglo-American group. Mexicans have tended to remain separate by choice as well as by necessity. Like many other ethnic groups, they have often found this the easier course, since they need not strain to learn another language or to change their ways and manners. The isolation practices of the Mexican group are as relevant to an understanding of intergroup relations as are the exclusion practices of the Anglo-Americans.

This should not, however, obscure the fact that to a wide extent the majority of Mexican-Americans share the patterns of living of Anglo-American society; many of their ways are already identical. Regardless of the degree of their insulation from the larger society, the demands of life in the United States have required basic modifications of the Mexicans' cultural tradition. In material culture, Mexicans are hardly to be distinguished from Anglo-Americans, and there have been basic changes in medical beliefs and practices and in the customs regarding godparenthood. Mexicans have acquired English in varying degrees, and their Spanish has become noticeably Anglicized. Although the original organization of the family has persisted, major changes have occurred in patterns of traditional authority, as well as in child training and courtship practices. Still, it is the exceedingly rare Mexican-American, no matter how acculturated he may be to the dominant society, who does not in some degree retain the more subtle characteristics of his Mexican heritage, particularly in his conception of time and in other fundamental value orientations, as well as in his modes of participation in interpersonal relations. Many of the most acculturated Mexican-Americans have attempted to exemplify what they regard as "the best of both ways." They have become largely Anglo-American in their way of living, but they still retain fluent Spanish and a knowledge of their traditional culture, and they maintain an identification with their own heritage while participating in Anglo-American culture. Nevertheless, this sort of achievement still seems a long way off for many Mexican-Americans who regard it as desirable.

A predominant Anglo-American expectation is that the Mexicans will be eventually assimilated into the larger society; but this is contingent upon Mexicans' becoming just like Anglo-Americans. The Mexican counterpart to this expectation is only partially complementary. Mexicans want to be full members of the larger society, but they do not want to give up their cultural heritage. There is even less complementarity of expectation with regard to the present conduct of intergroup relations. Anglo-Americans believe they are justified in withholding equal access to the rewards of full acceptance as long as Mexicans remain "different," particularly since they interpret the differences (both those which have some basis in reality and those which have none) as evidence of inferiority. Mexicans, on the other hand, while not always certain that they are not inferior, clearly want equal opportunity and full acceptance now, not in some dim future, and they do not believe that their differences (either presumed or real) from Anglo-Americans offer any justification for the denial of opportunity and acceptance. Moreover, they do not find that acculturation is rewarded in any clear and regular way by progressive acceptance.

It is probable that both Anglo-Americans and Mexicans will have to modify their beliefs and practices if they are to realize more nearly their expectations of each other. Mutual stereotyping, as well as the exclusion practices of Anglo-Americans and the isolation practices of Mexicans, maintains the separateness of the two groups, and separateness is a massive barrier to the realization of their expectations. The process of acculturation is presently going on among Mexican-Americans and will continue, regardless of whether changes in Anglo-Mexican relations occur. Unless Mexican-Americans can validate their increasing command of Anglo-American ways by a free participation in the larger society, however, such acculturation is not likely to accelerate its present leisurely pace, nor will it lead to eventual assimilation. The *colonia* is a relatively safe place in which new cultural acquisitions may be tried out, and thus it has its positive functions; but by the same token it is only in intergroup contacts with Anglo-Americans that acculturation is validated, that the Mexican's level of acculturation is tested, and that the distance he must yet travel to assimilation is measured.

Conclusions

There are major inconsistencies in the assumptions that Anglo-Americans and Mexican-Americans hold about one another. Anglo-Americans assume that Mexican-Americans are their potential, if not actual, peers, but at the same time assume they are their inferiors. The beliefs that presumably demonstrate the Mexican-Americans' inferiority tend to place them outside the accepted moral order and framework of Anglo-American society by attributing to them undesirable characteristics that make it "reasonable" to treat them differently from their fellow Anglo-Americans. Thus the negative images provide not only a rationalized definition of the intergroup relation that makes it palatable for Anglo-Americans, but also a substantial support for maintaining the relation as it is. The assumptions of Mexican-Americans about Anglo-Americans are similarly inconsistent, and their images of Anglo-Americans are predominantly negative, although these are primarily defensive rather than justificatory. The mutual expectations of the two groups contrast sharply with the ideal of a complementarity of expectations, in that Anglo-Americans expect Mexicans to become just like themselves, if they are to be accorded equal status in the larger society, whereas Mexican-Americans want full acceptance, regardless of the extent to which they give up their own ways and acquire those of the dominant group.

Anglo-Americans and Mexicans may decide to stay apart because they are different, but cultural differences provide no moral justification for one group to deny to the other equal opportunity and the rewards of the larger society. If the full acceptance of Mexicans by Anglo-Americans is contingent upon the disappearance of cultural differences, it will not be accorded in the foreseeable future. In our American society, we have often seriously underestimated the strength and tenacity of early cultural conditioning. We have expected newcomers to change their customs and values to conform to American ways as quickly as possible, without an adequate appreciation of the strains imposed by this process. An understanding of the nature of culture and of its interrelations with personality can make us more realistic about the rate at which cultural change can proceed and about the gains and costs for the individual who is subject to the experiences of acculturation. In viewing cultural differences primarily as disabilities, we neglect their positive aspects. Mexican-American culture represents the most constructive and effective means Mexican-Americans have yet been able to develop for coping with their changed natural and social environment. They will further exchange old ways for new only if these appear to be more meaningful and rewarding than the old, and then only if they are given full opportunity to acquire the new ways and to use them.

18

The culture of poverty

OSCAR LEWIS

Poverty is more than lack of money — it is a way of life that is a response to impoverished economic conditions. In this article, Oscar Lewis outlines the main features of this culture: poverty, low esteem, woman-dominated families, fatalism, and hostility to the established society. And he briefly analyzes their implications for social change.

Poverty and the so-called war against it provide a principal theme for the domestic program of the present Administration. In the midst of a population that enjoys unexampled material well-being — with the average annual family income exceeding $7,000 — it is officially acknowledged that some 18 million families, numbering more than 50 million individuals, live below the $3,000 "poverty line." Toward the improvement of the lot of these people some $1,600 million of Federal funds are directly allocated through the Office of Economic Opportunity, and many hundreds of millions of additional dollars flow indirectly through expanded Federal expenditures in the fields of health, education, welfare, and urban affairs.

Along with the increase in activity on behalf of the poor indicated by these figures there has come a parallel expansion of publication in the social sciences on the subject of poverty. The new writings advance the same two opposed evaluations of the poor that are to be found in literature, in proverbs, and in popular sayings throughout recorded history. Just as the poor have been pronounced blessed, virtuous, upright, serene, independent, honest, kind and happy, so contemporary students stress

From "The Culture of Poverty," *Scientific American* 215 (October 1966): 19–25.
 An expanded version of this article appears in *La Vida* by Oscar Lewis. Illustrations are omitted.

their great and neglected capacity for self-help, leadership, and community organization. Conversely, as the poor have been characterized as shiftless, mean, sordid, violent, evil, and criminal, so other students point to the irreversibly destructive effects of poverty on individual character and emphasize the corresponding need to keep guidance and control of poverty projects in the hands of duly constituted authorities. This clash of viewpoints reflects in part the infighting for political control of the program between Federal and local officials. The confusion results also from the tendency to focus study and attention on the personality of the individual victim of poverty rather than on the slum community and family and from the consequent failure to distinguish between poverty and what I have called the culture of poverty.

The phrase is a catchy one and is used and misused with some frequency in the current literature. In my writings it is the label for a specific conceptual model that describes in positive terms a subculture of Western society with its own structure and rationale, a way of life handed on from generation to generation along family lines. The culture of poverty is not just a matter of deprivation or disorganization, a term signifying the absence of something. It is a culture in the traditional anthropological sense in that it provides human beings with a design for living, with a ready-made set of solutions for human problems, and so serves a significant adaptive function. This style of life transcends national boundaries and regional and rural-urban differences within nations. Wherever it occurs, its practitioners exhibit remarkable similarity in the structure of their families, in interpersonal relations, in spending habits, in their value systems, and in their orientation in time.

Not nearly enough is known about this important complex of human behavior. My own concept of it has evolved as my work has progressed and remains subject to amendment by my own further work and that of others. The scarcity of literature on the culture of poverty is a measure of the gap in communication that exists between the very poor and the middle-class personnel — social scientists, social workers, teachers, physicians, priests, and others — who bear the major responsibility for carrying out the antipoverty programs. Much of the behavior accepted in the culture of poverty goes counter to cherished ideals of the larger society. In writing about "multiproblem" families social scientists thus often stress their instability, their lack of order, direction, and organizaton. Yet, as I have observed them, their behavior seems clearly patterned and reasonably predictable. I am more often struck by the inexorable repetitiousness and the iron entrenchment of their lifeways.

The concept of the culture of poverty may help to correct misapprehensions that have ascribed some behavior patterns of ethnic, national or regional groups as distinctive characteristics. For example, a high incidence of common-law marriage and of households headed by women has been thought to be distinctive of Negro family life in this country and has been attributed to the Negro's historical experience of slavery. In actuality it turns out that such households express essential traits of the culture of poverty and are found among diverse peoples in many parts of the world and among peoples that have had no history of slavery. Although it is now possible to assert such generalizations, there is still much to be learned about this difficult and affecting subject. The absence of intensive anthropological studies of poor families in a wide variety of national contexts — particularly the lack of such studies in socialist countries — remains a serious handicap to the formulation of dependable cross-cultural constants of the culture of poverty.

My studies of poverty and family life have centered largely in Mexico. On occasion some of my Mexican friends have suggested delicately that I turn to a study of poverty in my own country. As a first step in this direction I am currently engaged in a study of Puerto Rican families. Over the past three years my staff and I have been assembling data on 100 representative families in four slums of Greater San Juan and some 50 families of their relatives in New York City.

Our methods combine the traditional techniques of sociology, anthropology and psychology. This includes a battery of nineteen questionnaires, the administration of which requires twelve hours per informant. They cover the residence and employment history of each adult; family relations; income and expenditure; complete inventory of household and personal possessions; friendship patterns, particularly the *compadrazgo,* or godparent, relationship that serves as a kind of informal social security for the children of these families and establishes special obligations among the adults; recreational patterns; health and medical history; politics; religion; world view and "cosmopolitanism." Open-end interviews and psychological tests (such as the thematic apperception test, the Rorschach test, and the sentence-completion test) are administered to a sampling of this population.

All this work serves to establish the context for close-range study of a selected few families. Because the family is a small social system, it lends itself to the holistic approach of anthropology. Whole-family studies bridge the gap between the conceptual extremes of the culture at one pole and of the individual at the other, making possible observation of both culture and personality as they are interrelated in real life. In a large metropolis such as San Juan or New York the family is the natural unit of study.

Ideally our objective is the naturalistic observation of the life of "our" families, with a minimum of intervention. Such intensive study, however, necessarily involves the establishment of deep personal ties. My assistants include two Mexicans whose families I had studied; their "Mexican's-eye view" of the Puerto Rican slum has helped to point up the similarities and differences between the Mexican and Puerto Rican subcultures. We have spent many hours attending family parties, wakes and baptisms, responding to emergency calls, taking people to the hospital, getting them out of jail, filling out applications for them, hunting apartments with them, helping them to get jobs or to get on relief. With each member of these families we conduct tape-recorded interviews, taking down their life stories and their answers to questions on a wide variety of topics. For the ordering of our material we undertake to reconstruct, by close interrogation, the history of a week or more of consecutive days in the lives of each family, and we observe and record complete days as they unfold. The first volume to issue from this study is to be published next month under the title of *La Vida, a Puerto Rican Family in the Culture of Poverty — San Juan and New York* (Random House).

There are many poor people in the world. Indeed, the poverty of the two-thirds of the world's population who live in the underdeveloped countries has been rightly called "the problem of problems." But not all of them by any means live in the culture of poverty. For this way of life to come into being and flourish it seems clear that certain preconditions must be met.

The setting is a cash economy, with wage labor and production for profit and with a persistently high rate of unemployment and underemployment, at low wages, for unskilled labor. The society fails to provide social, political and economic organization, on either a voluntary basis or by government imposition, for the low-income population. There is a bilateral kinship system centered on the nuclear progenitive family, as distinguished from the unilateral extended kinship system of lineage and clan. The dominant class asserts a set of values that prizes thrift and the accumulation of wealth and property, stresses the possibility of upward mobility and explains low economic status as the result of individual personal inadequacy and inferiority.

Where these conditions prevail the way of life that develops among some of the poor is the culture of poverty. That is why I have described it as a subculture of the Western social order. It is both an adaptation and a reaction of the poor to their marginal position in a class-stratified, highly individuated, capitalistic society. It represents an effort to cope with feelings of hopelessness and despair that arise from the realization by the members of the marginal communities in these societies of the improbability of their achieving success in terms of the prevailing values and goals. Many of the traits of the culture of poverty can be viewed as local, spontaneous attempts to meet needs not served in the case of the poor by the institutions and agencies of the larger society because the poor are not eligible for such service, cannot afford it, or are ignorant and suspicious.

Once the culture of poverty has come into existence it tends to perpetuate itself. By the time slum children are six or seven they have usually absorbed the basic attitudes and values of their subculture. Thereafter they are psychologically unready to take full advantage of changing conditions or improving opportunities that may develop in their lifetime.

My studies have identified some seventy traits that characterize the culture of poverty. The principal ones may be described in four dimensions of the system: the relationship between the subculture and the larger society; the nature of the slum community; the nature of the family; and the attitudes, values and character structure of the individual.

The disengagement, the nonintegration, of the poor with respect to the major institutions of society is a crucial element in the culture of poverty. It reflects the combined effect of a variety of factors including poverty, to begin with, but also segregation and discrimination, fear, suspicion and apathy, and the development of alternative institutions and procedures in the slum community. The people do not belong to labor unions or political parties and make little use of banks, hospitals, department stores, or museums. Such involvement as there is in the institutions of the larger society — in the jails, the army, and the public welfare system — does little to suppress the traits of the culture of poverty. A relief system that barely keeps people alive perpetuates rather than eliminates poverty and the pervading sense of hopelessness.

People in a culture of poverty produce little wealth and receive little in return. Chronic unemployment and underemployment, low wages, lack of property, lack of savings, absence of food reserves in the home, and chronic shortage of cash imprison the family and the individual in a vicious circle. Thus for lack of cash the slum householder makes frequent purchases of small quantities of food at higher prices. The slum economy turns inward; it shows a high incidence of pawning of personal goods, borrowing at usurious rates of interest, informal credit arrangements among neighbors, use of secondhand clothing and furniture.

There is awareness of middle-class values. People talk about them and even claim some of them as their own. On the whole, however, they do not live by them. They will declare that marriage by law, by the church or by both is the ideal form of marriage, but few will marry. For men who have no steady jobs, no property and no prospect of wealth to pass on to their children, who live in the present without expectations of the future, who want to avoid the expense and legal difficulties involved in marriage and divorce, a free union or consensual marriage makes good sense. The women, for their part, will turn down offers of marriage from men who are likely to be immature, punishing, and generally unreliable. They feel that a consensual union gives them some of the freedom and flexibility men have. By not giving the fathers of their children legal status as husbands, the women have a stronger claim on the children. They also maintain exclusive rights to their own property.

Along with disengagement from the larger society, there is a hostility to the basic institutions of what are regarded as the dominant classes. There is hatred of the police, mistrust of government and of those in high positions and a cynicism that extends to the church. The culture of poverty thus holds a certain potential for protest and for entrainment in political movements aimed against the existing order.

With its poor housing and overcrowding, the community of the culture of poverty is high in gregariousness, but it has a minimum of organization beyond the nuclear and extended family. Occasionally slum-dwellers come together in temporary informal groupings; neighborhood gangs that cut across slum settlements represent a considerable advance beyond the zero point of the continuum I have in mind. It is the low level of organization that gives the culture of poverty its marginal and anomalous quality in our highly organized society. Most primitive peoples have achieved a higher degree of sociocultural organization than contemporary urban slum dwellers. This is not to say that there may not be a sense of community and *esprit de corps* in a slum neighborhood. In fact, where slums are isolated from their surroundings by enclosing walls or other physical barriers, where rents are low and residence is stable and where the population constitutes a distinct ethnic, racial or language group, the sense of community may approach that of a village. In Mexico City and San Juan such territoriality is engendered by the scarcity of low-cost housing outside of established slum areas. In South Africa it is actively enforced by the *apartheid* that confines rural migrants to prescribed locations.

The family in the culture of poverty does not cherish childhood as a specially prolonged and protected stage in the life cycle. Initiation into sex comes early. With the instability of consensual marriage the family tends to be mother-centered and tied more closely to the mother's extended family. The female head of the house is given to authoritarian rule. In spite of much verbal emphasis on family solidarity, sibling rivalry for the limited supply of goods and maternal affection is intense. There is little privacy.

The individual who grows up in this culture has a strong feeling of fatalism, helplessness, dependence and inferiority. These traits, so often remarked in the current literature as characteristic of the American Negro, I found equally strong in slum dwellers of Mexico City and San Juan, who are not segregated or discriminated against as a distinct ethnic or racial group. Other traits include a high incidence of weak ego structure, orality, and confusion of sexual identification, all reflecting maternal deprivation; a strong present-time orientation with relatively little disposition to defer gratification and plan for the future, and a high tolerance for psychological pathology of all kinds. There is widespread belief in male superiority and among the men a strong preoccupation with *machismo,* their masculinity.

Provincial and local in outlook, with little sense of history, these people know only their own neighborhood and their own way of life. Usually they do not have the knowledge, the vision or the ideology to see the similarities between their troubles and those of their counterparts elsewhere in the world. They are not class-conscious, although they are sensitive indeed to symbols of status.

The distinction between poverty and the culture of poverty is basic to the model described here. There are numerous examples of poor people whose way of life I would not characterize as belonging to this subculture. Many primitive and preliterate peoples that have been studied by anthropologists suffer dire poverty attributable to low technology or thin resources or both. Yet even the simplest of these peoples have a high degree of social organization and a relatively integrated, satisfying and self-sufficient culture.

In India the destitute lower-caste peoples — such as the Chamars, the leatherworkers, and the Bhangis, the sweepers — remain integrated in the larger society and have their own panchayat institutions of self-government. Their panchayats and their extended unilateral kinship systems, or clans, cut across village lines, giving them a strong sense of identity and continuity. In my studies of these peoples I found no culture of poverty to go with their poverty.

The Jews of eastern Europe were a poor urban people, often confined to ghettos. Yet they did not have many traits of the culture of poverty. They had a tradition of literacy that placed great value on learning; they formed many voluntary associations and adhered with devotion to the central community organization around the rabbi, and they had a religion that taught them they were the chosen people.

I would cite also a fourth, somewhat speculative example of poverty dissociated from the culture of poverty. On the basis of limited direct observation in one country — Cuba — and from indirect evidence, I am inclined to believe the culture of poverty does not exist in socialist countries. In 1947 I undertook a study of a slum in Havana. Recently I had an opportunity to revisit the same slum and some of the same families. The physical aspect of the place had changed little, except for a beautiful new nursery school. The people were as poor as before, but I was impressed to find much less of the feelings of despair and apathy, so symptomatic of the culture of poverty in the urban slums of the United States. The slum was now highly organized, with block committees, educational committees, party committees. The people had found a new sense of power and importance in a doctrine that glorified the lower class as the hope of humanity, and they were armed. I was told by one Cuban official that the Castro government had practically eliminated delinquency by giving arms to the delinquents!

Evidently the Castro regime — revising Marx and Engels — did not write off the so-called *lumpenproletariat* as an inherently reactionary and antirevolutionary force but rather found in them a revolutionary potential and utilized it. Frantz Fanon, in his book *The Wretched of the Earth,* makes a similar evaluation of their role in the Algerian revolution: "It is within this mass of humanity, this people of the shantytowns, at the core of the *lumpenproletariat,* that the rebellion will find its urban spearhead. For the *lumpenproletariat,* that horde of starving men, uprooted from their tribe and from their clan, constitutes one of the most spontaneous and most radically revolutionary forces of a colonized people."

It is true that I have found little revolutionary spirit or radical ideology among low-income Puerto Ricans. Most of the families I studied were politically conservative, about half of them favoring the Statehood Republican Party, which provides opposition on the right to the Popular Democratic Party that dominates the politics of the commonwealth. It seems to me, therefore, that disposition for protest among people living in the culture of poverty will vary considerably according to the national context and historical circumstances. In contrast to Algeria, the independence movement in Puerto Rico has found little popular support. In Mexico, where the cause of independence carried long ago, there is no longer any such movement to stir the dwellers in the new and old slums of the capital city.

Yet it would seem that any movement — be it religious, pacifist or revolutionary — that organizes and gives hope to the poor and effectively promotes a sense of solidarity with larger groups must effectively destroy the psychological and social core of the culture of poverty. In this connection, I suspect that the civil rights movement among American Negroes has of itself done more to improve their self-image and self-respect than such economic gains as it has won although, without doubt, the two kinds of progress are mutually reinforcing. In the culture of poverty of the American Negro the additional disadvantage of racial discrimination has generated a potential for revolutionary protest and organization that is absent in the slums of San Juan and Mexico City and, for that matter, among the poor whites in the South.

If it is true, as I suspect, that the culture of poverty flourishes and is endemic to the free-enterprise, pre-welfare-state stage of capitalism, then it is also endemic in colonial societies. The most likely candidates for the culture of poverty would be the people who come from the lower strata of a rapidly changing society and who are already partially alienated from it. Accordingly the subculture is likely to be found where imperial conquest has smashed the native social and economic structure and held the natives, perhaps for generations, in servile status, or where feudalism is yielding to capitalism in the later evolution of a colonial economy. Landless rural workers who migrate to the cities, as in Latin America, can be expected to fall into this way of life more readily than migrants from stable peasant villages with a well-organized traditional culture, as in India. It remains to be seen, however, whether the culture of poverty has not already begun to develop in the slums of Bombay and Calcutta. Compared with Latin America also, the strong corporate nature of many African tribal societies may tend to inhibit or delay the formation of a full-blown culture of poverty in the new towns and cities of that continent. In South Africa the institutionalization of repression and discrimination under *apartheid* may also have begun to promote an immunizing sense of identity and group consciousness among the African Negroes.

One must therefore keep the dynamic aspects of human institutions forward in observing and assessing the evidence for the presence, the waxing or the waning of this subculture. Measured on the dimension of relationship to the larger society, some slum-dwellers may have a warmer identification with their national tradition even though they suffer deeper poverty than members of a similar community in another country. In Mexico City a high percentage of our respondents, including those with little or no formal schooling, knew of Cuauhtémoc, Hidalgo, Father Morelos, Juárez, Díaz, Zapata, Carranza and Cárdenas. In San Juan the names of Rámon Power, José de Diego, Baldorioty de Castro, Rámon Betances, Nemesio Canales, Lloréns Torres rang no bell; a few could tell about the late Albizu Campos. For the lower-income Puerto Rican, however, history begins with Muñoz Rivera and ends with his son Muñoz Marín.

The national context can make a big difference in the play of the crucial traits of fatalism and hopelessness. Given the advanced technology, the high level of literacy, the all-pervasive reach of the media of mass communications and the relatively high aspirations of all sectors of the population, even the poorest and most marginal communities of the

United States must aspire to a larger future than the slum dwellers of Ecuador and Peru, where the actual possibilities are most limited and where an authoritarian social order persists in city and country. Among the 50 million U.S. citizens now more or less officially certified as poor, I would guess that about 20 percent live in a culture of poverty. The largest numbers in this group are made up of Negroes, Puerto Ricans, Mexicans, American Indians and Southern poor whites. In these figures there is some reassurance for those concerned, because it is much more difficult to undo the culture of poverty than to cure poverty itself.

Middle-class people — this would certainly include most social scientists — tend to concentrate on the negative aspects of the culture of poverty. They attach a minus sign to such traits as present-time orientation and readiness to indulge impulses. I do not intend to idealize or romanticize the culture of poverty — "it is easier to praise poverty than to live in it." Yet the positive aspects of these traits must not be overlooked. Living in the present may develop a capacity for spontaneity, for the enjoyment of the sensual, which is often blunted in the middle-class, future-oriented man. Indeed, I am often struck by the analogies that can be drawn between the mores of the very rich — of the "jet set" and "café society" — and the culture of the very poor. Yet it is, on the whole, a comparatively superficial culture. There is in it much pathos, suffering, and emptiness. It does not provide much support or satisfaction; its pervading mistrust magnifies individual helplessness and isolation. Indeed, poverty of culture is one of the crucial traits of the culture of poverty.

The concept of the culture of poverty provides a generalization that may help to unify and explain a number of phenomena hitherto viewed as peculiar to certain racial, national or regional groups. Problems we think of as being distinctively our own or distinctively Negro (or as typifying any other ethnic group) prove to be endemic in countries where there are no segregated ethnic minority groups. If it follows that the elimination of physical poverty may not by itself eliminate the culture of poverty, then an understanding of the subculture may contribute to the design of measures specific to that purpose.

What is the future of the culture of poverty? In considering this question one must distinguish between those countries in which it represents a relatively small segment of the population and those in which it constitutes a large one. In the United States the major solution proposed by social workers dealing with the "hard core" poor has been slowly to raise their level of living and incorporate them in the middle class. Wherever possible psychiatric treatment is prescribed.

In underdeveloped countries where great masses of people live in the culture of poverty, such a social-work solution does not seem feasible.

The local psychiatrists have all they can do to care for their own growing middle class. In those countries the people with a culture of poverty may seek a more revolutionary solution. By creating basic structural changes in society, by redistributing wealth, by organizing the poor and giving them a sense of belonging, of power and of leadership, revolutions frequently succeed in abolishing some of the basic characteristics of the culture of poverty even when they do not succeed in curing poverty itself.

VI

Economic systems

Every society has developed ways to survive. The Eskimo make their parkas of sealskin for protection against bitter Arctic cold. In the Trobriand Islands, inland yam-growers broaden their diet by trade with coastal fishermen. From hunting and gathering to farming and manufacturing, man has found ways to provide for his needs. He creates a technology and produces food and other things to supply his wants; through systems of allocation, he distributes goods and services. These activities make up the substance of the economy.

But cultural subsystems do not exist in isolation, and this becomes especially clear as we consider the economic sphere. Every facet of life is linked to a culture's economy. In America, low status results from lack of money; among the Nayar, an exchange of goods must accompany weddings; in New Guinea, some curing rituals cannot occur without the expediture of a pig. Demands for goods and services creates bonds both within a society and between members of different cultures.

Thus, it is not surprising that contact in the economic sphere is a major cause of extensive culture change. Exchange within a society is fraught with cultural meanings. When intercultural exchange takes place, not only does it affect the raw materials or finished products being traded, but the meaning systems as well.

This linkage is clearly illustrated by the selections in this chapter. In complex societies the overall economic system does not affect all groups in the same way; in fact, those at the bottom of the social structure often find that the system actually works against them. This discrimination is especially true for the poor — both in India and the United States, to name but two areas of the world.

19

The changing economy of an Indian village

DAVID W. McCURDY

Every society must possess an economic system that provides for the production, exchange, and consumption of goods and services if the biological and social needs of its members are to be met. Also, the economy is closely integrated with the overall cultural system as is shown in this selection by David McCurdy. For the Bhils in India, exchange traditionally took place as part of a more general social interaction based on kinship and community roles. When a new form of market exchange was adopted, it altered some of these relationships.

Ratakote is a village that occupies a valley and adjacent ridge in the Aravalli Hills of Central India. While it resembles multi-caste Indian communities, it is not typical of them, for almost all of its eleven hundred inhabitants are Bhil tribal members. To be sure, one is immediately reminded of nontribal India when he visits the village. The people live in the mud- and dung-plastered stone huts, common in this part of southern Rajasthan, and the small fields, cattle, iron-tipped wooden plows and wells seen everywhere in India are in evidence. Men wear turban and *dhoti*; women, skirts and saris in the southern Rajasthani style. But an experienced eye can detect that the color and cut of the clothing differs from the usual local dress. Houses are built on a special plan, and there is no obvious village center as is common elsewhere; houses are set by themselves, scattered here and there about the community. These things tell us that some of the cultural rules that regulate Bhil life vary from those of nearby caste Indians. Through observation of the villagers and their actions, deeper and more significant differences can be discovered.

The villager's independent self-view is an example of Bhil unique-

This article was written especially for this volume and has never before been published.

ness. Although Bhils think that the world is made up of named ethnic groups like their own, they fail to make important distinctions among them. Caste groups found in multi-caste villages on the flatter and more arable lands in and around the hills are ordered in a hierarchical and interdependent system; they provide each other with services and goods and their members are concerned about caste rank within the hierarchy. Bhils are not locked in such a system. For the most part they produce what they need themselves. They value their independence. One man claimed, "We stay away from the city because if you live there, you must work for others." Another said, "You have no control over your needs in the city. You must beg from others." The fastness of their hills and the disdain of caste Indians, most of whom define Bhils as aboriginal, primitive rustics, have helped Ratakote's inhabitants maintain a separate identity.

The design of Ratakote's economy is affected by the village's traditional cultural and physical isolation. More than the inhabitants of most caste-Indian villages, those of Ratakote have managed to stay aloof from the larger social and economic system surrounding them. But economic change has begun to occur in Ratakote and has forced villagers to cope with the pull of a larger, market-oriented, Indian subsistence economy. The following incident which occurred in Ratakote illustrates this economic change.

> The event, a village meeting, took place on a warm sunny morning in January, 1963. Almost all the village men were there to meet with traders called Mahajans. The headman, who despite his advancing age, looked healthier and more robust than most, spoke first. "You know that the Mahajans have come to the village to argue with us," he began. "What shall we tell them? When we tried to set a fair price on the grain they take from us, they ignored it. Now that we have refused to give up any more grain as credit against our debts, they come and claim that we are unfair and that we should continue our relationship with them. What should we do?" Those present grew angry. They spoke of the injustices done to them by the Mahajans. They noted that they would be forever in their Mahajans' debt unless action were taken. They decided, with their headman, that debts should be cut in half, that they would pay no more interest, that they should never again borrow from a Mahajan, and that the remaining debts would be paid off quickly. The Mahajans who had come to speak to them that day were informed of this decision. The ensuing argument did them little good and they left the village beaten and dejected.

How can we explain this event? The answer would appear to lie in an understanding of Ratakote's economic system as it was, and of the changes that have come to it altering the meaning of the Bhil-Mahajan relationship. Thus, we must know how the people produce, exchange, and use things in Ratakote. We must review what place the Mahajans have in the traditional economic system, what happened to produce the impetus for change, and what the dynamics were by which the Bhils came to see their relationship with Mahajans in a new light.

Economic system

Economic life is not a sphere of activity separate from others in Ratakote. There are no factories, no professional organizations, no corporations as we know them. Villagers have no term equivalent to our word *economy*. They do have activities and viewpoints which anthropologists label as economic — a set of cultural norms that define the activities necessary to provide for physical and social needs. Because Bhils grow crops, exchange things, eat food, and consume goods, they have activities that are, for us, economic, but for them such acts are viewed as a part of other patterns for doing things. In short, these activities are categorized in other ways by Bhils and thereby have special and different meanings for them.

Production is a case in point. Bhils stress that they must grow crops and make goods in order to live. Physical survival partly defines the meaning, or better, the motivation for growing crops and manufacturing necessary items. One villager put it easily: "If we do not farm the land, we do not eat. If we do not build houses, we get wet when it rains." To meet their needs, every Bhil householder has a little land — on the average of two or three acres — that he and the able-bodied members of his nuclear family farm. Every year he grows a wet season crop between July and October. Maize is most commonly planted, but wheat, barley, millet, mustard, chillies, sugarcane, and a few other crops are also grown. Some men also plant a winter crop but few have fields well suited to it, for the main crop, winter wheat, must be irrigated. Once his grain is threshed, the farmer stores it in large cylindrical bins in his house. These crops are the main source of his food; the relationship between agricultural production and eating is unmistakable. The land is life.

Animal husbandry and handcrafted tools have the same kind of importance. Cattle, water buffaloes, and goats comprise the village herds, and are valued for their milk and, with the exception of cattle, their meat. Every family owns a few animals and some have more than fifty. Adults milk them every morning and evening, and prize the ghee (clarified butter) and buttermilk produced by churning.

Ratakote villagers also produce many tools and other items they need to live. Some things like stone walls, house posts, and roof tiles can be made by almost any grown man. Others, such as baskets, plow frames, butter churns, and bows and arrows are produced by part-time village specialists, who make these things for their neighbors when they have need for them.

The crucial relationship between production and survival is most vividly brought home to Bhils by the uncertainties of the agricultural enterprise. Rains often fail, animals grow sick and die, and cutworms invade the fields and eat the roots of young corn plants. Severe grain and milk shortages result. Villagers respond in the only way they know, by enlisting the aid of the gods; for in Ratakote, gods, godlings, spirits, and ancestors share the village and its products with men. There are godlings of field and weather. Ancestors live on the land and watch over the crops. All are worshipped regularly to insure an abundant yield, and some are selected for special propitiation in times of crisis. But, despite all such efforts, even the gods may fail and villagers know once again what it is like to be hungry.

This pragmatic approach to economic activities, the satisfaction of physical needs, is not the only reason Bhils produce goods and perform services. Their social identity is also at stake. First, a man is measured by the way he performs, and part of his performance involves production. He seeks to live up to village expectations defining the category *farmer*, into which all men fall. For example, he should be industrious and careful of his land; he should be able to detect the humidity that signals the time for sowing and plowing in summer, or the moisture content in ears of corn that tells him they are ready for harvest.

Second, he belongs to kinship groups that are associated with agriculture. His nuclear family holds direct rights to a portion of land, but his ability to assign those rights to others is limited by a group composed of his brothers and sometimes his father's brother's sons that decides how land is to be divided among its members. Group members also cooperate in the plowing and harvesting, and if one is short of food, the others will help him out if they have the resources.

Third and most important, an individual's social identity, in fact his ability to perform in social relationships, requires that he engage in reciprocal exchange. For Bhils, reciprocal exchange is not an institution by itself; instead, it occurs as part of one's expected behavior when playing a number of common and important roles. When a man gives his wife silver bangles, or offers his neighbor a *biri* to smoke, or serves a chicken to his visiting brother-in-law, he is engaged in reciprocal exchange. Each recipient is expected to return the favor, sometimes in equal measure, sometimes in a different way. To do so is required by the cultural norms defining the roles and relationships within Bhil society. Reciprocal exchange is important: it maintains the mutual obligations that tie people together in the social network.

The Bhil wedding ceremony clearly illustrates this point. Bhils are patrilocal and village exogamous; i.e., grooms live with or near their fathers and brides come to Ratakote from other communities. Because she must leave her father's house to live with her husband's family, a bride is an item of exchange. To compensate her father for his loss, the groom's father gives him a sum of money or "bride price," the amount being determined by tradition. Since it is usual for kinsmen to affirm their bond with one another through exchange, and since a wedding establishes a relationship between the families of the bride and groom, formal exchange between new in-laws must occur. In the same way, one invites his other relatives to a marriage and must also conduct exchanges with them before the wedding party leaves for the bride's village. Even unrelated neighbors will give money to help defray the cost of the wedding with the assurance that the groom will reciprocate the favor when there is a wedding in their family.

The occasion of marriage and the exchanges marking it not only provide for the expression of kinship and neighborhood roles, but allow for the acquisition of prestige. For example, the degree of approbation accorded members of a family who have conducted a wedding is dependent on a number of factors, the most important of which relate to the resources expended. Kinsmen, neighbors, and friends comment openly on the amount and quality of the food and liquor served at feasts, the excellence of the clothing exchanged, and the number of guests in attendance. Obviously a larger number of guests requires the expenditure of a greater amount of food, liquor, and exchange items. The people of Ratakote remember "really fine" weddings and those who gave them for many years.

The grain and goods necessary to support exchange come partly from the productive activities of villagers, but items like clothing and money are not available in the village. Who provides these goods and how? This is where the Mahajan fits into the picture. Mahajans come from the village of Nagar, twelve miles from Ratakote; their caste name stands for trader or merchant, their traditional occupation. In this part of India, they are Jains, members of an Indian religion espousing the sanctity of all life. Their relationship to the people of Ratakote seems simple enough. Each Mahajan serves a number of hereditary Bhil clients; at the death of a Mahajan father, his sons divide the list of his clients and continue the traditional service. They provide for their clients' needs — clothing, ritual items, food, spices, tobacco — on annual festival occasions and when there is an urgent need for them. In return, they collect part of their clients' crop. A Bhil's sons, on their part, inherit his debt and his Mahajan, and continue to depend on the merchant for their needs, while making repayment with grain, and such items as chillies or ghee which they feel can be spared.

The Bhil-Mahajan relationship has endured for at least a century and perhaps much longer. Traditionally it served to protect Ratakote Bhils from contact with the cash markets in Udaipur, the district capital located some twenty-one miles away. While in the past Bhils collected bamboo and other produce from the jungle and occasionally sold it for cash in the city, their urban contact was limited. The Mahajan was the middleman between city and village, and this function continues in modified form today. The Mahajan buys goods on the Udaipuri market and provides them on credit to his Bhil clients. He makes a profit in three ways: he charges his client more for an item than he pays for it in the bazaar; he also charges an annual interest of approximately 25 percent which he adds to the Bhil's account; and finally, he systematically undervalues his client's grain payment in relation to its sale value on the Udaipuri market.

As a way of fitting merchants into their traditional culture, Bhils model their relationship with Mahajans after the reciprocal ties characteristic of kinship roles, particularly those reflecting differential age, authority, and reciprocal obligation. Mahajans are like fathers or older brothers and receive the deferential behavior due such status. In return, Mahajans happily play the role of elder kinsmen and express their willingness to provide material support for their clients, "as a father would care for his sons." One Bhil informant described the degree of authority associated with the relationship in these terms: "In the past, people dressed only as well as their Mahajan would let them. What he gave them to wear, they wore. Everything else they had, he was responsible for."

In addition to providing Bhils with goods which are not made or grown in Ratakote, the Mahajan supplies security. From time to time crops fail, animals die, or some other catastrophe befalls the village, impairing its people's ability to survive. It is the Mahajan who comes to their rescue, who provides them with *subsistence security*. But more commonly the Mahajan offers *social security* to his clients. The people of Ratakote are not able to save the amounts of food and money necessary to underwrite a successful marriage ceremony or other important events. To meet the demands of such an occasion, Bhils look to the services of their Mahajans, who will provide the wedding suit, clothing, bride price, grain, and mahua flowers to make liquor. They are the only ones who can insure that a man's performance will not suffer in the eyes of his peers.

The process of change

Then, in 1963, this system of cultural rules and the social relationships they define changed abruptly. What generated the villagers' anger against their Mahajans? Why did the Bhils wish to end what appears to have been a necessary relationship? In its simplest form, the answer lies in a change of rules applied by villagers to their relationship with the moneylender-merchants. The meaning of Mahajans and the nature of exchange with them changed.

This change was precipitated by the building of a dirt road from

Udaipur southwest to the Panerva bamboo forests in the year 1935; the road cut through Ratakote. When the road was first under construction, a great many villagers of both sexes served on the labor gang. No one accurately recalls the rate of pay for this work, but all agree that it provided a significant increase in their supply of cash. The completion of the road opened the bamboo forest to exploitation, and over 100 Ratakote men began to make what has become a yearly migration to work in the forests during the winter. Since the national government has taken responsibility for the road, as many as 150 villagers are employed from time to time during the year as laborers to keep it in repair. The effect of this work has been to sustain an increased money supply and to attract merchants permanently to the village. These merchants sell many goods previously supplied by Mahajans, but do not offer extended credit.

In light of this information, we might attempt to explain the dissolution of the Bhil-Mahajan relationship on the grounds that Mahajans were functionally replaced by resident merchants; that city goods were now conveniently available in Ratakote, so the services of the Mahajan were no longer needed. But in fact, for a number of years prior to 1963 the Bhil-Mahajan relationship grew in importance, for several reasons. First, as the amount of money and the goods it could buy increased, so did the amount and quality of goods necessary for reciprocal exchange. Weddings became more expensive, as did exchanges associated with many other events. Men bemoaned the fact that their wives used to be happy with just silver anklets; now they wanted silver bracelets, bangles, neck rings, ear chains, and toe rings. Daughters were demanding more, too. The English word *fashion* became part of the Bhil language. At the annual spring Holi festival the young village belles competed for an unofficial "best dressed" award. Added to this was the growing desire on the part of many for city-made items such as flashlights, kerosene lamps, and tools. Where the new-found cash went is obvious.

While families anticipating an upcoming marriage do manage to save some cash against the cost of the ceremony, the newly inflated terms of exchange associated with the ritual almost always insure that they will have to turn to their Mahajan for help. The Mahajan is there, ready to lend them the necessary goods and cash. As a result, debts to Mahajans have continued to rise in concert with general inflation in India. Some persons in Ratakote owe as much as fifteen hundred rupees; most owe over five hundred.

If Mahajans became even more important sources of security and credit to villages following the advent of the road, what can explain villagers' disenchantment with them? Perhaps the answer can be found in the comments of those present at the meeting held in 1963, for these are accurate measures of the villagers' viewpoint. They angrily accused their

Mahajans of taking advantage of them. For example, a white-haired man in his fifties got up and complained, "I borrowed a *maund* [about 82 pounds] of corn from my Mahajan when I was married. I have been paying that bastard one maund of corn every year since, and he still claims that I owe him a maund of corn." Another rose and said, "We all know that Mahajans cheat us. They change units of measure when they weigh out our grain to confuse us. They know we cannot read and write so they put down any amount of debt they want in their little books. We work hard so that they can grow fat." Still another acknowledged the futility of ever getting free of a Mahajan's clutches. "When I got married," he said, "I inherited a three-hundred-rupee debt from my father and I borrowed two hundred rupees for my wedding. For the next four years crops were poor. I couldn't even pay off the interest and my debt grew to eight hundred rupees. The weather for the last three years has been good. Crops have been fine and I have paid off some of my debt, but seven years after I started, I owe the same amount I began with, five hundred rupees."

Anger due to exploitation is the theme of these comments. For Bhils, Mahajans are now cheats, not fathers. Why? Most probably, this view stems from growing experience with the rules defining market exchange in Udaipuri bazaars. Instead of reciprocity based on role-obligations, goods in the bazaar change hands on the basis of economizing, trying to get the most for the least. When the road was built through Ratakote, villagers began to spend their money in the city market with greater frequency. They discovered that *biris* sold for more money in the village than in the city; they learned that clothing, ritual items, spices, and their own grain had a value measured by their sale price. They tried to patronize the cheapest bazaars in Udaipur because money saved there could be spent for other desired things.

Even now, however, the market principal is not predominant in Ratakote. Neighbors and kinsmen still abide by the rules of reciprocal hospitality. In fact, the few Bhils who have attempted to establish small shops in the village have soon closed their doors; their neighbors simply dropped by to smoke and eat them out of business.

But Mahajans are not Bhils. Mahajans come from outside the village; they are not neighbors. While Bhils treated them as kinsmen, the relationship was obviously fictitious. Once villagers had experience in the city markets, the parallel between the services provided by the Mahajans and those available in the bazaar became clear. The Mahajans already kept their clients' accounts in the form of a money statement. Now the clients had the information they needed to interpret just what their debts meant; they discovered how and where their Mahajans were making a profit, and they did not like it. The Mahajans' services were not economical.

Thus began the search to end the relationship. For years the headman and other villagers had thought about dispensing with their Mahajans' services. What held them back was their need for security — credit was obviously necessary to them — and the fear that the Indian government would uphold the system. Their basis for this notion stemmed from the policies applied by the princely state of Mewar before Indian Independence when, indeed, traders were protected by law. But by 1963, villagers felt the government would take their side.

Confidence that new sources of credit could be found grew steadily during the few years preceding the meeting. When attempts by villagers to increase the price of the grain they exchanged with Mahajans failed, they contemplated alternatives, and recognizing that weddings caused the greatest need for credit, they decided at the meeting to manage these in a new way which had already been adopted for funerals. All the householders of the village ward in which the wedding was to take place would donate the necessary food, liquor, and funds to the father of the bride or groom; it was felt that if everyone in the ward cooperated, marriage credit could be raised on the traditional reciprocal basis.

A second suggestion proposed at the gathering involved borrowing marriage funds from the village forest cooperative, a group formed under government auspices but outside its immediate view. As the headman said, "We might as well use that cooperative for something, even if we don't do it legally." As the cooperative's funds were raised in the village, this approach included the same sense of reciprocity as the first proposal.

A third solution required the reduction of credit needs. If people could dispense with the bride price at weddings, and could reduce the amount and scope of feasts, credit would not be needed. People would have to convince prospective in-laws in other villages, but the result would be worthwhile. In fact, some villagers had already been critical of the bride price. Since they had learned the value of money on the market, they looked at the bride price as "buying a wife" rather than the exchange of a prestige item.

In short, Ratakote's economic system changed in response to contact with the urban market, but the change was toward a traditional as well as a market orientation. Falling back on cooperation to support weddings involves the use of traditional reciprocal norms. It preserves the ability of villagers to continue holding weddings in the face of unsatisfactory credit arrangements. This solution, however, costs the bride and groom and their parents as well, for weddings no longer retain as much power to confer prestige. The same may be said for the use of forest cooperative funds.

Cancellation of bride price and some other forms of wedding exchange is clearly a more drastic solution to the Mahajan problem because it seriously erodes the importance of the ritual. It is interesting to note that later this solution was not taken as seriously as when it was made. Villagers are not yet ready to part with tradition to this extent.

There are villages like Ratakote all over the world, not alike in the sense that their culture precisely parallels that found in Ratakote, but in the fact that they have traditionally not been integrated in a national market economy. As underdeveloped countries stress economic growth, the knowledge and impact of the market in rural areas will increase. The changes that result will necessarily disrupt traditional culture, causing villagers to make new accommodations. Cries of moral decay will emanate from those areas as traditional meanings change. In the end, cultural exchange rules based on role obligation must give way, at least a bit, to those found in the market.

20

Penny capitalism on an urban streetcorner

ELLIOT LIEBOW

In our complex Western economy, the job a man has and the value the society places on it determine his productive capability and measure his worth. Elliot Liebow examines the cultural meaning of jobs to men in the Black ghetto. Given the limitations placed on him by his immediate society, the Black "corner man" cannot hope to fill a job valued by the larger society. As a result his pay is low, his future dim, and his self-esteem diminished; he is unable to provide for the needs of his family or himself.

A pickup truck drives slowly down the street. The truck stops as it comes abreast of a man sitting on a cast-iron porch and the white driver calls out, asking if the man wants a day's work. The man shakes his head and the truck moves on up the block, stopping again whenever idling men come within calling distance of the driver. At the Carry-out corner, five men debate the question briefly and shake their heads no to the truck. The truck turns the corner and repeats the same performance up the next street. In the distance, one can see one man, then another, climb into the back of the truck and sit down. It starts and stops, the truck finally disappears.

What is it we have witnessed here? A labor scavenger rebuffed by his would-be prey? Lazy, irresponsible men turning down an honest day's pay for an honest day's work? Or a more complex phenomenon marking the intersection of economic forces, social values, and individual states of mind and body?

Let us look again at the driver of the truck. He has been able to recruit only two or three men from each twenty or fifty he contacts. To him, it is clear that the others simply do not choose to work. Singly or in groups, belly-empty or belly-full, sullen or gregarious, drunk or sober, they confirm what he has read, heard and knows from his own experience: these men wouldn't take a job if it were handed to them on a platter.[1]

Quite apart from the question of whether or not this is true of some of the men he sees on the street, it is clearly not true of all of them. If it were, he would not have come here in the first place; or having come, he would have left with an empty truck. It is not even true of most of them, for most of the men he sees on the street this weekday morning do, in fact, have jobs. But since, at the moment, they are neither working nor sleeping, and since they hate the depressing room or apartment they live in, or because there is nothing to do there,[2] or because they want to get away from their wives or anyone else living there, they are out on the street, indistinguishable from those who do not have jobs or do not want them. Some, like Boley, a member of a trash-collection crew in a suburban housing development, work Saturdays and are off on this weekday. Some, like Sweets, work nights cleaning up middle-class trash, dirt, dishes, and garbage, and mopping the floors of the office buildings, hotels, restaurants, toilets, and other public places dirtied during the day. Some men work for retail businesses such as liquor stores which do not begin the day until ten o'clock. Some laborers, like Tally, have already come back from the job because the ground was too wet for pick and shovel or because the weather was too cold for pouring concrete. Other employed men stayed off the job today for personal reasons: Clarence to go to a funeral at eleven this morning and Sea Cat to answer a subpoena as a witness in a criminal proceeding.

Also on the street, unwitting contributors to the impression taken away by the truck driver, are the halt and the lame. The man on the cast-iron steps strokes one gnarled arthritic hand with the other and says he doesn't know whether or not he'll live long enough to be eligible for Social Security. He pauses, then adds matter-of-factly, "Most times, I don't care whether I do or don't." Stoopy's left leg was polio-withered in childhood. Raymond, who looks as if he could tear out a fire hydrant,

[1] By different methods, perhaps, some social scientists have also located the problem in the men themselves, in their unwillingness or lack of desire to work: "To improve the underprivileged worker's performance, one must help him to learn *to want* . . . higher social goals for himself and his children. . . . The problem of changing the work habits and motivation of [lower class] people . . . is a problem of changing the goals, the ambitions, and the level of cultural and occupational aspiration of the underprivileged worker." (Emphasis in original.) Allison Davis, "The Motivation of the Underprivileged Worker," p. 90.

[2] The comparison of sitting at home alone with being in jail is commonplace.

coughs up blood if he bends or moves suddenly. The quiet man who hangs out in front of the Saratoga apartments has a steel hook strapped onto his left elbow. And had the man in the truck been able to look into the wine-clouded eyes of the man in the green cap, he would have realized that the man did not even understand he was being offered a day's work.

Others, having had jobs and been laid off, are drawing unemployment compensation (up to $44 per week) and have nothing to gain by accepting work which pays little more than this and frequently less.

Still others, like Bumdoodle the numbers man, are working hard at illegal ways of making money, hustlers who are on the street to turn a dollar any way they can: buying and selling sex, liquor, narcotics, stolen goods, or anything else that turns up.

Only a handful remains unaccounted for. There is Tonk, who cannot bring himself to take a job away from the corner, because, according to the other men, he suspects his wife will be unfaithful if given the opportunity. There is Stanton, who has not reported to work for four days now, not since Bernice disappeared. He bought a brand new knife against her return. She had done this twice before, he said, but not for so long and not without warning, and he had forgiven her. But this time, "I ain't got it in me to forgive her again." His rage and shame are there for all to see as he paces the Carry-out and the corner, day and night, hoping to catch a glimpse of her.

And finally, there are those like Arthur, able-bodied men who have no visible means of support, legal or illegal, who neither have jobs nor want them. The truck driver, among others, believes the Arthurs to be representative of all the men he sees idling on the street during his own working hours. They are not, but they cannot be dismissed simply because they are a small minority. It is not enough to explain them away as being lazy or irresponsible or both because an able-bodied man with responsibilities who refuses work is, by the truck driver's definition, lazy and irresponsible. Such an answer begs the question. It is descriptive of the facts; it does not explain them.

Moreover, despite their small numbers, the don't-work-and-don't-want-to-work minority is especially significant because they represent the strongest and clearest expression of those values and attitudes associated with making a living which, to varying degrees, are found throughout the streetcorner world. These men differ from the others in degree rather than in kind, the principal difference being that they are carrying out the implications of their values and experiences to their logical, inevitable conclusions. In this sense, the others have yet to come to terms with themselves and the world they live in.

Putting aside, for the moment, what the men say and feel, and looking at what they actually do and the choices they make, getting a job, keeping a job, and doing well at it is clearly of low priority. Arthur will not take a job at all. Leroy is supposed to be on his job at 4:00 P.M. but it is already 4:10 and he still cannot bring himself to leave the free games he has accumulated on the pinball machine in the Carry-out. Tonk started a construction job on Wednesday, worked Thursday and Friday, then didn't go back again. On the same kind of job, Sea Cat quit in the second week. Sweets had been working three months as a busboy in a restaurant, then quit without notice, not sure himself why he did so. A real estate agent, saying he was more interested in getting the job done than in the cost, asked Richard to give him an estimate on repairing and painting the inside of a house, but Richard, after looking over the job, somehow never got around to submitting an estimate. During one period, Tonk would not leave the corner to take a job because his wife might prove unfaithful; Stanton would not take a job because his woman had been unfaithful.

Thus, the man-job relationship is a tenuous one. At any given moment, a job may occupy a relatively low position on the streetcorner scale of real values. Getting a job may be subordinated to relations with women or to other non-job considerations; the commitment to a job one already has is frequently shallow and tentative.

The reasons are many. Some are objective and reside principally in the job; some are subjective and reside principally in the man. The line between them, however, is not a clear one. Behind the man's refusal to take a job or his decision to quit one is not a simple impulse or value choice but a complex combination of assessments of objective reality on the one hand, and values, attitudes and beliefs drawn from different levels of his experience on the other.

Objective economic considerations are frequently a controlling factor in a man's refusal to take a job. How much the job pays is a crucial question but seldom asked. He knows how much it pays. Working as a stock clerk, a delivery boy, or even behind the counter of liquor stores, drug stores, and other retail businesses pays one dollar an hour. So, too, do most busboy, car-wash, janitorial, and other jobs available to him. Some jobs, such as dishwasher, may dip as low as eighty cents an hour and others, such as elevator operator or work in a junk yard, may offer $1.15 or $1.25. Take-home pay for jobs such as these ranges from $35 to $50 a week, but a take-home pay of over $45 for a five-day week is the exception rather than the rule.

One of the principal advantages of these kinds of jobs is that they offer fairly regular work. Most of them involve essential services and are therefore somewhat less responsive to business conditions than are some higher paying, less menial jobs. Most of them are also inside jobs not dependent on the weather, as are construction jobs and other higher-paying outside work.

Another seemingly important advantage of working in hotels, restaurants, office and apartment buildings, and retail establishments is that they frequently offer an opportunity for stealing on the job. But stealing can be a two-edged sword. Apart from increasing the cost of the goods or services to the general public, a less obvious result is that the practice usually acts as a depressant on the employee's own wage level. Owners of small retail establishments and other employers frequently anticipate employee stealing and adjust the wage rate accordingly. Tonk's employer explained why he was paying Tonk $35 for a 55–60 hour workweek. These men will all steal, he said. Although he keeps close watch on Tonk, he estimates that Tonk steals from $35 to $40 a week.[3] What he steals, when added to his regular earnings, brings his take-home pay to $70 or $75 per week. The employer said he did not mind this because Tonk is worth that much to the business. But if he were to pay Tonk outright the full value of his labor, Tonk would still be stealing $35–$40 per week and this, he said, the business simply would not support.

This wage arrangement, with stealing built-in, was satisfactory to both parties, with each one independently expressing his satisfaction. Such a wage-theft system, however, is not as balanced and equitable as it appears. Since the wage level rests on the premise that the employee will steal the unpaid value of his labor, the man who does not steal on the job is penalized. And furthermore, even if he does not steal, no one would believe him; the employer and others believe he steals because the system presumes it.

Nor is the man who steals, as he is expected to, as well off as he believes himself to be. The employer may occasionally close his eyes to the worker's stealing but not often and not for long. He is, after all, a businessman and cannot always find it within himself to let a man steal from him, even if the man is stealing his own wages. Moreover, it is only by keeping close watch on the worker that the employer can control how much is stolen and thereby protect himself against the employee's stealing more than he is worth. From this viewpoint, then, the employer is not in wage-theft collusion with the employee. In the case of Tonk, for instance, the employer was not actively abetting the theft. His estimates of how much Tonk was stealing was based on what he thought Tonk was able to steal despite his own best efforts to prevent him from stealing anything at all. Were he to have caught Tonk in the act of stealing, he

[3] Exactly the same estimate as the one made by Tonk himself. On the basis of personal knowledge of the stealing routine employed by Tonk, however, I suspect the actual amount is considerably smaller.

would, of course, have fired him from the job and perhaps called the police as well. Thus, in an actual if not in a legal sense, all the elements of entrapment are present. The employer knowingly provides the conditions which entice (force) the employee to steal the unpaid value of his labor, but at the same time he punishes him for theft if he catches him doing so.

Other consequences of the wage-theft system are even more damaging to the employee. Let us, for argument's sake, say that Tonk is in no danger of entrapment; that his employer is willing to wink at the stealing and that Tonk, for his part, is perfectly willing to earn a little, steal a little. Let us say, too, that he is paid $35 a week and allowed to steal $35. His money income — as measured by the goods and services he can purchase with it — is, of course, $70. But not all of his income is available to him for all purposes. He cannot draw on what he steals to build his self-respect or to measure his self-worth. For this, he can draw only on his earnings — the amount given him publicly and voluntarily in exchange for his labor. His "respect" and "self-worth" income remains at $35 — only half that of the man who also receives $70 but all of it in the form of wages. His earnings publicly measure the worth of his labor to his employer, and they are important to others and to himself in taking the measure of his worth as a man.[4]

With or without stealing, and quite apart from any interior processes going on in the man who refuses such a job or quits it casually and without apparent reason, the objective fact is that menial jobs in retailing or in the service trades simply do not pay enough to support a man and his family. This is not to say that the worker is underpaid; this may or may not be true. Whether he is or not, the plain fact is that, in such a job, he cannot make a living. Nor can he take much comfort in the fact that these jobs tend to offer more regular, steadier work. If he cannot live on the $45 or $50 he makes in one week, the longer he works, the longer he cannot live on what he makes.[5]

[4] Some public credit may accrue to the clever thief but not respect.

[5] It might be profitable to compare, as Howard S. Becker suggests, gross aspects of income and housing costs in this particular area with those reported by Herbert Gans for the low-income working class in Boston's West End. In 1958, Gans reports, median income for the West Enders was just under $70 a week, a level considerably higher than that enjoyed by the people in the Carry-out neighborhood five years later. Gans himself rented a six-room apartment in the West End for $46 a month, about $10 more than the going rate for long-time residents. In the Carry-out neighborhood, rooms that could accommodate more than a cot and a miniature dresser — that is, rooms that qualified for family living — rented for $12 to $22 a week. Ignoring differences that really can't be ignored — the privacy and self-contained efficiency of the multi-room apartment as against the fragmented, public living of the rooming-house "apartment," with a public toilet on a floor always different from the one your room is on (no matter, it probably doesn't work, anyway) — and assuming comparable states of disrepair, the West Enders were paying $6 or $7 a month for a room that cost the Carry-outers at least $50 a month, and frequently

Construction work, even for unskilled laborers, usually pays better, with the hourly rate ranging from $1.50 to $2.60 an hour.[6] Importantly, too, good references, a good driving record, a tenth grade (or any high school) education, previous experience, the ability to "bring police clearance with you" are not normally required of laborers as they frequently are for some of the jobs in retailing or in the service trades.

Construction work, however, has its own objective disadvantages. It is, first of all, seasonal work for the great bulk of the laborers, beginning early in the spring and tapering off as winter weather sets in.[7] And even during the season the work is frequently irregular. Early or late in the season, snow or temperatures too low for concrete frequently sends the laborers back home, and during late spring or summer, a heavy rain on Tuesday or Wednesday, leaving a lot of water and mud behind it, can mean a two or three day workweek for the pick-and-shovel men and other unskilled laborers.[8]

The elements are not the only hazard. As the project moves from one construction stage to another, laborers — usually without warning — are laid off, sometimes permanently or sometimes for weeks at a time. The more fortunate or the better workers are told periodically to "take a walk for two, three days."

---

more. Looking at housing costs as a percentage of income — and again ignoring what cannot be ignored: that what goes by the name of "housing" in the two areas is not at all the same thing — the median income West Ender could get a six-room apartment for about 12 percent of his income, while his 1963 Carry-out counterpart, with a weekly income of $60 (to choose a figure from the upper end of the income range), often paid 20–33 percent of his income for one room. See Herbert J. Gans, *The Urban Villagers*, pp. 10–13.

[6] The higher amount is 1962 union scale for building laborers. According to the Wage Agreement Contract for Heavy Construction Laborers (Washington, D.C., and vicinity) covering the period from May 1, 1963 to April 30, 1966, minimum hourly wage for heavy construction laborers was to go from $2.75 (May 1963) by annual increments to $2.92, effective November 1, 1965.

[7] "Open-sky" work, such as building overpasses, highways, etc., in which the workers and materials are directly exposed to the elements, traditionally begins in March and ends around Thanksgiving. The same is true for much of the street repair work and the laying of sewer, electric, gas, and telephone lines by the city and public utilities, all important employers of laborers. Between Thanksgiving and March, they retain only skeleton crews selected from their best, most reliable men.

[8] In a recent year, the crime rate in Washington for the month of August jumped 18 percent over the preceding month. A veteran police officer explained the increase to David L. Bazelon, Chief Judge, U.S. Court of Appeals for the District of Columbia. "It's quite simple. . . . You see, August was a very wet month. . . . These people wait on the street corner each morning around 6:00 or 6:30 for a truck to pick them up and take them to a construction site. If it's raining, that truck doesn't come, and the men are going to be idle that day. If the bad weather keeps up for three days . . . we know we are going to have trouble on our hands — and sure enough, there invariably follows a rash of purse-snatchings, house-breakings and the like. . . . These people have to eat like the rest of us, you know." David L. Bazelon, Address to the Federal Bar Association, p. 3.

Both getting the construction job and getting to it are also relatively more difficult than is the case for the menial jobs in retailing and the service trades. Job competition is always fierce. In the city, the large construction projects are unionized. One has to have ready cash to get into the union to become eligible to work on these projects and, being eligible, one has to find an opening. Unless one "knows somebody," say a foreman or a laborer who knows the day before that they are going to take on new men in the morning, this can be a difficult and disheartening search.

Many of the nonunion jobs are in suburban Maryland or Virginia. The newspaper ads say, "Report ready to work to the trailer at the intersection of Rte. 11 and Old Bridge Rd., Bunston, Virginia (or Maryland)," but this location may be ten, fifteen, or even twenty-five miles from the Carry-out. Public transportation would require two or more hours to get there, if it services the area at all. Without access to a car or to a car-pool arrangement, it is not worthwhile reading the ad. So the men do not. Jobs such as these are usually filled by word of mouth information, beginning with someone who knows someone or who is himself working there and looking for a paying rider. Furthermore, nonunion jobs in outlying areas tend to be smaller projects of relatively short duration and to pay somewhat less than scale.

Still another objective factor is the work itself. For some men, whether the job be digging, mixing mortar, pushing a wheelbarrow, unloading materials, carrying and placing steel rods for reinforcing concrete, or building or laying concrete forms, the work is simply too hard. Men such as Tally and Wee Tom can make such work look like child's play; some of the older work-hardened men, such as Budder and Stanton, can do it too, although not without showing unmistakable signs of strain and weariness at the end of the workday. But those who lack the robustness of a Tally or the time-inured immunity of a Budder must either forego jobs such as these or pay a heavy toll to keep them. For Leroy, in his early twenties, almost six feet tall but weighing under 140 pounds, it would be as difficult to push a loaded wheelbarrow, or to unload and stack 96-pound bags of cement all day long, as it would be for Stoopy with his withered leg.

Heavy, backbreaking labor of the kind that used to be regularly associated with bull gangs or concrete gangs is no longer characteristic of laboring jobs, especially those with the larger, well-equipped construction companies. Brute strength is still required from time to time, as on smaller jobs where it is not economical to bring in heavy equipment or where the small, undercapitalized contractor has none to bring in. In many cases, however, the conveyor belt has replaced the wheelbarrow or the Georgia buggy, mechanized forklifts have eliminated heavy, manual lifting, and a variety of digging machines have replaced the pick and shovel. The result is fewer jobs for unskilled laborers and, in many cases, a work speed-up for those who do have jobs. Machines now set the pace formerly set by men. Formerly, a laborer pushed a wheelbarrow of wet cement to a particular spot, dumped it, and returned for another load. Another laborer, in hip boots, pushed the wet concrete around with a shovel or a hoe, getting it roughly level in preparation for the skilled finishers. He had relatively small loads to contend with and had only to keep up with the men pushing the wheelbarrows. Now, the job for the man pushing the wheelbarrow is gone and the wet concrete comes rushing down a chute at the man in the hip boots who must "spread it quick or drown."

Men who have been running an elevator, washing dishes, or "pulling trash" cannot easily move into laboring jobs. They lack the basic skills for "unskilled" construction labor, familiarity with tools and materials, and tricks of the trade without which hard jobs are made harder. Previously unused or untrained muscles rebel in pain against the new and insistent demands made upon them, seriously compromising the man's performance and testing his willingness to see the job through.

A healthy, sturdy, active man of good intelligence requires from two to four weeks to break in on a construction job.[9] Even if he is willing somehow to bull his way through the first few weeks, it frequently happens that his foreman or the craftsman he services with materials and general assistance is not willing to wait that long for him to get into condition or to learn at a glance the difference in size between a rough 2" x 8" and a finished 2" x 10". The foreman and the craftsman are themselves "under the gun" and cannot "carry" the man when other men, who are already used to the work and who know the tools and materials, are lined up to take the job.

Sea Cat was "healthy, sturdy, active and of good intelligence." When a judge gave him six weeks in which to pay his wife $200 in back child-support payments, he left his grocery-store job in order to take a higher-paying job as a laborer, arranged for him by a foreman friend. During the first week the weather was bad and he worked only Wednesday and Friday, cursing the elements all the while for cheating him out of the money he could have made. The second week, the weather was fair but he quit at the end of the fourth day, saying frankly that the work was too hard for him. He went back to his job at the grocery store and took a second job working nights as a dishwasher in a restaurant,[10] earning little if any more at the two jobs than he would have earned as a laborer, and keeping at both of them until he had paid off his debts.

[9] Estimate of Mr. Francis Greenfield, President of the International Hod Carriers, Building and Common Laborers' District Council of Washington, D.C., and Vicinity. I am indebted to Mr. Greenfield for several points in these paragraphs dealing with construction laborers.

[10] Not a sinecure, even by streetcorner standards.

Tonk did not last as long as Sea Cat. No one made any predictions when he got a job in a parking lot, but when the men on the corner learned he was to start on a road construction job, estimates of how long he would last ranged from one to three weeks. Wednesday was his first day. He spent that evening and night at home. He did the same on Thursday. He worked Friday and spent Friday evening and part of Saturday draped over the mailbox on the corner. Sunday afternoon, Tonk decided he was not going to report on the job the next morning. He explained that after working three days, he knew enough about the job to know that it was too hard for him. He knew he wouldn't be able to keep up and he'd just as soon quit now as get fired later.

Logan was a tall, two-hundred-pound man in his late twenties. His back used to hurt him only on the job, he said, but now he can't straighten up for increasingly longer periods of time. He said he had traced this to the awkward walk he was forced to adopt by the loaded wheelbarrows which pull him down into a half-stoop. He's going to quit, he said, as soon as he can find another job. If he can't find one real soon, he guesses he'll quit anyway. It's not worth it, having to walk bent over and leaning to one side.

Sometimes, the strain and effort is greater than the man is willing to admit, even to himself. In the early summer of 1963, Richard was rooming at Nancy's place. His wife and children were "in the country" (his grandmother's home in Carolina), waiting for him to save up enough money so that he could bring them back to Washington and start over again after a disastrous attempt to "make it" in Philadelphia. Richard had gotten a job with a fence company in Virginia. It paid $1.60 an hour. The first few evenings, when he came home from work, he looked ill from exhaustion and the heat. Stanton said Richard would have to quit, "he's too small [thin] for that kind of work." Richard said he was doing O.K. and would stick with the job.

At Nancy's one night, when Richard had been working about two weeks, Nancy and three or four others were sitting around talking, drinking, and listening to music. Someone asked Nancy when was Richard going to bring his wife and children up from the country. Nancy said she didn't know, but it probably depended on how long it would take him to save up enough money. She said she didn't think he could stay with the fence job much longer. This morning, she said, the man Richard rode to work with knocked on the door and Richard didn't answer. She looked in his room. Richard was still asleep. Nancy tried to shake him awake. "No more digging!" Richard cried out. "No more digging! I can't do no more God-damn digging!" When Nancy finally managed to wake him, he dressed quickly and went to work.

Richard stayed on the job two more weeks, then suddenly quit, ostensibly because his pay check was three dollars less than what he thought it should have been.

In summary of objective job considerations, then, the most important fact is that a man who is able and willing to work cannot earn enough money to support himself, his wife, and one or more children. A man's chances for working regularly are good only if he is willing to work for less than he can live on, and sometimes not even then. On some jobs, the wage rate is deceptively higher than on others, but the higher the wage rate, the more difficult it is to get the job, and the less the job security. Higher-paying construction work tends to be seasonal and, during the season, the amount of work available is highly sensitive to business and weather conditions and to the changing requirements of individual projects.[11] Moreover, high-paying construction jobs are frequently beyond the physical capacity of some of the men, and some of the low-paying jobs are scaled down even lower in accordance with the self-fulfilling assumption that the man will steal part of his wages on the job.[12]

Bernard assesses the objective job situation dispassionately over a cup of coffee, sometimes poking at the coffee with his spoon, sometimes staring at it as if, like a crystal ball, it holds tomorrow's secrets. He is twenty-seven years old. He and the woman with whom he lives have a baby son, and she has another child by another man. Bernard does odd jobs — mostly painting — but here it is the end of January, and his last job was with the Post Office during the Christmas mail rush. He would like postal work as a steady job, he says. It pays well (about $2.00 an hour) but he has twice failed the Post Office examination (he graduated from a Washington high school) and has given up the idea as an impractical one. He is supposed to see a man tonight about a job as a parking attendant for a large apartment house. The man told him to bring his birth certificate and driver's license, but his license was suspended because of a backlog of unpaid traffic fines. A friend promised to lend him some money this evening. If he gets it, he will pay the fines tomorrow

[11] The overall result is that, in the long run, a Negro laborer's earnings are not substantially greater — and may be less — than those of the busboy, janitor, or stock clerk. Herman P. Miller, for example, reports that in 1960, 40 percent of all jobs held by Negro men were as laborers or in the service trades. The average annual wage for nonwhite nonfarm laborers was $2,400. The average earning of nonwhite service workers was $2,500 (*Rich Man, Poor Man*, p. 90). Francis Greenfield estimates that in the Washington vicinity, the 1965 earnings of the union laborer who works whenever work is available will be about $3,200. Even this figure is high for the man on the streetcorner. Union men in heavy construction are the aristocrats of the laborers. Casual day labor and jobs with small firms in the building and construction trades, or with firms in other industries, pay considerably less.

[12] For an excellent discussion of the self-fulfilling assumption (or prophecy) as a social force, see "The Self-Fulfilling Prophecy," Ch. XI, in Robert K. Merton's *Social Theory and Social Structure*.

morning and have his license reinstated. He hopes the man with the job will wait till tomorrow night.

A "security job" is what he really wants, he said. He would like to save up money for a taxicab. (But having twice failed the postal examination and having a bad driving record as well, it is highly doubtful that he could meet the qualifications or pass the written test.) That would be "a good life." He can always get a job in a restaurant or as a clerk in a drugstore but they don't pay enough, he said. He needs to take home at least $50 to $55 a week. He thinks he can get that much driving a truck somewhere . . . Sometimes he wishes he had stayed in the army . . . A security job, that's what he wants most of all, a real security job . . .

When we look at what the men bring to the job rather than at what the job offers the men, it is essential to keep in mind that we are not looking at men who come to the job fresh, just out of school perhaps, and newly prepared to undertake the task of making a living, or from another job where they earned a living and are prepared to do the same on this job. Each man comes to the job with a long job history characterized by his not being able to support himself and his family. Each man carries this knowledge, born of his experience, with him. He comes to the job flat and stale, wearied by the sameness of it all, convinced of his own incompetence, terrified of responsibility — of being tested still again and found wanting. Possible exceptions are the younger men not yet, or just, married. They suspect all this but have yet to have it confirmed by repeated personal experience over time. But those who are or have been married know it well. It is the experience of the individual and the group; of their fathers and probably their sons. Convinced of their inadequacies, not only do they not seek out those few better-paying jobs which test their resources, but they actively avoid them, gravitating in a mass to the menial, routine jobs which offer no challenge — and therefore pose no threat — to the already diminished images they have of themselves.

Thus Richard does not follow through on the real estate agent's offer. He is afraid to do on his own — minor plastering, replacing broken windows, other minor repairs, and painting — exactly what he had been doing for months on a piecework basis under someone else (and which provided him with a solid base from which to derive a cost estimate).

Richard once offered an important clue to what may have gone on in his mind when the job offer was made. We were in the Carry-out, at a time when he was looking for work. He was talking about the kind of jobs available to him.

> I graduated from high school [Baltimore] but I don't know anything. I'm dumb. Most of the time I don't even say I graduated, 'cause then somebody asks me a question and I can't answer it, and they think I was lying about graduating. . . . They graduated me but I didn't know

> anything. I had lousy grades but I guess they wanted to get rid of me.
>
> I was at Margaret's house the other night and her little sister asked me to help her with her homework. She showed me some fractions and I knew right away I couldn't do them. I was ashamed so I told her I had to go to the bathroom.

And so it must have been, surely, with the real estate agent's offer. Convinced that "I'm dumb . . . I don't know anything," he "knew right away" he couldn't do it, despite the fact that he had been doing just this sort of work all along.

Thus, the man's low self-esteem generates a fear of being tested and prevents him from accepting a job with responsibilities or, once on a job, from staying with it if responsibilities are thrust on him, even if the wages are commensurately higher. Richard refuses such a job, Leroy leaves one, and another man, given more responsibility and more pay, knows he will fail and proceeds to do so, proving he was right about himself all along. The self-fulfilling prophecy is everywhere at work. In a hallway, Stanton, Tonk and Boley are passing a bottle around. Stanton recalls the time he was in the service. Everything was fine until he attained the rank of corporal. He worried about everything he did then. Was he doing the right thing? Was he doing it well? When would they discover their mistake and take his stripes (and extra pay) away? When he finally lost his stripes, everything was all right again.

Lethargy, disinterest, and general apathy on the job, so often reported by employers, has its streetcorner counterpart. The men do not ordinarily talk about their jobs or ask one another about them.[13] Although most of the men know who is or is not working at any given time, they may or may not know what particular job an individual man has. There is no overt interest in job specifics as they relate to this or that person, in large part perhaps because the specifics are not especially relevant. To know that a man is working is to know approximately how much he makes and to know as much as one needs or wants to know about how he makes it. After all, how much difference does it make to know whether a man is pushing a mop or pulling trash in an apartment house, a restaurant, or an office building, or delivering groceries, drugs, or liquor, or, if he's a laborer, whether he's pushing a wheelbarrow, mixing mortar, or digging a hole. So much does one job look like every other that there is little to choose between them. In large part, the job market

[13] This stands in dramatic contrast to the leisure-time conversation of stable, working-class men. For the coal miners (of Ashton, England), for example, "the topic [of conversation] which surpasses all others in frequency is work — the difficulties which have been encountered in the day's shift, the way in which a particular task was accomplished, and so on." Josephine Klein, *Samples from English Cultures*, Vol. I, p. 88.

consists of a narrow range of nondescript chores calling for nondistinctive, undifferentiated, unskilled labor. "A job is a job."

A crucial factor in the streetcorner man's lack of job commitment is the overall value he places on the job. *For his part, the streetcorner man puts no lower value on the job than does the larger society around him.* He knows the social value of the job by the amount of money the employer is willing to pay him for doing it. In a real sense, every pay day, he counts in dollars and cents the value placed on the job by society at large. He is no more (and frequently less) ready to quit and look for another job than his employer is ready to fire him and look for another man. Neither the streetcorner man who performs these jobs nor the society which requires him to perform them assesses the job as one "worth doing and worth doing well." Both employee and employer are contemptuous of the job. The employee shows his contempt by his reluctance to accept it or keep it, the employer by paying less than is required to support a family.[14] Nor does the low-wage job offer prestige, respect, interesting work, opportunity for learning or advancement, or any other compensation. With few exceptions, jobs filled by the streetcorner men are at the bottom of the employment ladder in every respect, from wage level to prestige. Typically, they are hard, dirty, uninteresting, and underpaid. The rest of society (whatever its ideal values regarding the dignity of labor) holds the job of the dishwasher or janitor or unskilled laborer in low esteem if not outright contempt.[15] So does the streetcorner man. He cannot do otherwise. He cannot draw from a job those social values which other people do not put into it.[16]

Only occasionally does spontaneous conversation touch on these matters directly. Talk about jobs is usually limited to isolated statements of intention, such as "I think I'll get me another gig [job]," "I'm going to look for a construction job when the weather breaks," or "I'm going to quit. I can't take no more of his shit." Job assessments typically consist

[14] It is important to remember that the employer is not entirely a free agent. Subject to the constraints of the larger society, he acts for the larger society as well as for himself. Child labor laws, safety and sanitation regulations, minimum wage scales in some employment areas, and other constraints, are already on the books; other control mechanisms, such as a guaranteed annual wage, are to be had for the voting.

[15] See, for example, the U.S. Bureau of the Census, *Methodology and Scores of Socioeconomic Status*. The assignment of the lowest SES ratings to men who hold such jobs is not peculiar to our own society. A low SES rating for "the shoeshine boy or garbage man . . . seems to be true for all [industrial] countries." Alex Inkeles, "Industrial Man," p. 8.

[16] That the streetcorner man downgrades manual labor should occasion no surprise. Merton points out that "the American stigmatization of manual labor . . . *has been found to hold rather uniformly in all social classes*" (emphasis in original; *Social Theory and Social Structure*, p. 145). That he finds no satisfaction in such work should also occasion no surprise: "[There is] a clear positive correlation between the over-all status of occupations and the experience of satisfaction in them." Inkeles, "Industrial Man," p. 12.

of nothing more than a noncommittal shrug and "It's O.K." or "It's a job."

One reason for the relative absence of talk about one's job is, as suggested earlier, that the sameness of job experience does not bear reiteration. Another and more important reason is the emptiness of the job experience itself. The man sees middle-class occupations as a primary source of prestige, pride, and self-respect; his own job affords him none of these. To think about his job is to see himself as others see him, to remind him of just where he stands in this society.[17] And because society's criteria for placement are generally the same as his own, to talk about his job can trigger a flush of shame and a deep, almost physical ache to change places with someone, almost anyone, else.[18] The desire to be a person in his own right, to be noticed by the world he lives in, is shared by each of the men on the streetcorner. Whether they articulate this desire (as Tally does below) or not, one can see them position themselves to catch the attention of their fellows in much the same way as plants bend or stretch to catch the sunlight.[19]

Tally and I were in the Carry-out. It was summer, Tally's peak earning season as a cement finisher, a semiskilled job a cut or so above that of the unskilled laborer. His take-home pay during these weeks was well over a hundred dollars — "a lot of bread." But for Tally, who no longer had a family to support, bread was not enough.

> "You know that boy came in last night? That Black Moozlem? That's what I ought to be doing. I ought to be in his place."
>
> "What do you mean?"
>
> "Dressed nice, going to [night] school, got a good job."
>
> "He's no better off than you, Tally. You make more than he does."
>
> "It's not the money. [Pause] It's position, I guess. He's got position. When he finish school he gonna be a supervisor. People respect him. . . . Thinking about people with position and education gives me a feeling right here [pressing his fingers into the pit of his stomach]."
>
> "You're educated, too. You have a skill, a trade. You're a cement finisher. You can make a building, pour a sidewalk."

[17] "[In our society] a man's work is one of the things by which he is judged, and certainly one of the more significant things by which he judges himself. . . . A man's work is one of the more important parts of his social identity, of his self; indeed, of his fate in the one life he has to live." Everett C. Hughes, *Men and Their Work*, pp. 42–43.

[18] Noting that lower-class persons "are constantly exposed to evidence of their own irrelevance," Lee Rainwater spells out still another way in which the poor are poor: "The identity problems of lower class persons make the soul-searching of middle class adolescents and adults seem rather like a kind of conspicuous consumption of psychic riches" ("Work and Identity in the Lower Class," p. 3).

[19] Sea Cat cuts his pants legs off at the calf and puts a fringe on the raggedy edges. Tonk breaks his "shades" and continues to wear the horn-rimmed frames minus the lenses. Richard cultivates a distinctive manner of speech. Lonny gives himself a birthday party. And so on.

"That's different. Look, can anybody do what you're doing? Can anybody just come up and do your job? Well, in one week I can teach you cement finishing. You won't be as good as me 'cause you won't have the experience but you'll be a cement finisher. That's what I mean. Anybody can do what I'm doing and that's what gives me this feeling. [Long pause] Suppose I like this girl. I go over to her house and I meet her father. He starts talking about what he done today. He talks about operating on somebody and sewing them up and about surgery. I know he's a doctor 'cause of the way he talks. Then she starts talking about what she did. Maybe she's a boss or a supervisor. Maybe she's a lawyer and her father says to me, 'And what do you do, Mr. Jackson?' [Pause] You remember at the courthouse, Lonny's trial? You and the lawyer was talking in the hall? You remember? I just stood there listening. I didn't say a word. You know why? 'Cause I didn't even know what you was talking about. That's happened to me a lot."

"Hell, you're nothing special. That happens to everybody. Nobody knows everything. One man is a doctor, so he talks about surgery. Another man is a teacher, so he talks about books. But doctors and teachers don't know anything about concrete. You're a cement finisher and that's your specialty."

"Maybe so, but when was the last time you saw anybody standing around talking about concrete?"

The streetcorner man wants to be a person in his own right, to be noticed, to be taken account of, but in this respect, as well as in meeting his money needs, his job fails him. The job and the man are even. The job fails the man and the man fails the job.

Furthermore, the man does not have any reasonable expectation that, however bad it is, his job will lead to better things. Menial jobs are not, by and large, the starting point of a track system which leads to even better jobs for those who are able and willing to do them. The busboy or dishwasher in a restaurant is not on a job track which, if negotiated skillfully, leads to chef or manager of the restaurant. The busboy or dishwasher who works hard becomes, simply, a hard-working busboy or dishwasher. Neither hard work nor perseverance can conceivably carry the janitor to a sitdown job in the office building he cleans up. And it is the apprentice who becomes the journeyman electrician, plumber, steam fitter or bricklayer, not the common unskilled Negro laborer.

Thus, the job is not a stepping-stone to something better. It is a dead end. It promises to deliver no more tomorrow, next month or next year than it does today.

Delivering little, and promising no more, the job is "no big thing." The man appears to treat the job in a cavalier fashion, working and not working as the spirit moves him, as if all that matters is the immediate satisfaction of his present appetites, the surrender to present moods, and the indulgence of whims with no thought for the cost, the consequences, the future. To the middle-class observer, this behavior reflects a "present-time orientation" — an "inability to defer gratification." It is this "present-time" orientation — as against the "future orientation" of the middle-class person — that "explains" to the outsider why Leroy chooses to spend the day at the Carry-out rather than report to work; why Richard, who was paid Friday, was drunk Saturday and Sunday and penniless Monday; why Sweets quit his job today because the boss looked at him "funny" yesterday.

But from the inside looking out, what appears as a "present-time" orientation to the outside observer is, to the man experiencing it, as much a future orientation as that of his middle-class counterpart.[20] The difference between the two men lies not so much in their different orientations to time as in their different orientations to future time or, more specifically, to their different futures.[21]

The future orientation of the middle-class person presumes, among other things, a surplus of resources to be invested in the future and a belief that the future will be sufficiently stable both to justify his investment (money in a bank, time and effort in a job, investment of himself in marriage and family, etc.) and to permit the consumption of his investment at a time, place and manner of his own choosing and to his greater satisfaction. But the streetcorner man lives in a sea of want. He does not, as a rule, have a surplus of resources, either economic or psychological. Gratification of hunger and the desire for simple creature comforts cannot be long deferred. Neither can support for one's flagging self-esteem. Living on the edge of both economic and psychological subsistence, the streetcorner man is obliged to expend all his resources on maintaining himself from moment to moment.[22]

[20] Taking a somewhat different point of view, S. M. Miller and Frank Riessman suggest that "the entire concept of deferred gratification may be inappropriate to understanding the essence of workers' lives" ("The Working Class Subculture: A New View," p. 87).

[21] This sentence is a paraphrase of a statement made by Marvin Cline at a 1965 colloquium at the Mental Health Study Center, National Institute of Mental Health.

[22] And if, for the moment, he does sometimes have more money than he chooses to spend or more food than he wants to eat, he is pressed to spend the money and eat the food anyway since his friends, neighbors, kinsmen, or acquaintances will beg or borrow whatever surplus he has or, failing this, they may steal it. In one extreme case, one of the men admitted taking the last of a woman's surplus food allotment after she had explained that, with four children, she could not spare any food. The prospect that consumer soft goods not consumed by oneself will be consumed by someone else may be related to the way in which portable consumer durable goods, such as watches, radios, television sets, or phonographs, are sometimes looked at as a form of savings. When Shirley was on welfare, she regularly took her television set out of pawn when she got her monthly check. Not so much to watch it, she explained, as to have something to fall back on when her money runs out toward the end of the month. For her and others, the television set or the phonograph is her savings, the pawnshop is where she banks her savings, and the pawn ticket is her bankbook.

As for the future, the young streetcorner man has a fairly good picture of it. In Richard or Sea Cat or Arthur he can see himself in his middle twenties; he can look at Tally to see himself at thirty, at Wee Tom to see himself in his middle thirties, and at Budder and Stanton to see himself in his forties. It is a future in which everything is uncertain except the ultimate destruction of his hopes and the eventual realization of his fears. The most he can reasonably look forward to is that these things do not come too soon. Thus, when Richard squanders a week's pay in two days it is not because, like an animal or a child, he is "present-time oriented," unaware of or unconcerned with his future. He does so precisely because he is aware of the future and the hoplessness of it all.

Sometimes this kind of response appears as a conscious, explicit choice. Richard had had a violent argument with his wife. He said he was going to leave her and the children, that he had had enough of everything and could not take any more, and he chased her out of the house. His chest still heaving, he leaned back against the wall in the hallway of his basement apartment.

> "I've been scuffling for five years," he said. "I've been scuffling for five years from morning till night. And my kids still don't have anything, my wife don't have anything, and I don't have anything.
>
> "There," he said, gesturing down the hall to a bed, a sofa, a couple of chairs and a television set, all shabby, some broken. "There's everything I have and I'm having trouble holding onto that."
>
> Leroy came in, presumably to petition Richard on behalf of Richard's wife, who was sitting outside on the steps, afraid to come in. Leroy started to say something but Richard cut him short.
>
> "Look, Leroy, don't give me any of that action. You and me are entirely different people. Maybe I look like a boy and maybe I act like a boy sometimes but I got a man's mind. You and me don't want the same things out of life. Maybe some of the same, but you don't care how long you have to wait for yours and *I — want — mine — right — now.*" [23]

[23] This was no simple rationalization for irresponsibility. Richard had indeed "been scuffling for five years" trying to keep his family going. Until shortly after this episode, Richard was known and respected as one of the hardest-working men on the street. Richard had said, only a couple of months earlier, "I figure you got to get out there and try. You got to try before you can get anything." His wife Shirley confirmed that he had always tried. "If things get tough, with me I'll get all worried. But Richard get worried, he don't want me to see him worried. . . . He *will* get out there. He's shoveled snow, picked beans, and he's done some of everything. . . . He's not ashamed to get out there and get us something to eat." At the time of the episode reported above, Leroy was just starting marriage and raising a family. He and Richard were not, as Richard thought, "entirely different people." Leroy had just not learned, by personal experience over time, what Richard had learned. But within two years Leroy's marriage had broken up and he was talking and acting like Richard. "He just let go completely," said one of the men on the street.

Thus, apparent present-time concerns with consumption and indulgences — material and emotional — reflect a future-time orientation. "I want mine right now" is ultimately a cry of despair, a direct response to the future as he sees it.[24]

In many instances, it is precisely the streetcorner man's orientation to the future — but to a future loaded with "trouble" — which not only leads to a greater emphasis on present concerns ("I want mine right now") but also contributes importantly to the instability of employment, family and friend relationships, and to the general transient quality of daily life.

Let me give some concrete examples. One day, after Tally had gotten paid, he gave me four twenty-dollar bills and asked me to keep them for him. Three days later he asked me for the money. I returned it and asked why he did not put his money in a bank. He said that the banks close at two o'clock. I argued that there were four or more banks within a two-block radius of where he was working at the time and that he could easily get to any one of them on his lunch hour. "No, man," he said, "you don't understand. They close at two o'clock and they closed Saturday and Sunday. Suppose I get into trouble and I got to make it [leave]. Me get out of town, and everything I got in the world layin' up in that bank? No good! No good!"

In another instance, Leroy and his girl friend were discussing "trouble." Leroy was trying to decide how best to go about getting his hands on some "long green" (a lot of money), and his girl friend cautioned him about "trouble." Leroy sneered at this, saying he had had "trouble" all his life and wasn't afraid of a little more. "Anyway," he said, "I'm famous for leaving town." [25]

Thus, the constant awareness of a future loaded with "trouble" results in a constant readiness to leave, to "make it," to "get out of town,"

[24]There is no mystically intrinsic connection between "present-time" orientation and lower-class persons. Whenever people of whatever class have been uncertain, skeptical or downright pessimistic about the future, "I want mine right now" has been one of the characteristic responses, although it is usually couched in more delicate terms: e.g., Omar Khayyam's "Take the cash and let the credit go," or Horace's "*Carpe diem.*" In wartime, especially, all classes tend to slough off conventional restraints on sexual and other behavior (i.e., become less able or less willing to defer gratification). And when inflation threatens, darkening the fiscal future, persons who formerly husbanded their resources with commendable restraint almost stampede one another rushing to spend their money. Similarly, it seems that future-time orientation tends to collapse toward the present when persons are in pain or under stress. The point here is that, the label notwithstanding, (what passes for) present-time orientation appears to be a situation-specific phenomenon rather than a part of the standard psychic equipment of Cognitive Lower Class Man.

[25] And proceeded to do just that the following year when "trouble" — in this case, a grand jury indictment, a pile of debts, and a violent separation from his wife and children — appeared again.

and discourages the man from sinking roots into the world he lives in.[26] Just as it discourages him from putting money in the bank, so it discourages him from committing himself to a job, especially one whose payoff lies in the promise of future rewards rather than in the present. In the same way, it discourages him from deep and lasting commitments to family and friends or to any other persons, places or things, since such commitments could hold him hostage, limiting his freedom of movement and thereby compromising his security which lies in that freedom.

What lies behind the response to the driver of the pickup truck, then, is a complex combination of attitudes and assessments. The streetcorner man is under continuous assault by his job experiences and job fears. His experiences and fears feed on one another. The kind of job he can get — and frequently only after fighting for it, if then — steadily confirms his fears, depresses his self-confidence and self-esteem until finally, terrified of an opportunity even if one presents itself, he stands defeated by his experiences, his belief in his own self-worth destroyed and his fears a confirmed reality.

[26] For a discussion of "trouble" as a focal concern of lower-class culture, see Walter Miller, "Lower Class Culture as a Generating Milieu of Gang Delinquency," pp. 7, 8.

21

The impact of money on an African subsistence economy

PAUL J. BOHANNAN

In this article Paul Bohannan describes the early colonial economy of the Tiv of Nigeria and shows that it contained three spheres of exchange. These spheres — subsistence, prestige, and women in marriage — were separated by the rule that goods from one could not be used to purchase goods in another without loss of prestige to one of the parties in the exchange. When general-purpose money was introduced from the West, it became possible to equate the values of each of these spheres, and radical change took place. The author discusses in detail the nature of the changes resulting from the introduction of money.

It has often been claimed that money was to be found in much of the African continent before the impact of the European world and the extension of trade made coinage general. When we examine these claims, however, they tend to evaporate or to emerge as tricks of definition. It is an astounding fact that economists have, for decades, been assigning three or four qualities to money when they discuss it with reference to our own society or to those of the medieval and modern world, yet the moment they have gone to ancient history or to the societies and economies studied by anthropologists they have sought the "real" nature of money by allowing only one of these defining characteristics to dominate their definitions.

All economists learned as students that money serves at least three purposes. It is a means of exchange, it is a mode of payment, it is a standard of value. Depending on the vintage and persuasion of the author of the book one consults, one may find another money use — storage of

From "The Impact of Money on an African Subsistence Economy," *The Journal of Economic History* 19 (December 1959): 491–503. Reprinted by permission of the publisher and the author. Some footnotes, the bibliographic citations, and the bibliography are omitted.

wealth. In newer books, money is defined as merely the means of unitizing purchasing power, yet behind that definition still lie the standard, the payment, and the exchange uses of money.

It is interesting that on the fairly rare occasions that economists discuss primitive money at all — or at least when they discuss it with any empirical referrent — they have discarded one or more of the money uses in framing their definitions. Paul Einzig,[1] to take one example for many, first makes a plea for "elastic definitions," and goes on to point out that different economists have utilized different criteria in their definitions; he then falls into the trap he has been exposing: he excoriates Menger for utilizing only the "medium of exchange" criterion and then himself omits it, utilizing only the standard and payment criteria, thus taking sides in an argument in which there was no real issue.

The answer to these difficulties should be apparent. If we take no more than the three major money uses — payment, standard, and means of exchange — we will find that in many primitive societies as well as in some of the ancient empires, one object may serve one money use while quite another object serves another money use. In order to deal with this situation, and to avoid the trap of choosing one of these uses to define "real" money, Karl Polanyi [2] and his associates have labeled as "general-purpose money" any item which serves all three of these primary money uses, while an item which serves only one or two is "special-purpose money." With this distinction in mind, we can see that special-purpose money was very common in pre-contact Africa, but that general-purpose money was rare.

This paper is a brief analysis of the impact of general-purpose money and increase in trade in an African economy which had known only local trade and had used only special-purpose money.

The Tiv are a people, still largely pagan, who live in the Benue Valley in central Nigeria, among whom I had the good fortune to live and work for well over two years. They are prosperous subsistence farmers and have a highly developed indigenous market in which they exchanged their produce and handicrafts, and through which they carried on local trade. The most distinctive feature about the economy of the Tiv — and it is a feature they share with many, perhaps most, of the pre-monetary peoples — is what can be called a multi-centric economy. Briefly, a multicentric economy is an economy in which a society's exchangeable goods fall into two or more mutually exclusive spheres, each marked by

[1] Paul Einzig, *Primitive Money in Its Ethnological, Historical and Economic Aspects* (London: Eyre and Spottiswoode, 1949), pp. 319–26.

[2] Karl Polanyi, "The Economy as Instituted Process," in Karl Polanyi, Conrad M. Arensberg, and Harry W. Pearson, eds. *Trade and Market in the Early Empires* (Glencoe, Ill.: The Free Press and The Falcon's Wing Press, 1957), pp. 264–66.

different institutionalization and different moral values. In some multi-centric economies these spheres remain distinct, though in most there are more or less institutionalized means of converting wealth from one into wealth in another.

Indigenously there were three spheres in the multi-centric economy of the Tiv. The first of these spheres is that associated with subsistence, which the Tiv call *yiagh*. The commodities in it include all locally produced foodstuffs: the staple yams and cereals, plus all the condiments, vegetable side-dishes, and seasonings, as well as small livestock — chickens, goats, and sheep. It also includes household utensils (mortars, grindstones, calabashes, baskets, and pots), some tools (particularly those used in agriculture), and raw materials for producing any items in the category.

Within this sphere, goods are distributed either by gift giving or through marketing. Traditionally, there was no money of any sort in this sphere — all goods changed hands by barter. There was a highly developed market organization at which people exchanged their produce for their requirements, and in which today traders buy produce in cheap markets and transport it to sell in dearer markets. The morality of this sphere of the economy is the morality of the free and uncontrolled market.

The second sphere of the Tiv economy is one which is in no way associated with markets. The category of goods within this sphere is slaves, cattle, ritual "offices" purchased from the Jukun, that type of large white cloth known as *tugudu*, medicines and magic, and metal rods. One is still entitled to use the present tense in this case, for ideally the category still exists in spite of the fact that metal rods are today very rare, that slavery has been abolished, that European "offices" have replaced Jukun offices and cannot be bought, and that much European medicine has been accepted. Tiv still quote prices of slaves in cows and brass rods, and of cattle in brass rods and *tugudu* cloth. The price of magical rites, as it has been described in the literature, was in terms of *tugudu* cloth or brass rods (though payment might be made in other items); payment for Jukun titles was in cows and slaves, *tugudu* cloths and metal rods.[3]

None of these goods ever entered the market as it was institutionalized in Tivland, even though it might be possible for an economist to find the principle of supply and demand at work in the exchanges which characterized it. The actual shifts of goods took place at ceremonies, at more or less ritualized wealth displays, and on occasions when "doctors" performed rites and prescribed medicines. Tiv refer to the items and the ac-

[3] B. Akiga Sai, *Akiga's Story* (London: International Institute of African Languages and Cultures, 1939), p. 382 and passim.

sphere #1

sphere #2

tivities within this sphere by the word *shagba,* which can be roughly translated as prestige.

Within the prestige sphere there was one item which took on all of the money uses and hence can be called a general-purpose currency, though it must be remembered that it was of only a *very limited range.* Brass rods were used as means of exchange *within the sphere;* they also served as a standard of value within it (though not the only one), and as a means of payment. However, this sphere of the economy was tightly sealed off from the subsistence goods and its market. After European contact, brass rods occasionally entered the market, but they did so only as means of payment, not as medium of exchange or as standard of valuation. Because of the complex institutionalization and morality, no one ever sold a slave for food; no one, save in the depths of extremity, ever paid brass rods for domestic goods.

The supreme and unique sphere of exchangeable values for the Tiv contains a single item: rights in human beings other than slaves, particularly rights in women. Even twenty-five years after official abolition of exchange marriage, it is the category of exchange in which Tiv are emotionally most entangled. All exchanges within this category are exchanges of rights in human beings, usually dependent women and children. Its values are expressed in terms of kinship and marriage.

Tiv marriage is an extremely complex subject. Again, economists might find supply and demand principles at work, but Tiv adamantly separate marriage and market. Before the coming of the Europeans all "real" marriages were exchange marriages. In its simplest form, an exchange marriage involves two men exchanging sisters. Actually, this simple form seldom or never occurred. In order for every man to have a ward *(ingol)* to exchange for a wife, small localized agnatic lineages formed ward-sharing groups ("those who eat one Ingol" — *mbaye ingol i mom*). There was an initial "exchange" — or at least, distribution — of wards among the men of this group, so that each man became the guardian *(tien)* of one or more wards. The guardian, then, saw to the marriage of his ward, exchanging her with outsiders for another woman (her "partner" or *ikyar*) who becomes the bride of the guardian or one of his close agnatic kinsmen, or — in some situations — becomes a ward in the ward-sharing group and is exchanged for yet another woman who becomes a wife.

Tiv are, however, extremely practical and sensible people, and they know that successful marriages cannot be made if women are not consulted and if they are not happy. Elopements occurred, and sometimes a woman in exchange was not forthcoming. Therefore, a debt existed from the ward-sharing group of the husband to that of the guardian.

These debts sometimes lagged two or even three generations behind actual exchanges. The simplest way of paying them off was for the eldest daughter of the marriage to return to the ward-sharing group of her mother, as ward, thus cancelling the debt.

Because of its many impracticalities, the system had to be buttressed in several ways in order to work: one way was a provision for "earnest" during the time of the lag, another was to recognize other types of marriage as binding to limited extents. These two elements are somewhat confused with one another, because of the fact that right up until the abolition of exchange marriage in 1927, the inclination was always to treat all non-exchange marriages as if they were "lags" in the completion of exchange marriages.

When lags in exchange occurred, they were usually filled with "earnests" of brass rods or, occasionally, it would seem, of cattle. The brass rods or cattle in such situations were *never* exchange equivalents *(ishe)* for the woman. The only "price" of one woman is another woman.

Although Tiv decline to grant it antiquity, another type of marriage occurred at the time Europeans first met them — it was called "accumulating a woman/wife" (*kem kwase*). It is difficult to tell today just exactly what it consisted in, because the terminology of this union has been adapted to describe the bridewealth marriage that was declared by an administrative fiat of 1927 to be the only legal form.

Kem marriage consisted in acquisition of sexual, domestic and economic rights in a woman — but not the rights to filiate her children to the social group of the husband. Put in another way, in exchange marriage, both rights *in genetricem* (rights to filiate a woman's children) and rights *in uxorem* (sexual, domestic and economic rights in a woman) automatically were acquired by husbands and their lineages. In *kem* marriage, only rights *in uxorem* were acquired. In order to affiliate the *kem* wife's children, additional payments had to be made to the woman's guardians. These payments were for the children, not for the rights *in genetricem* in their mother, which could be acquired only by exchange of equivalent rights in another woman. *Kem* payments were paid in brass rods. However, rights in women had no equivalent or "price" in brass rods or in any other item — save, of course, identical rights in another woman. *Kem* marriage was similar to but showed important differences from bridewealth marriage as it is known in South and East Africa. There rights in women and rights in cattle form a single economic sphere, and could be exchanged directly for one another. Among Tiv, however, conveyance of rights in women necessarily involved direct exchange of another woman. The Tiv custom that approached bridewealth was not an exchange of equivalents, but payment in a medium that was specifically not equivalent.

Thus, within the sphere of exchange marriage there was no item that fulfilled any of the uses of money; when second-best types of marriage were made, payment was in an item which was specifically not used as a standard of value.

That Tiv do conceptualize exchange articles as belonging to different categories, and that they rank the categories on a moral basis, and that most but not all exchanges are limited to one sphere, gives rise to the fact that two different kinds of exchanges may be recognized: exchange of items contained within a single category, and exchanges of items belonging to different categories. For Tiv, these two different types of exchange are marked by separate and distinct moral attitudes.

To maintain this distinction between the two types of exchanges which Tiv mark by different behavior and different values, I shall use separate words. I shall call those exchanges of items within a single category "conveyances" and those exchanges of items from one category to another "conversions." Roughly, conveyances are morally neutral; conversions have a strong moral quality in their rationalization.

Exchanges within a category — particularly that of subsistence, the only one intact today — excite no moral judgments. Exchanges between categories, however, do excite a moral reaction: the man who exchanges lower category goods for higher category goods does not brag about his market luck but about his "strong heart" and his success in life. The man who exchanges high category goods for lower rationalizes his action in terms of high-valued motivation (most often the needs of his kinsmen).

The two institutions most intimately connected with conveyance are markets and marriage. Conveyance in the prestige sphere seems (to the latter-day investigator, at least) to have been less highly institutionalized. It centered on slave dealing, on curing, and on the acquisition of status.

Conversion is a much more complex matter. Conversion depends on the fact that some items of every sphere could, on certain occasions, be used in exchanges in which the return was *not* considered equivalent (*ishe*). Obviously, given the moral ranking of the spheres, such a situation leaves one party to the exchange in a good position, and the other in a bad one. Tiv says that it is "good" to trade food for brass rods, but that it is "bad" to trade brass rods for food, that it is good to trade your cows or brass rods for a wife, but very bad to trade your marriage ward for cows or brass rods.

Seen from the individual's point of view, it is profitable and possible to invest one's wealth if one converts it into a morally superior category: to convert subsistence wealth into prestige wealth and both into women is the aim of the economic endeavor or individual Tiv. To put it into economists' terms: conversion is the ultimate type of maximization.

We have already examined the marriage system by which a man could convert his brass rods to a wife: he could get a *kem* wife and *kem* her children as they were born. Her daughters, then, could be used as wards in his exchange marriages. It is the desire of every Tiv to "acquire a woman" (*ngoho kwase*) either as wife or ward in some way other than sharing in the ward-sharing group. A wife whom one acquires in any other way is not the concern of one's marriage-ward sharing group because the woman or other property exchanged for her did not belong to the marriage-ward group. The daughters of such a wife are not divided among the members of a man's marriage-ward group, but only among his sons. Such a wife is not only indicative of a man's ability and success financially and personally, but rights in her are the only form of property which is not ethically subject to the demands of his kinsmen.

Conversion from the prestige sphere to the kinship sphere was, thus, fairly common; it consisted in all the forms of marriage save exchange marriage, usually in terms of brass rods.

Conversion from the subsistence sphere to the prestige sphere was also usually in terms of metal rods. They, on occasion, entered the market place as payment. If the owner of the brass rods required an unusually large amount of staples to give a feast, making too heavy a drain on his wives' food supplies, he might buy it with brass rods.

However, brass rods could not possibly have been a general currency. They were not divisible. One could not receive "change" from a brass rod. Moreover, a single rod was worth much more than the usual market purchases for any given day of most Tiv subsistence traders. Although it might be possible to buy chickens with brass rods, one would have to have bought a very large quantity of yams to equal one rod, and to buy an item like pepper with rods would be laughable.

Brass rods, thus, overlapped from the prestige to the subsistence sphere on some occasions, but only on special occasions and for large purchases.

Not only is conversion possible, but it is encouraged—it is, in fact, the behavior which proves a man's worth. Tiv are scornful of a man who is merely rich in subsistence goods (or, today, in money). If, having adequate subsistence, he does not seek prestige in accordance with the old counters, or if he does not strive for more wives, and hence more children, the fault must be personal inadequacy. They also note that they all try to keep a man from making conversions; jealous kinsmen of a rich man will bewitch him and his people by fetishes, in order to make him expend his wealth on sacrifices to repair the fetishes, thus maintaining economic equality. However, once a conversion has been made, demands of kinsmen are not effective — at least, they take a new form.

Therefore, the man who successfully converts his wealth into higher categories is successful — he has a "strong heart." He is both feared and respected.

In this entire process, metal rods hold a pivotal position, and it is not surprising that early administrators considered them money. Originally imported from Europe, they were used as "currency" in some part of southern Nigeria in the slave trade. They are dowels about a quarter of an inch in diameter and some three feet long; they can be made into jewelry, and were used as a source of metal for castings.

Whatever their use elsewhere, brass rods in Tivland had some but not all of the attributes of money. Within the prestige sphere, they were used as a standard of equivalence, and they were a medium of exchange; they were also a mode for storage of wealth, and were used as payment. In short, brass rods were a general-purpose currency *within the prestige sphere.* However, outside of the prestige sphere — markets and marriage were the most active institutions of exchange outside it — brass rods fulfilled only one of these functions of money: payment. We have examined in detail the reasons why equivalency could not exist between brass rods and rights in women, between brass rods and food.

We have, thus, in Tivland, a multi-centric economy of three spheres, and we have a sort of money which was general-purpose money within the limited range of the prestige sphere, and a special-purpose money in the special transactions in which the other spheres overlapped it.

The next question is: what happened to this multi-centric economy and to the morality accompanying it when it felt the impact of the expanding European economy in the nineteenth and early twentieth centuries, and when an all-purpose money of very much greater range was introduced?

The Western impact is not, of course, limited to economic institutions. Administrative organizations, missions and others have been as effective instruments of change as any other.

One of the most startling innovations of the British administration was a general peace. Before the arrival of the British, one did not venture far beyond the area of one's kinsmen or special friends. To do so was to court death or enslavement.

With government police systems and safety, road-building was also begun. Moving about the country has been made both safe and comparatively easy. Peace and the new road network led to both increased trade and a greater number of markets.

Not only has the internal marketing system been perturbed by the introduction of alien institutions, but the economic institutions of the Tiv have in fact been put into touch with world economy. Northern Nigeria, like much of the rest of the colonial world, was originally taken over by trading companies with governing powers. The close linkage of government and trade was evident when taxation was introduced into Tivland. Tax was originally paid in produce, which was transported and sold through Hausa traders, who were government contractors. A few years later, coinage was introduced; taxes were demanded in that medium. It became necessary for Tiv to go into trade or to make their own contract with foreign traders in order to get cash. The trading companies, which had had "canteens" on the Benue for some decades, were quick to cooperate with the government in introducing a "cash crop" which could be bought by the traders in return for cash to pay taxes, and incidentally to buy imported goods. The crop which proved best adapted for this purpose in Tivland was beniseed *(sesamum indicum)*, a crop Tiv already grew in small quantities. Acreage need only be increased and facilities for sale established.

There is still another way in which Tiv economy is linked, through the trading companies, to the economy of the outside world. Not only do the companies buy their cash crops, they also "stake" African traders with imported goods. There is, on the part both of the companies and the government, a desire to build up "native entrepreneurial classes." Imported cloth, enamelware, and ironmongery are generally sold through a network of dependent African traders. Thus, African traders are linked to the companies, and hence into international trade.

Probably no single factor has been so important, however, as the introduction of all-purpose money. Neither introduction of cash crops and taxes nor extended trading has affected the basic congruence between Tiv ideas and their institutionalization to the same extent as has money. With the introduction of money the indigenous ideas of maximization — that is, conversion of all forms of wealth into women and children — no longer leads to the result it once did.

General-purpose money provides a common denominator among all the spheres, thus making the commodities within each expressible in terms of a single standard and hence immediately exchangeable. This new money is misunderstood by Tiv. They use it as a standard of value in the subsistence category, even when — as is often the case — the exchange is direct barter. They use it as a means of payment of bridewealth under the new system, but still refuse to admit that a woman has a "price" or can be valued in the same terms as food. At the same time, it has become something formerly lacking in all save the prestige sphere of Tiv economy — a means of exchange. Tiv have tried to categorize money with the other new imported goods and place them all in a fourth economic sphere, to be ranked morally below subsistence. They have, of course, not been successful in so doing.

What in fact happened was that general-purpose money was introduced to Tivland, where formerly only special-purpose money had been known.

It is in the nature of a general-purpose money that it standardizes the exchangeability value of every item to a common scale. It is precisely this function which brass rods, a "limited-purpose money" in the old system, did not perform. As we have seen, brass rods were used as a standard in some situations of conveyance in the intermediate or "prestige" category. They were also used as a means of payment (but specifically not as a standard) in some instances of conversion.

In this situation, the early Administrative officers interpreted brass rods as "money," by which they meant a general-purpose money. It became a fairly easy process, in their view, to establish by fiat an exchange rate between brass rods and a new coinage, "withdraw" the rods, and hence "replace" one currency with another. The actual effect, as we have seen, was to introduce a general-purpose currency in place of a limited-purpose money. Today all conversions and most conveyances are made in terms of coinage. Yet Tiv constantly express their distrust of money. This fact, and another — that a single means of exchange has entered all the economic spheres — has broken down the major distinctions among the spheres. Money has created in Tivland a uni-centric economy. Not only is the money a general-purpose money, but it applies to the full range of exchangeable goods.

Thus, when semi-professional traders, using money, began trading in the foodstuffs marketed by women and formerly solely the province of women, the range of the market was very greatly increased and hence the price in Tiv markets is determined by supply and demand far distant from the local producer and consumer. Tiv react to this situation by saying that foreign traders "spoil" their markets. The overlap of marketing and men's long-distance trade in staples also results in truckload after truckload of foodstuffs exported from major Tiv markets every day they meet. Tiv say that food is less plentiful today than it was in the past, though more land is being farmed. Tiv elders deplore this situation and know what is happening, but they do not know just where to fix the blame. In attempts to do something about it, they sometimes announce that no women are to sell any food at all. But when their wives disobey them men do not really feel that they were wrong to have done so. Tiv sometimes discriminate against non-Tiv traders in attempts to stop export of food. In their condemnation of the situation which is depriving them of their food faster than they are able to increase production, Tiv elders always curse money itself. It is money which, as the instrument for selling one's life subsistence, is responsible for the worsened situation — money and the Europeans who brought it.

Of even greater concern to Tiv is the influence money has had on marriage institutions. Today every woman's guardian, in accepting money as bridewealth, feels that he is converting down. Although attempts are made to spend money which is received in bridewealth to acquire brides for one's self and one's sons, it is in the nature of money, Tiv insist, that it is most difficult to accomplish. The good man still spends his bridewealth receipts for brides — but good men are not so numerous as would be desirable. Tiv deplore the fact that they are required to "sell" *(te)* their daughters and "buy" *(yam)* wives. There is no dignity in it since the possibility of making a bridewealth marriage into an exchange marriage has been removed.

With money, thus, the institutionalization of Tiv economy has become uni-centric, even though Tiv still see it with multi-centric values. The single sphere takes many of its characteristics from the market, so that the new situation can be considered a spread of the market. But throughout these changes in institutionalization, the basic Tiv value of maximization — converting one's wealth into the highest category, women and children — has remained. And in this discrepancy between values and institutions, Tiv have come upon what is to them a paradox, for all that Westerners understand it and are familiar with it. Today it is easy to sell subsistence goods for money to buy prestige articles and women, thereby aggrandizing oneself at a rapid rate. The food so sold is exported, decreasing the amount of subsistence goods available for consumption. On the other hand, the number of women is limited. The result is that bridewealth gets higher: rights in women have entered the market, and since the supply is fixed, the price of women has become inflated.

The frame of reference given me by the organizer of this symposium asked for comments on the effects of increased monetization on trade, on the distribution of wealth and indebtedness. To sum up the situation in these terms, trade has vastly increased with the introduction of general-purpose money but also with the other factors brought by a colonial form of government. At the same time, the market has expanded its range of applicability in the society. The Tiv are, indigenously, a people who valued egalitarian distribution of wealth to the extent that they believed they bewitched one another to whittle down the wealth of one man to the size of that of another. With money, the degree and extent of differentiation by wealth has greatly increased and will probably continue to increase. Finally, money has brought a new form of indebtedness — one which we know, only too well. In the indigenous system, debt took either the form of owing marriage wards and was hence congruent with the kinship system, or else took the form of decreased prestige. There was no debt in the sphere of subsistence because there was no credit there save among kinsmen and neighbors whose activities were aspects of family status, not acts of money-lenders. The introduction of general-purpose money and the concomitant spread of the market has divorced debt from kinship and status and has created the notion of debt in the subsistence sphere divorced from the activities of kinsmen and neighbors.

In short, because of the spread of the market and the introduction of general-purpose money, Tiv economy has become a part of the world economy. It has brought about profound changes in the institutionalization of Tiv society. Money is one of the shatteringly simplifying ideas of all time, and like any other new and compelling idea, it creates its own revolution. The monetary revolution, at least in this part of Africa, is the turn away from the multi-centric economy. Its course may be painful, but there is very little doubt about its outcome.

22

Poverty is being poor

THOMAS GLADWIN

A market cash economy has adverse effects upon the poor of our nation, a theme explored by Thomas Gladwin in this selection. Because they have so little money to spend, they must make small day-to-day exchanges that increase the cost of doing business for the merchants who serve them. As a result, the poor endure higher costs and inferior quality; these burdens, in turn, generate the hostility of the poor toward local merchants.

One of the more extraordinary characteristics not only of the War on Poverty itself but also of the great amount currently being written about poverty in general is the relatively minor attention which is being given to the immediate and direct consequences of simply being poor. Being poor has a large number of secondary consequences such as powerlessness, inadequate access to resources, lack of education, and a poor diet. However, these follow and are derived from a primary condition of just being poor. Being poor, at least in the United States, consists in a lack of sufficient money to function effectively in the economic system through which everyone is forced to seek the necessities of life. Let us examine what this means for day-to-day living.

Having at any one time at most only a small amount of money, and never being sure that in the immediate future enough will be available to cover even minimum needs, the poor person is forced to spend whatever he has on the most urgent demands which arise each day, and thus to operate constantly through a succession of very small deals. Instead of a weekly trip in the car to a supermarket, food must be bought by walking to a neighborhood store and buying only enough for the next meal or two. The size and the adequacy of the purchase, and therefore of the meal to follow, depends on how much money can be scraped together on that particular day. Improvident, inefficient? Of course. But to do otherwise calls at least for a car, a reserve supply of money, and reliable refrigeration. Louise Richards in a recent article reexamined the standard guidelines which have been customarily recommended ever since Depression days for efficient handling of household finances: spend first for necessities and last for luxuries, buy the best quality of foods for the lowest price, budget carefully and plan purchases in advance and so on.[1] She then demonstrated that each one of these budgeting rules, although rational and sensible, is in fact difficult or impossible to follow when one works with a very small and uncertain income.

In an eloquent and angry article entitled "Keeping the Poor Poor" Paul Jacobs has described the variety of people and of commercial practices which surround the poor person and take his money.[2] Although they keep him poor they also provide the only channels open to him for spending the small sums of money which he can command at any one time. Without a car to get to work it is very hard to obtain a decent job (especially in an area without public transportation such as Watts), but without sufficient funds for a substantial down payment the only cars available are nearly worn out. When they break down the necessary expensive repairs will only be performed for cash. The poor person who needs to spend money to meet installments or pay bills cannot sustain a checking account and if he is lucky enough to be working cannot get to a bank or a post office for a money order. Consequently he must purchase a commercial money order at a rate governed only by what the traffic will bear, and of uncertain reliability. Food and other products are often available in the poverty areas at lower prices in less than standard qualities, but once these products are identified as below standard they often can go very far below without intervention of legal or other controls. The manner in which poor people are gouged and exploited by excessive installment payments and carrying charges has become notorious. Mr. Jacobs describes a variety of other less well-known credit arrangements to which the poor are often forced and which in the long run soak up still more of their meager resources.

Mr. Jacobs is profoundly sympathetic toward poor people and their dilemmas. He has several times joined poor people in their daily lives after deliberately divesting himself of all but a pittance of money. Finding him-

[1] Louise G. Richards, "Consumer Practices of the Poor," in *Low Income Life Styles*, Lola M. Irelan, ed. (Washington, D.C.: Welfare Administration, 1966), pp. 67–86.

[2] In *Economic Progress and Social Welfare*, Leonard H. Goodman, ed. (New York: Columbia University Press, 1966), pp. 158–184.

self and his new friends surrounded by people ready to take every penny they have and give very little in return he not surprisingly has become angry. He holds those people who are exploiting the poor responsible for what they are doing and his anger is therefore directed at them. He is also angry with the rest of us who complacently let the exploiters go on about their business. This anger is felt by the poor themselves. It expresses itself among other things in the smashing and looting of stores which is now a standard feature of urban riots. These attacks on local merchants are not merely a means for obtaining otherwise unavailable goods but also rather clearly reflect a smoldering resentment against people who are seen as coming into the slums to prey upon their inhabitants.

Inherent in the angry resentment directed toward shopkeepers, loan agencies, landlords, and the like is an assumption that the mechanisms they use to extort money from poor people have been deliberately devised as a way to make large profits and grow rich. Put the other way around it is assumed that if they were willing to make a little less money they could give poor people deals as favorable as those which middle-class people enjoy. As we shall see, this is almost certainly not true.

Not only is exploitation perceived as deliberately contrived to maximize profit, it is also seen by its victims as discriminatory against whatever minority group occupies the slum area involved. It would be surprising if they saw it any other way. Members of minority groups in cities are constantly faced with insulting reminders of their inferior status and therefore inferior rights and privileges. It is thus only natural that they should also interpret the economic policies which they encounter as deliberately designed further to disadvantage them *because* they are Negro or Puerto Rican or Mexican-American or whatever. In addition, the car dealers and money lenders and landlords are more often than not English-speaking whites. As a consequence when there are riots not only are the stores of white merchants the principal targets for vandalism, but business enterprises run by members of the local ethnic group can usually escape damage simply by advertising prominently the ethnic affiliation of the proprietor. This is true even though in many cases the actual business practices of these establishments differ little if at all from those practiced by whites.

Undoubtedly ethnic discrimination contributes to the development of the commercial practices which so disadvantage poor people. It is hard to imagine white middle-class customers putting up with the usurious rates, shabby merchandise, and run-down facilities which poor Negroes, Puerto Ricans and Mexican-Americans usually accept without audible protest.

Beyond this, however, two much broader economic principles are at work, principles which must almost inevitably apply to any really poor people regardless of their color or speech or culture. The first and most crucial of these principles constitutes a central tenet of all commercial transactions in any free economy: the larger the deal the better the terms. At the upper end of the scale stands the man about whom we so often hear who can get it for you wholesale. However, attention is very seldom focused on the other end of the scale where the principle inevitably becomes the converse: *the smaller the deal the worse the terms.* Costs which tend to accrue at a fairly fixed level per deal or unit of business, costs such as handling, packaging, negotiating, carrying inventories, paying rent, and so forth, and the less tangible costs reflected in making judgments and accepting risks, all these costs are proportionately lower when a large number or high value of units are involved in each deal. Conversely, when these factors are all added into the cost of completing a very small deal this cost necessarily becomes highly inflated. Even riding a bus costs more when tokens must be bought one at a time to conserve cash. A larger markup is needed to pay the rent, the overhead and the wages of a full-time clerk in a neighborhood store whose daily volume is usually very small. In other kinds of transactions the size of the deal can become sufficiently small that entirely new bases for making profits must come into play. Despite the very high interest rates which are charged on small loans to poor people the risks are so high that it is not possible to make a profit from interest payments alone. The profit margin is therefore deliberately planned to come from the equities in repossessed merchandise which a succession of defaulting borrowers are forced to surrender. In other cases dishonest practices, like putting a thumb on the scale, become so widespread among retailers trying to assure their own living that they are almost taken for granted. At least they are accepted by poor people without protest, perhaps because protest would be in vain. But accepted or not these practices further rob the poor person of his rights, his money, and his dignity.

The high cost of doing business through a series of very small deals applies to anyone and is an inherent attribute of the economy of poverty. Unless there is some way to make the deals bigger or else to reduce the risk and high costs involved in transacting business with people who have practically no money, it is hard to see how even the most kindly of businessmen could support themselves in a poor neighborhood without charging exorbitant rates and prices or offering substandard goods or services or both.

A second major principle almost as crippling for a poor person as the first is the need in many kinds of transactions for substantial financial resources before being able to enter into any kind of deal at all. Sometimes this takes the form of a requirement for actual cash, as in the down payment on an automobile or the deposit required for a telephone. Because they are unable to assemble the necessary amounts of cash at one time, persons who could afford the monthly charges for telephone services or the monthly payments on a fairly good car are often denied these facilities, yet these are facilities critical for effective articulation with the larger commercial world. Both a telephone and a car are essential in applying for and obtaining a job, finding out about and capitalizing on sales and other sources of bargains, or obtaining medical and other services without wasting a good part of a day on them. If it were somehow possible to compute the monthly cost in added expenses and lost income of not having a car and telephone it is probable that this figure would not differ widely from the monthly cost of operating and paying for both.

The resources necessary to get a transaction under way need not take the form of cash. An obvious alternative is to obtain credit at reasonable cost. However, this can usually be achieved only through already having substantial assets that are convertible into cash, or else someone prepared to guarantee repayment of the loan if it is defaulted. Since poor people are very unlikely to have many convertible assets or rich relatives they cannot obtain these guarantees. There is of course another basis for obtaining credit. This is to have a steady and reliable income at a level high enough to pay for necessities with a little left over. Welfare payments are often fairly steady, but are usually at levels so low they do not really cover necessities, much less leave a little over, so they are no help. The only steady income which can leave some extra cash over is a good job, but this is precisely what the poor person almost by definition does not have and usually cannot get. Therefore poor people who have to buy something of some size must either do so on credit at very high interest rates and with the constant threat (and cost) of repossession, get it dishonestly, or else do without. When it comes to essentials, doing without usually means that needs have to be met through alternatives which in the long run are even more costly. Inability to obtain a mortgage frequently results in paying rent at a higher level than mortgage payments, in return for which there is instead of a growing equity only the prospect of a lifetime of shabby accommodations.

Another class of deals which can only be consummated if cash or credit are available in some quantity involves the provision of professional services, especially legal and medical services. Some effort is made to provide both of these for poor people through governmental programs, but they are usually poor in quality, limited in scope, and obtained only through the exercise of patience and persistence. Outside of criminal cases, legal services are virtually unavailable to a poor person who, for example, wishes to sue for damages (except in cases of clear liability with a fairly certain outcome) or to recover something which he believes was taken from him by fraud. With respect to health, the miserable and humiliating medical care which poor people must expect is too well known to require comment. Positive and personal medical or legal attention to the problems of a poor person, regardless of his race or language, is usually available only if he is clearly in risk of dying, or is about to go to jail, or has cash.

If, to borrow Paul Jacobs's phrase, the poor are kept poor not simply because of deliberate exploitation and discrimination, but also because being poor is economically so inefficient that people are usually unable to escape from poverty by their own efforts no matter what they do, what does this suggest with respect to planning programs to help poor people? One conclusion which emerges compellingly is that even complete elimination of discrimination against members of any minority group will not substantially improve their life circumstances if they are genuinely poor. Leaving aside questions of personal ability and training, and regardless of the sentimental history of how our Italian or Irish or Jewish ancestors made it from rags to riches, it seems inescapable that if you are born in the mid-twentieth century of really poor parents in an urban slum (or on a sharecropper's farm) the purely economic dice are loaded so heavily against you that the likelihood of your achieving a position of real dignity or security is almost precluded. Put in another way, if only *equal* opportunities are extended to the minority poor and they are therefore subject to the same rules of business which govern middle-class people their limited cash resources will prevent them from deriving any lasting advantage from this "equality." Thus many of the demands which are currently being made by civil rights leaders in northern as well as southern cities appear impossible of fulfillment within our economic system as it presently operates.

The solution furthermore does not seem to lie in trying to coerce businessmen to offer to poor people deals on as favorable terms as they would offer to middle-class customers. The cost both direct and indirect of doing business exclusively in small deals prohibits the offer of terms as good as those which govern large deals without either a subsidy, or else bankruptcy. In other words, regardless of the moral character of businessmen who operate in the slums as bankers or employers or merchants, there is no basis on which they can do business which will simultaneously be fair to them and their customers. At least one has to lose. If this is true it points unequivocally to the need for some new additional factor in the economic life of poor people through which they can at least have a chance to become self-starting along the road toward improving their circumstances. What this new factor should be is probably already evident, because it consists in an already familiar proposal.

Everything which has been said thus far points strongly in the direction others have been pointing with increasing urgency over the past several years. This is toward the adoption of a policy of guaranteeing for everyone some minimum level of income sufficient to assure at least modest decency and security. A number of different ways have been proposed for accomplishing this and all have been analyzed for their relative cost and effectiveness from a variety of points of view. Although advantages of one sort or another accrue to each of these proposed plans, for our present purposes their relatively minor differences are far less important than the central principle of guaranteed income maintenance.

Formidable problems of administrative policy, political and moral acceptability, and fiscal feasibility must be resolved before a guaranteed income can become a reality. Yet with increasing unanimity people who are looking at the problems of poverty from almost any point of view, whether they are social scientists or economists or blue ribbon advisory commissions, are arriving at the conclusion that a guaranteed income must be a part of the solution. Without it people in our society who are disfranchised by poverty and discrimination will never achieve full participation in the way of life which is supposed to be the right of every American to enjoy. Various arguments are advanced to support this position. The one set forth here rests upon the relative efficiency of economic transactions as a function of income. To recapitulate in summary form, below a certain level transactions become so small that their nature changes and sinks into rapidly increasing inefficiency. In addition, at this level of income there can be no surplus, hence no savings, no real control over the future and therefore no advantage in trying to plan ahead, and no security. Some means must therefore be found to permit people to stabilize their economic activity at a minimal level of efficiency and predictability. The only way to do this is to see that enough money is regularly available to sustain this level of activity. The guaranteed minimum income is the only mechanism thus far proposed which will effectively meet this requirement. . . .

VII

Religion and world view

As the preceding chapters have shown, culture provides man with rules for dealing with his natural and social environment. Traditional knowledge brings security by allowing man to achieve his purposes and explain his experience. Culture provides alternatives when a strategy for dealing with life is only partially successful in meeting its problems.

But then, illness strikes indiscriminately and the best methods for its remedy fail . . . earthquakes destroy entire communities without warning . . . children from the best families turn to a life of crime. Such events, as well as the persistent question of life's meaning, create fear, anxiety, and a feeling of helplessness. At these crucial points in life, man fills the gap in his knowledge with answers of another kind. His symbolic skills have created a supernatural dimension, as well as a comprehensive view of the world, to help account for the vagaries of human experience. Unknown forces are, in a sense, controlled when they are identified as spirits, deities, and witches. Evil, unexpected tragedy, and human weakness are all explained by a society's world view and controlled, in part, by magic and religion.

Although religion usually involves worship, it is often linked to more mundane human purposes. Americans pray for peace, Kwakiutl Indians perform rituals to increase the salmon run, Bhils slaughter animals to drive away spirits that bring disease, Azande poison chickens to divine causes of tragedy, and St. Christopher rides the dashboard of some automobiles as a symbolic insurance policy. When faced with inequality and discrimination, religion may become the handmaiden of rapid culture change. The civil-rights movement in our society gained legitimacy by its association with the church, and cargo cults of the South Pacific are often inspired by faith in the supernatural. Many of these functions can be seen in this chapter.

23

When technology fails: Magic and religion in New Guinea

PHILIP L. NEWMAN

All men experience anxiety when confronted with situations they cannot control, and in many societies natural methods of influencing and predicting events work only part of the time. In such instances, supernatural forces are invoked to account for such events and man's relation to them. In this article, Philip Newman describes the use of magic and witchcraft by a highland New Guinea people and shows that they employ such practices throughout their lives whenever faced with uncertainty. He suggests that magical procedures can be ranked according to their ability to release tension, and that the choice of particular magical practices correlates with the degree of anxiety to be reduced.

Man has created many forms in his quest for means of dealing with the world around him. Whether these forms be material tools, social groups, or intangible ideas, they are all, in a sense, "instruments": each is a means to some end; each has a purpose that it fulfills. When we think of such things as magical rites, a belief in ghosts, or accusations of sorcery, however, the matter of purpose becomes less obvious. In the descriptions and in the case history that follow, we will try both to show something of the magical and religious beliefs of a New Guinea people and to demonstrate the purposes that these beliefs have for the men who hold them.

In the mountainous interior of Australian New Guinea, the Asaro River has its headwaters some thirty miles to the north of Goroka, a European settlement that serves as the administrative center for the Central

From "Sorcery, Religion and the Man," *Natural History* 71 (February 1962): 21–28. Illustrations are omitted.

Highlands District. Near Goroka, the Asaro flows through a wide valley where the ground cover is mostly grasses and reeds. In its upper reaches, this valley narrows into a gorge where steep, heavily forested ridges reach out toward the river from mountain masses on either side. Some 12,000 people live on this part of the river, occupying an area of approximately 200 square miles. While these people are culturally and linguistically similar, they do not form a single political unit. Indeed, before contact with Europeans, the area was characterized by incessant intertribal warfare. Even now, when active warfare is no longer part of their lives, the pattern of alliances and animosities among the tribes is a factor in social intercourse.

Except for the cessation of warfare, life in the valley today is little changed from what it was before the Australian government began active pacification of the area after the end of World War II. Almost daily, the people climb up from the valley floor to enter the dense forest on the mountain slopes. It is here that building wood is gathered; birds and small marsupials are shot for meat, plumage, or fur; plants that provide for many needs are collected.

Below an altitude of some 7,000 feet, the forest has been cut back to make room for gardens that cling to the sides of steep ridges and crowd together in the narrow valley floors. These gardens provide the people's staple foods — sweet potatoes, yams, sugar cane, and a variety of green vegetables. A woman spends most of her time at garden work, preparing new planting areas, weeding the crop, and harvesting mature plants. In fallow areas nearby she can turn loose the pigs her husband has entrusted to her care. If they wander too far afield by evening, her call will bring them back on the run. They know that a meal awaits them, as well as a snooze by the fire in their "mother's" house.

While each family may have one or more houses near the forest or in their garden, the center of social life is the village. The villages are located on the tops of ridges in spots usually selected with an eye to their defensibility against enemies. The fifteen to twenty houses that compose each village usually march in single file along the narrow ridge. But, if space permits, they are formed into a square. All the houses are much alike — round, about fifteen feet in diameter, made of double rows of five-foot stakes. The space between the stakes is filled with grass and the outside covered with strips of bark. The roof is thatched and topped with a long, tasseled pole.

Two or three houses always stand out. They are larger, they are not in line with the rest, and they may have as many as eight poles protruding through their roofs. These are the men's houses. As a rule, men and women do not live together, for the men fear that too much contact with women is weakening. For this reason, a man builds a house for his wife — or each of them, if he has more than one — and then helps in the construction of the larger house where he and the other men of the village will sleep apart. Ideally, all the men who live together in a single house can trace their descent back to a known, common ancestor. They thus constitute a lineage. Such a lineage is connected to the other village men's houses by descent links, but in many cases the links are so amorphous that no one can actually tell what they are. Similarly, several villages will be linked together into a clan, but geneological ties may be more imputed than real.

Just as the forest and the garden represent the physical framework within which each individual lives, so too these various orders of grouping — the lineage, the village, the clan, and the tribe — represent the social framework of existence. The members of these groups are the people with whom each individual is in daily contact. They nurture him, teach him, and assist him in times of crisis. It is from these groups that he derives such things as his name, his rights to the land for gardening and hunting, and the financial help that he needs when it is time to purchase a wife. They hail his birth and mourn his death.

In turn, each individual has obligations to the other members of these groups. He acts as a representative of his group when dealing with outsiders. In this way, he enters into a whole series of relationships with individuals and groups outside his own immediate circle. He may visit a neighboring clan to help one of his own clansmen win the admiration of a prospective bride by sitting up all night near the hot fire singing love songs to her. Or a trip may take him to a nearby tribe, where he dances mightily with other men to show that his group is appreciative of the gift of food and valuables they are about to receive. He may walk several days over difficult ground to reach a completely alien group, where he can barter for shells, plumes, or foodstuffs not available in his own group. As in all societies, the groups comprising the society provide for the individual, while the individual, in turn, contributes some of his efforts to the life of the group.

Man not only has his tools and his society to help cope with the world: he also has his ideas. There are some problems presented by the environment for which the people of the upper Asaro have not yet devised a mechanical or technical solution. There are other problems for which a technical solution seems not enough. Finally, there are problems for which an idea seems to be an inherently better solution than a physical or social tool. It is here that we enter the realm of magic and religion.

A great many of the activities among the upper Asaro people have a magical or religious component. When a child is born, it is cleaned, fed, and covered with grease to help protect it from the cool mountain air. It is also protected, nonphysically, by burying its umbilical cord in some secluded spot — so that sorcerers cannot later use this piece of the newformed being to cause illness or death by magical means. During the first few days of life, the infant is also made to accept, via magic, his first social responsibility — not to cry at night and disturb its mother. A small bundle of sweet-smelling grass is placed on the mother's head and her desire for uninterrupted slumber is blown into the grass by an attendant. The grass is then crushed over the head of the child and its pungent odor released so that the infant will breathe in the command along with the scent of the plant.

Throughout an individual's life there will be magical rites to protect him from various dangers, to overcome difficulties, and to assist his growth. When a young boy kills his first animal, his hand will be magically "locked" in the position that first sent an arrow on a true course. When he reaches puberty and moves out of his mother's house to begin his life in the men's house, he will be ritually cleansed of the contamination he has been subjected to during his years of association with women. If he were not so cleansed, he would never become strong enough to engage in men's activities. During the years when a young man is trying to win the favor of a girl, he not only relies on his prowess in singing love songs and his decorations, but on his knowledge of love magic as well. If all the usual spells and potions fail, he may utilize one especially powerful form that is thought to make him appear to his beloved with an entirely new face — the face of someone he knows she likes.

In his mature years, when a man's attention turns to the growth of pigs and gardens, he will have magical as well as technical skills to help him. Gardens are not difficult to grow in this fertile land, but it is still wise to put a certain series of leaves across one's fences, so that any thief will find his arms and legs paralyzed should he decide to raid the garden. It also behooves one whose gardens are near the main trails and settlements to give them magical assistance, for a slow-growing garden in such a conspicuous place could be an embarrassment.

The raising of pigs is a more difficult matter, and it is here that magical and religious rites become greatly elaborated. Some of these rites are performed by an individual for his own pigs. It may be a simple performance, as when smoke is blown into the ear of a wild pig to tame it. The theory is that the smoke cools and dries the pig's "hot" disposition. On the other hand, these individual rites may attain considerable complexity, as in the propitiation of forest spirits called *nokondisi.* These spirits are capricious in nature — sometimes playing malicious tricks on men and sometimes performing acts of kindness. Each man, therefore, maintains a small, fenced enclosure in which he builds a miniature earth oven and a tiny house. By placing food in the earth oven he may be able to entice a *nokondisi* to come live near his pigs and watch after them. In return for the food, the spirit will help bring in lost pigs, protect the herd from thieves, and carry the animals safely across flooded streams during the rainy season.

In addition to the magic performed by an individual on behalf of his own pigs, some rather elaborate rites are performed by the lineage and clan for all the pigs belonging to these groups. The largest of these is the *gerua* ceremony, performed at intervals of from five to seven years. In this ritual, hundreds of pigs are killed and used to pay off various kinds of economic obligations to other clans. It is a time for feasting and dancing, for courting and reunion. It is also a time for propitiating the ghosts of the dead in the hope that they will help the living grow their pigs. All the pigs are killed in the name of particular ghosts. The songs are pleas for ghostly assistance. The wooden *gerua* boards, with their colorful geometric designs, are visible symbols to the ghosts that they have not been forgotten. It is not tender sentiment that motivates this display, however. Rather, it is the fear that failure to do so will engender the wrath of the ever watchful dead.

The magical and religious beliefs that we have so far examined are all used in conjunction with other practices of a nonmagical nature. There are some areas, however, where no purely technical solutions are available, and where magic and religion are the only "tools" available. One such area is sickness. The people of the upper Asaro are not generally aware of modern medical practices, although efforts are being made in that direction. The nonmagical techniques available to them, such as inhaling the steam from fragrant plants to relieve a stopped-up nose, are few. These remedies do not extend to more serious maladies. When serious illness strikes, the only recourse is to magic.

The magical solutions available are many and varied. There are herbs with magical properties that are administered in much the same way as are medicines in our own society. I made a cursory check, however, which seems to show that few of the plants possess any curative value.

Ghosts and forest spirits are frequently thought to be the causes of illness, for they are deemed capable of entering the body and devouring a person's inner organs. Cures for such illnesses usually involve propitiation of the offending supernatural.

Witches and sorcerers are believed to be another major cause of illness, for they are supposedly capable of injecting foreign bodies into a victim, or performing black magic on objects that have been in association with the victim. To cure illness caused in this way involves calling in a magical specialist who can either extract the foreign bodies or retrieve the objects being operated upon.

While the ideas and rites listed here do not exhaust the entire inventory available to the group under discussion, they give some sense of the variety that exists. The notions are interesting in themselves, but the question of how an individual makes use of these notions is even more fascinating. Let us look at a crisis in the life of one of these people, and see how he picks and chooses among the various "tools" at his disposal.

Ombo was a young man in his early thirties. He had been married for about five years, but was childless. Early one April, it was announced in the traditional style that his wife, Magara, was with child. On such an occasion, a food distribution is held in the village and the announcement, along with gifts of food, was sent out to related villages. Ombo was instructed in the food taboos he would have to undergo during the period of his wife's pregnancy to protect himself from her increased contamination.

All went well for the first few weeks and then Magara became ill. It is doubtful that her illness was associated with her pregnancy, for her symptoms were the classic signs of malaria — a rather rare disease in this part of the highlands. The first attempts to cure her involved a variety of highly regarded pseudomedications.

A potion of sweet-smelling leaves was administered. A command to the effect that the illness should depart was blown into the leaves, and the leaves were eaten. It was thought that the command, thus internalized, would drive out the illness.

At various other times, attempts were made to relieve her headaches and body pains by rubbing the afflicted areas with stinging nettles. It was held that when the welts and the pain caused by the nettles subsided, the pains in her body would also leave. On one occasion her husband blew smoke over her during a period of fever because, as we have seen, smoke is held to have a cooling and drying effect. He also painted various parts of her body with mud in an effort to cause the pain to dry up at the same time the mud dried.

This kind of treatment continued until early May without any noticeable improvement in Magara's condition. After almost a month had passed and it became apparent that the illness was not going away, Ombo began to speculate on a possible cause. During the next few weeks he came up with several solutions. While he had been away from the village, working for Europeans in Goroka, he had acquired some charms to help him win at a card game popular among the sophisticated younger men.

One of these charms was fairly new and he was worried that he might not have gained sufficient control over it. Since he kept it hidden in his wife's house, his conclusion was that the charm was exerting its influence on her and causing the illness. He therefore removed it from her house and sent it away to a friend in another tribe. There was no improvement in his wife's condition.

Ombo's next action was to destroy his spirit house. He had not kept it in good repair and had not been diligent in feeding the *nokondisi* that lived there. His father suggested that the angered spirit was taking revenge on Magara. By destroying the house of the spirit, Ombo caused it to retreat to the forest where it could do no harm. Finally, he burned the costly paraphernalia of a potent sorcery technique he had purchased some years before, fearing it affected his wife.

By now it was late in May. Magara had become so ill that she stopped all but the most minimal work in her garden. Concern about her illness began to increase, and people outside the immediate family began to speculate about its cause. Ombo's older brother mentioned one day that a malevolent ghost might be behind it. It was not long after this that a meeting was held in the men's houst and Fumai, a member of the lineage, recounted a dream he had had the night before. In it, he had seen the ghost of Ombo's great-grandmother sitting in the forest near the spot where *gerua* boards are displayed for the ancestors. She had covered herself with ashes and, in a fit of self-pity, was wailing loudly because no one had made a *gerua* board in her honor at the last *gerua* ceremony, and no one had killed a pig in her name. Since ashes are put on at the death of a near relative as a sign of mourning, while clay is put on if the deceased is more distantly related, and since ghosts are thought to be capable of causing death, it was concluded that the dream was prophetic. It implied the imminent death of Magara at the great-grandmother's hands unless something were done.

The next day, Ombo and his wife, along with his parents and siblings, set out for the spot where the ghost had been "seen." A pig was killed there in honor of the ghost. It was cooked in an earth oven filled with valued food items — the largest sweet potatoes, the most succulent yams, and the most highly prized varieties of taro. While water was being poured into the oven, a speech was addressed to the ghost. It was pointed out that the food had been prepared and donated in her honor at considerable trouble to those present. The feeling was expressed that she should be satisfied with the amount and the quality of the offering. She was then told to refrain from causing trouble in the future. As the food steamed in the oven, a *gerua* board was made in the ghost's honor and placed among others in a nearby tree. Some of the food was eaten and the rest was later distributed among members of the lineage.

Things seemed to go well for the next few weeks. Magara improved and was able to return to her work in the garden. Discussion of the topic was dropped. Then, late in June, she suddenly became ill again. Ombo was greatly upset. I suggested to him that she might have malaria and should be taken to the medical aid post. But Ombo did not want to do this, for by now he was convinced that his wife was being attacked by a sorcerer. To deal with this threat, a magical specialist had to be called in. It was several days before he arrived, for he lived some distance away in another tribe. As with any good "doctor," his first acts were aimed at relieving his patient's pain and fever. With much physical strain, he literally pulled the pain from her body and cast it into the ground where it could do no further harm. His next task was to find out what was causing her illness. For over two hours he sat chatting with Ombo and Magara, discussing the history of the illness, the treatments that had been used, and their own life histories. All the while, he puffed on a tobacco pipe made of a bamboo tube. The degree of irritation caused by the smoke in his throat signalized the appearance in the conversation of significant diagnostic events. Finally, he announced his conclusion — illness by black magic.

To eliminate the effects of the imputed black magic, the object being manipulated by the sorcerer had to be recovered. To do this, the magical specialist first had a bundle of long, thin leaves prepared. Into the bundle were put cooked pork and a variety of plants with magical properties. The specialist never directly touched the bundle himself, but directed Ombo in its preparation. When the bundle was completed, it and a specially prepared bamboo tube were both carried into Magara's house. She was given the tube to hold and the bundle was hung in the rafters near the center pole. After a rite to protect her from further sorcery, Ombo and Magara were locked together in the house.

The specialist remained outside. He walked round and round the house, reciting spells and whirling a special plant around his head. He was pulling the unknown object away from the sorcerer and bringing it back home. The ceremony became a real struggle: the object would come tantalizingly close, only to slip away. Then the specialist announced that the object had arrived. Magara was instructed to open the bundle in the rafters. Inside, among the bits of meat, were a small spider and a piece of string of the type used to hang ornaments around the neck.

The spider, Magara and Ombo were told, was an assistant to the specialist. It had taken the string out of the sorcerer's house and into the open where the specialist could reach it with his powers. The sorcerer was thought to be a young man who had once wanted to marry Magara. The existence of a disappointed suitor was one fact that had come out during the specialist's long interview. When Magara had married Ombo, the suitor had become angry and cut a bit of her necklace string to use for sorcery. The specialist placed the recovered string in the bamboo tube that Magara had been holding, and the tube was then hidden away among the thatch.

From that time until late September, when I left the area, Magara did not experience any further attacks of illness, although she was not in the best of health. The community considered her cured. Significantly, her child was born prematurely in September and died two days later, but no one saw any connection between this death and her illness.

What, then, can we say about the purpose of such ideas and behavior patterns? A situation such as Magara's creates a great deal of tension in an individual who experiences it. If magic does nothing more, it allows the bearer of this tension to act. Both the patient and those concerned feel that something is being done. The pioneer anthropologist Bronislaw Malinowski long ago made the point: "Magic expresses the greater value for man of confidence over doubt, of steadfastness over vacillation, of optimism over pessimism."

It is a rare man indeed, however, who can maintain his confidence and optimism in the face of repeated failure. The question then arises, why is it that magic is not more readily given up? Three answers have traditionally been given to this question, all of them valid. In the first place, for people such as these, there is no alternative. Secondly, for the believer in the efficacy of magic, the occasional chance successes are more significant than repeated failure. Finally, explanations for failures are always at hand. Inadvertent errors in spells or formulas that must be performed precisely, or imagined countermagic, are ready explanations that are necessarily built into the very nature of magic.

The case history we have seen suggests still a fourth answer. This answer becomes apparent, however, only if we examine the way in which an individual makes use of the magical notions available to him. In the progression of the various magical techniques and explanations employed by Ombo, we can see that they call for behavior patterns allowing for increasingly aggressive release of the tension built up in him by the failure of previously selected techniques.

The simple pseudomedicinal rites, such as rubbing with nettles and painting with mud, were enough to reduce the tension of the initial crisis. The treatment was symptomatic and there was no attempt to identify the cause of the illness. When it became apparent that these techniques had failed, we find Ombo resorting to the more drastic measure of destroying valuable property. The frustration was not yet great enough to cause him to seek outlets in other people: that which he destroyed and removed from his use belonged only to him. In the next phase, we find that a ghost is predicated as the causative agent. One need not be nice to ghosts. They, like the living, are thought to be a mercenary lot who do not much care what is said about them as long as they get their just due. The speech made to the great-grandmother was studded with commands and expressions of anger at the trouble the ghost had caused. This was an excellent mechanism for the release of tension, just as was the physical act of killing the pig.

Finally, we see the most aggressive act of all — accusing a specific individual of sorcery. The accused individual was a member of an enemy tribe and lived some distance away. It was, therefore, unlikely that accuser and accused would often meet. But if the two had come together, a fight would have been inevitable. In former times, this could have led to open warfare. Thus, Ombo not only used magic as a tool against disease, but also selected the magical tools in such an order that his own increasing anxiety was relieved by increasingly aggressive actions. It is thus not only the forms created by man that enable him to cope with the world he meets, but the very way in which he manipulates those forms that are available to him.

24

Urban witches

EDWARD J. MOODY

Witchcraft is usually seen as a feature of underdeveloped societies, but it is also present in the urban centers of the United States. Edward Moody presents empirical data on the person who uses black magic, and analyzes the function it has for the magician. Even in "civilized" societies, some men try to explain events in their lives and to compensate for personal inadequacies and anxieties by a belief in witchcraft.

Every Friday evening just before midnight, a group of men and women gathers at a home in San Francisco; and there, under the guidance of their high priest, a sorcerer or magus sometimes called the "Black Pope of Satanism," they study and practice the ancient art of black magic. Precisely at midnight they begin to perform Satanic rituals that apparently differ little from those allegedly performed by European Satanists and witches at least as early as the seventh century. By the dim and flickering light of black candles, hooded figures perform their rites upon the traditional Satanic altar — the naked body of a beautiful young witch — calling forth the mysterious powers of darkness to do their bidding. Beneath the emblem of Baphomet, the horned god, they engage in indulgences of flesh and sense for whose performance their forebears suffered death and torture at the hands of earlier Christian zealots.

Many of these men and women are, by day, respected and responsible citizens. Their nocturnal or covert practice of the black art would, if exposed, make them liable to ridicule, censure, and even punishment. Even though we live in an "enlightened" age, witches are still made a

This article was written especially for this volume and has never before been published. The research on which this article is based was conducted during the period from October 1967 to August 1969. Since that time changes in the institutional structure of the Church have taken place and the composition of the membership has altered slightly. The patterns of behavior, the therapeutic interactions described remain, in the author's opinion, essentially unchanged.

focus of a community's aggression and anxiety. They are denounced from the pulpit, prosecuted to the limit of the law, and subjected to extralegal harassment by the fearful and ignorant.

Why then do the Satanists persist? Why do they take these risks? What benefits do they derive from membership in a Satanic church, what rewards are earned from the practice of witchcraft? What indulgences are enjoyed that they could not as easily find in one of the more socially acceptable arenas of pleasure available in our "permissive" society?

The nearly universal allegation of witchcraft in the various cultures of the world has excited the interest of social scientists for years and the volume of writing on the topic is staggering. Most accounts of witchcraft, however, share the common failing of having been written from the point of view of those who do not themselves practice the black art. Few, if any, modern authors have had contact with witches, black magicians, or sorcerers, relying instead on either the anguished statements of medieval victims of inquisition torture, or other types of secondhand "hearsay" evidence for their data. To further confuse the issue, authoritative and respected ethnologists have reported that black magic and witchcraft constitute an imaginary offense because it is impossible — that because witches cannot do what they are supposed to do, they are nonexistent.

WITCHES AND MAGICIANS

But the witches live. In 1965 while carrying out other research in San Francisco, California, I heard rumors of a Satanic cult which planned to give an All-Hallows Eve blessing to a local chamber of horrors. I made contact with the group through its founder and high priest and thus began over two years of participant-observation as a member of a contemporary black magic group. As a member of this group I interacted with my fellow members in both ritual and secular settings. The following description is based on the data gathered at that time.

The witches and black magicians who were members of the group came from a variety of social class backgrounds. All shades of political opinion were represented from Communist to American Nazi. Many exhibited behavior identified in American culture as "pathological," such as homosexuality, sadomasochism, and transvestism. Of the many characteristics that emerged from psychological tests, extensive observations, and interviews, the most common trait, exhibited by nearly all Satanic novices, was a high level of general anxiety related to low self-esteem and a feeling of inadequacy. This syndrome appears to be related to intense interpersonal conflicts in the nuclear family during socialization. Eighty-five percent of the group, the administrative and magical hierarchy of the church, reported that their childhood homes were split by alcoholism, divorce, or some other serious problem. Their adult lives were in turn marked by admitted failure in love, business, sexual, or social relationships. Before entering the group each member appeared to have been battered by failure in one or more of the areas mentioned, rejected or isolated by a society frightened by his increasingly bizarre and unpredictable behavior, and forced into a continuing struggle to comprehend or give meaning to his life situation.

Almost all members, prior to joining the group, had made some previous attempt to gain control over the mysterious forces operating around them. In order to give their environment some structure, in order to make it predictable and thus less anxiety-provoking, they dabbled in astrology, the Tarot, spiritualism, or other occult sciences, but continued failure in their everyday lives drove them from the passive and fatalistic stance of the astrologer to consideration of the active and manipulative role of sorcerer or witch. In articles in magazines such as *Astrology* and *Fate*, the potential Satanist comes into direct contact with magic, both white and black. Troubled by lack of power and control, the pre-Satanist is frequently introduced to the concept of magic by advertisements which promise "Occult power . . . now . . . for those who want to make real progress in understanding and working the forces that rule our Physical Cosmos . . . a self-study course in the practice of Magic." Or, Ophiel will teach you how to "become a power in your town, job, club, etc. . ," how to "create a familiar [a personal magic spirit servant] to help you through life," how to "control and dominate others." "The Secret Way" is offered free of charge, and the Esoteric Society offers to teach one how herbs, roots, oils, and rituals may be used, through "white magic," to obtain love, money, power, or a peaceful home. They will also teach one self-confidence and how to banish "unwanted forces." The reader is invited to join the Brotherhood of the White Temple, Inc.; the Monastery of the Seven Rays (specializing in sexual magic); the Radiant School; and numerous other groups that promise to reveal the secrets of success in business, sex, love, and life — the very secrets the potential or pre-Satanist feels have eluded him. Before joining the group, the pre-Satanist usually begins to perform magic ceremonies and rituals whose descriptions he receives for a fee from one of the various groups noted above, from magical wholesale houses, or from occult book clubs. These practices reinforce his "magical world view," and at the same time bring him in contact with other practitioners of the magical arts, both white and black.

Although most of the mail-order magic groups profess to practice "white" magic — benevolent magic designed only to benefit those involved and never aggressive or selfish, only altruistic — as opposed to "black," malevolent, or selfish magic, even white magic rituals require ingredients that are rare enough so they can be bought only at certain specialty stores. These stores, usually known to the public as candle shops although some now call themselves occult art supply houses, provide not only the raw materials — oils, incenses, candles, herbs, parchments, etc. — for the magical workings, but serve as meeting places for those interested in the occult. A request for some specific magic ingredient such as "John the Conqueror oil," "Money-come" powder, "crossing" powder, or black candles usually leads to a conversation about the magical arts and often to introductions to other female witches and male warlocks. The realization that there are others who privately practice magic, white or black, supports the novice magician in his new-found interest in magical manipulation. The presence of other witches and magicians in his vicinity serves as additional proof that the problems he has personally experienced may indeed be caused by witchcraft, for the pre-Satanist has now met, firsthand, witches and warlocks who previously were only shadowy figures, and if there are a few known witches, who knows how many there might be practicing secretly?

Many witches and magicians never go beyond the private practice of white or black magic, or at most engage in a form of magic "recipe" swapping. The individual who does join a formal group practicing magic may become affiliated with such a group in one of several ways. In some cases he has been practicing black magic with scant success. Perhaps he has gone no further than astrology or reading the designs on the ancient Tarot cards, a type of socially acceptable magic which the leader of the Satanic church disparagingly calls "god in sport clothes." But the potential Satanist has come to think of the cosmos as being ordered, and ordered according to magical — that is, imperceptible — principles. He is prompted by his sense of alienation and social inadequacy to try to gain control of the strange forces that he feels influence or control him and, hearing of a Satanic church, he comes to learn magic.

Others join because of anxiety and inadequacy of a slightly different nature. They may be homosexual, nymphomaniac, sadist, or masochist. They usually have some relatively blatant behavioral abnormality which, though they personally may not feel it wrong, is socially maladaptive and therefore disruptive. As in many "primitive" societies, magic and witchcraft provide both the "disturbed" persons and, in some cases, the community at large with a ready and consistent explanation for those "forces" or impulses which they themselves have experienced. Seeking control, or freedom, the social deviants come ultimately to the acknowledged expert in magic of all kinds, the head of the Satanic church, to have their demons exorcised, the spells lifted, and their own powers restored.

Others whose problems are less acute come because they have been brought, in the larger religious context, to think of themselves as "evil." If their struggle against "evil" has been to no avail, many of the individuals in question take this to mean that the power of "evil" is greater than the power of "good" — that "God is dead" — and so on. In their search for a source of strength and security, rather than continue their vain struggle with that "evil" force against which they know themselves to be powerless, they seek instead to identify themselves with evil, to join the "winning" side. They identify with Satan — etymologically the "opposition" — and become "followers of the left-hand path," "walkers in darkness."

Finally, there are, of course, those who come seeking thrills or titillation, lured by rumors of beautiful naked witches, saturnalian orgies, and other strange occurrences. Few of these are admitted into the group.

Black magic

For the novice, initial contact with the Satanists is reassuring. Those assisting the "Prince of Darkness" who heads the church are usually officers in the church, long-term members who have risen from the rank and file to positions of trust and authority. They are well-dressed, pleasant persons who exude an aura of confidence and adequacy. Rather than having the appearance of wild-eyed fanatics or lunatics, the Satanists look like members of the middle-class, but successful middle-class. The Prince of Darkness himself is a powerfully built and striking individual with a shaven head and black, well-trimmed beard. Sitting among the implements of magic, surrounded by books that contain the "secrets of the centuries," he affirms for those present what they already know: that there is a secret to power and success which can and must be learned, and that secret is black magic.

All magic is black magic according to the Satanists. There is no altruistic or white magic. Each magician intends to benefit from his magical manipulation, even those workings performed at someone else's behest. To claim to be performing magic only for the benefit of others is either hypocrisy — the cardinal sin in Satanic belief — or naiveté, another serious shortcoming. As defined by the Satanists, magic itself is a surprisingly common-sense kind of phenomenon: "the change in situations or events in accordance with one's will, which would, using normally accepted methods, be unchangeable." Magic can be divided into two categories: ritual (ceremonial) and nonritual (manipulative).

Ritual, or "the greater magic," is performed in a specified ritual area and at a specific time. It is an emotional, not an intellectual act. Although the Satanists spend a great deal of time intellectualizing and rationalizing magic power, they state specifically that "any and all intellectual activity must take place *before* the ceremony, not during it." [1]

[1] The official doctrine of several Satanic groups within the continental United States is contained in the *Satanic Bible* by Anton Szandor LaVey (New York: Avon Books, 1969), p. 111.

The "lesser magic," nonritual (manipulative) magic, is, in contrast, a type of transactional manipulation based upon a heightened awareness of the various processes of behavior operative in interaction with others, a Satanic "games people play." The Satanist in ritual interaction is taught to analyze and utilize the motivations and behavioral Achilles' heels of others for his own purposes. If the person with whom one is interacting has masochistic tendencies, for example, the Satanist is taught to adopt the role of sadist, to "indulge" the other's desires, to be dominant, forceful, and even cruel in interaction with him.

Both the greater and the lesser magic is predicated upon a more general "magical" world view in which all elements of the "natural world" are animate, have unique and distinctive vibrations that influence the way they relate to other natural phenomena. Men, too, have vibrations, the principal difference between men and inanimate objects being that men can alter their pattern of vibrations, sometimes consciously and at will. It is the manipulation and the modification of these vibrations, forces, or powers that is the basis of all magic. There are "natural magicians," untrained and unwitting manipulators of magic power. Some, for example, resonate in harmony with growing things; these are people said to have a "green thumb," gardeners who can make anything grow. Others resonate on the frequency of money and have the "Midas touch" which turns their every endeavor into a profit-making venture. Still others are "love magnets"; they automatically attract others to them, fascinate and charm even though they may be physically plain themselves. If one is a "natural magician," he does some of these things unconsciously, intuitively, but because of the intellectual nature of our modern world, most people have lost their sensitivity to these faint vibrations. Such individuals may, if they become witches, magicians or Satanists, regain contact with that lost world just as tribal shamans are able to regain contact with another older world where men communicated with animals and understood their ways. It is this resensitization to the vibrations of the cosmos that is the essence of magical training. It takes place best in the "intellectual decompression chamber" of magical ritual, for it is basically a "subjective" and "nonscientific" phenomenon.

Those who have become members of the inner circle learn to make use of black magic, both greater and lesser, in obtaining goals which are the antithesis of Christian dogma. The seven deadly sins of Christian teaching — greed, pride, envy, anger, gluttony, lust, and sloth — are depicted as Satanic virtues. Envy and greed are, in the Satanic theology, natural in man and the motivating forces behind ambition. Lust is necessary for the preservation of the species and not a Satanic sin. Anger is the force of self-preservation. Instead of denying natural instincts the Satanist learns to glory in them and turn them into power.

Satanists recognize that the form of their ritual, its meanings and its functions are largely determined by the wider society and its culture. The novitiate in the Satanic cult is taught, for example, that the meaning of the word "Satan" etymologically is "the opposition," or "he who opposes," and that Satanism itself arose out of opposition to the demeaning and stultifying institutions of Christianity. The cult recognizes that had there been no Christianity there would be no Satanism, at least not in the form it presently takes, and it maintains that much of the Satanic ritual and belief is structured by the form and content of Christian belief and can be understood only in that larger religious context. The Satanists choose black as their color, not white, precisely because white is the symbol of purity and transcendence chosen by Christianity, and black therefore has come to symbolize the profane earthy indulgences central to Satanic theodicy. Satanists say that their gods are those of the earth, not the sky; that their cult is interested in making the sacred profane, in contrast to the Judeo-Christian cults which seek to make the profane sacred. Satanism cannot, in other words, be understood as an isolated phenomenon, but must be seen in a larger context.

The Satanic belief system, not surprisingly, is the antithesis of Christianity. Their theory of the universe, their cosmology, is based upon the notion that the desired end state is a return to a pagan awareness of the mystical forces inhabiting the earth, a return to an awareness of their humanity. This is in sharp contrast to the transcendental goals of traditional Christianity. The power associated with the pantheon of gods is also reversed: Satan's power is waxing; God's, if he still lives, waning. The myths of the Satanic church purport to tell the true story of the rise of Christianity and the fall of paganism, and there is a reversal here too. Christ is depicted as an early "con man" who tricked an anxious and powerless group of individuals into believing a lie. He is typified as "pallid incompetence hanging on a tree." [2] Satanic novices are taught that early church fathers deliberately picked on those aspects of human desire that were most natural and made them sins, in order to use the inevitable transgressions as a means of controlling the populace, promising them salvation in return for obedience. And finally, their substantive belief, the very delimitation of what is sacred and what is profane, is the antithesis of Christian belief. The Satanist is taught to "be natural; to revel in pleasure and in self-gratification. To emphasize indulgence and power in this life."

The opposition of Satanists to Christianity may be seen most clearly in the various rituals of greater magic. Although there are many different types of rituals all aimed at achieving the virtues that are the inverted

[2] LaVey 1969:31.

sins of the Christian, we shall examine briefly only two of these: blasphemy and the invocation of destruction. By far the most famous of Satanic institutions, the Black Mass and other forms of ritual blasphemy serve a very real and necessary function for the new Satanist. In many cases the exhortations and teachings of his Satanic colleagues are not sufficient to alleviate the sense of guilt and anxiety he feels when engaging in behavior forbidden by Judeo-Christian tradition. The novice may still cower before the charismatic power of Christian symbols; he may still feel guilty, still experience anxiety and fear in their presence. It is here that the blasphemies come into play, and they take many forms depending on the needs of the individuals involved.

A particular blasphemy may involve the most sacred Christian rituals and objects. In the traditional Black Mass powerful Christian symbols such as the crucifix are handled brutally. Some Black Masses use urine or menstrual flow in place of the traditional wine in an attempt to evoke disgust and aversion to the ritual. If an individual can be conditioned to respond to a given stimulus, such as the communion wafer or wine, with disgust rather than fear, that stimulus's power to cause anxiety is diminished. Sexuality is also used. A young man who feared priests and nuns was deliberately involved in a scene in which two witches dressed as nuns interacted with him sexually; his former neurotic fear was replaced by a mildly erotic curiosity even in the presence of real nuns. The naked altar — a beautiful young witch — introduces another deliberate note of sexuality into a formerly awe-inspiring scene.

By far the most frequently used blasphemy involves laughter. Awe-inspiring or fear-producing institutions are made the object of ridicule. The blasphemous rituals, although still greater magic, are frequently extremely informal. To the outsider they would not seem to have any structure; the behavior being exhibited might appear to be a charade, or a party game. The Satanists decide ahead of time the institution to be ridiculed and frequently it is a Christian ritual. I have seen a group of Satanists do a parody of the Christmas manger scene, or dress in clerical garb while performing a satire of priestly sexual behavior. The target of blasphemy depends upon the needs of the various Satanists. If the group feels it is necessary for the well-being of one member, they will gladly, even gleefully, blaspheme anything from psychiatry to psychedelics.

In the invocation of destruction black magic reaches its peak. In some cases an individual's sense of inadequacy is experienced as victimization, a sense of powerlessness before the demands of stronger and more ruthless men. The Satanic Bible, in contrast to Christian belief, teaches the fearful novice that "Satan represents vengeance instead of turning the other cheek." In the Third Chapter of the Book of Satan, the reader is exhorted to "hate your enemies with a whole heart, and if a man smite you on one cheek, SMASH him on the other . . . he who turns the other cheek is a cowardly dog."[3]

One of the most frequently used rituals in such a situation is the Conjuration of Destruction, or Curse. Contrary to popular belief, black magicians are not indiscriminately aggressive. An individual must have harmed or hurt a member of the church before he is likely to be cursed. Even then the curse is laid with care, for cursing a more powerful magician may cause one's curse to be turned against oneself. If, in the judgment of the high priest and the congregation, a member has been unjustly used by a non-Satanist, even if the offender is an unaffiliated witch or magician, at the appropriate time in the ritual the member wronged may step forward and, with the aid and support of the entire congregation, ritually curse the transgressor. The name of the intended "sacrifice" is usually written on parchment made of the skin of unborn lamb and burned in the altar flame while the member himself speaks the curse; he may use the standard curse or, if he so desires, prepare a more powerful, individualistic one. In the curse he gives vent to his hostility and commands the legions of hell to torment and sacrifice his victim in a variety of horrible ways. Or, if the Satanist so desires, the High Priest will recite the curse for him, the entire group adding their power to the invocation by spirited responses.

The incidence of harmful results from cursing is low in the church of Satan because of two factors: first, one does not curse other members of the church for fear that their superior magic might turn the curse back upon its user; second, victims outside the congregation either do not believe in the power of black magic or do not recognize the esoteric symbols that should indicate to them they are being cursed.

On only one occasion was I able to see the effect of a curse on a "victim." A member attempted to use the church and its members for publicity purposes without their permission. When the leader of the group refused to go along with the scheme, the man quit — an action that would normally have brought no recrimination — and began to slander the church by spreading malicious lies throughout San Francisco social circles. Even though he was warned several times to stop his lies, the man persisted; so the group decided to level the most serious of all curses at him, and a ritual death rune was cast.

Casting a death rune, the most serious form of greater magic, goes considerably beyond the usual curse designed to cause only discomfort or unhappiness, but not to kill. The sole purpose of the death rune is to cause the total destruction of the victim. The transgressor's name is written in blood (to the Satanist, blood is power — the very power of life) on

[3] LaVey 1969:33.

special parchment, along with a number of traditional symbols of ceremonial magic. In a single-minded ritual of great intensity and ferocity, the emotional level is raised to a peak at which point the entire congregation joins in ritually destroying the victim of the curse. In the case in question, there was an orgy of aggression. The lamb's-wool figurine representing the victim was stabbed by all members of the congregation, hacked to pieces with a sword, shot with a small calibre pistol, and then burned.

A copy of the death rune was sent to the man in question, and every day thereafter an official death certificate was made out in his name and mailed to him. After a period of weeks during which the "victim" maintained to all who would listen that he "did not believe in all that nonsense," he entered the hospital with a bleeding ulcer. Upon recovery he left San Francisco permanently.

In fairness, I must add that the "victim" of the curse had previously had an ulcer, was struggling with a failing business, and seemed hypertense when I knew him. His knowledge of the "curse" may have hastened the culmination of his difficulties. The Satanic church, however, claimed it as a successful working, a victory for black magic, and word of it spread among the adherents of occult subculture, enhancing the reputation of the group.

Conclusion

Contemporary America is presently undergoing a witchcraft revival. On all levels, from teenagers to octogenarians, interest in, or fear of, witchcraft has increased dramatically over the past two years. It is hardly possible to pass a popular magazine rack without seeing an article about the revival of the black arts. Covens and cults multiply, as does the number of exorcisms and reconsecrations. England, France, Germany, and a host of other countries all report a rebirth of the black art. Why? Those who eventually become Satanists are attempting to cope with the everyday problems of life, with the here and now, rather than with some transcendental afterlife. In an increasingly complex world which they do not fully understand, an anxiety-provoking world, they seek out a group dedicated to those mysterious powers that the sufferers have felt moving them. Fearful of what one witch calls "the dark powers we all feel moving deep within us," they come seeking either *release* or *control.* They give various names to the problems they bring, but all, anxious and afraid, come to the Satanic cult seeking help in solving problems beyond their meager abilities. Whatever their problem — bewitchment, business failure, sexual impotence, or demonic possession — the Satanists, in the ways I have mentioned and many more, *can* and *do* help them. Witchcraft, the witches point out, "is the most practical of all beliefs. According to its devotees, its results are obvious and instantaneous. No task is too high or too lowly for the witch." Above all, the beliefs and practices provide the witch and the warlock with a sense of power, a feeling of control, and an explanation for personal failure, inadequacy, and other difficulties.

Moreover, a seeker's acceptance into the Inner Circle provides a major boost for his self-esteem; he has, for the first time, been accepted into a group as an individual despite his problems and abnormalities. Once within the Inner Circle that support continues. The Satanic group is, according to the cultural standards of his society, amoral, and the Satanist frequently finds himself lauded and rewarded for the very impulses and behavior that once brought shame and doubt.

Each Satanist is taught, and not without reason, that the exposure of his secret identity, of the fact that he is a powerful and adequate black magician, means trouble from a fearful society. Therefore, in keeping with the precepts of lesser magic, he learns to transform himself magically by day (for purposes of manipulation) into a bank clerk, a businessman, or even a college professor. He wears the guise and plays the role expected by society in order to manipulate the situation to his own advantage, to reach his desired goals. Members of society at large, aware only of his "normal" role behavior and unaware of the secret person within, respond to him positively instead of punishing him or isolating him. Then, in the evening, in the sanctity of his home, or when surrounded by his fellow magicians, he reverts to his "true" role, that of Satanic priest, and becomes himself once again. Inadequate and anxious persons, guilty because of socially disapproved impulses, are accepted by the Satanists and taught that the impulses they feel are natural and normal, but must be contained within certain spatial and temporal boundaries — the walls of the ritual chamber, the confines of the Inner Circle.

25

An African world view

JAMES H. VAUGHAN, JR.

World view pervades all aspects of culture. It includes assumptions regarding the world and man's place in it. James Vaughan describes the theology and ritual of the Marghi tribe in northern Nigeria, and shows how these are related to this people's broader view of the world. Of major concern is the Marghi cultural reconciliation between the concepts of fate and of independent personal action.

The concept of "world view" implies that societies organize natural and supernatural phenomena into integrated, meaningful systems — what might be called philosophic systems. Though the process of integration is unquestionably psychological in nature and permeates all behavior, the system is manifest most clearly in the sociological institution of religion. Since our interest is so broad, it is important that we consider both the ideational and the behavioral components of religion, that is, both theology and ritual. This is particularly necessary in this presentation, for each aspect emphasizes a different, and somewhat contrasting, relationship between the natural and the supernatural. The world view is indicated only in the integration of the two.

The Marghi, one of the highland tribes of Northern Nigeria, are found in the Mandara Mountains, which form a part of the border between Nigeria and Cameroun, and in the adjacent Chad basin of Nigeria. They do not possess a homogeneous culture — partly because of several distinct historical traditions among the clans, partly because they are organized into autonomous and frequently hostile kingdoms, and finally because of differential acculturation with Muslim tribes to the north and west. The central and eastern kingdoms are, however, relatively homo-

From "The Religion and the World View of the Marghi," *Ethnology* 3, no. 4 (1964):389–397. Reprinted by permission of the publisher and the author. Bibliographic citations and bibliography are omitted.

geneous and unacculturated. The material herein is drawn from the eastern Marghi, who are considered, both by themselves and by other Marghi, to be the most conservative branch of the tribe.

Theology

Marghi theology recognizes three classes of supernatural beings or forces. The supreme supernatural entity is *iju*, the ultimate cause of all, both good and bad. In some myths, proverbs, and figures of speech, *iju* is personalized, but on the whole the term is better translated "fate" than "god." Since *iju* is omnipotent and omnipresent, it is beyond the manipulations of men. There is no logical system which encompasses *iju*; a scoundrel may prosper, or a good man fail, and the explanation is *iju*. When an individual suffered a dramatic, accidental injury, he was consoled by comments of "*iju, iju*." Inquiry revealed that two things were implied in the comments: first, that the accident was attributable to *iju* and, second, that the victim's survival was likewise attributable to *iju*.

Iju is not, however, intimately concerned with the lives of individuals. One of the most widely known myths recounts the alienation of man and *iju*. According to this myth, in the beginning man and *iju* (personalized in this myth) lived together, *iju* providing food for all, but through the carelessness and ingratitude of a woman the daughter of *iju* was fatally injured, and he withdrew from the world of men for all time. This tale validates the remoteness of *iju*. Despite the supremacy of the power of *iju*, it is a generalized power, only implicitly concerned with daily routines and the problems of men. The *raison d'être* of all is *iju*, but this fact exists as an unspecified axiom underlying all other theological concepts.

The other two classes of supernatural beings are less remote and are actively malevolent or mischievous. The good which they do is entirely passive; that is, they do good by not doing evil. It is significant, I believe, that neither of them is believed to be present in the afterworld. These supernaturals are anthropomorphic in habits though not always in appearance. They are more manlike in personality and are capable of being pleased or angered. They also have places of residence in proximity to man. The importance of these spirits and their localized nature give Marghi religion a distinctly provincial character; it is a religion bound to specific places. This provincialism, which is undoubtedly characteristic of other societies, has important implications for attempts to understand social and cultural change among societies of this type, but these lie outside the scope of this paper.

The first of these classes of supernaturals is comprised of the *yal*. They are the most dangerous of spirits, capable of causing serious illness and death. They live in extraordinary places — in unusual rocks or trees, in springs or caves, or occasionally atop deserted mountains. Clairvoyants *(salkur)* have in the past revealed some of the specific residences of *yal*. These bear thereafter the names of their residences and form a group which we might call "public *yal*." Usually priests *(zuli)* look after the shrines of these *yal* and conduct annual ceremonies which recognize and attempt to placate them. Public *yal* are associated with the villages near which they are found, and the priesthood is usually hereditary in the senior clan of the village. In a sense such a *yal* belongs to the village, and in some cases where mountain villages have become deserted the *zuli* must return annually to the shrine of the *yal* — a fact which emphasizes the provincialism of the religion.

Another class of supernaturals is called *shatar*. They are quite similar to *yal* except that they are less dreadful and occasionally only mischievous. It is said, however, that a *shatar* can give a person to a *yal*. There are no "public *shatar*," and though they are thought to be more numerous than *yal* they are in many ways less specific. *Shatar* are not named, they have no shrines, nor are priests associated with them. Although *shatar* have no specific abodes, ant hills are in general considered to be their residences, and one often sees offerings left there.

One type of *shatar* is more specialized — the *kikyuwi*, dwarfs who live in tiny compounds in the earth. (The walls of their allegedly deserted compounds are occasionally found and look suspiciously like cross sections of large water pots.) These dwarfs are notorious for causing people to become lost. It is said that they urinate across paths and that when one crosses such a spot the world becomes reversed, right becoming left, etc. The only way to reorient oneself is to place one's left foot on an anthill.

Ancestor worship has a place in Marghi religion, though more as an appendage than as an integral part. Only the most recently deceased ancestor is revered and believed to have any direct sway over the affairs of the living. The eldest living son is the keeper of the shrine of a deceased father, while a deceased woman's youngest son keeps her shrine. The attention paid to female ancestors is trivial and not universal among the Marghi. The ancestral shrine is used only once a year, and in general there is only a minimal concern for the ancestors in a religious context.

The afterworld, *ivuhu (ivu,* inside; *hu,* grave), is vaguely conceived. There is agreement that it is a place very much like this world and is located in the mountains to the east. *Ivuhu* is a better world, a world without hunger and sickness, though it is not the paradise of Christian belief. The souls *(mambəl* of all persons go to *ivuhu,* though there is some disagreement as to what happens to an evil person once there. The Marghi do not seem overly concerned with the notion of good versus evil or with divine punishment. It seems possible that evil may simply be expurgated.

Mambəl must work and farm and, in general, live as do mortals. Many logical difficulties are resolved in reliance upon *iju*, who will "judge" all disputes in *ivuhu*.

In the organization of Marghi theology *iju* is the locus of all power. Men may question and supplicate, *yal* and *shatar* may execute, but everything is caused by *iju*. We must caution again, however, that a theology and its structure are not the totality of a world view.

Ritual

Overt religious behavior can be divided into public and private ceremonies, neither of which occupies a large portion of the people's time. Most of the public ceremonies and some of the private ones are calendrical, but others vary with circumstances or the needs of the individual. The number and name of the public ceremonies vary from kingdom to kingdom, but there is a considerable similarity between them, in function if not in form. The ceremonies briefly described herewith are the principal ones in the Kingdom of Gulagu, and this paper will attempt to cover only the major events.

The Marghi calendar begins with the new moon near the end of March or the beginning of April. There is no rationale for this beginning, though we may note that it virtually corresponds with the first moon after the vernal equinox and that during this month the first rains of the new year may be expected to fall. One ceremony occurs during this month, but, since it bears such an intrinsic relation to the ceremonies of the past year, we shall discuss it as the last of the public ceremonies.

The major religious ceremony of the Marghi is *yawal*, a three-day festival occurring at the end of the fourth moon. All planting is completed by this time. The rains are at their peak, and the fields and mountainsides are green with the growth of the new year. Formerly this was the time of the year when wars were fought, and — significantly, I believe — it was traditionally the time when the Marghi killed or forcibly removed the old king and installed their new one. *Yawal* is a time of virility and growth.

The ceremonies are notable for the feasting that accompanies them. Large quantities of beef are consumed, although the Marghi do not in general keep cattle. The feature of the first day's ritual is the sacrificing of the "spirit cow" *(mambəl thla)* by the king, who performs the act wearing the traditional dress of a ram-skin loin garment and a cape of hyrax skin. In addition, his head is uncovered, and the royal hairlock is plainly visible; at no other time may subjects see the king's head uncovered. The meat from the "spirit cow" is divided ritually among the members of the king's council, who are representatives of clans and other divisions of the kingdom.

The second day's ceremonies begin before sunrise when the king throws a lighted torch into a tree, an act which is interpreted as prophetic of the coming year. If the torch should quickly go out or fall from the tree, a poor year would be indicated. This is followed by dancing, by mock battles, and finally by a staged combat between the uninitiated boys and the adult males. The boys withdraw from the royal village and then march on the royal compound. After refusing to be placated by an offering of food from the king, which they eat nonetheless, they attack the men of the village, who are defeated. After further dancing the people adjourn to their homes to gather in neighborhood groups for feasting. The king sits outside his compound during these activities, encouraging the dancing and fighting, and retires only after taking a mouthful of food. This event is likewise unique, for ordinarily no one is permitted to observe the king eating; there is even a legend of a king who fled his kingdom in shame after having been tricked into eating in public.

The main feature of the final day of *yawal* is a "minature" grain threshing. Three heads of guinea corn are threshed with tiny sticks, as a drummer sets the pace of the work and the spectators drink beer and chat. The corn is deposited in the king's granary, and a goat is sacrificed. In all respects this is identical to the threshing ceremonies which will occur after harvest except that the amount of corn threshed is restricted to only three heads.

The second major ceremonial event is the boys' initiation *(dəkwa)*. Because of the general festivity involved, this affects virtually everyone in the community for at least two days. It occurs one month after *yawal* and consists of a one-week mountain retreat and a less formal period lasting for the rest of the month. This custom is more appropriate to a consideration of rites of passage, and its complexities are too great for the present discussion.

The *aŋgarawai* is a harvest ceremony which takes place during the eleventh moon and features females, particularly new mothers. In many ways the central role belongs to the king's senior wife, called *thladawa*, who in general plays an important part in the ritual life of the kingdom. In this ceremony the women, with their infants on their backs, go out along the paths into the fields and return, dancing and singing, to the king's compound. They are led by the *birma*, the royal steward, who is a slave. He carries a sword and a basket in which are placed a ceremonial sickle and three heads of corn — those which will be threshed at the next *yawal*. The *thladawa* walks behind the *birma* dressed as though she were a young maid and carrying a calabash of food. They all salute the king, after which the ceremony dissolves into general dancing and beer drinking.

The final public celebration in Gulagu occurs at the end of the first moon. It is called *digu digal*, "great threshing." On the morning of the selected day the three heads of corn are again separated from the king's harvest, and the remaining corn is threshed in the conventional manner. This is the last threshing of the year; soon it will be time to start planting again. In the afternoon the people gather in front of the royal compound, where the king, in his most elaborate dress, sits and talks with the visitors. When the crowd is sufficiently large, he takes his sacred staff and moves away from the royal compound to the edge of the fields. All the men in attendance then go and "bring" him back to his compound. They lead and he follows; no one may remain behind — not even observing anthropologists. He is the last to come from the field, the last to enter the village. The men then dance, and there is a great deal of drinking and conversation. On the whole, the participants in this ceremony are males as those of the *aŋgarawai* had been female.

There is but one other class of public religious observances, and these are not a part of the calendrical cycle of ceremonies. From time to time, in response to forebodings, warnings, disasters, or the like, villages or kingdoms declare an *asadaka* or holiday, during which no work is done and individuals may propitiate the *yal* and *shatar* with sacrifices and offerings. (The same term is used among some Marghi to designate a particular funeral celebration, by others to denote any holiday from work.)

Individual ceremonies frequently overlap public ceremonies. In all individual ceremonies the proper dress for males is a ram-skin loin garment. Marghi shrines, typically, are specially made pots called *i'iwa* — usually six to eight inches in diameter with narrow elongated necks. Each man has one such shrine, called *iju kir* (*kir*, head), at which he should sacrifice a goat once a year during the month of the *yawal* celebration. These sacrifices are for the general well-being of the compound and thus in practice tend to be confined to household heads. Theoretically, however, a man may sacrifice at his *iju kir* at any time after his initiation.

A similar shrine is the *koptu tada* (*koptu*, shrine; *tada*, father), at which the eldest son must sacrifice each year. The ceremony takes place on the day following the *iju kir* custom and is considered to be more important. Men not infrequently sacrifice goats to their *koptu tada* but only cocks at their *iju kir*, and it is said that if a man can perform only one sacrifice it is better to render the former. This, however, probably implies less about the relative importance of ancestors and *iju* than it does about Marghi notions concerning respect toward fathers. The *koptu tada* shrine is usually slightly larger than that of the *iju kir*, but the distinctive difference is the occurrence of two or three small protuberances on the upper portion of the pot — two indicating that the deceased's first child was female, three that it was male. The *koptu tada* shrine is preserved more carefully than the *iju kir* and is kept outside the owner's house, often in a tiny house of its own. Otherwise the ceremony is quite similar to that at the *iju kir*. A mother's shrine *(koptu mama)* is rarely an *i'iwa;* it is often only a piece of broken calabash and at most receives a sacrifice of a hen. On the whole this custom is very irregularly and incompletely observed.

A *koptu bzir* (*bzir,* children) is usually only the neck of a cooking pot placed to the right of the entrance to the compound. A chicken is sacrificed at this shrine on the first day of *yawal* and on the seventh day following the birth of the child. This custom is manifestly intended to insure the good health and well-being of the youngest child in the family, but by extension it applies to all children in the family. It is probably a minor fertility shrine as well, for in one instance during *yawal* I observed a barren woman performing a rite at the household *koptu bzir*.

The remaining category of ceremonies is that of private, noncalendrical approaches to the supernatural, which in fact constitute the major part of Marghi religious behavior. All things are caused by *iju,* of course, but misfortunes, including illness, are quite likely to be due to *yal* and *shatar*. Since these latter spirits are amenable to human intervention, almost all misfortunes are met by attempts at propitiation. In practice, routine and common illnesses are usually treated from a common store of knowledge without reference to supernatural powers, but more serious or unusual illnesses require both symptomatic and causal treatment. To the Marghi causality is supernatural. Misfortune in general is directly referable to supernatural causation, and the specific supernatural cause is usually determined by a diviner. The term for diviner, *malaga,* is also the word for crab, undoubtedly because the most common mode of divination utilizes a crab. Once divination has indicated a cause for the ill, the diviner suggests a course of propitiation for its alleviation. Occasionally a client requires a personal medicine for his protection or to increase his abilities, but the most common prescription of diviners is an offering. Two types of offerings are recognized: *nadləsu (nadlu,* coarsely ground guinea corn; *su,* thing) *zibəsu* or *zibsu (zibə,* to come out; *su,* thing). The former is usually some form of grain or seed, whereas the latter is an offering of meat, preferably from a sacrificed goat or chicken.

The following generalizations about offerings are based upon observations but do not form a conscious part of Marghi belief. There is a correlation between the type of offering and the seriousness of the problem, *zibəsu* being more powerful than *nadləsu*. Similarly, there is a tendency for *zibəsu* to be associated with *yal* and *nadləsu* with *shatar*. In addition, it would seem that women often offer *nadləsu,* whereas *zibəsu,* and certainly sacrifice, are rendered by men.

Funerals, too, are a part of ritual life, though, like initiations, they might better be discussed as rites of passage. Funerals require community participation, primarily dancing and singing. The entire village participates in intense public mourning, which lasts for about twenty-four hours or until interment. General mourning continues for at least seven more days, but this is observed more in fashion and decorum than in overt mourning behavior. The funeral itself is energetically cathartic; mourning is vigorous, and references to "the long journey," death, and *iju* are frequent. Mourners at funerals frequently carry sprigs of thorn to protect them from loitering evil spirits. The frailty and uncertainty of life are made apparent to all who attend.

Though religion permeates their lives, the Marghi do not spend a great deal of their time in overt religious behavior. The public ceremonies occupy only seven days. The more formal individual rituals add only two more, since the *koptu tada* and *koptu mama* rituals occur on the same day and the *koptu bzir* takes place on the first day of *yawal*. The variable ceremonies, the *asadaka* or rest days, funerals, and individual propitiations account for the greater part of the religious life of Marghi. *Asadaka* may vary widely, but a range from five to ten days is possibly typical. Funerals are less variable, except that the older one becomes and the wider his contacts the more funerals he is likely to attend; an adult male may attend perhaps twelve per year. The actual number of days devoted to specific supernatural propitiation is not great. This fact may, however, be misleading since two other circumstances seem more indicative of the importance of individual propitiation. First, the ominous threat of misfortune and illness is so pervasive and persistent that it constantly intrudes in thought and behavior, so that the potentiality for this type of religious behavior overrides its actual occurrence. Second, the distribution of such behavior throughout the population is such that everyone is constantly aware of it, quite apart form his personal involvement, thus giving it greater importance than might be assumed from the involvement of particular individuals.

The calendrical ceremonies, both public and private, are not directed to immediate or conscious ends. In most instances no overt reason is given for holding them. Plausible interpretations of them have doubtless occurred to the reader, but the aims of this presentation are served if we indicate that these ceremonies all establish or reaffirm the relationship of man and *iju*. The benefit sought is the general harmony or well-being of the world. This lack of specificity perhaps explains why many of the ceremonial acts have little manifest meaning; they are mere parts of a total configuration toward a generalized end.

The variable ceremonies are directed more toward specific ends. They are therefore more concerned with *yal* and *shatar* than with *iju*. Funerals and *asadaka*, to be sure, may be thought of as reaffirmations of the relationship of man to *iju*, but they are always closely tied to specific misfortunes and crises and thus actually emphasize the importance of the relationship of man to *yal* and *shatar*. Since the variable ceremonies, as previously indicated, constitute the most pervasive part of Marghi religion, we may conclude that the emphasis of Marghi ritual life is on the malevolent *yal* and *shatar*. This is in opposition to the primacy accorded *iju* in Marghi theology.

World view

An understanding of the way Marghi view the world is possible only if we accept the prevalence of both the fatalism manifest in their theology and the individualism apparent in their rituals and see the relationship of each theme to the other. The greatest strength of Marghi philosophy may lie in the integration of these contrasting themes, which may be summarized as follows. *Iju* is an omnipotent power, but it is remote and impersonal. The affairs and fortunes of individuals are only generally the concern of *iju* and are much more directly and explicitly governed by *yal*, *shatar*, and occasionally the ancestors. These powers are much more personal in their habits and specific in their actions, and they are not intractable but may be influenced by the ceremonies of men. Consequently, despite the fatalistic theme of Marghi theology, man is not helpless in the face of misfortune caused by supernatural powers, except to the extent that all things are, in the end, preordained by *iju*. This system, which is typical of other West African cultures, permits man to attempt to control his fortunes while it offers him a final explanation of human failure that does not destroy his belief in the efficacy of religious ceremony. This explains the activist system of ceremonies which masks a fatalistic theology. Man may engage in propitiatory ceremonies for the alleviation of specific ills without contradicting his ultimate reliance upon *iju*.

As a consequence of these contrasting themes, the Marghi are extremely reserved, even defensive, in their religion; and because it forms the basis of their world view, defensiveness permeates all their behavior. Each act of propitiation masks a semiconscious awareness that such an act may be futile. Though they never give in to passivity, they seem always to expect the worst. Looked at from another point of view, this attitude might be characterized as a means of control whereby they attempt to prepare themselves for the eventualities of life. This view is illustrated in the frequent and casual references to pregnant women as "dead women," a practice which prepares them for the possibility of death in childbirth. By predicting, as it were, this unhappy eventuality, they attain a measure of control over the situation. It is preferable in some instances to have a known unhappy destiny than simply an unknown destiny. At a spot on a trail leading to a large market one may pull a leaf and place it upon a rock and thereby incur the fate of this coming market day for future market days. Clearly, the Marghi have a low tolerance for ambiguity.

Comparable attempts at control are manifest in interpersonal relations as well. Any action which makes an individual uncharacteristically dependent upon another — particularly an unrelated person — is an obvious manifestation of loss of control and hence creates an intolerable situation. Consequently arguments are interminable, for no one will admit to being bested. Individuals are reluctant to ask the simplest favors for the same reason. Requests are usually made through an intermediary or are phrased so indirectly that the favor may be granted without the recipient's having made an overt request. Public embarrassment is a dire event, and the Marghi carefully avoid causing embarrassment to others.

Conspicuous pretense characterizes some of this defensiveness, since certain patterns seem to indicate a lack of concern in the very things about which the Marghi care the most. Pretense or masking is an important part of their behavior. The more one emotionally invests in a thing, the more one has to lose should it be removed; and the more one loses, the more he loses control of the situation. This pattern is evident in the characteristically deprecating comments concerning infants. The *zibumbwa* (*zib*, to come out; *umbwa,* house) ceremony makes the same point somewhat more subtly. This ritual, which takes place seven days after the birth of a child, and at which the child is seen publicly for the first time, marks the social birth of the individual. If the infant dies before this ceremony, it is as though it were never born; biological birth counts for naught. It is, of course, during these seven days that death is most likely; thus in a sense the probability of a child's social survival is increased by delaying its social birth. If the child dies before the ceremony, people can deny that, socially, it ever lived and thus lessen their loss.

This world view is adaptive for the circumstances in which the Marghi live. The high rates of infant and maternal mortality, the rates of morbidity, and historical conditions of warfare, slavery, and exploitation are reconciled with their own activist traditions. Their religion and world view reflect these circumstances but in turn provide the rationale for pursuing their way of life. They perceive a world, not of their making, full of natural and supernatural dangers. But their conception of the relationship of man to supernatural permits them to meet these dangers. Should they fail, then that was their fate, but they succeed in enough instances to insure the persistence of their beliefs. Such a world view is tolerant of changes in natural or material conditions, which the Marghi meet with characteristic aggressiveness. On the other hand, it is a world view rigidly intolerant of changes that threaten its philosophic basis.

The importance of society's world view is indicated in these observations, for it goes beyond the field of religion. A world view is more accurately a matrix which channels and encompasses the totality of cultural experience. It is a part of the unconscious basis of the process of social life, as relevant to discussions of cultural change as to discussions of cultural content.

26

The world view of street warriors

R. LINCOLN KEISER

We customarily think of religion and world view as supernaturally based, but no such limitation is mandatory, as the ideology of the Vice Lords indicates. The Vice Lords are a Black street gang located in the Lawndale area of Chicago's West Side ghetto. This selection is taken from a more complete description of the social and cultural system of this urban gang. In his description of Vice Lord cultural categories, Lincoln Keiser makes clear the impact of ideology on the meaning of life. "Heart," "soul," "brotherhood," and "the game" are all shown to be valued cultural properties.

Vice lords define their world and guide their actions in terms of a particular ideological framework. This constitutes Vice Lord culture. Our concern . . . is to describe some of the beliefs and values comprising this framework, and to show how they relate to social behavior. I found four general ideological sets which constitute Vice Lord culture. They can be designated: heart ideology, soul ideology, brotherhood ideology, and game ideology. Each of these sets functions to divide Vice Lord reality into a number of compartments we can call cultural scenes, and to guide and judge behavior within these scenes.

Heart ideology

> A Cobra swung on one of the fellows, and he come down with his knife out. That means he's not scared to take that man's life if he wished to. That's what you call a lot of heart — not scared to go to jail and pay whatever the consequences is.

> If a group of boys say, going to break into a store or truck, and I tell this boy to do it and he does it, the people say he got a whole lot of heart — he not afraid of anything. He'll just go on and do everything the other person tell him to do.
>
> A person who got heart, he not scared to do anything. Like we break in a liquor lounge or something, he not worried about being busted. He's game for it. Or like we in a fight, and we outnumbered say four to two. This man will stand up there and fight with you no matter what. If you all go down, he there with you. You all both go down together.
>
> If you don't show heart people call you a punk, and they don't want to hang with you. A punk is a person who like get into a fight with somebody and he don't fight back. Or like if say me and you and somebody else, we going to rob somebody, and one of us be scared and won't do it. Then they say he punked out.

From these explanations we can understand what Vice Lords mean by "heart." It is apparent that generally "heart" means bravery, but it means more than just this. It also means bravery in terms of being "game," that is, being willing to follow any suggestion regardless of personal risk. Having heart contrasts with punking out. A person who acts in a cowardly way — that is, who is not "game" for any suggestion — is a punk. Vice Lords believe that having heart is good, while being a punk, or punking out is bad. Heart, in other words, is one of the values of Vice Lord culture.

The heart-punk contrast defines a particular segment of Vice Lord reality. If we look at the explanations given by Vice Lords, it is apparent that the heart-punk contrast is relevant to situations where there is personal risk. Individuals are judged in terms of heart ideology only in situations which involve personal risk, and thus these situations are set off as distinct segments of Vice Lord Life. A further look at our Vice Lords' explanations shows a division in risk situations — those involving fighting, and those involving robbing. Vice Lords call fighting humbugging, and robbing hustling. Humbugging is further subdivided: fighting between rival clubs is gangbanging, fighting between individuals is humbugging, and fighting which results when a group of club members goes out to jump on anyone they can find is wolf packing. We can show this more clearly by constructing a typology comprised of contrast sets.

<table>
<tr><td colspan="3">Personal Risk Situations</td><td rowspan="3">Other Situations</td></tr>
<tr><td></td><td>Humbugging$_1$</td><td rowspan="2">Hustling</td></tr>
<tr><td>Gangbanging</td><td>Humbugging$_2$ Wolfpacking</td></tr>
</table>

Personal risk situations contrast with other situations. Within the former, humbugging$_1$ contrasts with hustling. Within humbugging$_1$ situations, gangbanging, humbugging$_2$, and wolf packing all contrast. I should explain the difference between humbugging$_1$ and humbugging$_2$. Vice Lords refer to all kinds of fighting as humbugging. A fight between a boy and his father, a fight between males and females, a fight between rival clubs, or any other kind of fight can be referred to as a humbug. However, Vice Lords further distinguish between kinds of fighting. Gangbanging refers only to fights between enemy clubs. When individuals wish to distinguish between fights involving two individuals and fights involving rival clubs, they refer to the former as humbugs and the latter as gangbangs. Thus humbugging means any kind of fighting when contrasted with hustling, but means only fighting between individuals when contrasted with gangbanging. Therefore, I have used humbugging$_1$ to designate fighting in general and humbugging$_2$ to specify fighting between individuals.

Situations which involve humbugging$_2$, gangbanging, wolf packing, and hustling form distinct segments of Vice Lord reality that can be called cultural scenes. The use of scene is an analogy to the scenes of a play. As the action of a play is divided into scenes, so the action of Vice Lord behavior is structured into units we can call cultural scenes. My data on humbugging$_2$, wolf packing, and hustling is too limited to provide a detailed description of the pattern of action that takes place within these scenes. We can, however, study the cultural scene gangbang in greater detail. . . . We made the distinction between gangbangs that resulted from accidental encounters between members of an enemy club and those that involved prior planning. Here, we are concerned with the latter.

There are four phases in a gangbang. The first we can call the prefight gathering. Before actual fighting begins, Vice Lords meet in their territory to plan strategy. During this phase there is drinking, singing, shouting, and bragging. Besides planning strategy Vice Lords are emotionally preparing to face the dangers of actual fighting. The second phase is the confrontation between enemy clubs. During the confrontation the groups stand facing each other, while the two rival war counselors are in between exchanging threats and insults. When the rival war counselors begin fighting, the first phase begins. This we can call the encounter. During the encounter the actual fighting takes place. The final phase is the postfight gathering. During this phase Vice Lords again gather in their territory to drink and brag of their exploits. The following account illustrates in greater detail what happens during the second and third phases.

> Now a fight like this really looks funny when it starts, but it turns out to be terrifying. When it's just coming night is when most of the fighting occurs so if the Man come, then everybody can get away.
>
> You get a stick, or maybe a knife, or a chain. And some fools got shotguns. What you really do, you stand there and the counselors are the

> first ones up. You stand back and you wait and see if they come to an agreement and talk. Now everybody standing there watching everybody else to see what's going to happen. And all of a sudden maybe a blow will be passed, and if it is, a fight start right there. Let's say this is what happened. Now nine out of ten you know everybody in your club, or everybody who came with you. You standing just like you'd met in a crowd and you were talking. It's really almost a semicircle. You just standing there and you're looking — you're watching the counselor. And if a blow pass, automatically the first thing you do is hit the man closest to you. After that if things get too tight for you then you get out of there. If it look like you getting whupped, you get out. It's all according to your nerve. The first who runs, that's it right there. Naturally if you're standing there and you're fighting, and you see half the club starting to run, you know the other half going to run soon. All it takes is one to run and the whole crowd breaks up. That's how a club gets its rep — by not running, by standing its ground.

The beliefs and values of heart ideology underlie the action of the gangbang scene. Esteem among Vice Lords corresponds to rep. Rep, in turn, depends on how others judge one's behavior in relation to heart ideology. These judgments are made on the behavior that takes place during the second and third phases of the gangbang scene. Heart ideology is also important in the first and third phases of a gangbang. Here, the beliefs and values of heart are reinforced through expression in ritualistic behavior. The basic tenets of heart ideology are contained in a poem composed by several of the original members of the club:

> From back out to south came the King of the Gestapoes, Lord of the Sabotage, Ruler of the Astronauts, knocking down fifty-sixty lanes.
>
> I say, for any man make attempt to take a Vice Lord down, he got to first find a rock to kill Goliath, overturn the pillars of Sampson, name the stone that David stood on, name the three little children that walked the burning fires of hell, stand in front of the Lord and say, "I have no fear."
>
> For the Vice Lords, I say for all Vice Lords, sixty-two across the chest, don't fear nothing, God and death, got a tombstone opportunity, a grave-yard mind, he must be a Vice Lord 'cause he don't mind dying.
>
> Vice Lord! Mighty Vice Lord!

During the first and third phases of a gangbang this poem is repeated by members of the club. The group divides itself into sections and each repeats alternating phrases. The final refrain — "Vice Lord! Mighty Vice Lord!" — is said by the entire group. In this manner the beliefs and values contained in the poem are given public expression, and heart ideology is reinforced.

Soul ideology

There are several aspects to the Vice Lord concept of "soul." In one sense it refers to a general sort of Negritude. One who acts in a "hip" manner is said to have soul. However, it means more than this. Soul also refers to a way of doing something. When someone puts real effort into what he is doing, he is said to have soul. Stripping away superficiality and getting to the essence (or, in ghetto jargon, getting down to the real "nitty-gritty") is also involved in soul. Thus, for example, someone who sings with real effort and real feeling, and in so doing succeeds in capturing the essence of Black experience, has soul. His musical ability as such is irrelevant to the amount of his soul. Charles Keil has made an intensive study of the soul concept among Blacks in Chicago, and his research shows that the Vice Lord meaning of soul is the same as that found in ghetto culture as a whole. For a deeper analysis of the soul concept the reader is referred to Keil's monograph *The Urban Blues.* For our purposes, however, it is only necessary to note these three elements — Negritude, intense effort; and stripping away superficiality, or getting down to the real nitty-gritty — for Vice Lords base their judgments of soul on these elements.

Vice Lords value soul. To tell someone he has soul is a compliment, while to say he has "a hole in his soul" is a definite criticism. There are certain social situtions in which judgments are made in terms of soul. These are contexts involving music. Music is an extremely important part of Vice Lord life. Vice Lords closely follow the music from Chicago's Black radio stations, and are constantly singing the songs that are broadcasted there. Many have formed their own singing groups which hold regular practices and perform at certain times. Dancing is even more important in Vice Lord life. Almost all Vice Lords take intense pride in their dancing ability, and lose few opportunities to demonstrate it.

Vice Lords judge one another's singing and dancing in terms of soul ideology, and thus that segment of Vice Lord life in which singing and dancing is found is set off from other social situations. Singing and dancing are important activities in two Vice Lord scenes. These are called by Vice Lords sets and hanging on the corner. A set can be translated as a party. Vice Lords usually display their dancing ability in this scene, and it is here that judgments are made in terms of soul. Singing takes place in many situations. Riding in a car, or meeting at a member's house, are a few examples of when singing occurs. However, judgments about singing are usually made during performances that take place while hanging on the corner. When large groups of Vice Lords gather on the corner of 16th and Lawndale, for example, various groups demonstrate their singing abilities, and soul judgments are made on these performances.

Brotherhood ideology

. . . Mutual help is an important value in the Vice Lord cultural framework. Vice Lords often express this in terms of brotherhood. "Man, we're just like brothers" is an often-heard phrase. One Vice Lord scene in which the values of brotherhood are especially relevant is drinking wine. There is a special ritual to wine-drinking, and through this ritual the values of brotherhood are expressed and reinforced.

A wine-drinking scene is initiated when a small group of Vice Lords gathers and someone suggests having a taste, or pulling some jive. The next phase is gathering the money. The individual who made the first suggestion usually acts as collector. Everyone in the group donates what he feels he can afford. Often it is necessary to go around the group several times before enough money is collected. Vice Lords passing by are also asked to contribute money and join in the wine-drinking activities. After the money is collected and the wine is purchased, the next phase of the scene begins. This consists of "cracking the bottle." The bottle of wine is given to one of the group, who points it toward the ground and strikes the bottom of the bottle two times with the palm of his hand. This cracks the seal. Next, a small portion of the wine is poured out on the ground either in the letters CVL, or simply the letter V. This is interpreted as a symbolic gift to all the Vice Lords who have been killed or who are in jail. Finally, the bottle is passed around to everyone in the group, and each drinks the same amount regardless of how much money he contributed toward buying the wine.

There are two aspects of the wine-drinking scene that give expression to brotherhood ideology. The first is the wine that is poured out in the Vice Lord letters. Vice Lords place a high value on wine, and pouring out even a little is a form of sacrifice. This sacrifice is interpreted as a symbolic giving to other Vice Lords in need. Vice Lords who are dead and in jail can't get wine for themselves, but this way there is symbolically something for them to drink too. The second aspect that reinforces brotherhood values is the way the wine is distributed and the way it is drunk. Every person in the group is entitled to an equal amount of wine regardless of the amount of money he contributed. Each gives whatever he has or whatever he can afford, but all, as Vice Lords put it, "share like brothers" in the consumption of the wine. Further, the wine is drunk from the same bottle. Each person does not take his portion in a separate glass, but everyone drinks from the same bottle. To Vice Lords this sharing further symbolizes the unity and brotherhood between members of the group. Thus the wine-drinking ritual expresses and reinforces the values of mutual help — the values of brotherhood.

Game ideology

. . . In certain situations the ability to successfully manipulate others, or, as Vice Lords say, "whupping the game," is an activity which sets off a particular part of Vice Lord life. We can call this segment a "game." The way individuals behave during a game scene is judged by other Vice Lords in terms of game ideology. Individuals who are thought to be good at whupping the game are said to have a "heavy game," while those who are judged to be poor at this activity are said to have a "lightweight game." The technique one uses in whupping the game is called a "front," and the quality of various individuals' fronts is often a topic of conversation.

Various Vice Lords often tried to whup the game on me with various degrees of success. A few examples will help illustrate the kinds of situations that constitute the game scene. Washington was known for having a lightweight game. He was seldom successful in beating anyone out of anything, but was often taken himself for various items of value. His attempt to whup the game on me consisted of simply requesting money: "Hey man, can you give me a quarter?" My answer was, "Sorry Washington, I don't have it today." This exchange constituted a game scene in Vice Lord life.

Blue Goose, in contrast to Washington, was known to have a heavy game. Once he convinced me that a group of older men who were not members of the Vice Lords were planning to jump on me. He assured me, however, that I had nothing to fear because he would see to it that they did not bother me. He made a big show of chasing two old wineheads who he purported were plotting against me down the street. A little while later he asked me to loan him fifty cents and a shirt so he could make his "gig" (job) the next day. Of course, in gratitude, I was more than glad to help in any way possible. Later I learned I had taken part in a game scene and had been the victim of a successful front. . . .

27

Cargo cults

PETER M. WORSLEY

When one cultural group becomes dominated by another, its original meaning system may seem thin, ineffective, and contradictory. The resulting state of deprivation often causes members to rebuild their culture along more satisfying lines. In this article Peter Worsley describes such a movement among the peoples of New Guinea and adjacent islands, an area where Western influence has caused cultural disorientation and where cargo cults have provided the basis for reorganization.

Patrols of the Australian Government venturing into the "uncontrolled" central highlands of New Guinea in 1946 found the primitive people there swept up in a wave of religious excitement. Prophecy was being fulfilled: The arrival of the Whites was the sign that the end of the world was at hand. The natives proceeded to butcher all of their pigs — animals that were not only a principal source of subsistence but also symbols of social status and ritual preeminence in their culture. They killed these valued animals in expression of the belief that after three days of darkness "Great Pigs" would appear from the sky. Food, firewood, and other necessities had to be stockpiled to see the people through to the arrival of the Great Pigs. Mock wireless antennae of bamboo and rope had been erected to receive in advance the news of the millennium. Many believed that with the great event they would exchange their black skins for white ones.

This bizarre episode is by no means the single event of its kind in the murky history of the collision of European civilization with the indigenous cultures of the southwest Pacific. For more than one hundred years traders and missionaries have been reporting similar disturbances among the peoples of Melanesia, the group of Negro-inhabited islands (including New

From "Cargo Cults," *Scientific American* 200 (May 1959): 117–128. Reprinted with permission of the publisher and the author. Illustrations are omitted.

Guinea, Fiji, the Solomons, and the New Hebrides) lying between Australia and the open Pacific Ocean. Though their technologies were based largely upon stone and wood, these peoples had highly developed cultures, as measured by the standards of maritime and agricultural ingenuity, the complexity of their varied social organizations, and the elaboration of religious belief and ritual. They were nonetheless ill prepared for the shock of the encounter with the Whites, a people so radically different from themselves and so infinitely more powerful. The sudden transition from the society of the ceremonial stone ax to the society of sailing ships and now of airplanes has not been easy to make.

After four centuries of Western expansion, the densely populated central highlands of New Guinea remain one of the few regions where the people still carry on their primitive existence in complete independence of the world outside. Yet as the agents of the Australian Government penetrate into ever more remote mountain valleys, they find these backwaters of antiquity already deeply disturbed by contact with the ideas and artifacts of European civilization. For "cargo" — Pidgin English for trade goods — has long flowed along the indigenous channels of communication from the seacoast into the wilderness. With it has traveled the frightening knowledge of the white man's magical power. No small element in the white man's magic is the hopeful message sent abroad by his missionaries: the news that a Messiah will come and that the present order of Creation will end.

The people of the central highlands of New Guinea are only the latest to be gripped in the recurrent religious frenzy of the "cargo cults." However variously embellished with details from native myth and Christian belief, these cults all advance the same central theme: the world is about to end in a terrible cataclysm. Thereafter God, the ancestors, or some local culture hero will appear and inaugurate a blissful paradise on earth. Death, old age, illness, and evil will be unknown. The riches of the white man will accrue to the Melanesians.

Although the news of such a movement in one area has doubtless often inspired similar movements in other areas, the evidence indicates that these cults have arisen independently in many places as parallel responses to the same enormous social stress and strain. Among the movements best known to students of Melanesia are the "Taro Cult" of New Guinea, the "Vailala Madness" of Papua, the "Naked Cult" of Espiritu Santo, the "John Frum Movement" of the New Hebrides, and the "Tuka Cult" of the Fiji Islands.

At times the cults have been so well organized and fanatically persistent that they have brought the work of government to a standstill. The outbreaks have often taken the authorities completely by surprise and have confronted them with mass opposition of an alarming kind. In the 1930's, for example, villagers in the vicinity of Wewak, New Guinea, were stirred by a succession of "Black King" movements. The prophets announced that the Europeans would soon leave the island, abandoning their property to the natives, and urged their followers to cease paying taxes, since the government station was about to disappear into the sea in a great earthquake. To the tiny community of Whites in charge of the region, such talk was dangerous. The authorities jailed four of the prophets and exiled three others. In yet another movement, that sprang up in declared opposition to the local Christian mission, the cult leader took Satan as his god.

Troops on both sides in World War II found their arrival in Melanesia heralded as a sign of the Apocalypse. The G.I.'s who landed in the New Hebrides, moving up for the bloody fighting on Guadalcanal, found the natives furiously at work preparing airfields, roads and docks for the magic ships and planes that they believed were coming from "Rusefel" (Roosevelt), the friendly king of America.

The Japanese also encountered millenarian visionaries during their southward march to Guadalcanal. Indeed, one of the strangest minor military actions of World War II occurred in Dutch New Guinea, when Japanese forces had to be turned against the local Papuan inhabitants of the Geelvink Bay region. The Japanese had at first been received with great joy, not because their "Greater East Asia Co-Prosperity Sphere" propaganda had made any great impact upon the Papuans, but because the natives regarded them as harbingers of the new world that was dawning, the flight of the Dutch having already given the first sign. Mansren, creator of the islands and their peoples, would now return, bringing with him the ancestral dead. All this had been known, the cult leaders declared, to the crafty Dutch, who had torn out the first page of the Bible where these truths were inscribed. When Mansren returned, the existing world order would be entirely overturned. White men would turn black like Papuans, Papuans would become Whites; root crops would grow in trees, and coconuts and fruits would grow like tubers. Some of the islanders now began to draw together into large "towns"; others took Biblical names such as "Jericho" and "Galilee" for their villages. Soon they adopted military uniforms and began drilling. The Japanese, by now highly unpopular, tried to disarm and disperse the Papuans; resistance inevitably developed. The climax of this tragedy came when several canoe-loads of fanatics sailed out to attack Japanese warships, believing themselves to be invulnerable by virtue of the holy water with which they had sprinkled themselves. But the bullets of the Japanese did not turn to water, and the attackers were mowed down by machine-gun fire.

Behind this incident lay a long history. As long ago as 1857 missionaries in the Geelvink Bay region had made note of the story of Mansren. It is typical of many Melanesian myths that became confounded with Christian doctrine to form the ideological basis of the movements. The legend tells how long ago there lived an old man named Manamakeri ("he who itches"), whose body was covered with sores. Manamakeri was extremely fond of palm wine, and used to climb a huge tree every day to tap the liquid from the flowers. He soon found that someone was getting there before him and removing the liquid. Eventually he trapped the thief, who turned out to be none other than the Morning Star. In return for his freedom, the Star gave the old man a wand that would produce as much fish as he liked, a magic tree and a magic staff. If he drew in the sand and stamped his foot, the drawing would become real. Manamakeri, aged as he was, now magically impregnated a young maiden; the child of this union was a miracle-child who spoke as soon as he was born. But the maiden's parents were horrified, and banished her, the child, and the old man. The trio sailed off in a canoe created by Mansren ("The Lord"), as the old man now became known. On this journey Mansren rejuvenated himself by stepping into a fire and flaking off his scaly skin, which changed into valuables. He then sailed around Geelvink Bay, creating islands where he stopped, and peopling them with the ancestors of the present-day Papuans.

The Mansren myth is plainly a creation myth full of symbolic ideas relating to fertility and rebirth. Comparative evidence — especially the shedding of his scaly skin — confirms the suspicion that the old man is, in fact, the Snake in another guise. Psychoanalytic writers argue that the snake occupies such a prominent part in mythology the world over because it stands for the penis, another fertility symbol. This may be so, but its symbolic significance is surely more complex than this. It is the "rebirth" of the hero, whether Mansren or the Snake, that exercises such universal fascination over men's minds.

The nineteenth-century missionaries thought that the Mansren story would make the introduction of Christianity easier, since the concept of "resurrection," not to mention that of the "virgin birth" and the "second coming," was already there. By 1867, however, the first cult organized around the Mansren legend was reported.

Though such myths were widespread in Melanesia, and may have sparked occasional movements even in the pre-White era, they took on a new significance in the late nineteenth century, once the European powers had finished parceling out the Melanesian region among themselves. In many coastal areas the long history of "blackbirding" — the seizure of islanders for work on the plantations of Australia and Fiji — had built up a reservoir of hostility to Europeans. In other areas, however, the arrival of the Whites was accepted, even welcomed, for it meant access to bully beef and cigarettes, shirts and paraffin lamps, whisky and bicycles. It also meant access to the knowledge behind these material goods, for the Europeans brought missions and schools as well as cargo.

Practically the only teaching the natives received about European life came from the missions, which emphasized the central significance of religion in European society. The Melanesians already believed that man's activities — whether gardening, sailing canoes, or bearing children — needed magical assistance. Ritual without human effort was not enough. But neither was human effort on its own. This outlook was reinforced by mission teaching.

The initial enthusiasm for European rule, however, was speedily dispelled. The rapid growth of the plantation economy removed the bulk of the able-bodied men from the villages, leaving women, children, and old men to carry on as best they could. The splendid vision of the equality of all Christians began to seem a pious deception in face of the realities of the color bar, the multiplicity of rival Christian missions and the open irreligion of many Whites.

For a long time the natives accepted the European mission as the means by which the "cargo" would eventually be made available to them. But they found that acceptance of Christianity did not bring the cargo any nearer. They grew disillusioned. The story now began to be put about that it was not the Whites who made the cargo, but the dead ancestors. To people completely ignorant of factory production, this made good sense. White men did not work; they merely wrote secret signs on scraps of paper, for which they were given shiploads of goods. On the other hand, the Melanesians labored week after week for pitiful wages. Plainly the goods must be made for Melanesians somewhere, perhaps in the Land of the Dead. The Whites, who possessed the secret of the cargo, were intercepting it and keeping it from the hands of the islanders, to whom it was really consigned. In the Madang district of New Guinea, after some forty years' experience of the missions, the natives went in a body one day with a petition demanding that the cargo secret should now be revealed to them, for they had been very patient.

So strong is this belief in the existence of a "secret" that the cargo cults generally contain some ritual in imitation of the mysterious European customs which are held to be the clue to the white man's extraordinary power over goods and men. The believers sit around tables with bottles of flowers in front of them, dressed in European clothes, waiting for the cargo ship or airplane to materialize; other cultists feature magic pieces of paper and cabalistic writing. Many of them deliberately turn their backs on the past by destroying secret ritual objects, or exposing them to the gaze of uninitiated youths and women, for whom formerly even a glimpse of the sacred objects would have meant the severest penalties, even death. The belief that they were the chosen people is further reinforced by their reading of the Bible, for the lives and customs of the people in the Old Testament resemble their own lives rather than those of the Europeans. In the New Testament they find the Apocalypse, with its prophecies of destruction and resurrection, particularly attractive.

Missions that stress the imminence of the Second Coming, like those of the Seventh Day Adventists, are often accused of stimulating millenarian cults among the islanders. In reality, however, the Melanesians themselves rework the doctrines the missionaries teach them, selecting from the Bible what they themselves find particularly congenial in it. Such movements have occurred in areas where missions of quite different types have been dominant, from Roman Catholic to Seventh Day Adventist. The reasons for the emergence of these cults, of course, lie far deeper in the life-experience of the people.

The economy of most of the islands is very backward. Native agriculture produces little for the world market, and even the European plantations and mines export only a few primary products and raw materials: copra, rubber, gold. Melanesians are quite unable to understand why copra, for example, fetches thirty pounds sterling per ton one month and but five pounds a few months later. With no notion of the workings of world-commodity markets, the natives see only the sudden closing of plantations, reduced wages and unemployment, and are inclined to attribute their insecurity to the whim or evil in the nature of individual planters.

Such shocks have not been confined to the economic order. Governments, too, have come and gone, especially during the two world wars: German, Dutch, British, and French administrations melted overnight. Then came the Japanese, only to be ousted in turn largely by the previously unknown Americans. And among these Americans the Melanesians saw Negroes like themselves, living lives of luxury on equal terms with white G.I.'s. The sight of these Negroes seemed like a fulfillment of the old prophecies to many cargo cult leaders. Nor must we forget the sheer scale of this invasion. Around a million U.S. troops passed through the Admiralty Islands, completely swamping the inhabitants. It was a world of meaningless and chaotic changes, in which anything was possible. New ideas were imported and given local twists. Thus in the Loyalty Islands people expected the French Communist Party to bring the millennium. There is no real evidence, however, of any Communist influence in these movements, despite the rather hysterical belief among Solomon Island planters that the name of the local "Masinga Rule" movement was derived from the word "Marxian"! In reality the name comes from a Solomon Island tongue, and means "brotherhood."

Europeans who have witnessed outbreaks inspired by the cargo cults are usually at a loss to understand what they behold. The islanders throw away their money, break their most sacred taboos, abandon their gardens, and destroy their precious livestock; they indulge in sexual license or, alternatively, rigidly separate men from women in huge communal establishments. Sometimes they spend days sitting gazing at the horizon for a glimpse of the long-awaited ship or airplane; sometimes they dance, pray and sing in mass congregations, becoming possessed and "speaking with tongues."

Observers have not hesitated to use such words as "madness," "mania," and "irrationality" to characterize the cults. But the cults reflect quite logical and rational attempts to make sense out of a social order that appears senseless and chaotic. Given the ignorance of the Melanesians about the wider European society, its economic organization and its highly developed technology, their reactions form a consistent and understandable pattern. They wrap up all their yearning and hope in an amalgam that combines the best counsel they can find in Christianity and their native belief. If the world is soon to end, gardening or fishing is unnecessary; everything will be provided. If the Melanesians are to be part of a much wider order, the taboos that prescribe their social conduct must now be lifted or broken in a newly prescribed way.

Of course the cargo never comes. The cults nonetheless live on. If the millennium does not arrive on schedule, then perhaps there is some failure in the magic, some error in the ritual. New breakaway groups organize around "purer" faith and ritual. The cult rarely disappears, so long as the social situation which brings it into being persists.

At this point it should be observed that cults of this general kind are not peculiar to Melanesia. Men who feel themselves oppressed and deceived have always been ready to pour their hopes and fears, their aspirations and frustrations, into dreams of a millennium to come or of a golden age to return. All parts of the world have had their counterparts of the cargo cults, from the American Indian ghost dance to the Communist-millenarist "reign of the saints" in Münster during the Reformation, from medieval European apocalyptic cults to African "witch-finding" movements and Chinese Buddhist heresies. In some situations men have been content to wait and pray; in others they have sought to hasten the day by using their strong right arms to do the Lord's work. And always the cults serve to bring together scattered groups, notably the peasants and urban plebeians of agrarian societies and the peoples of "stateless" societies where the cult unites separate (and often hostile) villages, clans, and tribes into a wider religio-political unity.

Once the people begin to develop secular political organizations, however, the sects tend to lose their importance as vehicles of protest. They begin to relegate the Second Coming to the distant future or to the next world. In Melanesia ordinary political bodies, trade unions and native councils are becoming the normal media through which the islanders express their aspirations. In recent years continued economic prosperity and political stability have taken some of the edge off their despair. It now seems unlikely that any major movement along cargo-cult lines will recur in areas where the transition to secular politics has been made, even if the insecurity of prewar times returned. I would predict that the embryonic nationalism represented by cargo cults is likely in future to take forms familiar in the history of other countries that have moved from subsistence agriculture to participation in the world economy.

VIII

Politics, law, and conflict

No culture effects perfect social harmony. The resolution of conflict is a major preoccupation of men in every society. It may appear that in heated political debate, demand for equal rights, or warfare between nations, there is no common ground among disputants. But even modern warfare can be like a game with each side consenting to periods of rest, holidays, and the limited use of some weapons. In every human conflict, cultural rules guide attempted resolution. Politics, law, and warfare are some of the major activities aimed at conflict resolution.

The articles in this chapter not only deal with these spheres of culture, but they show the contrasts between our own society and others very clearly. Courts of law are present in our cities as well as among the Kpelle in Africa; however, the underlying values are quite different. When social change occurs, laws often fail to keep up with the pace of change. In American culture, this may be seen in difficulties over draft resistance and marijuana use — as well as in the way alcoholics are treated.

A study of warfare in human societies — and its function — may enable us to discover alternatives to war. Margaret Mead has suggested that a form of world organization, built so that its constituent groups cannot maintain exclusive self-identities or in any sense compete as rivalrous equals, can end war on this earth once and for all. Others have already constructed structural models designed to embody these characteristics.

28

Poor man, rich man, big-man, chief

MARSHALL D. SAHLINS

Melanesia and Polynesia provide an interesting contrast in political complexity, which is described by Marshall Sahlins in the following article. The Melanesian "big-man" is the self-made leader of his small localized kinship group, while the Polynesian chief is a "born" leader. The Polynesian system, which depends upon the ascribed right of its chief to lead, attains far larger proportions than the Melanesian structure, which depends on the ability of certain individuals to influence others.

With an eye to their own life goals, the native peoples of Pacific Islands unwittingly present to anthropologists a generous scientific gift: an extended series of experiments in cultural adaptation and evolutionary development. They have compressed their institutions within the confines of infertile coral atolls, expanded them on volcanic islands, created with the means history gave them cultures adapted to the deserts of Australia, the mountains and warm coasts of New Guinea, the rain forests of the Solomon Islands. From the Australian Aborigines, whose hunting and gathering existence duplicates in outline the cultural life of the later Paleolithic, to the great chiefdoms of Hawaii, where society approached the formative levels of the old Fertile Crescent civilizations, almost every general phase in the progress of primitive culture is exemplified.

Where culture so experiments, anthropology finds its laboratories — makes its comparisons.

In the southern and eastern Pacific two contrasting cultural provinces have long evoked anthropological interest: *Melanesia*, including New Guinea, the Bismarcks, Solomons, and island groups east to Fiji; and

From "Poor Man, Rich Man, Big-Man, Chief: Political Types in Melanesia and Polynesia," *Comparative Studies in Society and History* 5 (April 1963): 285–303. Reprinted by permission of the publisher and the author. Many footnotes, the bibliographic citations, and the bibliography are omitted.

Polynesia, consisting in its main portion of the triangular constellation of lands between New Zealand, Easter Island, and the Hawaiian Islands. In and around Fiji, Melanesia and Polynesia intergrade culturally, but west and east of their intersection the two provinces pose broad contrasts in several sectors: in religion, art, kinship groupings, economics, political organization. The differences are the more notable for the underlying similarities from which they emerge. Melanesia and Polynesia are both agricultural regions in which many of the same crops — such as yams, taro, breadfruit, bananas, and coconuts — have long been cultivated by many similar techniques. Some recently presented linguistic and archaeological studies indeed suggest that Polynesian cultures originated from an eastern Melanesian hearth during the first millennium B.C. Yet in anthropological annals the Polynesians were to become famous for elaborate forms of rank and chieftainship, whereas most Melanesian societies broke off advance on this front at more rudimentary levels.

It is obviously imprecise, however, to make out the political contrast in broad culture-area terms. Within Polynesia, certain of the islands, such as Hawaii, the Society Islands and Tonga, developed unparalleled political momentum. And not all Melanesian polities, on the other side, were constrained and truncated in their evolution. In New Guinea and nearby areas of western Melanesia, small and loosely ordered political groupings are numerous, but in eastern Melanesia, New Caledonia and Fiji for example, political approximations of the Polynesian condition become common. There is more of an upward west to east slope in political development in the southern Pacific than a step-like, quantum progression. It is quite revealing, however, to compare the extremes of this continuum, the western Melanesian underdevelopment against the greater Polynesian chiefdoms. While such comparison does not exhaust the evolutionary variations, it fairly establishes the scope of overall political achievement in this Pacific phylum of cultures.

Measurable along several dimensions, the contrast between developed Polynesian and underdeveloped Melanesian polities is immediately striking for differences in scale. H. Ian Hogbin and Camilla Wedgwood concluded from a survey of Melanesian (mostly western Melanesian) societies that ordered, independent political bodies in the region typically include seventy to three hundred persons; more recent work in the New Guinea Highlands suggests political groupings of up to a thousand, occasionally a few thousand, people.[1] But in Polynesia sovereignties of two thousand or three thousand are run-of-the-mill, and the most advanced chiefdoms, as in Tonga or Hawaii, might claim ten thousand, even tens of

[1] H. Ian Hogbin and Camilla H. Wedgwood, "Local Groupings in Melanesia," *Oceania* 23 (1952–53): 241–276; 24 (1953–54): 58–76.

thousands. Varying step by step with such differences in size of the polity are differences in territorial extent: from a few square miles in western Melanesia to tens or even hundreds of square miles in Polynesia.

The Polynesian advance in political scale was supported by advance over Melanesia in political structure. Melanesia presents a great array of social-political forms: here political organization is based upon patrilineal descent groups, there on cognatic groups, or men's club-houses recruiting neighborhood memberships, on a secret ceremonial society, or perhaps on some combination of these structural principles. Yet a general plan can be discerned. The characteristic western Melanesian "tribe," that is, the ethnic-cultural entity, consists of many autonomous kinship-residential groups. Amounting on the ground to a small village or a local cluster of hamlets, each of these is a copy of the others in organization, each tends to be economically self-governing, and each is the equal of the others in political status. The tribal plan is one of politically unintegrated segments — segmental. But the political geometry in Polynesia is pyramidal. Local groups of the order of self-governing Melanesian communities appear in Polynesia as subdivisions of a more inclusive political body. Smaller units are integrated into larger through a system of intergroup ranking, and the network of representative chiefs of the subdivisions amounts to a coordinating political structure. So instead of the Melanesian scheme of small, separate, and equal political blocs, the Polynesian polity is an extensive pyramid of groups capped by the family and following of a paramount chief. (This Polynesian political upshot is often, although not always, facilitated by the development of ranked lineages. Called *conical clan* by Kirchhoff, at one time *ramage* by Firth and *status lineage* by Goldman, the Polynesian ranked lineage is the same in principle as the so-called *obok* system widely distributed in Central Asia, and it is at least analogous to the Scottish clan, the Chinese clan, certain Central African Bantu lineage systems, the house-groups of Northwest Coast Indians, perhaps even the "tribes" of the Israelites. Genealogical ranking is its distinctive feature: members of the same descent unit are ranked by genealogical distance from the common ancestor; lines of the same group become senior and cadet branches on this principle; related corporate lineages are relatively ranked, again by genealogical priority.)

Here is another criterion of Polynesian political advance: historical performance. Almost all of the native peoples of the South Pacific were brought up against intense European cultural pressure in the late eighteenth and the nineteenth centuries. Yet only the Hawaiians, Tahitians, Tongans, and to a lesser extent the Fijians, successfully defended themselves by evolving countervailing, native-controlled states. Complete with public governments and public law, monarchs and taxes, ministers and minions, these nineteenth-century states are testimony to the native Polynesian political genius, to the level and the potential of indigenous political accomplishments.

Embedded within the grand differences in political scale, structure and performance is a more personal contrast, one in quality of leadership. An historically particular type of leader-figure, the "big-man" as he is often locally styled, appears in the underdeveloped settings of Melanesia. Another type, a chief properly so-called, is associated with the Polynesian advance. Now these are distinct sociological types, that is to say, differences in the powers, privileges, rights, duties, and obligations of Melanesian big-men and Polynesian chiefs are given by the divergent societal contexts in which they operate. Yet the institutional distinctions cannot help but be manifest also in differences in bearing and character, appearance and manner — in a word, personality. It may be a good way to begin the more rigorous sociological comparison of leadership with a more impressionistic sketch of the contrast in the human dimension. Here I find it useful to apply characterizations — or is it caricature? — from our own history to big-men and chiefs, however much injustice this does to the historically incomparable backgrounds of the Melanesians and Polynesians. The Melanesian big-man seems so thoroughly bourgeois, so reminiscent of the free-enterprising rugged individual of our own heritage. He combines with an ostensible interest in the general welfare a more profound measure of self-interested cunning and economic calculation. His gaze, as Veblen might have put it, is fixed unswervingly to the main chance. His every public action is designed to make a competitive and invidious comparison with others, to show a standing above the masses that is product of his own personal manufacture. The historical caricature of the Polynesian chief, however, is feudal rather than capitalist. His appearance, his bearing is almost regal; very likely he just *is* a big man — "'Can't you see he is a chief? See how big he is?'"[2] In his every public action is a display of the refinements of breeding, in his manner always that *noblesse oblige* of true pedigree and an incontestable right of rule. With his standing not so much a personal achievement as a just social due, he can afford to be, and he is, every inch a chief.

In the several Melanesian tribes in which big-men have come under anthropological scrutiny, local cultural differences modify the expression of their personal powers. But the indicative quality of big-man authority is everywhere the same: it is *personal* power. Big-men do not come to office; they do not succeed to, nor are they installed in, existing positions of leadership over political groups. The attainment of big-man status is rather the outcome of a series of acts which elevate a person above the

[2] Edward Winslow Gifford, *Tongan Society* (Honolulu: Bernice P. Bishop Museum Bulletin 61, 1926).

common herd and attract about him a coterie of loyal, lesser men. It is not accurate to speak of "big-man" as a political title, for it is but an acknowledged standing in interpersonal relations — a "prince among men" so to speak as opposed to "The Prince of Danes." In particular Melanesian tribes the phrase might be "man of importance" or "man of renown," "generous rich-man," or "center-man," as well as "big-man."

A kind of two-sidedness in authority is implied in this series of phrases, a division of the big-man's field of influence into two distinct sectors. "Center-man" particularly connotes a cluster of followers gathered about an influential pivot. It socially implies the division of the tribe into political in-groups dominated by outstanding personalities. To the in-group, the big-man presents this sort of picture:

> The place of the leader in the district group [in northern Malaita] is well summed up by his title, which might be translated as "centre-man" . . . He was like a banyan, the natives explain, which, though the biggest and tallest in the forest, is still a tree like the rest. But, just because it exceeds all others, the banyan gives support to more lianas and creepers, provides more food for the birds, and gives better protection against sun and rain.[3]

But "man of renown" connotes a broader tribal field in which a man is not so much a leader as he is some sort of hero. This is the side of the big-man facing outward from his own faction, his status among some or all of the other political clusters of the tribe. The political sphere of the big-man divides itself into a small internal sector composed of his personal satellites — rarely over eighty men — and a much larger external sector, the tribal galaxy consisting of many similar constellations.

As it crosses over from the internal into the external sector, a big-man's power undergoes qualitative change. Within his faction a Melanesian leader has true command ability, outside of it only fame and indirect influence. It is not that the center-man rules his faction by physical force, but his followers do feel obliged to obey him, and he can usually get what he wants by haranguing them — public verbal suasion is indeed so often employed by center-men that they have been styled "harangue-utans." The orbits of outsiders, however, are set by their own center-men. " 'Do it yourself. I'm not *your* fool,' " would be the characteristic response to an order issued by a center-man to an outsider among the Siuai.[4] This fragmentation of true authority presents special political difficulties, particularly in organizing large masses of people for the prosecution of such collective ends as warfare or ceremony. Big-men do instigate mass action,

[3] H. Ian Hogbin, "Native Councils and Courts in the Solomon Islands," *Oceania* 14 (1943–44): 258–283.

[4] Douglas Oliver, *A Solomon Islands Society* (Cambridge: Harvard University Press, 1955).

but only by establishing both extensive renown and special personal relations of compulsion or reciprocity with other center-men.

Politics is in the main personal politiking in these Melanesian societies, and the size of a leader's faction as well as the extent of his renown are normally set by competition with other ambitious men. Little or no authority is given by social ascription: leadership is a creation — a creation of followership. "Followers," as it is written of the Kapauku of New Guinea, "stand in various relations to the leader. Their obedience to the headman's decisions is caused by motivations which reflect their particular relations to the leader." [5] So a man must be prepared to demonstrate that he possesses the kinds of skills that command respect — magical powers, gardening prowess, mastery of oratorical style, perhaps bravery in war and feud. Typically decisive is the deployment of one's skills and efforts in a certain direction: towards amassing goods, most often pigs, shell monies and vegetable foods, and distributing them in ways which build a name for cavalier generosity, if not for compassion. A faction is developed by informal private assistance to people of a locale. Tribal rank and renown are developed by great public giveaways sponsored by the rising big-man, often on behalf of his faction as well as himself. In different Melanesian tribes, the renown-making public distribution may appear as one side of a delayed exchange of pigs between corporate kinship groups; a marital consideration given a bride's kinfolk; a set of feasts connected with the erection of a big-man's dwelling, or of a clubhouse for himself and his faction, or with the purchase of higher grades of rank in secret societies; the sponsorship of a religious ceremony; a payment of subsidies and blood compensations to military allies; or perhaps the giveaway is a ceremonial challenge bestowed on another leader in the attempt to outgive and thus outrank him (a potlatch).

The making of the faction, however, is the true making of the Melanesian big-man. It is essential to establish relations of loyalty and obligation on the part of a number of people such that their production can be mobilized for renownbuilding external distribution. The bigger the faction the greater the renown; once momentum in external distribution has been generated the opposite can also be true. Any ambitious man who can gather a following can launch a societal career. The rising big-man necessarily depends initially on a small core of followers, principally his own household and his closest relatives. Upon these people he can prevail economically: he capitalizes in the first instance on kinship dues and by finessing the relation of reciprocity appropriate among close kinsmen. Often it becomes necessary at an early phase to enlarge one's household. The rising leader goes out of his way to incorporate within his family

[5] Leopold Pospisil, *Kapauku Papuans and Their Law* (New Haven: Yale University Press, Yale University Publications in Anthropology, no. 54, 1958).

"strays" of various sorts, people without familial support themselves, such as widows and orphans. Additional wives are especially useful. The more wives a man has the more pigs he has. The relation here is functional, not identical: with more women gardening there will be more food for pigs and more swineherds. A Kiwai Papuan picturesquely put to an anthropologist in pidgin the advantages, economic and political, of polygamy: "'Another woman go garden, another woman go take firewood, another woman go catch fish, another woman cook him — husband he sing out plenty people come kaikai [i.e., come to eat].'"[6] Each new marriage, incidentally, creates for the big-man an additional set of in-laws from whom he can exact economic favors. Finally, a leader's career sustains its upward climb when he is able to link other men and their families to his faction, harnessing their production to his ambition. This is done by calculated generosities, by placing others in gratitude and obligation through helping them in some big way. A common technique is payment of bridewealth on behalf of young men seeking wives.

The great Malinowski used a phrase in analyzing primitive political economy that felicitously describes just what the big-man is doing: amassing a "fund of power." A big-man is one who can create and use social relations which give him leverage on others' production and the ability to siphon off an excess product — or sometimes he can cut down their consumption in the interest of the siphon. Now although his attention may be given primarily to short-term personal interests, from an objective standpoint the leader acts to promote long-term societal interests. The fund of power provisions activities that involve other groups of the society at large. In the greater perspective of that society at large, big-men are indispensable means of creating supralocal organization: in tribes normally fragmented into small independent groups, big-men at least temporarily widen the sphere of ceremony, recreation and art, economic collaboration, of war too. Yet always this greater societal organization depends on the lesser factional organization, particularly on the ceilings on economic mobilization set by relations between center-men and followers. The limits and the weaknesses of the political order in general are the limits and weaknesses of the factional in-groups.

And the personal quality of subordination to a center-man is a serious weakness in factional structure. A personal loyalty has to be made and continually reinforced; if there is discontent it may well be severed. Merely to create a faction takes time and effort, and to hold it, still more effort. The potential rupture of personal links in the factional chain is at the heart of two broad evolutionary shortcomings of western Melanesian political orders. First, a comparative instability. Shifting dispositions

[6] Gunnar Landtman, *The Kiwai Papuans of British New Guinea* (London: Macmillan, 1927).

and magnetisms of ambitious men in a region may induce fluctuations in factions, perhaps some overlapping of them, and fluctuations also in the extent of different renowns. The death of a center-man can become a regional political trauma: the death undermines the personally cemented faction, the group dissolves in whole or in part, and the people re-group finally around rising pivotal big-men. Although particular tribal structures in places cushion the disorganization, the big-man political system is generally unstable over short terms: in its superstructure it is a flux of rising and falling leaders, in its substructure of enlarging and contracting factions. Secondly, the personal political bond contributes to the containment of evolutionary advance. The possibility of their desertion, it is clear, often inhibits a leader's ability to forceably push up his followers' output, thereby placing constraints on higher political organization, but there is more to it than that. If it is to generate great momentum, a big-man's quest for the summits of renown is likely to bring out a contradiction in his relations to followers, so that he finds himself encouraging defection — or worse, an egalitarian rebellion — by encouraging production.

One side of the Melanesian contradiction is the initial economic reciprocity between a center-man and his followers. For his help they give their help, and for goods going out through his hands other goods (often from outside factions) flow back to his followers by the same path. The other side is that a cumulative build-up of renown forces center-men into economic extortion of the faction. Here it is important that not merely his own status, but the standing and perhaps the military security of his people depend on the big-man's achievements in public distribution. Established at the head of a sizeable faction, a center-man comes under increasing pressure to extract goods from his followers, to delay reciprocities owing them, and to deflect incoming goods back into external circulation. Success in competition with other big-men particularly undermines internal-factional reciprocities: such success is precisely measurable by the ability to give outsiders more than they can possibly reciprocate. In well delineated big-man polities, we find leaders negating the reciprocal obligations upon which their following had been predicated. Substituting extraction for reciprocity, they must compel their people to "eat the leader's renown," as one Solomon Island group puts it, in return for productive efforts. Some center-men appear more able than others to dam the inevitable tide of discontent that mounts within their factions, perhaps because of charismatic personalities, perhaps because of the particular social organizations in which they operate. But paradoxically the ultimate defense of the center-man's position is some slackening of his drive to enlarge the funds of power. The alternative is much worse. In the anthropological record there are not merely instances of big-man chicanery and of material deprivation of the faction in the interests of renown, but some also of overloading of social relations with followers: the generation of antagonisms, defections, and in extreme cases the violent liquidation of the center-man. Developing internal constraints, the Melanesian big-man political order brakes evolutionary advance at a certain level. It sets ceilings on the intensification of political authority, on the intensification of household production by political means, and on the diversion of household outputs in support of wider political organization. But in Polynesia these constraints were breached, and although Polynesian chiefdoms also found their developmental plateau, it was not before political evolution had been carried above the Melanesian ceilings. The fundamental defects of the Melanesian plan were overcome in Polynesia. The division between small internal and larger external political sectors, upon which all big-man politics hinged, was suppressed in Polynesia by the growth of an enclaving chiefdom-at-large. A chain of command subordinating lesser chiefs and groups to greater, on the basis of inherent societal rank, made local blocs or personal followings (such as were independent in Melanesia) merely dependent parts of the larger Polynesian chiefdom. So the nexus of the Polynesian chiefdom became an extensive set of offices, a pyramid of higher and lower chiefs holding sway over larger and smaller sections of the polity. Indeed the system of ranked and subdivided lineages (conical clan system), upon which the pyramid was characteristically established, might build up through several orders of inclusion and encompass the whole of an island or group of islands. While the island or the archipelago would normally be divided into several independent chiefdoms, high-order lineage connections between them, as well as kinship ties between their paramount chiefs, provided structural avenues for at least temporary expansion of political scale, for consolidation of great into even greater chiefdoms.

The pivotal paramount chief as well as the chieftains controlling parts of a chiefdom were true office holders and title holders. They were not, like Melanesian big-men, fishers of men: they held positions of authority over permanent groups. The honorifics of Polynesian chiefs likewise did not refer to a standing in interpersonal relations, but to their leadership of political divisions — here "The Prince of Danes" *not* "the prince among men." In western Melanesia the personal superiorities and inferiorities arising in the intercourse of particular men largely defined the political bodies. In Polynesia there emerged suprapersonal structures of leadership and followership, organizations that continued independently of the particular men who occupied positions in them for brief mortal spans.

And these Polynesian chiefs did not make their positions in society — they were installed in societal positions. In several of the islands, men did struggle to office against the will and stratagems of rival aspirants. But then they came *to* power. Power resided in the office; it was not made by the demonstration of personal superiority. In other islands, Tahiti was famous for it, succession to chieftainship was tightly controlled by inherent rank. The chiefly lineage ruled by virtue of its genealogical connections with divinity, and chiefs were succeeded by first sons, who carried "in the blood" the attributes of leadership. The important comparative point is this: the qualities of command that had to reside in men in Melanesia, that had to be personally demonstrated in order to attract loyal followers, were in Polynesia socially assigned to office and rank. In Polynesia, people of high rank and office *ipso facto* were leaders, and by the same token the qualities of leadership were automatically lacking — theirs was not to question why — among the underlying population. Magical powers such as a Melanesian big-man might acquire to sustain his position, a Polynesian high chief inherited by divine descent as the *mana* which sanctified his rule and protected his person against the hands of the commonalty. The productive ability the big-man laboriously had to demonstrate was effortlessly given Polynesian chiefs as religious control over agricultural fertility, and upon the ceremonial implementation of it the rest of the people were conceived dependent. Where a Melanesian leader had to master the compelling oratorical style, Polynesian paramounts often had trained "talking chiefs" whose voice was the chiefly command.

In the Polynesian view, a chiefly personage was in the nature of things powerful. But this merely implies the objective observation that his power was of the group rather than of himself. His authority came from the organization, from an organized acquiescence in his privileges and organized means of sustaining them. A kind of paradox resides in evolutionary developments which detach the exercise of authority from the necessity to demonstrate personal superiority: organizational power actually extends the role of personal decision and conscious planning, gives it greater scope, impact, and effectiveness. The growth of a political system such as the Polynesian constitutes advance over Melanesian orders of interpersonal dominance in the human control of human affairs. Especially significant for society at large were privileges accorded Polynesian chiefs which made them greater architects of funds of power than ever was any Melanesian big-man.

Masters of their people and "owners" in a titular sense of group resources, Polynesian chiefs had rights of call upon the labor and agricultural produce of households within their domains. Economic mobilization did not depend on, as it necessarily had for Melanesian big-men, the *de novo* creation by the leader of personal loyalties and economic obligations. A chief need not stoop to obligate this man or that man, need not by a series of individual acts of generosity induce others to support him, for economic leverage over a group was the inherent chiefly due. Consider the implications for the fund of power of the widespread chiefly privilege, related to titular "ownership" of land, of placing an interdiction, a tabu, on the harvest of some crop by way of reserving its use for a collective project. By means of the tabu the chief directs the course of production in a general way: households of his domain must turn to some other means of subsistence. He delivers a stimulus to household production: in the absence of the tabu further labors would not have been necessary. Most significantly, he has generated a politically utilizable agricultural surplus. A subsequent call on this surplus floats chieftainship as a going concern, capitalizes the fund of power. In certain islands, Polynesian chiefs controlled great storehouses which held the goods congealed by chiefly pressures on the commonalty. David Malo, one of the great native custodians of old Hawaiian lore, felicitously catches the political significance of the chiefly magazine in his well-known *Hawaiian Antiquities:*

> It was the practice for kings [i.e., paramount chiefs of individual islands] to build store-houses in which to collect food, fish, tapas [bark cloth], malos [men's loin cloths] pa-us [women's loin skirts], and all sorts of goods. These store-houses were designed by the Kalaimoku [the chief's principal executive] as a means of keeping the people contented, so they would not desert the king. They were like the baskets that were used to entrap the *hinalea* fish. The *hinalea* thought there was something good within the basket, and he hung round the outside of it. In the same way the people thought there was food in the store-houses, and they kept their eyes on the king. As the rat will not desert the pantry . . . where he thinks food is, so the people will not desert the king while they think there is food in his store-house.[7]

Redistribution of the fund of power was the supreme art of Polynesian politics. By well-planned *noblesse oblige* the large domain of a paramount chief was held together, organized at times for massive projects, protected against other chiefdoms, even further enriched. Uses of the chiefly fund included lavish hospitality and entertainments for outside chiefs and for the chief's own people, and succor of individuals or the underlying population at large in times of scarcities — bread and circuses. Chiefs subsidized craft production, promoting in Polynesia a division of technical labor unparalleled in extent and expertise in most of the Pacific. They supported also great technical construction, as of irrigation complexes, the further returns to which swelled the chiefly fund. They initiated large-scale religious construction too, subsidized the great ceremonies, and organized logistic support for extensive military campaigns.

[7] David Malo, *Hawaiian Antiquities* (Honolulu: Hawaiian Gazette Co., 1903).

Larger and more easily replenished than their western Melanesian counterparts, Polynesian funds of power permitted greater political regulation of a greater range of social activities on greater scale.

In the most advanced Polynesian chiefdoms, as in Hawaii and Tahiti, a significant part of the chiefly fund was deflected away from general redistribution towards the upkeep of the institution of chieftainship. The fund was siphoned for the support of a permanent administrative establishment. In some measure, goods and services contributed by the people precipitated out as the grand houses, assembly places, and temple platforms of chiefly precincts. In another measure, they were appropriated for the livelihood of circles of retainers, many of them close kinsmen of the chief, who clustered about the powerful paramounts. These were not all useless hangers-on. They were political cadres: supervisors of the stores, talking chiefs, ceremonial attendants, high priests who were intimately involved in political rule, envoys to transmit directives through the chiefdom. There were men in these chiefly retinues — in Tahiti and perhaps Hawaii, specialized warrior corps — whose force could be directed internally as a buttress against fragmenting or rebellious elements of the chiefdom. A Tahitian or Hawaiian high chief had more compelling sanctions than the harangue. He controlled a ready physical force, an armed body of executioners, which gave him mastery particularly over the lesser people of the community. While it looks a lot like the big-man's faction again, the differences in functioning of the great Polynesian chief's retinue are more significant than the superficial similarities in appearance. The chief's coterie, for one thing, is economically dependent upon him rather than he upon them. And in deploying the cadres politically in various sections of the chiefdom, or against the lower orders, the great Polynesian chiefs sustained command where the Melanesian big-man, in his external sector, had at best renown.

This is not to say that the advanced Polynesian chiefdoms were free of internal defect, of potential or actual malfunctioning. The large political-military apparatus indicates something of the opposite. So does the recent work of Irving Goldman [8] on the intensity of "status rivalry" in Polynesia, especially when it is considered that much of the status rivalry in developed chiefdoms, as the Hawaiian, amounted to popular rebellion against chiefly despotism rather than mere contest for position within the ruling-stratum. This suggests that Polynesian chiefdoms, just as Melanesian big-man orders, generate along with evolutionary development countervailing anti-authority pressures, and that the weight of the latter may ultimately impede further development.

The Polynesian contradiction seems clear enough. On one side, chief-

[8] Irving Goldman, "Status Rivalry and Cultural Evolution in Polynesia," *American Anthropologist* 57 (1957): 680–697; "Variations in Polynesian Social Organization," *Journal of the Polynesian Society* 66 (1957): 374–390.

tainship is never detached from kinship moorings and kinship economic ethics. Even the greatest Polynesian chiefs were conceived superior kinsmen to the masses, fathers of their people, and generosity was morally incumbent upon them. On the other side, the major Polynesian paramounts seemed inclined to "eat the power of the government too much," as the Tahitians put it, to divert an undue proportion of the general wealth toward the chiefly establishment. The diversion could be accomplished by lowering the customary level of general redistribution, lessening the material returns of chieftainship to the community at large — tradition attributes the great rebellion of Mangarevan commoners to such cause. Or the diversion might — and I suspect more commonly did — consist in greater and more forceful exactions from lesser chiefs and people, increasing returns to the chiefly apparatus without necessarily affecting the level of general redistribution. In either case, the well-developed chiefdom creates for itself the dampening paradox of stoking rebellion by funding its authority.

In Hawaii and other islands cycles of political centralization and decentralization may be abstracted from traditional histories. That is, larger chiefdoms periodically fragmented into smaller and then were later reconstituted. Here would be more evidence of a tendency to overtax the political structure. But how to explain the emergence of a developmental stymie, of an inability to sustain political advance beyond a certain level? To point to a chiefly propensity to consume or a Polynesian propensity to rebel is not enough: such propensities are promoted by the very advance of chiefdoms. There is reason to hazard instead that Parkinson's notable law is behind it all: that progressive expansion in political scale entailed more-than-proportionate accretion in the ruling apparatus, unbalancing the flow of wealth in favor of the apparatus. The ensuing unrest then curbs the chiefly impositions, sometimes by reducing chiefdom scale to the nadir of the periodic cycle. Comparison of the requirements of administration in small and large Polynesian chiefdoms helps make the point.

A lesser chiefdom, confined say as in the Marquesas Islands to a narrow valley, could be almost personally ruled by a headman in frequent contact with the relatively small population. Melville's partly romanticized — also for its ethnographic details, partly cribbed — account in *Typee* makes this clear enough. But the great Polynesian chiefs had to rule much larger, spatially dispersed, internally organized populations. Hawaii, an island over four thousand square miles with an aboriginal population approaching one hundred thousand, was at times a single chiefdom, at other times divided into two to six independent chiefdoms, and at all times each chiefdom was composed of large subdivisions under powerful subchiefs. Sometimes a chiefdom in the Hawaiian group extended beyond the confines of one of the islands, incorporating part of another through conquest. Now, such extensive chiefdoms would have to be coordinated; they would have to be centrally tapped for a fund of power, buttressed against internal disruption, sometimes massed for distant, perhaps overseas, military engagements. All of this to be implemented by means of communication still at the level of word-of-mouth, and means of transportation consisting of human bodies and canoes. (The extent of certain larger chieftainships, coupled with the limitations of communication and transportation, incidentally suggests another possible source of political unrest: that the burden of provisioning the governing apparatus would tend to fall disproportionately on groups within easiest access of the paramount.) A tendency for the developed chiefdom to proliferate in executive cadres, to grow top-heavy, seems in these circumstances altogether functional, even though the ensuing drain on wealth proves the chiefdom's undoing. Functional also, and likewise a material drain on the chiefdom at large, would be widening distinctions between chiefs and people in style of life. Palatial housing, ornamentation and luxury, finery and ceremony, in brief, conspicuous consumption, however much it seems mere self-interest always has a more decisive social significance. It creates those invidious distinctions between rulers and ruled so conducive to a passive — hence quite economical! — acceptance of authority. Throughout history, inherently more powerful political organizations than the Polynesian, with more assured logistics of rule, have turned to it — including in our time some ostensibly revolutionary and proletarian governments, despite every pre-revolutionary protestation of solidarity with the masses and equality for the classes.

In Polynesia then, as in Melanesia, political evolution is eventually shortcircuited by an overload on the relations between leaders and their people. The Polynesian tragedy, however, was somewhat the opposite of the Melanesian. In Polynesia, the evolutionary ceiling was set by extraction from the population at large in favor of the chiefly faction, in Melanesia by extraction from the big-man's faction in favor of distribution to the population at large. Most importantly, the Polynesian ceiling was higher. Melanesian big-men and Polynesian chiefs not only reflect different varieties and levels of political evolution, they display in different degrees the capacity to generate and to sustain political progress.

Especially emerging from their juxtaposition is the more decisive impact of Polynesian chiefs on the economy, the chiefs' greater leverage on the output of the several households of society. The success of any primitive political organization is decided here, in the control that can be developed over household economies. For the household is not merely the principal productive unit in primitive societies, it is often quite capable of autonomous direction of its own production, and it is oriented towards production for its own, not societal consumption. The greater potential of Polynesian chieftainship is precisely the greater pressure it could exert on household output, its capacity both to generate a surplus and to deploy it out of the household towards a broader division of labor, cooperative construction, and massive ceremonial and military action. Polynesian chiefs were the more effective means of societal collaboration on economic, political, indeed all cultural fronts. Perhaps we have been too long accustomed to perceive rank and rule from the standpoint of the individuals involved, rather than from the perspective of the total society, as if the secret of the subordination of man to man lay in the personal satisfactions of power. And then the breakdowns too, or the evolutionary limits, have been searched out in men, in "weak" kings or megalomaniacal dictators — always, "who is the matter?" An excursion into the field of primitive politics suggests the more fruitful conception that the gains of political developments accrue more decisively to society than to individuals, and the failings as well are of structure not men.

29

The weak and the strong: Native leaders under colonial rule

HARRIET J. KUPFERER

As part of its social function, a political system must define who has the right to make decisions. When a colonial power annexes the people and territory of another society, traditional leadership roles must change. The new political roles often reflect the original character of the culture as well as the administrative needs of the colonial government, as is shown by this selection by Harriet Kupferer. A Cree Indian chief, whose office is a colonial government creation, is unable to lead in the absence of legitimate support from colonial officials or other Crees, a people for whom there is no tradition of strong leadership. By contrast, headmen designated by the colonial administration in New Guinea have managed to gain personally from their position in a society where such gain is traditionally a male imperative.

Introduction

There have been several occasions in which colonial powers or stronger societies have imposed political systems on native peoples where none had existed previously. Most frequently, a native leader is appointed by an agent of the dominant society, or the mechanics of balloting are introduced and officers are elected. The introduction of elementary political systems has had varying consequences in specific societies. Such differences are probably functionally related to the cultures and social systems of the colliding societies. One may examine the ramifications of such an

Reprinted from Marc J. Swartz, Victor W. Turner, and Arthur Tuden, editors, *Political Anthropology*, pp. 61–71. Chicago: Aldine Publishing Company, 1966; copyright © 1966 by Aldine Publishing Company. This article was originally entitled "Impotency and Power: A Cross-Cultural Comparison of the Effect of Alien Rule," and is reprinted by permission of the publisher and the author. Some footnotes, the bibliographic citations, and the bibliography are omitted.

introduction on the subordinate peoples, on the agents of the superordinate society, or on the native leaders.

In this paper we will attempt to analyze the various leadership and authority expectations attendant upon the status of "band chief," and their effects upon role performance. Further, by contrasting this case study with one from another culture area, we will suggest that a number of variables may be operative in the role behavior of native officials.

In Rupert's House, which is the sub-Arctic Cree settlement from which these data come, the position of chief is achieved rather than ascribed. Role behavior, growing out of the normative expectations accompanying the status, plus idiosyncratic behavior that results from individual perceptions and definitions of the situation, are not enough to explain the enactment of role in this setting. The particular characteristics of this social system result in a typical or "modal role behavior" that is largely ineffectual.

Rupert's House, founded in 1668, is located on the east coast of James Bay, Quebec, at the mouth of the Rupert River. Approximately five hundred Indians and twenty resident Euro-Canadians make up the settlement. Significant among them are the Hudson's Bay Company manager, the game warden, a fundamentalist Protestant missionary, an Oblate priest, three school teachers, two nurses, and the widow of a former Hudson's Bay Company manager. Unlike the Indians on the west coast of James Bay, Rupert's House people are not treaty Indians and do not occupy a reservation. All the land that the Indians exploit, exclusive of that owned by the missions and the Hudson's Bay Company, belongs to the province.

Originally, the sub-Arctic Cree wandered over a hunting territory in small, kin-based bands. Honigmann [1] states that there were few groups larger than the family with which individuals enjoyed any sense of solidarity. The core culture of all northern Algonkians was described by Spindler [2] as consisting of hunting, fishing, gathering family groups, with an atomistic social structure. There was no aboriginal source of authority and legitimate power save that of the head of the family. A kind of informal leadership was recognized, however, in that a "good man," wise in the ways of the people or skilled in the hunt, might be sought out for counsel, but he did not have the power to coerce. There was no mechanism to enforce a headman's decisions or wishes.

Just as the phenomena of authority and power were largely unknown to the Cree, the idea of large permanent settlements or villages

[1] John J. Honigmann, "The Attawapiscat Swampy Cree: An Ethnographic Reconstruction," *Anthropological Papers of the University of Alaska* 5 (1956): 23–79.

[2] Louise S. Spindler, *Menomini Women and Culture Change*, American Anthropological Association Memoir, no. 92, 1962.

was foreign to them. In fact, there was no word in the Cree vocabulary that is equivalent to "village" or "band," although a word for the latter term developed from a growing dependency upon the Hudson's Bay Company and the Indian Affairs Branch of Canada. Those Indians who over the years returned to summer at the same Hudson's Bay post were eventually designated as bands by the Canadian government for purposes of administration. Power and authority were also introduced by the practices of the Hudson's Bay Company and the Indian Affairs Branch, and the branch recently instituted the position of "band chief" in Rupert's House.

Since the introduction of the position of chief, there have been three officeholders, each selected by the men and women of the band. The present incumbent has been chief for ten years. There is one living ex-chief, now serving on the council, which is an "advisory body" to the chief. Prior to the institution of the position, the Hudson's Bay Company manager served as "chief." The extent to which this function of the manager was made explicit is unknown, but the arrangement had at least the tacit consent of the Canadian Government.

The seasonal cycle of the people is now only semimigratory. During the winter, most mature men — those who are not otherwise employed — leave the post for their trapping territories. Some men take their families, but others do not; therefore some older persons, some wives, and many children are left in the settlement. At the close of the trapping season the trappers return to the post to await the spring fishing. When the fish are abundant, spring fishing camps are set up. As the weather grows warmer, fishing decreases, and the campers return to the settlement for the summer — during which time sporadic wage-labor is available, but not enough to provide employment for all. Early fall brings a return of the fish, and later in the fall migratory birds appear. Once more the people move a few miles from the village to establish camps for fishing and fowling. With the return of winter the cycle starts again. Despite this seasonal change in sources of food and money, the post is never totally abandoned by the Indians; there are always — for one reason or another — some who do not leave.

Of the Euro-Canadians, the teachers leave during the summer, and the others have annual holidays at different times during the year. Depending upon the status — nurses or Hudson's Bay Company manager — temporary replacements are sent in; so there is always a nucleus of resident whites.

Normative role expectations of the band chief

The differences in expectations of a chief are both cultural and structural, with Indians and Euro-Canadians holding conflicting views. The Indians' perception of the status and role of chief has its roots in the aboriginal concept of leadership; and differences in present expectations are a matter of degree, not of kind. The necessary qualities for chief, as far as the Indians are concerned, can be summed up in the phrase "He must be a good man." One informant, when asked whether he would like to be chief, said: "I am not good enough. A chief has to be a good man — one who doesn't do anything bad." The meaning of "a good man," although difficult to ascertain, implies an ethic of morality not unlike that associated with the traditional type of leader.

In addition to this ethic, the people have developed a clear idea of what they expect the chief to do, or what his normative role is consonant with their contemporary socioeconomic situation. He must look out for the people, take care of the children, order rations for the poor, send those who are ill to the hospital, and share his own food if need be. It is apparent from these expectations that the ideal role of chief involves not only assistance and counseling, it requires sufficient power and acumen to maneuver in the Euro-Canadian world.

As we have pointed out, the position of chief was imposed through official white action, and although such a status in Western society would normally imply both leadership and legitimate authority for initiating action, local Euro-Canadians do not hold these expectations of the role. Their comments and behavior suggest that they perceive the chief's role as largely that of liaison between Euro-Canadians and Indians. The whites view both authority and leadership as resting largely with themselves. Indeed, Dunning [3] notes that in northern Indian posts the Indian Agent frequently vetoes the nomination of candidates whose names have been proposed in the normal democratic process. These agents delegate little authority; more often, they exert their authority over the Indians through the chief.

On the other hand, the Euro-Canadians reflect some ambivalence in regard to the chief's role. Many of their comments indicate that they think the present chief is a more effective leader than his predecessors, and he was often described as the best chief in the James Bay area. At the same time, he was accused of being too bossy and too demanding. One informant contended that the chief did not like whites and that the band might be better off if it had a "leader" who did. The evidence of an inconsistency in white expectations of the status of chief can be related, in part, to the "democratic ideal" that such a position should carry some power and authority, but, because this would conflict with their own power and authority, they are reluctant to yield their superordinate place in the social structure.

[3] R. W. Dunning, "Some Aspects of Governmental Indian Policy and Administration," *Anthropologica* 4 (1962): 209–231.

ROLE PERFORMANCE OF THE CHIEF

Ideally, all aspects of Indian life — economic, health, education, and social — are responsibilities of the chief. There are, however, only a few spheres within the life of the settlment over which the chief has legitimate authority — independent of the Euro-Canadian residents. Among these are planning the wedding feasts and other social events, control of the children, and preliminary funeral arrangements. The wedding feasts and dances are excellent vehicles for demonstrating his administrative and leadership ability. He names the women who are to prepare the food; the arrangement of the benches and festive table are made under his supervision; and the guests are seated at his direction. As people enter the hall for the dance, he shouts orders in Cree. (Some of his comments are not flattering: "You, fat lady, sit down.")

He assumes responsibility for children in several ways. He has the bell rung at night, which is a signal for them to return to their homes. He visits the school occasionally to inquire about their behavior, and he once placed a notice in the store notifying the women to keep the children away from the motorized sleds. Such, then, are the kinds of behavior the chief can undertake without Euro-Canadian intervention.

However, the segments of life that are of utmost concern to contemporary Indians are those over which the chief has little or no control: economics, health, and education.

Economics

Economic matters — employment, beaver quotas and payment, and government assistance — have the highest priority for the Indians, and it is in this aspect of life that the chief is most impotent. The predictable pattern of interaction between Euro-Canadians and the chief in matters of employment can be seen in the following situations.

A government-owned sawmill operates during the spring and summer months, and the Indian Affairs Branch appointed the chief to oversee the mill. This responsibility includes the hiring of men, but *only those whom the Hudson's Bay manager approves.* The manager records the men's time, and provides credit at the store for their work, and the Indian Affairs Branch then recompenses the company.

In other situations it may be other Euro-Canadians whose superordinate position controls the chief's behavior. An engineer came to the post to make a survey for a new floating dock, and to run a survey for a new school. He elected to work through the Oblate priest rather than the Hudson's Bay Company manager. In the presence of the writer and the engineer, the priest sent for the chief, who came to the mission cap in hand. The priest explained in Cree the nature of the work, and told the chief whom to hire. The chief departed, returned in about fifteen minutes, and said that all the men would report at eight the following morning.

A similar situation occurred when the Hudson's Bay Company employed the priest to oversee the building of a new home for the company clerk. The priest, in turn, hired the chief as foreman, and gave him instructions with regard to the hiring of Indian carpenters. This lack of autonomy of the chief in the area of employment elicits such comments from the men of the band as "He always hires the same men" or "He always sees to it that his relatives have work."

Beavers, although declining in numbers, still constitute a source of income for Indians who trap. Individual quotas are established by the government's Fish and Game Commission, and (unlike Ontario, where the pelts go to the open market) Quebec province buys the pelts and sets the price. Frequently, there is a long interval between the delivery of the pelts and receipt of payment. The chief, who has no authority in this area, is nevertheless a target for the discontent engendered by the long wait for payment. We witnessed one such episode when a long-standing member of the community (and a good trapper) went to the chief while intoxicated and angrily demanded his check. This is another example of the way in which people expect that the chief, as a "good man," will take care of his people — an expectation, given the structure of the system, that he is unable to meet.

Money from various assistance programs are an important part of the economy. In addition to regular assistance, emergency rations can be issued to those in acute circumstances. In such cases the procedure is to go to the chief, who is empowered by the Indian Branch to wire or call the Indian agent, who will issue the rations. Because of language and other technical problems, the chief informs the Hudson's Bay manager, who makes the call. However, the manager interferes in the formalized channels of the chief's legitimate authority by exercising his discretion in this matter. If, in the manager's judgment, the family requesting emergency assistance is "undeserving," "lazy," or "improvident," he may neglect to relay the request.

It is difficult to know whether this informal subverting of the chief's power is done with the tacit permission of the Indian agent. There is some evidence, however, that the chief is unaware that interference has occurred with his request for action. The deprived family, after waiting for rations that do not appear, will turn on the chief in anger. Although he has acted according to his own and the Indians' normative role expectations, his responsibilities are abrogated.

Health

Health is second to economics as a focus of the band's concern or anxiety. Births and minor illnesses are ordinarily handled by the nursing station. Periodically, people are dissatisfied with the attention they receive there, or they may, for various reasons, wish to bypass this service and be flown out to the hospital at Moose Factory. They communicate their desires to the chief, who then intercedes for them with the nurse in charge. Only she has the authority to have a patient sent out, and, depending upon the seriousness of the condition, she may or may not act according to the chief's request. Here again he is blocked, for he has neither the knowledge necessary to decide whether or not to ask that the sick person be flown out nor the power to implement these requests when he does make them.

Education

The school at the settlement has six grades. From the seventh grade on, children are sent away to boarding schools, but it is not possible for all who complete the sixth grade to continue their education. Decisions with regard to continuing are made by the principal of the school, in a courtesy consultation with the chief. At present, all of the chief's younger children are, or have been, in "outside" schools. Parents who have aspirations for their children, and who are refused the principal's permission, accuse the chief of favoritism and capriciousness. In actual fact, he has little or nothing to say about who will be permitted to go on, although he may report the aims of certain families for their children. Decisions are based largely upon scholastic aptitude and performance of the children.

Attitudes of the chiefs toward their status and role

The consequences of the chief's subordinate status to the superordinate whites in many crucial situations inevitably brings about discontent with his role performance. I was told that when each of the three chiefs was elected, he had the popular support of the people. In time, each had found that, unable to meet certain role expectations, his popularity decreased and in some circumstances open hostility manifested itself. They have been accused of "looking out" for themselves and their families and of failing to take care of the people. Whether the chiefs ever fully recognized the causes for their dilemma, the two still living express disenchantment with the position.

The former chief asserted that he would never run again. His feeling about the conflicting expectations of his role can be seen in the following comments.

> The chief works for nothing and they [Indians] think he should give them everything. The first chief we had here, he wasn't too bad; he did his best but the band says he's no good. After him they chose me, then they say I'm not good. Now they say the same thing about Malcomb. You have to be a pretty good man to please these people.

The current chief, Malcomb, also shows discontent with his position. His daughter reported:

> He is getting fed up with it. People come over to his house drunk and jump on him, accuse him of telling lies, then the next day when he goes over to see them they swear up and down that they were never there.

Malcomb is frustrated by his inability to provide rations, effect employment, or meet all the Indians' needs. There is evidence that he also resents demands placed upon him by the whites, which he does not have the ability to resist. The simple plan of setting up a fishing camp for himself may be thwarted by pressure from a member of the Euro-Canadian community to remain in the settlement to oversee a construction job. This is an economic loss for him, for — although he is paid — the money is no substitute for a good supply of fresh fish.

Complexities of role enactment

The role enactment of an individual occurs largely in face-to-face situations with other people, who can be referred to as "role others." Because everyone occupies a position or status with definable behavior constellations, human interaction is a matter of the meeting and interplay of roles. Our data demonstrate that the status of chief at Rupert's House carries more than one set of role expectations. The chief — in his role as chief — has two clusters of "role others" with which he must interact. Each cluster of "role others" has expectations of the chief that are opposite and irreconcilable insofar as his rights and duties are concerned.

The Euro-Canadians comprise one cluster of "role others." Each of them occupies a status — nurse, teacher, priest, manager — and each acts in a more or less typical manner, consistent with his position. But there is another status that is common to all these people, that of the Euro-Canadian in an Indian settlement. This dimension — added to their particular statuses — places them in a superordinate position in the Rupert's House social system. Thus the combination of particular functions, plus the role that is inherent in the status of Euro-Canadian, comprises the power group with which the chief must interact. This segment of the "role others" has implicitly, if not explicitly, defined the role of chief as a liaison between the Euro-Canadians and the Indians, and he acts accordingly.

The other segment of the "role others" with which the chief interacts is the band members, who have normative expectations that the chief tries — with varying success — to meet. As we have demonstrated, his efforts are usually nullified. The Indians recognize that the Euro-Canadians are in power positions. A telling point here is that the Hudson's Bay Company manager is referred to as "the boss." The Indians are aware that he issues directives, and they know that the game warden acts as policeman for the settlement, and that others in the post have legitimate or illegitimate power. What they do not understand, however, is that their expectations of the chief, which do not include the exercise of power over them, include authority and decision-making ability that he simply does not have.

The effect of operating in a social structure that is composed of two different culture groups may be, as in this case, differential role definitions of one status. When one of these groups is dominant, the subordinate expectations are not likely to be met. In the case of the band chief, regardless of the abilities of the specific incumbent, it results in what we have called a "modal role" behavior that is largely ineffectual from the Indians' perspective — and perhaps also from that of Euro-Canadians if it is measured against the gap between their ideal and real norms for the role. The net results are the band's gradual disaffection for the chief and the chief's increasing sense of frustration. Effective role performance can seldom be executed where there are two sets of role expectations, of the same status, in a social structure that is characterized by superordinate-subordinate organizations.

When we compare our findings with a case study in New Guinea, some interesting differences are uncovered. Brown suggests that the imposition of foreign rule does not always restrict the power of aboriginal authority: the opposite can be true — alien rule can lend new power to the indigenous officials it establishes.[4]

Her material is drawn from the Chimbu area of New Guinea, where, until the arrival of colonial powers, the societies were stateless. Settlements in New Guinea are small and dispersed; and "leadership is not formalized and political units are not fixed." [5] Unlike the Cree, whose basic cooperative unit is the nuclear family, clans and subclans are the cooperative units. Authority rests largely with the heads of clans or subclans. Other leaders ("big men") achieve their position through good exchange relationships with other men. They are effective speakers, and possess the personality traits that are necessary to perform the tasks by which wealth is acquired. Few of them remain leaders throughout their adult life, and none of them can be sure their fellows will support their opinions and positions.

After the arrival of colonial powers (Germany initially, followed by Australia), community and district leaders were appointed, many of whom were former headmen. These men remained in office only as long as the Australian agent from the government station regarded them as ef-

[4] Paula Brown, "From Anarchy to Satrapy," *American Anthropologist* 65 (1963): 1–15.

[5] *Ibid.*, p. 2.

fective. Ultimately, these officials were replaced by younger men less aware of tradition, and at least partially acculturated. Like the Cree band chief, these leaders had to please two parties; but, unlike the Cree, the frequent result of their behavior was advancement of their self-interests at the expense of others. The consequence of alien rule in New Guinea was the creation of a new power structure. "Tribal leadership changed in a generation from the absence of any fixed authority ('anarchy') to a system giving the officials the opportunity to dominate ('satrapy')."[6]

It is apparent that the current role of the New Guinea headman is not conflict-inducing, nor does it result in impotence. In addition, the status carries significantly more permanent power than the traditional "big men" possessed.

Conclusion

Because of the great differences in the results of the innovations of political leaders in these two societies, we must assume that other factors — in addition to the absence of indigenous political structures — are operative; and we may put this in the form of tentative or working hypotheses.

> There is a relationship between the presence of resident aliens and the role of the native official.
>
> There is some congruence between the traditional expectations of a leader and the role of an imposed one.
>
> There is a correspondence between the role enactment of the contemporary leader and the modal overt personality characteristic of the culture.
>
> There is a connection between the behavior of the "chief" and the exploitation of the ecology and attendant social organization.
>
> There is a relationship between the manner in which an official comes into the status — appointed or elected — and his behavior.

It well may be that there is a functional association among some or all of the variables and the predictable behavior of the native power figures.

[6] *Ibid.*, p. 3.

30

Poro values and courtroom procedures

JAMES L. GIBBS, JR.

In every society, people break rules and every group has ways of sanctioning its offenders. One of these methods involves a formal court system before which those who break the law are brought for judgment. In this article James Gibbs describes a Kpelle court and links behavior there to fundamental values held by members of the large and sacred "Poro" society into which the Kpelle are divided.

Secret societies have long captured the imagination of observers of exotic cultures. This paper attempts to shed light on the subtle connection between a secret society — more properly a tribal fraternity — and legal procedures in one African culture.

Adjoining portions of Sierra Leone, Liberia, and the Ivory Coast form a homogeneous culture area, long recognized as distinctive, which has recently been termed "Kru and Peripheral Mande" by Murdock.[1] One of the most significant diagnostic traits for this area, and for certain adjoining portions of the Western Sudan, is the presence of tribal fraternities and secret societies of the Poro type which have drawn much attention because of their identification with initiation schools and exotic rites.

Analyses of the Poro and other tribal fraternities widespread in the region have demonstrated that these societies are core, integrative institutions which are inherently conservative. As d'Azevedo [2] has indicated,

From "Poro Values and Courtroom Procedures in a Kpelle Chiefdom," *Southwestern Journal of Anthropology* 18, no. 4 (1962): 341–350. Reprinted by permission of the author and the editors of the *Southwestern Journal of Anthropology*. Many footnotes, the bibliographic citations, and the bibliography are omitted.

[1] George P. Murdock, *Africa: Its People and Their Culture History* (New York: McGraw-Hill, 1959).

[2] Warren L. d'Azevedo, "Common Principles of Variant Kinship Structures among the Gola," *American Anthropologist* 64 (1962): 504–520.

one of the major functions is to preserve the status quo, even in situations of acculturation or social flux. In such situations, they attempt to maintain adherence to the traditional norms, not the competing intruding ones. This is done through the use of tribal oaths which enjoin all members of the Poro (by definition all men in the tribe) from taking certain actions; by secret trials of those who violate secret society rules, and by other social control measures. Such measures presuppose an unquestioning and unqualified acceptance of authority.

Authority in these cultures is exercised by elders who, in their decision-making, are governed by a basic postulate which holds that power is valuable; its mere possession is its own legitimation, for it is always used for important ends, even if this is not apparent. Harley,[3] in his description of the Poro among the Mano, has shown that the graded internal structure of the society requires and reinforces submission to authority, and that this is inculcated in the initiation schools. Because officials in the Poro have ritual as well as secular duties, respect for their authority is taught in the symbolic and binding idiom of ritual, as well as through direct instruction. This makes the attitude of authoritarian submission all the more compelling.

The fusion of Poro roles with religious and political roles also results in an overlapping of Poro functions and those of other institutions. Moreover, Poro *values* with their authoritarian focus also influence the operation of other institutions. My own field research was directed toward an understanding of this latter process.

In 1957 and 1958 I carried out a field study of the legal system of the Kpelle, one of the Poro-centered cultures of West Africa. I began the study with several preliminary or sensitizing hypothses. One of them was: that the character of the process for the formal settlement of disputes would be influenced in some manner by the presence of the Poro as a tribal fraternity. My results follow.

The Kpelle, a Mande-speaking, patrilineal group of some 175,000 rice cultivators, live in Liberia and the adjoining region of Guinea (where they are known as Guerzé). The present paper is based on field data collected among the Kpelle of Panta Chiefdom in northeastern Central Province of Liberia.

Kpelle political organization is centralized, although there is no single king or paramount chief, but a series of autonomous paramount chiefs of the same level of authority, each of whom is superordinate over district chiefs and town chiefs. Some political functions are vested in the Poro which, as indicated above, is still vigorous in the area. Thus, this form of political organization can best be termed the "polycephalous associational state."

[3] George W. Harley, *Masks as Agents of Control in Northeast Liberia* (Cambridge: Peabody Museum Papers, Vol. 22, [1950] No. 2).

In Liberia, the highest court of a tribal authority and the highest tribal court chartered by the Government of Liberia is that of a paramount chief. Courts of district chiefs (or "clan chiefs" as they are known in Liberia) are also chartered by the Liberian government. These are courts of original jurisdiction which also hear cases appealed from lower courts. Disputes may also be settled in nonchartered courts, those of town chiefs or ward elders. Finally, grievances are also adjusted in informal family moots, and sometimes by associational groupings such as church councils, or cooperative work groups.

The most significant of these Kpelle courts is that of a paramount chief and I undertook a study of the court of the late Chief Dolo Ken Pei, Paramount Chief of Panta Chiefdom. My method was to collect case material in as complete a form as possible. Accordingly, immediately after a court session, using notes and recall, my interpreter and I would prepare verbatim transcripts of each case that we heard. These transcripts were supplemented with accounts — obtained from respondents — of past cases or cases which I did not hear litigated.

In essence, the procedures employed in a Kpelle paramount chief's court are simple. A complainant goes to the paramount chief and/or his clerk. In a casual and informal pretrial hearing, the chief and the clerk decide whether or not the matter is justiciable. If it is, a summons is issued for the defendant. At this preliminary hearing the chief acquires his first judicial knowledge of the case, mentally sorts out the issues, and probably makes a provisional determination of how he will conduct the hearing. Normally, he hears only one party, the one who brings the complaint. In addition, he will supplement what he is told with what he may know of the case through local gossip and his knowledge of the character of the parties through personal acquaintance. His basis for deciding whether a case is justiciable, or what courtroom strategy he will follow, is necessarily somewhat limited.

The hearing itself follows four steps common to all types of Kpelle dispute settlement. The plaintiff speaks first, making his accusation. He is then questioned by the chief and his council. Next, the defendant answers and is also questioned. Where there are witnesses, they are then called and interrogated. Finally, a decision is announced.

The transcripts of the cases heard before Dolo Ken Pei impress the Western observer as being somewhat coercive and arbitrary in tone. He will even judge (albeit informally, *in camera*) a case in which he is a party. Grounds for one's intuitive feelings about the hearings in this court become apparent when the transcripts are analyzed in terms of a framework derived from both jurisprudence and ethno-law.

First, it can be noted that hearings seldom take place immediately after a breach has occurred. There is often a delay before a plaintiff can arrange to travel to the paramount chief's headquarters to institute suit.

The immediacy of the hearing is important because where a hearing takes place soon after a dispute has occurred, grievance tension does not have a chance to grow and to harden to the point where it cannot be effectively dissipated.

Cases are heard in the paramount chief's court house, the largest building in the chiefdom, an imposing structure almost forty feet tall, although it is of wattle and daub construction.

Hearings are attended by the paramount chief, sometimes one or both district chiefs, several town chiefs, and numerous spectators. A litigant thus has to air his affairs both before those who are directly involved in the case, and before a series of political notables and various "strangers." A public hearing is effective in deterring spectators from committing similar offenses, but it is also likely to inhibit litigants from fully expressing themselves.

Millar [4] and other jurists point out that more of the pertinent points of dissension between two parties are likely to emerge when the investigatory initiative lies with the parties or their advocates, rather than with the judge. In Panta Chiefdom, the chief, as adjudicator, has investigatory initiative in his hands. The transcripts often reveal a puzzling line of questioning rooted in information which did not emerge in the courtroom testimony. Such questions are often based on community gossip or on information gained in the pretrial hearing where only the plaintiff was present. At the same time, other points mentioned in the testimony may be ignored. Thus, in the Case of the Couple Who Used Love Charms, the wife asked for a divorce, claiming that she did not love her husband anymore. However, she did not refute his testimony that she had used love charms to cause him to love her more than his other wives and, ultimately, to drive them away. The husband, for his part, consulted a diviner, and also secured "medicine" to cause this wife to love him very much. In spite of this evident mutual concern for the marriage, the chief granted a divorce without delving into the reasons for the deterioration of the marital relationship. Since investigatory initiative lies with him, rather than with the parties, he may conduct the hearing in such a way that some grievances fail to emerge at all, while others — felt not to be pertinent — emerge, but are not ventilated.

Although Dolo Ken Pei often takes judicial notice of information which does not appear in the testimony, he usually operates with a narrow range of relevance, as noted in the reference to the Case of the Couple Who Used Love Charms. In the Case of the Wife Who Displeased the Court, another divorce case, he felt that the wife had precipitated the discord by not cohabiting with her husband and, perhaps, seeking lovers.

[4] Robert Millar, "The Formative Principles of Civil Procedure," *The Illinois Law Review* 18 (1923): 1–36, 94–117, 150–168.

Therefore, he ignored her denial and counter-assertion that the difficulty lay in the practice of witchcraft against her by a co-wife; witchcraft confessed by the co-wife and confirmed in court by the husband's testimony. She did not deny her husband's assertion that she stayed out late at night and had taken one lover. This, for the chief, was the crucial issue — the matter determining fault. He did not air the witchcraft matter at all. As Gluckman's [5] Barotse study indicates, where the range of information considered pertinent is wide, the exposure of grievances is likely to be more complete. Conversely, where it is narrow, grievances are not completely aired.

Dolo Ken Pei, the adjudicator, is both judge and chief, fusing judicial and political roles. He can impose a solution on the parties by backing a decision both with judicial authority and with the power underlying his political role. In the Case of the Man Who Beat His Wife, he threatened to send the defendant for his required public works duty before his normal time, saying: "We always give porters to the government. If the time has not come for you to do porter work, you must behave yourself and not always look for trouble."

The chief presides wearing robes emblematic of his office and status and is treated with deferential etiquette. Court sessions are attended and policed by the chief's uniformed mesengers known to the populace as "soldiers." These men are familiar in their roles as jailors, summoners of witnesses and persons accused of crimes such as tax delinquency. They are visible evidence of the chief's political authority, and the fact that this authority is backed by the possible application of physical force. The robes, messengers — even the courtroom itself — are all expressive symbols of his authority, reminders of the ultimate judicial and political sanctions underlying the legal process. As such, they tend to inhibit litigants from a full ventilation of the issues, for their presence is mildly intimidating.

In normal circumstances in a Kpelle court, the decision must necessarily be awarded to one party. The informal reprimands and admonitions which accompany the decision are directed primarily at the losing litigant. Fining the husband as the guilty party in the Case of the Man Who Beat His Wife, the Chief said to him:

> You are behaving badly. A man lives according to his heart, and everything that a man does wrong comes from a bad heart. Therefore, you have a bad heart all the time. . . . I planted greens in my own garden and my wives finished eating all of them, but I didn't say anything about it. You, little boy, what kind of wrong thing can a woman do to make you cut her?

[5] Max Gluckman, The Judicial Process among the Barotse of Northern Rhodesia (Manchester: Manchester University Press, 1955).

In handing down the decision on this note, the chief did not chastise the wife for her action described by the husband in an uncontested plea of self-defense, namely, that she had grabbed a stick and attempted to strike him on his penis. Dolo Ken Pei's droll reply was: "Why didn't you wait and see if she was really going to hit you?"

Such strongly unilateral ascription of blame is common in Kpelle courts, even though some fault usually lies with both parties, and it often creates resentment which raises a new reason for bad feeling between the parties. However, the decision is made less arbitrary by the lecture to the litigants. As illustrated above, it is phrased in homilies (and, often, proverbs) as a way of indicating the meaning of the decision and pointing out its roots in tradition.

Bad feeling between the parties raised by one-sided allocation of fault is often reinforced by the imposition of a harsh penalty. Such severe sanctions are more likely to be imposed by an adjudicator who holds political office and power. A most effective sanction employed by Dolo Ken Pei was to take the guilty party's fine and distribute it among the spectators in the courtroom as a windfall. Where the parties feel that the sanctions imposed as part of the settlement are unduly harsh, they will not truly concur in the solution.

The strong focus on the authority of the paramount chief in a Kpelle court is also mirrored in the fact that there is seldom a recess for deliberation between argumentation and the handing down of a decision. In fact, a decision may come very early in the proceedings, only to be finally pronounced in a formal manner at the end of a hearing. Moreover, even though a paramount chief has a "council" of lesser chiefs and elders whose formal function is to help in judicial deliberations, there is rarely a significant degree of overt consultation among them in reaching a judicial decision.

In sum, the above descriptive analysis of courtroom procedure in the Panta Chiefdom Paramount Chief's court indicates how some of the actions in the courtroom contribute to the coercive tone one notes there — and, to a certain extent, in courts in any society. Two dimensions of the dispute settlement process were studied: the completeness of the airing of grievances and the extent of party concurrence in the settlement. Each of these dimensions or rubrics presupposes several more minute attributes of a hearing which contribute to the outcome of the hearing.

It was noted that any dispute settlement is likely to be more stable when all of the grievances between the parties are completely aired. Four factors were held to contribute to this result: the immediacy of the hearing, the publicity of the hearing, the locus of investigatory initiative, and the range of relevance. Where all four of the features mark the conduct of a hearing, all of the grievances lodged between the parties are likely to be heard and adjusted.

Similarly, jurisprudence suggests that when a decision in a case is not simply imposed by the adjudicator but truly concurred in by both parties, it is more likely to be durable. We noted that the extent of party concurrence is also the result of four more detailed features of a hearing: authoritative personnel, expressive symbols of authority, unilateral ascription of blame, and sanctions of marked severity. The presence of these four features may lead to parties acquiescing in a settlement — even though it does not satisfy them. This is because the settlement is backed by authority strong enough to hand down a decision without waiting for a feeling of consensus to emerge.

Having noted the features which give hearings in this court their coercive cast, I can turn to the matter of the adequacy of the settlements reached there. Jurisprudence and ethno-law both offer guideposts by which one can measure this — albeit roughly.

Although the transcripts indicate that the hearings in the Panta Chiefdom court are arbitrary and coercive in tone, settlements effected are often satisfactory. A field period of only seventeen months does not permit meaningful conclusions as to the long term durability of settlements, but it is clear that the court is particularly effective in settling cases such as assault, theft, or possession of illegal charms. In matters like these, where the litigants are not linked in a relationship which must continue after the trial, the significant issues are isolated and the decision is announced in the form of a rule. The fact that some grievance tension remains and that the dissension sometimes spreads to other persons does not seem to undermine the decision. In short, the outcome in some types of disputes is not affected by the court's coercive tone.

However, most of the cases heard before a Kpelle paramount chief involve parties whose relationship is not transitory. They are cases of disputed rights over women. Here, the court is clearly less effective. In the majority of marital disputes brought before it, the court grants a divorce. Marital disputes seldom result in a willing reconciliation, because this requires restoration of genuine harmony between the parties. This is impossible because the coercive cast of courtroom procedures yields an incomplete airing of grievances, and faulty isolation of issues. Moreover, the coercive tone of the hearing itself *adds* to the grievance tension between the spouses and drives them farther apart. Precluded from arranging a concordant reconciliation, the court may effect an acquiescent reconciliation, perhaps by the drastic measure of threatening to jail a woman who will not return to her husband. One doubts the durability of such reconciliations.

This limited role of the court in settling matrimonial cases contrasts with that of the informal moot of kinsmen which, being more conciliatory in tone, can bring about concordant reconciliations.

I can now return to my initial problem and preliminary hypothesis. How does the presence of the Poro contribute to the coercive tone of the courtroom hearing in Panta Chiefdom? Some of the arbitrary nature of Kpelle court proceedings is due to the type of cases with which it has to deal. Matrimonial disputes become as cut and dried to the Kpelle judge as the Monday morning docket of drunken driving cases to an American traffic court judge. Marital disputes are handled with dispatch, which appears arbitrary, for once a judge sees that the two spouses are not reconcilable, he need not inquire further into their behavior, but proceed to arrange a divorce.

An equally significant cause of the coercive and arbitrary tone of courtroom procedure is the influence of Poro values. Respect for authority conditioned in the Poro bush leads ligitants to expect a certain amount of arbitrariness in court procedures and decisions. A young man in the initiation school cannot question what he is told by the masked figures or the older men because, not having been initiated into the higher degrees, he knows little of the rationale supporting actions he is ordered to perform. He must — and does — accept on faith the notion that those who command know what is right and act with the highest moral and spiritual aims. The same attitude toward authoritarian actions is carried into the courtroom.

This is significant because it apparently limits the manner with which the court can deal with some types of disputes, especially marital disputes. However, it also makes it possible for the court to serve as a forceful and unchallenged instrument for sanctioning deviant actions which threaten traditional values or traditional authority.

The present paper is based on the detailed and systematic analysis of a few selected cases rather than a mass of quantitive data. It uses an eclectic but organized collection of concepts to establish a relationship between one of a society's basic values, i.e., strong and unchallenged respect for authority, and the nature of that society's judicial procedures and results. An intervening variable is the presence of the Poro as a tribal fraternity which is the primary structural device through which this value is so effectively instilled and so strongly maintained. The hypothesis suggested is a tentative one. Further research should involve applying the same analytical scheme to detailed case material from other Kpelle courts and courts in other Poro-centered societies and to data from societies in other world culture areas which are similarly integrated around secret societies and rituals, such as the Pueblos of the American Southwest.

31

Beating the drunk charge

JAMES P. SPRADLEY

In the urban American court used in the following study, nearly 12,000 men are charged each year with public drunkenness. While many post bail and go free, most of the poor appear in court and place themselves at the mercy of the judge. They are not entirely destitute, however, and have an elaborate set of strategies for "beating the drunk charge." James Spradley analyzes these strategies, shows their differential effectiveness, and demonstrates how they reflect certain values of American culture.

It could be Miami, New York, Chicago, Minneapolis, Denver, Los Angeles, Seattle, or any other American city. The criminal court may be in the basement of a massive public building constructed at the turn of the century, or high above the city in a modern skyscraper. The judges who hear the never-ending list of cases may be veterans of the bench or men whose memories of law school are fresh and clear. But one scene does not change. Each weekday morning a group of unshaven men file into court with crestfallen faces, wrinkled clothing, and bloodshot eyes. They stand before the prosecuting attorney and hear him say, "You have been charged with public drunkenness, how do you plead?"

The most staggering problem of law and order in America today is public drunkenness. In 1968 the F.B.I. reported that one and a half million arrests for this crime made up nearly one third of all arrests. This means that every twenty seconds another person is arrested and charged with being drunk in public. During 1967, in Seattle, Washington, 51 per-

This article was written especially for this volume and has never before been published. Some of the data presented here is also published in a more complete study of this culture, entitled *You Owe Yourself a Drunk: An Ethnography of Urban Nomads*, 1970, Little, Brown and Company, Boston. Those interested in the meaning of various terms not explained here should consult this ethnographic study.

cent of all arrests and 65 percent of all cases that appeared in the criminal court were for intoxication. In that same year the chief of police stated, "As a public official I have no choice. Whether alcoholism is a disease or not would not affect my official position. Drunkenness is a crime. So we must enforce the law by arresting people. We know in the Police Department that probably right at this moment there are more than two hundred men in the city jail serving sentences for drunkenness who have never posed any threat to the community in any fashion at all."

Who are these men that are repeatedly arrested for drunkenness? Who are the ones who spend much of their lives in jail for their public behavior? The first task in this study was to discover how these men identified themselves. This was necessary because the police, courts, social scientists, and most citizens see them as criminals, homeless men, derelicts, and bums who have lost the ability to organize their behavior in the pursuit of goals. The word these men used to identify their subcultural membership was the term *tramp*. There were several different kinds of tramps recognized by informants; for example, a "mission stiff" is a tramp who frequents the skid-road missions, while a "rubber tramp" travels about in his own car. This category system constitutes one of the major social identity domains in the subculture.

Tramps have other ways to conceptualize their identity when they "make the bucket," or are incarcerated. As an inmate in jail one is either a *drunk*, a *trusty*, a *lockup*, a *kickout*, or a *rabbit*. In the particular jail studied there are over sixty different kinds of trusties. This fact led some tramps to believe they were arrested to provide cheap labor for the police department. In their capacity as trusties, nearly 125 men provide janitorial service for the city hall, outlying police precincts, and the jail. They assist in the preparation of food, maintain the firing range, care for police vehicles, and do numerous other tasks. Most men soon learn that doing time on a drunk charge is not a desirable occupation, so they use many strategies to escape the confines of the jail or to reduce the length of their sentence. When a man is arrested he is placed in the drunk tank where he awaits his arraignment in court. Those sentenced to do time will spend it in close association with other tramps. If a man is not experienced in the ways of this culture, he will learn them while he is in jail, for it is a veritable storehouse of invaluable information for those who are repeatedly arrested for public intoxication. He will learn to think of himself as a tramp and to survive on the street by employing more than a dozen "ways of making it." More important, as he discovers that the jailhouse has a revolving door for drunks, he will do his best to "beat the drunk charge." The casual observer in court may find the arraignment and sentencing of drunk cases to be a cut-and-dried process. From the perspective of these men, however, it is more like a game of skill and chance being played by the tramp and law-enforcement agencies. In this article we shall examine the rules of this game, the strategies employed by tramps, and the underlying American cultural values that make it intelligible to the outsider.

Plans for beating the drunk charge

Every culture contains one type of shared knowledge called *plans*. These are related to the achievement of goals. A plan is a set of rules that specifies a goal, conditions under which the goal will be chosen, techniques for the attainment of the goal, and conditions under which a particular technique will be used to attain the goal. The methods of ethnoscience are designed to map culturally shared systems of knowledge, and were used in this study to discover the plans tramps employ in their relationship to law-enforcement agencies.

The goal: Maximize freedom — minimize incarceration. There are many goals which tramps pursue. Most aims are referred to in a specific manner, such as "making a flop," "making a jug," "getting a dime," or "bailing out." Freedom is a general objective that includes such specific goals as rabbiting from jail, concealing one's identity, making a pay-off to a bull, leaving town, avoiding the police, and beating a drunk charge. Men do not always select one of these goals in order to maximize freedom — they sometimes even choose paths leading to *incarceration*. In a sample of a hundred men, 10 percent reported they had gone to jail and asked to be locked up in order to stop drinking. At other times a tramp will go to jail on his own to request a place to sleep or something to eat. Such cases are rare, and most tramps abhor imprisonment because they have learned a life style of mobility and the restrictions in the bucket lead to intense frustration. A testimonial to the fact that men do not seek imprisonment, as some outsiders believe, is the large number of strategies this culture has for avoiding incarceration. Almost every experience in the tramp world is defined, in part, by noting the degree of risk it entails for being jailed.

Techniques for the attainment of the goal. Because of the public nature of their life style, sooner or later most of these men end up in jail. Their specific objective at that time is to "beat the drunk charge." If successful, this could mean freedom in a few hours or at least a sentence of shorter duration than they would otherwise have received. The techniques for reaching this goal were discovered during interviews in which informants were asked: "Are there different ways to beat a drunk charge?" They responded with many specific instances in which they had taken action to beat the charge. These were classified as follows:

1. Bail out.
2. Bond out.
3. Request a continuance.

4. Have a good record.
5. Use an alias.
6. Plead guilty.
7. Hire a defense attorney.
8. Plead not guilty.
9. Submit a writ of habeas corpus.
10. Make a statement:
    a. Talk of family ties.
    b. Talk of present job.
    c. Talk of intent to work.
    d. Tell of extenuating circumstances.
    e. Offer to leave town.
11. Request the treatment center (alcoholic).

Each of these techniques labels a *category* of many different acts that are considered equivalent. For example, a man may bail out by using money he had with him when arrested, by borrowing from another man in jail, by contacting an employer who loans or gives him the money, and so on. There are several ways to "have a good record": a man must stay out of jail for at least six months for his record to begin to affect the length of his jail sentence. In order to do this a man may travel, quit drinking, stay off skid road, or go to an alcoholism treatment center for a long stay. Each kind of statement includes specific instances, varying from one man to another and from one time to the next. This category system is extremely important to tramps. Once they have learned these techniques, they practice them until their skill increases. Judges may consider an old-time tramp as a "con artist," but in this culture he is a man with expertise in carrying out these culturally shared techniques.

Conditions influencing selection. When a man is arrested he must process a great deal of information before he makes a decision to employ one or more of these techniques. He must assess his own resources, the probabilities of success, the risk of doing more time, etc. He needs to know the sentencing practices of the judge, the population of the jail, and the weather conditions. The most important factors that influence his decision are shown in Table I.

American cultural values

Every society is based upon shared values — conceptions of the desirable in human experience. They are the basis for rewards and punishments. It is not surprising to most Americans that our culture, like most others, has rules about the undesirability of certain behavior *in public.* We have outlawed nudity, begging, drinking, elimination of wastes, and intoxication in public places. We are offended by many other acts — if they occur in public. Tramps are booked for public intoxication, but they are often

TABLE I. *Conditions influencing selection of a way to beat a drunk charge*

Strategy	*Risk of outcome?*	*Risk offending bulls?*	*Risk getting more time?*	*Risk doing dead time?*	*Money needed?*
Bail out	No	No	No	No	$20
Bond out	No	No	No	No	$20+
Request a continuance	Yes	Yes	No	Yes	Yes
Have a good record	No	No	No	No	No
Use an alias	Yes	Yes	Yes	No	No
Plead guilty	Yes	No	No	No	No
Hire a defense attorney	Yes	Yes	No	Yes	Yes
Plead not guilty	Yes	Yes	Yes	Yes	No
Submit a writ of habeas corpus	Yes	Yes	Yes	Yes	No
Make a statement	Yes	No	Yes	No	No
Request a treatment center	Yes	Yes	Yes	Yes	No

arrested because they urinate, sleep, or drink in some public place. Poverty has made it impossible for them to conceal their behavior behind the walls of a home. The extent of these restrictions upon *public* acts are in contrast to many non-Western societies where there is a wider range of acceptable public behavior. Because public drunkenness, which covers a multitude of other public sins, involves more arrests each year than any other crime, we may conclude that *privacy* is an important value in our culture.

Above the judge's bench in the criminal court where this study took place, there is a large wooden plaque inscribed "Equal Justice for All Under the Law." Given the laws prohibiting public behavior of various kinds, we might still expect that the punishment for violation would be distributed *equally*. Thus, if two men with the same criminal record are found guilty of the same crime, they should receive the same punishment. If two men are found drunk in public for the first time, it would be unfair to fine one a few dollars and require the other to pay several hundred dollars. Upon examining the penalties given for public drunkenness, we discover a rather startling fact: *the less a man conforms to other American values, the more severe his punishment* — not because he violates other laws, but because he does not conform to the values of *materialism, moralism,* and *work*. These values are the basis for a set of implicit "punishment rules." Although they are unwritten, those who administer justice in our society have learned to punish the drunk offender on the basis of these rules.

Rule 1: *When guilty of public drunkenness, a man deserves greater punishment if he is poor.* In every society, when individuals violate legal norms they are punished. Physical torture, public humiliation, incarceration, and banishment from the society are some of the forms this punishment takes. It is not surprising that in our society, with its emphasis upon the value of material goods, violators are punished by making them give up some form of property. An individual may be fined after he has been convicted of public drunkenness. Most offenders pay money in the form of a "bail" prior to conviction. A few hours after being arrested, most men are able to be released from jail in a sober condition. They are still innocent before the law and an arraignment is scheduled at which time they may plead guilty or not guilty. If they enter the later plea, they must appear in court at another time for a trial. In order to insure that a man returns for his arraignment he is asked to deposit bail money with the court, which will be returned to him when he is sentenced or acquitted. In most courts a man may choose to ignore the arraignment and thereby "forfeit" his bail. It is still within the power of the court to issue a warrant for his arrest in this case and compel him to appear in court, but this is seldom done. Instead, much like bail for a traffic violation, forfeiture of the drunk bail is considered as a just recompense to society for appearing drunk in public.

When arrested, tramps are eager to post bail since it means an immediate release from jail. They do not need to wait for the arraignment which may not occur for several days. The bail is $20 and is almost always forfeited. This system of punishment treats offenders equally — *unless a man does not have $20.*

Those who are caught in the grip of poverty are usually convicted, and their punishment is "doing time" instead of "paying money." In America, the rich have money, the poor have time. It might be possible to punish men equitably using these two different commodities but such is not the case. If a man is poor he must be unwilling to expend his energies in the pursuit of materialism, and therefore his punishment should be more severe than that given to those with money. How does this occur? Each time a man is arrested his bail is always twenty dollars, but if he is indigent, his sentences become longer with each conviction. A man can be arrested hundreds of times and bail out for only twenty dollars, but not if he is poor. Consider the case of one man who was arrested in Seattle over one hundred times during a twenty-one-year period. On many arrests he bailed out, but for about seventy convictions he was sentenced to jail, and gradually his sentences grew to the maximum of six months for a single arrest. During this period he was sentenced to nearly fourteen years in jail — a punishment he could have avoided for only a hundred dollars for each of those years. This man was given a life sentence on the installment plan, not for being drunk but for being poor. There are many cases where a rich man and a poor man are arrested and booked for drunkenness on the same night. The rich man is released in a few hours because he had twenty dollars. The poor man is released in a few months because he did not have twenty dollars. One way then to beat a drunk charge is to bail out. If you do not have money, it is still possible to use this strategy by bonding out or asking for a continuance. A bond requires some collateral or assurance that the twenty dollars *plus* a fee to the bondsman will be paid. A continuance enables you to wait a few more days before being sentenced, and during that time, it may be possible to get money from a friend or an employer. Whether he can use these ways to beat a drunk charge or not, the tramp who is repeatedly arrested soon learns he is being punished because he does not conform to the value of materialism.

Rule 2: *When guilty of public drunkenness, a man deserves greater punishment if he has a bad reputation.* Most cultures have a moralistic quality that often leads to stereotyping and generalizing about the quality of a man's character. In our society once a person has been convicted of a crime, he is viewed by others with suspicion. He may never violate legal norms again, but for all practical purposes he is morally reprehensible. Since judges increase the length of a man's sentence with each arrest, he must engage in behavior designed to give him a "good record" if he is to beat the drunk charge. One way to do this is by travelling. For example, if a man stayed out of jail in Seattle for six months, subsequent convictions would begin again with short sentences; thus, when arrested several times, he often decided it would be better if he went to another town. When his arrest record began to grow in this new place, he would move on; after a period of time he would return to Seattle. Men learn to calculate the number of "days hanging" for each city where they are arrested, and their mobility is determined by the magnitude of the next sentence. Some men use an alias when arrested in an attempt to obscure the fact that they have a long record. If this ploy is successful, a man who, because of his record, deserves a sentence of six months, may only be given two or three days. Another way to beat a drunk charge is to volunteer to go to an alcoholism treatment center. A man may not believe that he is an alcoholic or even that he has a "drinking problem," but if he will agree with society's judgment — that his long record of arrests shows he is morally debased — and ask to be helped, his incarceration will be reduced. But not all men are candidates for treatment. Those with the worst records are rejected and must do their time in jail. A man with a bad reputation thus will be given a more severe punishment for the same crime than one with a good reputation.

Rule 3: *When guilty of public drunkenness, a man deserves greater punishment if he does not have a steady job.* American culture places great value on work as an end in itself. Resistance to hippies and welfare programs alike is based, in part, on the value of work. Tramps know that judges punish more severely those who do not have steady employment.

If a man cannot beat a drunk charge in some other way, he will make a statement telling the judge that he will find a job, return to a former job, or provide evidence that he is currently employed in a respectable occupation. Tramps often earn a living by "junking" to find things to sell, "spot jobbing," or "panhandling" (begging on the street) — but all these "occupations" are not admired in our society and cannot be used as evidence that one is conforming to the value of work. When a man appears in court with evidence that he is working, the judge will often suspend or shorten his sentence.

Tramps who have been unable to beat the drunk charge before being sentenced may capitalize on this value in another way. One man reported that he had written a letter to himself while in jail. The letter appeared to have been written by an employer in another city offering the man a steady job. The inmate asked another man who was being released from jail to carry the letter to that city and mail it from there. When it arrived, he used it to convince the judge that he should receive an early release in order to accept steady employment. Another inmate, when released from jail, went personally to the judge and pretended to be a contractor; he told him that a man who had worked for him was in jail and he would employ him if he were released. The judge complied with the request, and the two tramps left town together — proud of their achievement, surer than ever that one of the best ways to beat a drunk charge was to understand the value of work in American culture.

The values our culture places upon privacy, materialism, moralism, and work are not the only ones affecting the lives of tramps. These are men who live in a society that holds no place for them. Their life style is offensive to most Americans, and for this reason they are arrested, jailed, and punished by standards that do not apply to the rest of society. In response to these practices they have learned a culture with well-developed plans for survival. They have adopted a nomadic style of life — moving from one urban center to another to maximize their freedom. In spite of their efforts, sooner or later, most tramps find themselves arrested, and it is then that the techniques for beating a drunk charge will be found most useful.

32

Cannibalistic revenge in Jalé warfare

KLAUS-FRIEDRICH KOCH

To many Westerners, war is explained as an outgrowth of greed for territory and power, and cannibalism reflects man's brutal origins and denies his humanity. The Jalé of New Guinea are cannibals and almost continuously at war, but their military activity reflects a breakdown of procedures for solving conflicts and their cannibalism is an act of revenge on enemies slain in war. Klaus-Frederich Koch traces the cultural norms of warfare and the eating of human flesh. He speculates that these categories result from a characteristic of Jalé child-training, and are related to the lack of a broadly based political organization.

In October, 1968, two white missionaries on a long trek between two stations were killed in a remote valley in the Snow Mountains of western New Guinea, and their bodies were eaten. A few days later, warriors armed with bows and arrows gave a hostile reception to a group of armed police flown to the site by helicopter. These people, described by the newspapers as "savages living in a stone-age culture," belong to a large population of Papuans among whom I lived for nearly two years, from 1964 to 1966.

People living to the west, in the high valley of the Balim River, call them "Jalé," and this is the name that I use for them. When I read of the killing of the missionaries I was reminded of how I had first heard that the people whom I had selected for ethnographic study had anthropophagic (man-eating) predilections. After arriving at Sentani airport on the north coast, I began negotiations for transport to a mission airstrip located in the Jalémó, the country of the Jalé. "I hope the Jalé will give us per-

From "Cannibalistic Revenge in Jalé Warfare," *Natural History* 79 (February 1970): 41–43, 47, 49–50. Fieldwork in Jalémó was supported by the Social Science Research Council and the Wenner-Gren Foundation for Anthropological Research. Illustrations are omitted.

mission to land," one pilot said to me. "Just a few weeks ago the airstrip was blocked because the Jalé needed the ground for a dance and a cannibalistic feast to celebrate a military victory."

Our cultural heritage predisposes many people to view the eating of human meat with extreme horror. No wonder then that the literature on the subject is permeated with grossly erroneous and prejudicial ideas about the practice. Few anthropologists have been able to study cannibalism because missions and colonial governments have generally succeeded in eradicating a custom considered to epitomize, more than any other, the alleged mental primitiveness and diabolical inspirations of people with simple technologies. However, the Jalé, completely isolated from foreign influences until 1961, still practice cannibalism as an institutionalized form of revenge in warfare, which is itself an integral aspect of their life.

The Jalé live in compact villages along several valleys north and south of the Snow Mountains in east-central West New Guinea. Until the first missionaries entered the Jalémó in 1961, the Jalé were ignorant of the "outside" world. Five years later, when I left the area, many Jalé villages still had never been contacted, and culture change among the people living close to a mission station was largely limited to the acceptance of a few steel tools and to an influx of seashells imported by the foreigners.

Two weeks after I had set up camp in the village of Pasikni, a yearlong truce with a neighboring village came to an end. Three days of fierce fighting ensued, during which the Pasikni warriors killed three enemies (among them a small boy), raided the defeated settlement, and drove its inhabitants into exile with friends and relatives in other villages of the region. At that time I understood little of the political realities of Jalé society, where neither formal government nor forensic institutions exist for the settlement of conflicts. Later, when I had learned their language, I began to comprehend the conditions that make military actions an inevitable consequence of the absence of an effective system of political control.

From an anthropological perspective any kind of war is generally a symptom of the absence, inadequacy, or breakdown of other procedures for resolving conflicts. This view is especially applicable to Jalé military operations, which aim neither at territorial gains and the conquest of resources nor at the suppression of one political or religious ideology and its forceful replacement by another. All armed conflicts in Jalémó occur as a result of bodily injury or killing suffered in retaliation for the infliction of a wrong. Violent redress may be exacted for adultery or theft or for a breach of obligation — usually a failure to make a compensatory payment of pigs.

Jalé warfare is structured by a complex network of kin relationships. The Jalé conceptually divide their society into two parts (moieties) whose members must marry someone from the opposite side. By a principle of patrilineal descent a person always belongs to the moiety of his father. Links between kin groups created by intervillage marriages — about half the wives in a village were born elsewhere — provide the structure of trade networks and alliance politics.

Most villages contain two or more residential compounds, or wards. One hut among the group of dwellings forming a ward is considerably bigger than all the others. This is the men's house, a special domicile for men and for boys old enough to have been initiated. Women and uninitiated boys live in the smaller huts, each of which usually houses the family of one man. The residents of a men's house constitute a unified political and ritual community, and it is this community, not the village as a whole, that is the principal war-making unit.

As in all societies, there are some individuals who have more influence over the affairs of their fellows than most. In Jalémó a man gains a position of authority (which never extends much beyond the immediate kin group) through his acquisition of an esoteric knowledge of performing rituals and through the clever management of his livestock to the benefit of his relatives, for every important event demands the exchange of pigs — to solemnify or legitimate the creation of a new status or to settle a conflict. Most disputes are over women, pigs, or gardens, and any one of them may generate enough political enmity to cause a war in which many people may lose their lives and homes.

In every Jalé war one person on either side, called the "man-at-the-root-of-the-arrow," is held responsible for the outbreak of hostilities. These people are the parties to the original dispute, which ultimately escalates into armed combat. Being a man-at-the-root-of-the-arrow carries the liability of providing compensation for all injuries and deaths suffered by supporters on the battlefield as well as by all others — including women and children — victimized in clandestine revenge raids. This liability acts as a built-in force favoring an early end of hostilities.

On rare occasions blood revenge has been prevented by delivery of wergild compensation, in the form of a pig to the kinsmen of a slain person. But only those people who, for one reason or another, cannot rally support for a revenge action and who shy away from solitary, surreptitious ambush attacks will accept such an offer if it is made at all. A negotiated peace settlement of this nature is most likely if the disputants are from the same village or if the whole settlement is at war with a common outside enemy.

When two villages are at war with each other, periods of daily combat are interrupted by short "cease-fires" during which the warriors attend to the more mundane task of garden work, but they are always prepared to counter a surprise attack launched by the enemy. After several weeks of discontinuous fighting, however, the threat of famine due to the prolonged neglect of proper cultivation induces the belligerents to maintain an informal and precarious truce. During this time small bands of kinsmen and members of the men's house of a victim whose death could not be avenged on the battlefield will venture clandestine expeditions into enemy territory, from which a successful raiding party may bring back a pig as well. It is a revenge action of this kind that often precipitates a resumption of open warfare.

Fighting on the battlefield follows a pattern of haphazardly coordinated individual engagements, which rely on the tactic of "shoot-and-run." This technique requires a warrior to advance as far as the terrain affords him cover, discharge an arrow or two, and then run back to escape from the reach of enemy shots. When one side has been forced to retreat to its village, the fighting turns into sniping from behind huts and fences. Women and children always leave the village if an invasion is imminent and take refuge with friends and relatives in other villages. As a last resort the men retreat into the men's house, which a taboo protects from being burned. When a battle reaches this stage, the victorious warriors often plunder and burn family huts. Following a catastrophe of this extent the defeated side usually elects to abandon their village, and the warfare ceases, but the hostilities linger on until a formal peace ceremony reconciles the principal parties. Arranging the ceremony, which features the ritual slaughter and consumption of a pig, may take years of informal negotiations between people who have relatives on both sides. Afterward, dances in both villages and pig exchanges on a large scale consolidate the termination of the conflict.

"People whose face is known must not be eaten," say the Jalé. Consequently, cannibalism is normally not tolerated in wars between neighboring villages, and the few incidents that did occur during the lifetime of the oldest Pasikni men are remembered as acts of tragic perversion. In wars between villages separated by a major topographic boundary such as a mountain ridge, however, cannibalistic revenge is an integral part of the conflict.

While territorially confined hostilities usually end within a few years, interregional wars may last for more than a generation. During this long period revenge parties from either side venture sporadic expeditions into hostile areas, keenly avoiding any confrontation in battle and seeking instead to surprise lone hunters or small groups of women working in distant gardens. The geography of interregional wars favors long-lasting military alliances that have a stability quite unlike the temporary and shifting allegiances that personal kin connections and trading partnerships create in local conflicts.

If an enemy is killed during a foray into hostile territory, the raiders will make every effort to bring the body home. If tactical exigencies demand that the revenge party retreat without the victim, an attempt is made to retrieve at least a limb. The avengers always present the body to an allied kin group that has lost a member in the war. In return they receive pigs and are feted at a victory dance, during which the victim's body is steam-cooked in an earth oven dug near the village. Before the butchering begins, the head is specially treated by ritual experts: eyelids and lips are clamped with the wing bones of a bat to prevent the victim's ghost from seeing through these apertures. Thus blinded, it will be unable to guide a revenge expedition against its enemies.

After the head has been severed, it is wrapped in leaves. To insure more revenge killings in the future, some men shoot reed arrows into the head while it is dragged on the ground by a piece of vine. Then the head is unwrapped and swung through the fire to burn off the hair. This is accompanied by loud incantations meant to lure the victim's kinsmen into sharing his fate.

Following this ritual overture the butchers use stone adzes and bamboo knives to cut the body apart. The fleshy portions are removed from the skull, and in an established order of step-by-step incisions, the limbs are separated from the trunk, which is split open to allow removal of the gastronomically highly prized entrails. Some small, choice cuts, especially rib sections, are roasted over the fire, but the bulk of the meat is cooked with a variety of leafy vegetables.

Before and during the operation, people who are preparing the oven, tending the fire, or just standing around appraise the victim. A healthy, muscular body is praised with ravenous exclamations, but a lesser grade body is also applauded.

When the meat is done, the pit is opened and the "owners of the body," as the Jalé call the recipients of a slain enemy, distribute much of the food among the attending relatives of the person whose death the killing has avenged. It is also distributed to the allied kin groups of a person maimed or killed in the war. Eligible people from other villages who could not participate in the celebrations are later sent pieces reserved for them. If mood so moves the Jalé, they may place some of the victim's bones in a tree near the cooking site to tell travelers of their brave deed.

In the course of the dancing and singing, a poetically gifted man may introduce a new song. If the lyrics appeal to others, it becomes a standard piece in the repertoire. The songs commemorate fortunate and tragic events from past wars, and a typical verse goes like this:

> Ngingi, your mother
> bakes only tiny potatoes for you.
> Isel, your mother too
> bakes only the ends of potatoes for you.

We shall bake big potatoes for you
On the day of Kingkaen's return.

Ngingi and Isel are the names of two men from a hostile village, the home of a young woman named Kingkaen who was killed in an ambush attack in September, 1964. The lines make fun of the men who, because of Kingkaen's death, have to eat poor food prepared by the inept hands of senile women.

When the festival of revenge is over, the members of the men's house group of the owners of the body arrange for the ritual removal of the victim's ghost from their village. Rhythmically voicing efficacious formulas and whistling sounds, a ceremonial procession of men carries a special arrow into the forest, as far into enemy territory as is possible without risk. A small lump of pig's fat is affixed to the arrow by an expert in esoteric lore. (Pig's fat used for ritual purposes becomes a sacred substance that is applied in many different contexts.) The arrow is finally shot toward the enemy village. This, the Jalé believe, will make the ghost stay away from their own village, but as a further precaution they block the path with branches and plants over which spells are said.

Protective rites of this kind, and the vengeance ritual described above, are the only aspects of Jalé cannibalism that may be viewed as "religious." The actual consumption of human meat and organs does not constitute an act with intrinsic "supernatural" effects. Instead, as my Jalé friends repeatedly assured me, their reason for eating an enemy's body is that man tastes as good as pork, if not better. And they added that the bad enemies in the other valley had eaten some of their people.

These descriptions of Jalé rituals and beliefs do not sufficiently explain the practice of cannibalism. To do so would necessitate the compilation of all available information about this custom from every part of the world. On the basis of these data an extensive study would have to be made of the ecological and cultural variables found to be associated with institutionalized cannibalism. Perhaps it would then be possible to recognize specific ecological and sociological features that appear to be correlated with the consumption of human meat, but the task of interpreting the custom as a sociopsychological phenomenon would still remain.

It is obvious that the enigmatic nature of cannibalism has invited many writers to speculate about its origin and its biopsychic basis. Aristotle attributed anthropophagy among tribes around the Black Sea to their feral bestiality and morbid lust. In 1688 a treatise was published in Holland entitled *De natura et moribus anthropohagorum* ("On the Nature and Customs of Anthropophagi"), and some ethnographers writing in the nineteenth century still regarded the rejection of cannibalism as the "first step into civilization." Certainly, the consumption by man of a member of his own species is as much a problem for evolutionary bioanthropology as it is for ethnology and psychology. I have made an extensive survey of the various theories proposed by earnest scholars to elucidate the phenomenon, and I have found that, at best, a few hypotheses appear plausible for the interpretation of certain aspects of some cannibalistic practices.

In Jalémó the eating of a slain enemy, in addition to its dietary value, certainly indicates a symbolic expression of spite incorporated into an act of supreme vengeance. Violent retaliation, in turn, must be seen as a consequence of certain sociopsychological conditions that determine the de-degree of aggressive behavior expected and tolerated in their culture. Cross-cultural studies by anthropologists have supported theories that are applicable to Jalé society. An accepted model of personality development demonstrates that societies in which boys grow up in intimate association with their mothers, who dominate a household situation in which the boy's male elders, especially their fathers, do not take part, are characterized by a high level of physical violence. Sociological models developed from large-scale comparative research predict that in societies in which small kin groups operate as relatively independent political units, warfare within the society is a common means of resolving conflict.

Both models squarely apply to Jalé society. First, young boys, separated from the community of the men's house until their initiation, are socialized in a female environment. Second, the wards of a village are not integrated by a centralized system of headmanship, and no political cooperation exists between them until they are threatened by, or faced with, actual hostility from other villages. These are the critical variables that partially determine the bellicosity and violence I have observed.

No specific hypothesis can be given to explain the cannibalism that the Jalé incorporate in their vengeance. It is certain, however, that no understanding can be achieved by applying precepts of Western thought. In a missionary's travelogue published seventy years ago, the author, speaking of an African tribe, recounted:

> Once, when told by a European that the practice of eating human flesh was a most degraded habit, the cannibal answered, "Why degraded? You people eat sheep and cows and fowls, which are all animals of a far lower order, and we eat man, who is great and above all; it is you who are degraded!"

33

Civilized warfare: Why men fight

CHARLES C. MOSKOS, JR.

People who dwell on the "home front" of war in Western society like to think that bravery, the salvation of democracy, and the preservation of freedom motivate their soldiers on the battlefield. In this study, information gathered about the views of soldiers in combat during the Second World War and today indicates otherwise. The American soldier fights to survive in Vietnam. His proximity to constant danger causes him to learn the skills necessary to stay alive, some of which involve effective fighting. Charles Moskos shows that American soldiers usually attribute their presence in battle to fate, rather than to the noble ideals espoused by those at home.

Few stories to come out of the Vietnam War are so poignant as the story of Company A of the 196th Light Infantry Brigade, Third Battalion. As told by Associated Press reporters Horst Fass and Peter Arnett in a cable dated August 26, 1969, Company A had been pushing for five days through enemy-held territory in an effort to recover the bodies of eight Americans killed in a helicopter crash thirty-one miles south of Da Nang. Now, its strength halved to sixty men, its platoon leaders dead or wounded, Company A was ordered to move down a jungled rocky slope of Nuilon Mountain. They refused. Most of the men were nineteen to twenty years old, draftees, and many of them had only a short time to go before being rotated back to the States. They were ordered to move out and they refused.

The rest of the story is unimportant; as far as the military command is concerned the whole story is unimportant. But for many Americans,

From "Vietnam: Why Men Fight," *Trans*-action 7 (November 1969): 13–23.
 Illustrations and bibliography are omitted.

Company A's refusal to fight that day must have raised terrible questions — perhaps above all questions about one's own personal courage, but questions too about how and why American soldiers continue to expose themselves to death and pain in a war that few civilians any longer believe in.

The most popular notion of how men are brought to kill and be killed in combat has to do with the presumed national character of the soldiers. Different national armies perform better or worse according to the putative martial spirit of their respective citizenries. Italians make "poor" soldiers, Germans "good" ones. Another view has it that combat performance is basically a consequence of the operation of the formal military organization — the strict discipline, military training, unit esprit de corps, and so forth. This viewpoint is, naturally enough, found in traditional military thought, but the importance of military socialization is similarly emphasized — albeit from different premises — by antimilitarists concerned with the perversions that military life allegedly inflicts on men's minds. Another interpretation — often the hallmark of political rhetoric — holds that combat performance depends on the soldier's conscious allegiance to the stated purposes of the war. Whether motivated by patriotism or a belief that he is fighting for a just cause, the effective soldier is ultimately an ideologically inspired soldier.

Yet another explanation of combat motivation developed out of the social science studies of World War II. This interpretation deemphasizes cultural, formal socialization and ideological factors and focuses attention instead on the crucial role of face-to-face or "primary" groups. The motivation of the individual combat soldier rests on his solidarity and social intimacy with fellow soldiers at small-group levels. This viewpoint was characteristic of the studies that Samuel Stouffer and his associates reported in *The American Soldier,* as well as of the analysis of the *Wehrmacht* by Edward Shils and Morris Janowitz. The rediscovery of the importance of primary groups by social scientists was paralleled in the accounts given by novelists and other writers about combat behavior such as Norman Mailer, James Jones, J. Glenn Gray, and S. L. A. Marshall. In a few of the more extreme elaborations of this theory, primary relations among men in combat were viewed as so intense that they overrode not only preexisting civilian values and formal military goals, but even the individual's own sense of self-preservation.

My own research among American soldiers in Vietnam has led me to question the dominant influence of the primary group in combat motivation on at least two counts. First, the self-serving aspects of primary relations in combat units must be more fully appreciated. War is a Hobbesian world and, in combat, life is truly short, nasty, and brutish. But, to carry Hobbes a step farther, primary group processes in combat are a kind of rudimentary social contract, a contract that is entered into because of its advantages to oneself. Second, although the American soldier has a deep aversion to overt political symbols and patriotic appeals, this fact should not obscure his even deeper commitments to other values that serve to maintain the soldier under dangerous conditions. These values — misguided or not — must be taken into account in explaining the generally creditable combat performance American soldiers have given. Put most formally, I would argue that combat motivation arises out of the linkages between individual self-concern and the shared beliefs of soldiers as these are shaped by the immediate combat situation.

The combat situation

To convey the immediacy of the combat situation is hard enough for the novelist, not to say the sociologist. But to understand the fighting soldier's attitudes and behavior, it is vital to comprehend the extreme physical conditions under which he must try to live. It is only in the immediate context of battle that one can grasp the nature of the group processes developed in combat squads. For within the network of his relations with fellow squad members, the combat soldier is also fighting a very private war, a war he desperately hopes to leave alive and unscathed.

The concept of relative deprivation — interpreting an individual's evaluation of his situation by knowing the group he compares himself with — has been one of the most fruitful in social inquiry. We should not, however, forget that there are some conditions of life in which deprivation is absolute. In combat, a man's social horizon is narrowly determined by his immediate life chances in the most literal sense. The fighting soldier, as an absolutely deprived person, responds pragmatically to maximize any and all short-run opportunities to improve his chances of survival. For the soldier the decisions of state that brought him into combat are irrelevant, meaningless.

Under fire, the soldier not only faces an imminent danger of his own death and wounding; he also witnesses the killing and suffering of his buddies. And always there are the routine physical stresses of combat life — the weight of the pack, tasteless food, diarrhea, lack of water, leeches, mosquitos, rain, torrid heat, mud, and loss of sleep. In an actual firefight with the enemy, the scene is generally one of terrible chaos and confusion. Deadening fear intermingles with acts of bravery and, strangely enough, even moments of exhilaration and comedy. If prisoners are taken, they may be subjected to atrocities in the rage of battle or its immediate aftermath. The soldier's distaste for endangering civilians is overcome by his fear that any Vietnamese, of any age or sex, could very well want him dead. Where the opportunity arises, he will often loot. War souvenirs are frequently collected, either to be kept or later sold to rear-echelon servicemen.

As Stendahl and Tolstoy noted long ago, once the fight is over, the soldier still has little idea of what has been accomplished in a strategic sense. His view of the war is limited to his own observations and subsequent talks with others in the same platoon or company. The often-noted reluctance of soldiers to discuss their war experiences when back home doesn't hold true in the field. They talk constantly, repetitiously, of the battles and skirmishes they have been through. They talk about them not just to talk, but more importantly to nail down tactics that may save their lives in future encounters with the enemy.

"DEROS" AND AGAPE

For the individual soldier, the paramount factor affecting combat motivation is the operation of the rotation system. Under current assignment policies Army personnel serve a twelve-month tour of duty in Vietnam. Barring his being killed or severely wounded, then, every soldier knows exactly when he will leave Vietnam. His whole being centers on reaching his personal "DEROS" (Date Expected Return Overseas). It is impossible to overstate the soldier's constant concern with how much more time — down to the day — he must remain in Vietnam.

Within the combat unit, the rotation system has many consequences for social cohesion and individual motivation. The rapid turnover of personnel hinders the development of primary group ties, even as it rotates out of the unit men who have attained fighting experience. It also, however, mitigates those strains (noted in World War II in *The American Soldier*) that occur when new replacements are confronted by seasoned combat veterans. Yet because of the tactical nature of patrols and the somewhat random likelihood of encountering the enemy, a new arrival may soon experience more actual combat than some of the men in the same company who are nearing the end of their tour in Vietnam. Whatever its effects on the long-term combat effectiveness of the American forces as a whole however, the rotation system does largely account for the generally high morale of the combat soldier.

During his one-year stint in Vietnam, the fighting soldier finds his attitude undergoing definite changes. Although attitudes depend a good deal on individual personality and combat exposure, they usually follow a set course. Upon arrival at his unit and for several weeks thereafter, the soldier is excited to be in the war zone and looks forward to engaging the enemy. After the first serious encounter, however, he loses his enthusiasm for combat. He becomes highly respectful of the enemy's fighting abilities and begins to fear and scorn the South Vietnamese. He grows skeptical of victory statements from headquarters and of the official reports of enemy casualties. From about the third to the eighth month of his tour, the soldier operates on a kind of plateau of moderate commitment to his combat role.

Toward the ninth and tenth months, the soldier begins to regard himself as an "old soldier," and it is usually at this point that he is generally most effective in combat. As he approaches the end of his tour in Vietnam, however, he begins noticeably to withdraw his efficiency. He now becomes reluctant to engage in offensive combat operations; and increasingly, he hears and repeats stories of men killed the day they were to rotate back home.

It is significant, though, that "short-timer's fever" is implicitly recognized by the others, and demands on short-timers are informally reduced. The final disengagement period of the combat soldier is considered a kind of earned prerogative which those earlier in the rotation cycle hope eventually to enjoy.

Overall, the rotation system reinforces a perspective which is essentially private and self-concerned. Somewhat remarkably, for example, I found little difference in the attitudes of combat soldiers in Vietnam over a two-year interval. The consistency was largely due, I believe, to the fact that each soldier goes through a similar rotation experience. The end of the war is marked by the date a man leaves Vietnam, and not by its eventual outcome — whether victory, defeat, or stalemate. Even discussion of broader military strategy and the progress of the war — except when directly impinging on one's unit — appears irrelevant to the combat soldier: "*My* war is over when I go home."

When the soldier feels concern over the fate of others, it is for those he personally knows in his own outfit. His concern does not extend to those who have preceded him or will eventually replace him. Rather, the attitude is typically, "I've done my time; let the others do theirs." Or, as put in the soldier's vernacular, he is waiting to make the final entry on his "FIGMO" chart — "Fuck it, got my order [to return to the United States]." Whatever incipient identification there might be with abstract comrades-in-arms is flooded out by the private view of the war fostered by the rotation system.

Conventionally, the primary group is described as a network of interpersonal relationships in which the group's maintenance is valued for its own sake rather than as a mechanism that serves one's own interests. And, as has been noted, social science descriptions of combat motivation in World War II placed particular emphasis on the importance of groupings governed by intimate face-to-face relations. Roger Little's observations of a rifle company during the Korean War differed somewhat by pointing to the two-man or "buddy system" as the basic unit of cohesion rather than the squad or platoon.

My observations in Vietnam, however, indicate that the concept of primary groups has limitations in explaining combat motivation even beyond that suggested by Little. The fact is that if the individual soldier is realistically to improve his survival chances, he must *necessarily* develop and take part in primary relationships. Under the grim conditions of ground warfare, an individual's survival is directly dependent upon the support — moral, physical and technical — he can expect from his fellow soldiers. He gets such support to the degree that he reciprocates to the others in his unit. In other words, primary relations are at their core mutually pragmatic efforts to minimize personal risk.

Interpreting the solidarity of combat squads as an outcome of individual self-interest can be corroborated by two illustrations. The first deals with the behavior of the man on "point" in a patrolling operation. The point man is usually placed well in front of the main body, in the most exposed position. Soldiers naturally dread this dangerous assignment, but a good point man is a safeguard for the entire patrol. What happens, as often as not, is that men on point behave in a noticeably careless manner in order to avoid being regularly assigned to the job. At the same time, of course, the point man tries not to be so incautious as to put himself completely at the mercy of an encountered enemy force. In plain language, soldiers do not typically perform at their best when on point; personal safety overrides group interest.

The paramountcy of individual self-interest in combat units is also indicated by the letters soldiers write. Squad members who have returned to the United States seldom write to those remaining behind. In most cases, nothing more is heard from a soldier after he leaves the unit. Perhaps even more revealing, those still in the combat area seldom write their former buddies. Despite protestations of lifelong friendship during the shared combat period, the rupture of communication is entirely mutual, once a soldier is out of danger. The soldier writes almost exclusively to those he expects to see when he leaves the service: his family and relatives, girl friends, and civilian male friends.

Do these contrasting interpretations of the network of social relations in combat units — the primary groups of World War II, the two-man relationships of the Korean War, and the essentially individualistic soldier in Vietnam described here — result from conceptual differences on the part of the commentators, or do they reflect substantive differences in the social cohesion of the American soldiers being described? If substantive differences do obtain, particularly between World War II and the wars in Korea and Vietnam, much of this variation could be accounted for by the disruptive effects on unit solidarity caused by the introduction of the rotation system in the latter two wars.

Latent ideology

Even if we could decide whether combat primary groups are essentially entities *sui generis* or outcomes of pragmatic self-interest, there remain other difficulties in understanding the part they play in maintaining organizational effectiveness. For it has been amply demonstrated in many contexts that primary groups can hinder as well as serve to attain the formal goals of the larger organization. Thus, to describe effective combat motivation principally in terms of primary group ties leaves unanswered the question of why various armies — independent of training and equipment — perform differently in times of war. Indeed, because of the very ubiquity of primary groups in military organizations, we must look for supplementary factors to explain variations in combat motivation.

I propose that primary groups maintain the soldier in his combat role only when he has an underlying commitment to the worth of the larger social system for which he is fighting. This commitment need not be formally articulated, nor even perhaps consciously recognized. But the soldier must at some level accept, if not the specific purposes of the war, then at least the broader rectitude of the society of which he is a member. Although American combat soldiers do not espouse overtly ideological sentiments and are extremely reluctant to voice patriotic rhetoric, this should not obscure the existence of more latent beliefs in the legitimacy, and even superiority, of the American way of life. I have used the term "latent ideology" to describe the social and cultural sources of those beliefs about the war held by American soldiers. Latent ideology, in this context, refers to those widely shared sentiments of soldiers which, though not overtly political, nor even necessarily substantively political, nevertheless have concrete consequences for combat motivation.

Students of political behavior have too often been uninterested in answers that do not measure up to their own standards of expressiveness. When a person responds in a way that seems either ideologically confused or apathetic, he is considered to have no political ideology. But since any individual's involvement in any polity is usually peripheral, it is quite likely that his political attitudes will be organized quite differently from those of ideologists or political theorists. Yet when one focuses on underlying value orientations, we find a set of attitudes having a definite coherence — especially within the context of that individual's life situation.

Quite consistently, the American combat soldier displays a profound skepticism of political and ideological appeals. Somewhat paradoxically, then, anti-ideology itself is a recurrent and integral part of the soldier's belief system. They dismiss patriotic slogans or exhortations to defend democracy with "What a crock," "Be serious, man," or "Who's kidding who?" In particular, they have little belief that they are protecting an outpost of democracy in South Vietnam. United States Command Information pronouncements stressing defense of South Vietnam as an outpost of the "Free World" are almost as dubiously received as those of Radio

Hanoi which accuse Americans of imperialist aggression. As one soldier put it, "Maybe we're supposed to be here and maybe not. But you don't have time to think about things like that. You worry about getting zapped and dry socks tomorrow. The other stuff is a joke."

In this same vein, when the soldier responds to the question of why he is in Vietnam, his answers are couched in a quite individualistic frame of reference. He sees little connection between his presence in Vietnam and the national policies that brought him there. Twenty-seven of the thirty-four combat soldiers I interviewed defined their presence in the war in terms of personal misfortune. Typical responses were: "My outfit was sent over here and me with it," "My tough luck in getting drafted," "I happened to be at the wrong place at the wrong time," "I was fool enough to join this man's army," and "My own stupidity for listening to the recruiting sergeant." Only five soldiers mentioned broader policy implications — to stop Communist aggression. Two soldiers stated they requested assignment to Vietnam because they wanted to be "where the action is."

Because of the combat soldier's overwhelming propensity to see the war in private and personal terms, I had to ask them specifically what they thought the United States was doing in Vietnam. When the question was phrased in this manner, the soldiers most often said they were in Vietnam "to stop Communism." This was about the only ideological slogan these American combat soldiers could be brought to utter; nineteen of the thirty-four interviewed soldiers saw stopping Communism as the purpose of the war. But when they expressed this view it was almost always in terms of defending the United States, not the "Free World" in general and certainly not South Vietnam. They said: "The only way we'll keep them out of the States is to kill them here," "Let's get it over now, before they're too strong to stop," "They have to be stopped somewhere," "Better to zap this country than let them do the same to us."

Fifteen of the soldiers gave responses other than stopping Communism. Three gave frankly cynical explanations of the war by stating that domestic prosperity in the United States depended on a war economy. Two soldiers held that the American intervention was a serious mistake initially; but that it was now too late to back out because of America's reputation. One man even gave a Malthusian interpretation, arguing that war was needed to limit population growth. Nine of the soldiers could give no reason for the war even after extensive discussion. Within this group, one heard responses such as: "I only wish I knew," "Maybe Johnson knows, but I sure don't," and "I've been wondering about that ever since I got here."

I asked each of the nineteen soldiers who mentioned stopping Communism as the purpose of the war what was so bad about Communism that it must be stopped at the risk of his own life. The first reaction to such a question was usually perplexity or rueful shrugging. After thinking about it, and with some prodding, twelve of the men expressed their distaste for Communism by stressing its authoritarian aspects in social relations. They saw Communism as a system of excessive social regimentation which allows the individual no autonomy in the pursuit of his own happiness. Typical descriptions of Communism were: "That's when you can't do what you want to do," "Somebody's always telling you what to do," or "You're told where you work, what you eat, and when you shit." As one man wryly put it, "Communism is something like the army."

While the most frequently mentioned features of Communism concerned individual liberty, other descriptions were also given. Three soldiers mentioned the atheistic and antichurch aspects of Communism; two specifically talked of the absence of political parties and democratic political institutions; and one man said Communism was good in theory, but could never work in practice because human beings were "too selfish." Only one soldier mentioned the issues of public versus private property ownership.

I should stress once again that the soldiers managed to offer reasons for the war or descriptions of Communism only after extended discussion and questioning. When left to themselves, they rarely discussed the goals of America's military intervention in Vietnam, the nature of Communist systems, or other political issues.

Americanism

To say that the American soldier is not overtly ideological is not to deny the existence of salient values that do contribute to his motivation in combat. Despite the soldier's lack of ideological concern and his pronounced embarrassment in the face of patriotic rhetoric, he nevertheless displays an elemental American nationalism in the belief that the United States is the best country in the world. Even though he hates being in the war, the combat soldier typically believes — with a kind of joyless patriotism — that he is fighting for his American homeland. When the soldier does articulate the purposes of the war, the view is expressed that if Communist aggression is not stopped in Southeast Asia, it will be only a matter of time before the United States itself is in jeopardy. The so-called domino theory is just as persuasive among combat soldiers as it is among the general public back home.

The soldier definitely does *not* see himself fighting for South Vietnam. Quite the contrary, he thinks South Vietnam is a worthless country, and its people contemptible. The low regard in which the Vietnamese — "slopes" or "gooks" — are held is constantly present in the derogatory comments on the avarice of those who pander to G.I.'s, the treachery of all Vietnamese, and the numbers of Vietnamese young men in the cities who are not in the armed forces. Anti-Vietnamese sentiment is most glaringly apparent in the hostility toward the ARVN (Army of the Republic of Vietnam, pronounced "Arvin") who are their supposed military allies. Disparaging remarks about "Arvin's" fighting qualities are endemic.

A variety of factors underlie the soldier's fundamental pro-Americanism, not the least of them being his immediate reliance on fellow Americans for mutual support in a country where virtually all indigenous people are seen as actual or potential threats to his physical safety. He also has deep concern for his family and loved ones back home. These considerations, however, are true of any army fighting in a foreign land. It is on another level, then, that I tried to uncover those aspects of American society that were most relevant and important to the combat soldier.

To obtain such a general picture of the soldier's conception of his homeland, I asked the following question, "Tell me in your own words, what makes America different from other countries?" The overriding feature in the soldier's perception of America is the creature comforts that American life can offer. Twenty-two of the soldiers described the United States by its high-paying jobs, automobiles, consumer goods, and leisure activities. No other description of America came close to being mentioned as often as the high — and apparently uniquely American — material standard of living. Thus, only four of the soldiers emphasized America's democratic political institutions; three mentioned religious and spiritual values; two spoke of the general characteristics of the American people; and one said America was where the individual advanced on his own worth; another talked of America's natural and physical beauties; and one black soldier described America as racist. Put in another way, it is the materialistic — and I do not use the word pejoratively — aspects of life in America that are most salient to combat soldiers.

The big PX

The soldier's belief in the superiority of the American way of life is further reinforced by the contrast with the Vietnamese standard of living. The combat soldier cannot help making invidious comparisons between the life he led in the United States — even if he is working-class — and what he sees in Vietnam. Although it is more pronounced in the Orient, it must be remembered that Americans abroad — whether military or civilian — usually find themselves in locales that compare unfavorably with the material affluence of the United States. Indeed, should American soldiers ever be stationed in a country with a markedly higher standard of living than that of the United States, I believe they would be severely shaken in their belief in the merits of American society.

Moreover, the fighting soldier, by the very fact of being in combat, leads an existence that is not only more dangerous than civilian life, but more primitive and physically harsh. The soldier's somewhat romanticized view of life back home is buttressed by his direct observation of the Vietnamese scene, but also by his own immediate lower standard of living. It has often been noted that front-line soldiers bitterly contrast their plight with the physical amenities enjoyed by their fellow countrymen, both rear-echelon soldiers as well as civilians back home. While this is superficially true, the attitudes of American combat soldiers toward their compatriots are actually somewhat more ambivalent. For at the same time the soldier is begrudging the civilian his physical comforts, it is these very comforts for which he fights. Similarly, they envy rather than disapprove of those rear-echelon personnel who engage in sub rosa profiteering.

The materialistic ethic is reflected in another characteristic of American servicemen. Even among front-line combat soldiers, one sees an extraordinary amount of valuable paraphernalia. Transistor radios are practically *de rigueur*. Cameras and other photographic accessories are widely evident and used. Even the traditional letter-writing home is becoming displaced by tape recordings. It seems more than coincidental that American soldiers commonly refer to the United States as "The Land of the Big PX."

Another factor that plays a part in combat motivation is the notion of masculinity and physical toughness that pervades the soldier's outlook toward warfare. Being a combat soldier is a man's job. Front-line soldiers often cast aspersions on the virility of rear-echelon personnel ("titless WAC's"). A soldier who has not experienced combat is called a "cherry" (i.e., virgin). Likewise, paratroopers express disdain for "legs," as non-airborne soldiers are called. This he-man attitude is also found in the countless joking references to the movie roles of John Wayne and Lee Marvin. These definitions of masculinity are, of course, general in America and the military organization seeks to capitalize on them with such perennial recruiting slogans as "The Marine Corps Builds Men" and "Join the Army and Be a Man."

Needless to say, however, the exaggerated masculine ethic is much less evident among soldiers after their units have been bloodied. As the realities of combat are faced, more prosaic definitions of manly honor emerge. (Also, there is more frequent expression of the male role in manifestly sexual rather than combative terms, for example, the repeatedly heard "I'm a lover not a fighter.") That is, notions of masculinity serve to create initial motivation to enter combat, but recede once the life-and-death facts of warfare are confronted. Moreover, once the unit is tempered by combat, definitions of manly honor are not seen to encompass individual heroics. Quite the opposite, the very word "hero" is used to describe negatively any soldier who recklessly jeopardizes the unit's welfare. Men try to avoid going out on patrols with individuals who are overly anxious to make contact with the enemy. Much like the slacker at the other end of the spectrum, the "hero" is also seen as one who endangers the safety of others. As is the case with virtually all combat behavior, the ultimate standard rests on keeping alive.

THE FIGHTING MAN'S PEACE DEMONSTRATOR

On both of my trips to Vietnam I repeatedly heard combat soldiers — almost to a man — vehemently denounce peace demonstrators back in the United States. At first glance such an attitude might be surprising. After all, peaceniks and soldiers both fervently want the troops brought home. In fact, however, the troops I interviewed expressed overt political sentiments only when the antiwar demonstrations came up in the talk. Significantly, the soldier perceived the peace demonstrations as being directed against himself personally and not against the war. "Did I vote to come here? Why blame the G.I.?" There was also a widespread feeling that if peace demonstrators were in Vietnam they would change their minds. As one man stated: "How can they know what's happening if they're sitting on their asses in the States. Bring them here and we'd shape them up quick enough." Or as one of the more philosophically inclined put it, "I'd feel the same way if I were back home. But once you're here and your buddies are getting zapped, you have to see things different."

Much of the soldier's dislike of peace demonstrators is an outcome of class hostility. To many combat soldiers — themselves largely working-class — peace demonstrators are socially privileged college students. I heard many remarks such as the following: "I'm fighting for those candy-asses just because I don't have an old man to support me," "I'm stuck here and those rich draft dodgers are having a ball raising hell," "You'd think they'd have more sense with all that smart education."

The peace demonstrators, moreover, were seen as undercutting and demeaning the losses and hardships already suffered by American soldiers. Something of this sort undoubtedly contributed to the noticeable hawklike sentiments of combat soldiers. "If we get out now, then every G.I. died for nothing. Is this why I've been putting my ass on the line?" Here we seem to have an illustration of a more general social phenomenon: the tendency in human beings to justify to themselves sacrifices they have already made. Sacrifice itself can create legitimacy for an organization over a short period of time. It is only after some point when sacrifices suddenly seem too much, that the whole enterprise comes under critical reevaluation. But sharp questioning of past and future sacrifices does not generally occur among combat soldiers in Vietnam. I believe this is because the twelve-month rotation system removes the soldier from the combat theater while his personal stake remains high and before he might begin to question the whole operation. The rotation system, in other words, not only maintains individual morale but also fosters a collective commitment to justify American sacrifices.

The soldier's hostility toward peace demonstrators is reinforced by his negative reactions to the substance of certain antiwar arguments. For while the combat soldier is constantly concerned with his own and his fellow American's safety, as well as being a fundamental believer in the American way of life and profoundly apolitical to boot, the radical element of the peace movement mourns the suffering of the Vietnamese, is vehement in its anti-Americanism, and is self-consciously ideological. At almost every point, the militant peace movement articulates sentiments in direct opposition to the basic values of the American soldier. Statements bemoaning civilian Vietnamese casualties are interpreted as wishes for greater American losses. Assertions of the United States' immorality for its interventionism run contrary to the soldier's elemental belief in the rectitude of the American nation. Arguments demonstrating that the Viet Cong are legitimate revolutionaries have no credence both because of the soldier's ignorance of Vietnamese history and — more importantly — because the Viet Cong are out to kill him. As one man summed it up: "I don't know who are the good guys or the bad guys, us or the V.C. But anybody who shoots at me ain't my friend. Those college punks are going to answer to a lot of us when we get back."

It must be stressed, however, that the soldier's dislike of peace demonstrators is reactive and does not imply any preexisting support for the war. Paradoxically, then, the more militant peace demonstrations have probably created a level of support for the war among combat soldiers that would otherwise be absent. This is not to say that the soldier is immune to antiwar arguments. But the kind of arguments that would be persuasive among soldiers (e.g., Vietnam is not worth American blood, South Vietnam is manipulating the United States, the corruptness of the Saigon regime and ineptitude of the ARVN make for needless U.S. casualties) are not the ones usually voiced by radical peace groups. *The combat soldier is against peace demonstrators rather than for the war.* For it should also be known that he has scant affection for "support-the-boys" campaigns in the United States. Again, the attitude that "they don't know what it's all about" applies. As one soldier succinctly put it — and his words spoke for most: "The only support I want is out."

IX

The crisis of values

In the preceding chapters we have glimpsed a small sample of the many worlds of culture created by man. To those who have learned them, these ways of life appear natural and God-given. One's culture is not like a suit of clothing that can be discarded easily or exchanged for each new life style that comes along. It is rather like a security blanket, and though to some it may appear worn and tattered, outmoded and ridiculous, it has great meaning to its owner. Although there are many reasons for this fact, one of the most important is the value-laden nature of what we learn as a member of society. Whether it is acquired in a tribal band, a peasant village, or an urban neighborhood, each culture is like a giant iceberg. Beneath the surface of rules, norms, and behavior patterns there is a system of values. Some of these premises are easily stated by members of a society, while others are outside their awareness. Because most of the urgent crises in the modern world involve values, we must examine this concept in some detail.

A value is an arbitrary conception of what is *desirable* in human experience. During socialization every child is exposed to a constant barrage of evaluations — the arbitrary "rating system" of his culture. Nearly everything he learns is labeled in terms of its desirability. The value attached to each bit of information may result from the pain of a hot stove, the look of disapproval from a parent, the smile of appreciation from a teacher, or some specific verbal instruction. When a father tells his son, "You should not try to evade the draft; only cowards are unwilling to fight for their country," he is expressing a value. Those who do not conform to a society's rating system are identified with derogatory labels or punished in a more severe way. When a Tlingit Indian says to his nephew, "You should marry your father's sister," he is conforming to one of the core values of his culture. When a college student saves his earnings for a rainy day, he is living up to the American idea that the future is more important than the present. When a tramp urinates in an alley he is violating the value attached to privacy. All these concepts of what is desirable combine cognitive and affective meanings. Individuals internalize their ideas about right and wrong, good and bad, and invest them with strong feelings.

Why do values constitute an inevitable part of all human experience? That human potential is at odds with the requirements of social life is well known. Behavior within the realm of possibility is often outside the realm of necessity. There are numerous ways to resolve the conflict between what man *can do* as an individual, and what he *must do* as a member of society. It is a popular notion that prisons and other institutions are the primary means in our society to enforce conformity, but this is not the case. Socialization may be ineffective for a few and require such drastic action, but for the vast majority in any society, conformity results from the internalization of values. This is so, in part, because as one learns through imitation, identification, and instruction, values are internalized as part of his personality. They provide security and contribute to a sense of personal and social identity. For this reason, individuals in every society cling tenaciously to the ideals they have acquired and feel threatened when confronted with others who live according to radically different conceptions of what is desirable.

There are two popular misconceptions about the relationship between values and behavior. First, many believe that those who are different have lost all their values. Consider the following statement by a teacher: "Young people today have no values. They are smoking pot, growing long hair, and protesting the war!" It is often difficult to believe that those who hold different ideas about desirable behavior have any conceptions of good. Yet the teacher's statement indicates the very ideals held by those who are criticized as bereft of values. A minister declares, "We live in a moral crisis today in America — we are losing our sense of values!" We may be in a moral crisis — not due to a *loss*, but rather to a *shift* in values. If anything, when there are conflicts or changes in the structure of a society's value system, individuals have a heightened awareness of values.

A second misconception has been spawned by science and, in particular, the anthropological doctrine of cultural relativism. Some have maintained that it is possible to separate values from facts, and since science is limited to facts, it is possible to do "value free" research. Thus, by an exercise in mental gymnastics, the very scholars who admit the influence of values in the behavior of others sometimes deny it for themselves. Preferences operate whenever an individual must *select* one action from a multitude of possible courses. Anyone who decides to observe one thing and not another is making that decision on the basis of an implicit or explicit conception of desirability. Science is an activity that makes many value judgments including which approaches to gathering information are the best. When a biologist decides he will examine the structure of the DNA molecule using an empirical rather than a mystical, intuitive, or religious approach, he is doing so with reference to his sense of what is desirable. Even the decision to study DNA rather than some other substance involves an exercise of his values. The influence of one's ideals when doing research on human behavior is undeniable. The "objective observer" who is detached from his subject matter, who refrains from allowing his values to influence his observations, is a myth. This fact does not suggest a retreat from the *quest for objectivity*. It does not mean the social scientist is free to disparage the customs he encounters in another society, or to impose his morals upon those he studies. A skilled anthropologist is one who is aware of his own values and then approaches other cultures with tolerance and respect for theirs. He *identifies* rather than *denies* the influence of his own viewpoint. He strives to achieve the ideal of value-free research but with the realization that it would be naive to assume such a goal possible.

Cultural relativism rests on the premise that it is possible to remain aloof and free from making value judgments. To oversimplify this doctrine by a set of four interrelated propositions:

1. Each person's value system is a result of his experience, i.e., it is learned.
2. The values that individuals learn differ from one society to another because of different learning experiences.
3. Values, therefore, are relative to the society in which they occur.
4. There are no universal values but we should respect the values of each of the world's cultures.

Cultural relativism has enabled the uninformed to understand what appears to be strange and immoral behavior. For example, while we may not believe it is good to kill infants, this practice became intelligible in the context of a native Australian band. While Americans generally believe in the desirability of monogamous marriages (or at least serial monogamy), the practice of polygamy in other societies is comprehensible when related to their cultures. There are numerous difficulties with this position. Does one respect a society that believes it best to murder systematically six million of its members who happen to be Jewish? How does the anthropologist respect the values of a headhunting tribe when his own head is at stake? More important, all the statements in this doctrine of relativism are either based on implicit values (i.e., empiricism), or they are outright statements of desirability. The belief that it is good to *respect* the ideals of each of the world's cultures is itself a "relative" value. An extreme relativism is based on the philosophy that it is best to "let everyone do his own thing." Given unlimited resources and space this might have been possible, but in the modern world this philosophy represents a retreat from the realities facing us. It absolves the believer from the responsibility of finding some way to resolve conflicts among the world's different value systems. What is needed today is not a "live and let live" policy but a commitment to a higher, more inclusive, value system, and this requires changes that are extremely difficult to achieve.

Finally, values are the basis of all human societies. Every social system is a moral order — shared values act as the mortar binding together the structure of each human community. Rewards and punishments are based upon commonly held values; those persons achieving high status do so in terms of cultural rating systems. These ideals are expressed in symbolic ways — food, clothing, wealth, language, behavior — all carry the implicit message of good and bad. This pervasive quality of values gives each person a sense of belonging, a sense that he is a member of a community, the feeling that he is part of other human beings who share his commitment to the good life. But the moral nature of every culture has two sides — it facilitates adaptation and survival on the one hand, but often generates conflict and destruction on the other. Let us examine each of these possibilities.

For several million years man has successfully adapted to a variety of terrestrial environments. From the frozen tundra to the steaming jungle, he has built his home, reared his children, performed his rituals, and buried his dead. In recent years he has escaped the thin layer of atmosphere surrounding the earth to live, if only for a few days, in outer space and beneath the ocean. All these achievements have been possible because of his unique endowment — *a capacity for culture.* Wherever he wandered, man has developed patterns for organizing behavior, utilizing natural resources, relating to his fellow man, and creating a meaningful life. His genetic inheritance did not channel behavior into specialized responses but instead provided a reservoir of plasticity that was shaped by values into one of the many ways to be human. Children in every society do not learn the entire range of potential human behavior — they are taught to conform to a very limited number of behavior patterns which are appropriate to a particular society. Human survival depends upon a *culturally constituted society* and this requires that every individual must become a specialist, must become committed to a few values, and acquire the knowledge and skills of a single society.

This very specialization has led to diversity, resulting in a myriad of contrasting cultures. This volume presents only a small sample of these different symbolic worlds created by men in their attempt to cope with the common problems of human existence. We have seen how the generosity of the American Christmas spirit stands in contrast to the daily sharing among the Bushmen. Language styles among the Subanun could hardly function in the Black ghetto of American cities. The natives in the Brazilian jungle and Chicago suburbanites both adorn their bodies with paint, clothing, and rings — but neither can comprehend how the other defines these symbols. All elements of human experience — kinsmen, marriage, age, race, sexuality, food, warfare — are socially defined and valued. The difficulty of moving easily from one of these cultural worlds to another is immense.

Cultural diversity has fascinated mankind for centuries. Anthropology, as the study of strange and exotic peoples, has attracted the curious for many generations. In the isolation of a remote jungle village or South Sea island, the anthropologist found a natural laboratory for carrying out this work. His research reports often seemed more like novels than scientific studies and were read by both professionals and laymen; seldom did any reader feel threatened by the strange behavior of far off "savages."

But isolation rapidly disappeared — sometimes by virtue of the anthropologist's intrusion! Exploration gave way to colonization, trade, and the massive troop movements of modern warfare. Today it is impossible to find groups of people who are isolated from the remainder of the world. Instead we have a conglomeration of cultures within a single nation, and often within a single city. The anthropologist need only walk down the street from his university office to encounter those who have learned a culture unlike his own. Individuals with different language styles, sexual practices, religious rituals, and a host of other strange behavior patterns sit in his classroom or play with his children on the urban playground. Anthropology today is a science concerned with understanding how man can survive in a world where village, hamlet, city, and nation are all *multicultural.* In isolation each value system was interesting. Crowded into close and intimate contact, these distinct culture patterns often lead to conflict, oppression, and warfare. Barbara Ward has eloquently summed up our situation:

> In the last few decades, mankind has been overcome by the most fateful change in its entire history. Modern science and technology have created so close a network of communication, transport, economic interdependence — and potential nuclear destruction — that planet earth, on its journey through infinity, has acquired the intimacy, the fellowship, and the vulnerability of a spaceship.[1]

In a sense, man's greatest resource for adapting to different environments — a capacity to create different cultures — has become the source of his greatest danger. Diversity is required for survival in the ecological niches of earth, but it can be destructive when all mankind suddenly finds itself in the same niche. Numerous species have become extinct because of their inability to adapt to a changing *natural* environment. Culture was man's survival kit enabling him to meet these fluctuating conditions with flexibility, but now we are faced with a radically altered *human* environment. Successful adaptation will require changes that fly in the face of millions of years of cultural specialization. Man's ingenuity has been used to develop unique cultures, but thus far he has failed to develop satisfactory patterns and rules for articulating these differences. Can we survive in a world where our neighbors and even our children have different cultures? Can we adapt to the close, intimate fellowship of a spaceship when each group of passengers lives by different values?

These questions have special importance in the United States at this time in our history. During the 1960s the unity and harmony of former years seemed to disintegrate. Conflicting value systems have always been a part of the American scene, but there are many indications that our loss of community has reached a new level. While this loss is expressed in many specific issues — urban riots, antiwar protests, women's liberation and civil rights movements, sexual revolution, ecological concern, draft resistance, gaps between generations — it stems from a widespread defection from the pursuit of certain traditional values. The pervasive myth of the melting pot — *E Pluribus Unum* — is being destroyed by powerful social forces. This may be the beginning of a far-reaching revolution in the structure of our society, a change from a society based upon the unity of similarity to one in which cultural differences are fully recognized but somehow woven into the fabric of the social order.

What is required for such a change? In the first place, instead of suppressing cultural diversity by stressing assimilation into the mainstream of American life, we must recognize the extent to which our culture is pluralistic. We must become aware that Blacks, hippies, Chicanos, WASPs, construction workers, students, old people, and many other groups are committed to disparate and sometimes conflicting values. And

[1] Barbara Ward, *Spaceship Earth* (New York: Columbia University Press, 1966), p. vii.

this awareness is growing. Here is the view of an outsider, the French columnist Jean-François Revel, who recently visited the United States and on his return to France wrote the following commentary:

> Almost all portraits of America emphasize the uniformity, the monotonous sameness, the mechanization of life in the U.S. Now, even if this tendency is still evident . . . there is another force at work which today seems to be gaining the upper hand. This period in American history belongs to its minorities. Racial minorities above all: Black Power, Red Power, Chicano Power . . . And it is these cries that are being heard rather than demands for integrated equality on a social and economic level. These cries are an affirmation of the right to different ways of life, to a variety of life styles, rather than a single overwhelming "American way of life." American civilization is becoming more interested in the arts and religions of the Third World than in English literature. The melting pot is beginning to work in reverse: it is spattering outward, like a centrifuge.[2]

In the last few years Blacks and Chicanos have turned from seeking civil rights alone — they also want to recover and develop their special cultural heritages. In the city and on the reservation there are deep currents of cultural revival among American Indians. The much touted "generation gap" is not simply hostility between adults and their maturing children; Margaret Mead has aptly suggested that it is analogous to the situation of all immigrants. Contemporary parents see their children being socialized into a culture that, to the adult, is foreign and strange. The young and the old are not separated geographically, but even when they live in the same house they are cultural worlds apart. The realization that environmental problems are, in essence, the result of value conflicts is growing. Corporation leaders who seek unlimited economic growth are at odds with those who place more emphasis upon pure air and water. Private property values in our culture allow a man to cut down trees in his yard to satisfy his aesthetic preferences — but this suddenly conflicts with those who consider it desirable to preserve these natural sources of oxygen for future generations. As we become even more aware of the kaleidoscopic nature of American values, fear and confusion may increase. Peter Schrag writes in "The Decline of the Wasp," that "America is not on the verge of becoming two separate societies. . . . It is becoming, in all its dreams and anxieties, a nation of outsiders for whom no single style or ethic remains possible." [3] These changes appear to many as destructive; the segmenting and polarizing process seems to destroy the connective tissue of the social order. On the contrary, this process is more likely a

[2] Jean-François Revel, "Junking the Melting Pot," *Atlas*, April 1970. Translated from *L'Express*, Paris, pp. 31–32.

[3] Peter Schrag, "The Decline of the Wasp," *Harper's Magazine* 240, No. 1439 (1970): 85–91.

new and healthy awareness of cultural differences which are not new.

In addition to recognizing the extent of pluralism in our culture, the second requirement for a truly multicultural society is the continuous examination of the *consequences* of each value system. What is the long-range effect of our commitment to a "gospel of growth"? What are the results of a belief in male superiority? How do our values of privacy affect those without homes? What is the consequence for minority groups of teaching all students to use "standard English"? As we study American culture we must discover the effect of our dominant values on every sector of life. The ideals that have made this country great have also been destructive to some citizens. In our efforts to assimilate ethnic subcultures we have destroyed their pride and self-identity. In our efforts to offer the advantages of education to American Indians we have induced them to become failures because our schools are not able to educate for diversity. In order to demonstrate the goodness of American values we have created the "culturally deprived," but the sophistication of labels does not conceal our prejudice. The absence of men in the families of the urban poor is a logical consequence of welfare institutions created from a single value system. Tramps must travel, not because they are happy wanderers but because our "punishment rules" force them to adopt a life of mobility. The consumer suffers from dangerous products because productive enterprise is more important in our culture than his protection. We have only begun to understand some of the consequences of our values — and during the next few decades our survival will demand that the study of values be given top priority.

Finally, the most difficult task for our nation and the world is to induce mankind to relinquish those values with destructive consequences. While there are no simple ways to achieve this, it probably will not occur without a better understanding of the nature and function of the world's many value systems. Man's capacity to learn has not yet reached its full potential. In every society children learn to shift from *egocentric* behavior to *ethnocentric* behavior. Individuals give up those things they desire in deference to desirable community standards. And life in a particular society becomes secure and meaningful with conventional values acting as the warp and woof of social interaction. Can we now learn to shift from behavior that is *ethnocentric* to *homocentric* behavior? Can we relinquish values desirable from the standpoint of a single community but destructive to others in the wider world? This change will require a system of ideals greater than the conventions of each localized culture. It will necessitate a morality that can articulate among conflicting systems and create a climate of tolerance, respect, and cooperation. Only then will we survive the crises of values.